PLANNING PARKS FOR PEOPLE

John Hultsman
Arizona State University

Richard L. Cottrell
U.S. Forest Service,
Tennessee Valley Authority (retired)

Wendy Hultsman
Arizona State University

VENTURE PUBLISHING, INC.
State College, PA 16801

Design by Marilyn Shobaken
Cover Design by Sandra Sikorski
Copy Editing by Susan Lewis
Production Supervisor Bonnie Godbey
Typesetting by King Printing, State College, PA
Library of Congress Catalogue Card Number 86-50935
ISBN 0-910251-16-9

DEDICATION

The authors dedicate *Planning Parks for People* to the memory of a most outstanding and unique recreation professional — Mr. Ralph C. Wilson.

Ralph was an active, hard-working, and involved member of numerous professional organizations (including a few beyond America's shores). He was, at various times, chair or president of most of them and the recipient of numerous prestigious awards.

At his passing in May of 1985 he had just retired as assistant director of the Ecological Sciences Division of the USDA-Soil Conservation Service. Since the mid-1960's he had essentially been Chief of Recreation for the SCS.

Unlike most professionals who work within one or two interest areas in the recreation realm, Ralph had broad concerns about and impacts on outdoor, municipal, therapeutic, military, sports, private, and international recreation. He was involved in the development of new technologies through research and continuing education, along with the arts and historical preservation. Ralph advocated recreation progress in a broad sense: he disdained favoring advances for one user group at the expense of another, advocating both wilderness use and off-road vehicle riding, for example. Perhaps his greatest service to the recreation profession was his ability to link people who had problems with people who had answers — always in a spirit of advancing the value of recreation, parks, and leisure services.

If during your career you have the opportunity to help, encourage, or perhaps be a mentor to one or two younger professionals, you will have been most fortunate. Ralph was a mentor and an example to dozens of professionals across America and around the world.

Years ago he and others suggested we write a book about the mistakes we had all made in outdoor recreation planning, design, and programming, focusing on the negative effects these mistakes have had on park users, administrators, and the resources themselves. Throughout our long association with Ralph, he made sure we didn't forget his professional request. Ten days before he died he asked one of us about our early writing progress.

Many of the comments on professionalism we've included in this book are a part of Ralph's legacy to us and to you. He was a dynamic force in recreation, a professional's professional, and above all else a warm, close friend.

TABLE OF CONTENTS

OTHER BOOKS

BIOGRAPHICAL SKETCHES

John Hultsman is an Associate Professor of Leisure Studies at Arizona State University West, Phoenix, Arizona. He taught in the Department of Physical Education, Health, and Recreation Studies at Purdue University. He worked as a recreation planner for the Tennessee Valley Authority at Land Between the Lakes and in Norris, Tennessee. He enjoys (and occasionally suffers!) a domestic as well as a professional relationship with one of the other authors of this book.

Dick Cottrell spent a twenty-five-year career in outdoor recreation with the Forest Service and TVA at Land Between the Lakes. Since leaving the federal service, he has been active as a lecturer, author, and consultant, working with (among others) the Japanese government, the US Army in Europe, and the private sector.

Wendy Hultsman is an Assistant Professor of Leisure Studies at Arizona State University West. She taught in the Department of Forestry and Natural Resources at Purdue University, the Recreation and Parks Department of Bowling Green University, Clinton Community College, and Penn State University. She has raised a Golden Retriever named Toby as well as frequent questions about her husband's sense of humor.

ACKNOWLEDGEMENTS

If our experience in writing this book is at all typical, authors tend to take a parental perspective of their product. In one context, this view is appropriate, for any sins ascribed to *Planning Parks for People*, whether through commission or omission, are our responsibility. In a broader sense, however, this text represents the labor of a number of others. For these efforts, the authors wish to express appreciation to Frank Guadagnolo, president, and Geoffrey Godbey, managing editor, of Venture Publishing Inc., for the support, encouragement, and freedom they provided us; Bonnie Godbey, production supervisor, Sandra Sikorski, production assistant, and Susan Lewis, copy editor, who spun silk from literary sows' ears on innumerable occasions; Rob Rasor of the American Motorcyclist Association for his thoughtful suggestions; Marilyn McFatridge, who processed and revised what must have seemed an endless stream of chapters; and June Cottrell, who helped in ways too numerous to mention. Thank you all.

J.T.H.
R.L.C.
W.Z.H.

1

SETTING THE STAGE

Figure 1.1

Figure 1.2

Figure 1.3

INTRODUCTION

Welcome. Welcome to some of the most beautiful and important lands and waters in the world: the parks, lakes, forests, streams, and other resources we use for outdoor recreation. Those of us who choose recreation as a career have a responsibility to develop and manage these resources in ways which will provide the best possible experience for people. The challenge for park and recreation professionals, however, doesn't end with this task. Working in recreation also requires a commitment to *resource stewardship*. By this we mean that provision of recreation areas and facilities must be coupled with *protection* of the resources we develop. Thus, working in recreation implies a dual responsibility.

The first question we want to address is: "How well are we meeting this responsibility?" On the surface, it would seem our record is pretty good. Our resources are full of beautiful scenery, our trails are hiked, our campgrounds used, our beaches full. Unfortunately, a careful examination of our parks and other recreation areas would seem to indicate that the real answer to this question is one many of us would rather not hear. All too often our resources, which originally looked like those pictured in Figure 1.1, end up looking like the areas shown in Figures 1.2 and 1.3, with heavily compacted, poorly drained soil; erosion; dying, old-growth trees; and no aesthetic appeal. Too often we also tend to blame the users — the recreating public — for the environmental damage existing in our parks and recreation areas. Generally, the scenario runs something like this:

Time: Late September — after Labor Day
Place: A Virginia campground (The song is the same in Virginia, Indiana, Colorado, or Oregon.)
Cast: The "ranger" and maintenance crew
Plot: The *annual* job of rehabilitating Possum Hollow Campground begins

"Boy, I'm glad the season's over! Seems like this poor ole campground had twenty percent more of those city-born, city-raised critters called campers than ever before! Campers seemed even more determined than in past years to drive over and use any area they wanted. They even cut what few barrier posts we had left to get their trailers onto our tent pads and nearer the picnic tables. The soil is hard as concrete — dusty in dry times, with mud aplenty when it rains. The grass we planted around the camp units last September has long since died — a victim of the pad, pad, padding of feet, feet, feet! It's a real shame, since the green grass sure looked good this spring before the campers arrived."

"You know, Possum Hollow sure doesn't look like it did when we first built the campground. Remember the big trees — oaks, maple, white pine, hemlock? The mountain laurel, rhododendron, azalea, and other low shrubs were sure thick and pretty. Now look around. Shrubs and small trees are mighty scarce, and the big, beautiful trees have all got some kind of disease and are dying. I've sprayed them with all kinds of chemicals and spent a fortune having dead tops and limbs cut out; but nothing seems to work. We've got a sad area from all this overuse!"

"Well, folks, let's finish our lunch and get to work spreading grass seed and fertilizer around these tables!"

This sort of dialogue occurs in parks all over the world, including federal land-managing agencies like the National Park Service, the Corps of Engineers, the Forest Service, the Tennessee Valley Authority, and military installations. State parks, county parks, city parks, and private and commercial areas also face these maintenance challenges, and most of the good folks working in these parks make the same mistakes we described in our scenario. "Overuse" is a word we overuse! Park lands worldwide suffer from what is mistakenly called "overuse," meaning we blame visitors for our problems and maintenance woes. While users do create some difficulties for us, we frequently hold them responsible for far more damage than they cause.

If not "overuse," then what's the problem? More often than not, *poor planning, inadequate design,* and *lax administration* combine to give this appearance. Conscientious planning can minimize user impact, and a thorough understanding of design techniques, attention to detail, and application of knowledge from related areas of expertise can reduce maintenance costs drastically.

Over the years, resource managers have learned a good bit about stewardship. We know, for example, how to handle water movement on agricultural land through the use of ditches and berms; we know how to analyze soils and use the results for prescribing treatment for mineral imbalances to maximize agricultural production; we understand the carrying capacity of our resources to maintain domestic livestock and game species; we know how to manage forest lands for timber production. But when it comes to applying these same areas of expertise to managing resources for people — which is the goal of recreation resource management — we have either failed to use the information available to us or simply haven't realized that other disciplines, such as forestry and soil science, have application for recreation. Consider the situation we described at Possum Hollow Campground. The resources were in sad shape. What sort of "picture" did you get from the description? What were the *real* problems and what caused them? We can see many things, including:

— Heavily impacted and compacted soils caused by foot and vehicular traffic over the entire area;
— Accelerated runoff and erosion — soil with only 1/20 to 1/120 the percolation, or absorption, rate of water it once had;
— Once beautiful old-growth trees now dead or dying because their root systems

cannot absorb enough moisture and air through compacted soils;
— A continuing tendency to fight *effects* rather than *causes* by practices that include planting grass on known-impact areas such as campsites; and, perhaps the most serious error of all,
— A failure on the part of planners, designers, and administrators to blend together the *needs of the user and the environment* when developing and managing parks and other resource-based recreation areas.

It's easy to blame users for the types of problems we've just described. After all, Possum Hollow looked fine before it was opened to the public. Let's consider, however, others in the cast of characters — the planner, the designer, and the administrator — and see how they may have contributed to these problems.

The planners caused the first real error when they picked the grove of big trees as the site for the campground. You can't build park facilities in such groves (particularly among some species) without killing your attraction — those big trees. Trying to save old-growth trees by cutting out dead tops and limbs and by using chemical sprays is another example of fighting effects of recreation impact rather than causes. Generally, those of us who are planners have been treated well by the public and our agencies or organizations. Ofttimes we've had our pick of lands for development and have had few constraints placed on us in terms of design guidelines. Given this freedom, have we investigated alternative sites for suitability? Once a site has been tentatively selected, have we tested soils for composition and percolation rate? Chances are, we haven't.

What about designers, including landscape architects? Can these good folks be at fault as well? Often, designers subscribe to a philosophy of "If I like it, it must be right." This can lead to a failure to provide administrative and support personnel with *alternative* designs for park developments. With several alternatives to review, administrators and programmers responsible for managing an area can choose the best elements of each and synthesize them into a final, functional design. Most of the soil compaction described at Possum Hollow was a result of pedestrian and vehicular traffic — but not the fault of the user. The designers failed to *recognize* and *reinforce* areas they should have known would receive impact. Allowing users to drive over unreinforced areas changed the site environment. Also areas *not* intended for impact need to be protected from it. This is partly the responsibility of the designer. Since we were told visitors even cut barrier posts to get to tent pads and tables, the design — by ignoring the needs of users — actually forced them to cause maintenance problems. Designing a barricade between a parking spur and the camping pad it serves is analogous to an architect building a locked fence between your garage and living room; yet in recreation areas, this kind of *hindrance* to visitors occurs quite frequently.

It will perhaps surprise you to know that one of our most respected park agencies — the National Park Service — is quite guilty of the poor planning just described. (The authors plan to make sure you are surprised quite often throughout this text!) If you routinely ask your designers for only one solution to a design problem, e.g., a picnic area, more often than not they will accommodate you while "setting their feet in concrete" — insisting their design is the only feasible answer to your needs. Getting most of them to redesign or change their site plan, no matter how poor it is, will require quite a battle. Please take our advice and ask for three or four alternative solutions. With these in hand you and they can find avenues of agreement while egos remain intact.

Another portion of the responsibility for protecting recreation resources lies with administrators. At times, these managers may make changes in plans and designs without adequate thought, justification, or awareness of possible consequences for the environment. In fairness, political and budget problems may sometimes place constraints on managers and influence their decisions. However, park designs are periodically changed for the worse as a result of unnecessary managerial alterations. Also, a recreation area can be perfectly planned and designed and still fall apart if managerial staff allow visitors to misuse the area. Inadequate regulations, or failing to enforce existing ones, can create problems no design could avoid. Parks are *planned* by, *managed* by, and *used* by people. At times, planners and designers of recreation areas have failed to recognize the need to balance planning, parks, and people. As our title suggests, we'll consider the *interrelatedness* of these topics. Let's discuss each of these briefly, to set the stage for later chapters.

PLANNING. Our recipe for successful planning consists of three ingredients. The first is *technical knowledge.* To plan effectively, for example, it's necessary to understand contour lines and be able to interpret percent of slope. These types of skills, however, are relatively easy to acquire — slope is simply the change in elevation divided by the distance in which the change occurs. A four foot rise (or drop) in elevation along a line one hundred feet long would equal a four percent slope. Other types of technical knowledge, such as interpreting soils, are not as simple to learn. In fact, planners *shouldn't try* to learn all the skills necessary for planning. They should, however, be aware of what skills are necessary and know how to get information about these from sources who *are* experts in various areas.

The second element required for successful planning is a healthy dose of *common sense.* If a planner routes a trail immediately adjacent to a smooth-barked tree such as an aspen or beech, he or she shouldn't be too surprised to find people will carve their initials on it. Every element in the plan for a recreation area should have a purpose the planner can justify. Further, the purpose should make sense. Planners should be able to explain, in non-technical terms, *how* and *why* their designs function as they do. The architect Frank Lloyd Wright suggested that designs should adhere to the concept of "form follows function." In other words, while appearance (form) is a consideration, nothing is more important in a design than *purpose* or *function*. At times, park planners seem to have amended Wright's concept to "form follows function — Phooey!" Consider the concrete drainage ditch in a group camp in Tennessee shown in Figure 1.4. It has the *form* of a drainage ditch. It's also built *above* natural grade — water running down the slopes toward the ditch would have to rise *above* the sides of the ditch to drain into it, a fairly unlikely prospect. Elements of recreation plans must be functional.

While function must be the primary consideration for park designs, planners must also remember the recreational aspect of parks. To address this aspect, we need to include a third and final ingredient in our recipe for successful planning: a measure of *creativity*. Creativity in design is probably the most difficult element of planning to learn or to teach. Some people, and therefore some planners, are simply more creative than others. It is possible, however, to sharpen your creative design skills. The first trick is to *put yourself in the users' place:* how appealing is your design from their standpoint? The second method of improving your creativity is to make yourself *consider alternative designs*. Except for certain functional standards — length of a regulation tennis court, for example — there are no "rules" governing creative design. There may be a dozen alternative locations for the tennis court, all of which can satisfy technical requirements.

Figure 1.4

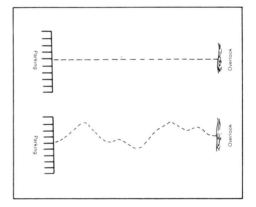

Figure 1.5

By developing the habit of looking at alternatives, you can become more creative. Figure 1.5 shows two ways of designing a path from a parking lot to a scenic overlook. Both designs get the public to the attraction, but, from the standpoint of building anticipation, providing an aura of mystery, and *creating* a positive recreational experience, which is the better design?

We have tried, throughout this book, to take a practical, here's-how-to-do-it approach to planning. It's important to understand the steps necessary for developing master plans for parks and recreation areas. However, there are other sources of information addressing needs assessments and broad planning issues. This text approaches planning from the standpoint of *designing* and *building*. When we discuss campgrounds, for example, we assume that the need for a campground has already been established — as part of the master planning process. This book concentrates on the actual development of facilities: how to *and* how not to lay out and construct parks and recreation areas.

PARKS. Our use of the word "Park" should be taken in the very broadest sense possible. This book is concerned primarily with resource-based, outdoor recreation areas. However, the planning *principles* we discuss apply to a much wider range of areas and facilities. It may take longer, for example, to plan a two-hundred-acre forest-based day-use area than it takes to plan an urban tot lot. But simply because the day-use area is larger doesn't imply that the tot lot deserves any less conscientious planning regarding its overall intended purpose. Conversely, the large day-use area should receive the same attention to detail and "fine tuning" as the tot lot. In fact, many of the planning concepts throughout this book may be applied to indoor settings as well. Designing a display area in a visitor center or environmental education building requires attention to factors such as intended audiences, zoning,

circulation, entry/exit points, and design psychology. All of these and other considerations are discussed in the following chapters. The types of facilities and available resources may vary, but the *principles* remain the same, regardless of whether the facility being planned is a major park or a minor parking lot.

To illustrate this point, consider what is perhaps the single most important principle in recreation planning and design: The KISS principle (**K**eep **I**t **S**imple, **S**tupid). Plans and designs for parks and recreation areas don't have to be, in fact *shouldn't* be, complex in order to be effective. Let's examine this principle for both a minor and a major design challenge. Figure 1.6 illustrates a potential problem at the exit point of a federal recreation area in Kentucky. Camping trailers and other recreational vehicles *exiting* the site tended to drive too near the check-out building, striking the overhanging roof of the building. Figure 1.7 shows the design "solution" recommended by a staff planner. Extending the curb as shown would have interfered with traffic for several days, thus causing inconvenience to users. Additionally, construction, including materials and labor, would have cost several hundred dollars. The KISS solution, shown in Figure 1.8, was to place a four-foot length of orange-painted railroad tie perpendicular to the building. Drivers steered to avoid the tie and the problem was solved. This solution took fifteen minutes to install at a minimum cost: Keep It Simple, Stupid!

On a larger scale, consider the design for the Indiana State Park campground shown as actually built in Figure 1.9. We'll discuss campground design in more detail in Chapter Seven; for now, let's concentrate on the problems created by the design. The road system has over twenty intersections, each of which is a potential source of confusion for users and an administrative problem for managers (safety, signing, and traffic control). The design also spreads the poten-

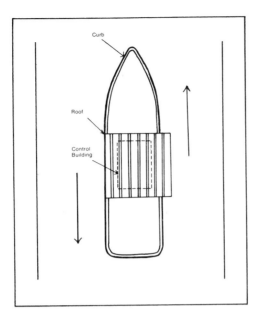

Figure 1.6

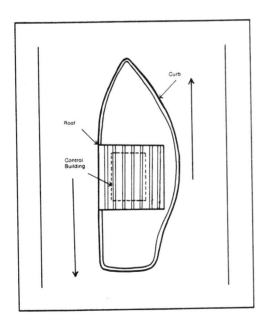

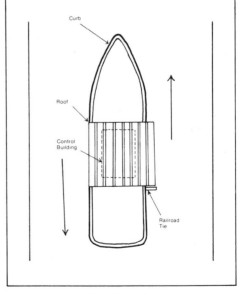

Figure 1.7   **Figure 1.8**

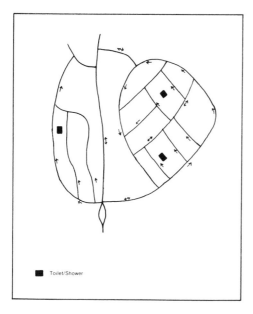

Toilet/Shower

Figure 1.9

tial for impact over the entire area. The KISS solution, shown in Figure 1.10, has reduced the number of intersections, simplified the circulation pattern, increased the potential for administrative control, minimized impact by moving users to and from toilet/shower buildings over the already hardened roadways, and reduced the cost of development by decreasing the amount of road. As these examples illustrate, design challenges for parks — measured in square miles or square feet — may differ in scope but not in need for simplicity of function.

PEOPLE. Of the three elements in our title, people are the most important. Before we discuss the kinds of people who need to be considered in park plans and designs, let's start by talking about the types of people for whom this book is written. First, each chapter is designed to serve as a quick reference for people who are directly responsible for developing plans and designs

for parks and recreation areas. For example, if someone assigns you the job of designing a campfire theater, you can turn to Chapter Eight and find answers to such questions as: "How many people should I expect to attend programs?" "How many linear feet of seating per person should I allow?" "How can I locate the theater to *complement* rather than *conflict with* other use areas?"

Second, and more important, this text is for people — both professionals and students — who aren't or don't expect to be recreation planners. This may sound like a different method of developing a book, which, after all, is about planning. There is, however, a reason behind this approach. The majority of people who practice in and study about recreation and parks are not planners — yet everyone involved with parks depends upon the designs planners create. This book considers planning from the perspective of those who are, in effect, *consumers* of the planning process — managers, programmers and maintenance personnel. Far too often, these people are left out of the planning process. Ask yourself this question: Who is a park for? The obvious answer — the visitor — is only partly correct. Users are the most visible recipients of the efforts of planners, but others benefit or suffer from park designs as well. This brings us to the types of people who should be considered during the planning and design process: users and staff.

People go to parks and recreation areas to relax, refresh themselves, and to have fun. Plans for these areas should be developed to *enhance* the experience of the user. Confusion should be minimized. Convenience, safety, and usability should be maximized. The way a park is designed can make the difference between an enjoyable or frustrating experience for visitors. It can also be discouraging to try to manage, maintain, or program a poorly designed recreation area. Park planners should remember their work is a *means* to an end rather than an end in itself. In other words, planning efforts should

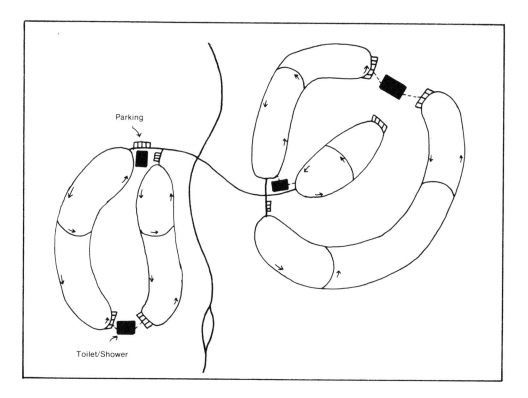

Parking

Toilet/Shower

Figure 1.10

support the work of those who operate park facilities. When planners fail to consider the *consequences* of their designs, the results can cause a variety of problems.

Many of the headaches associated with park planning result from a lack of *balance* between attention to the needs of people and the technical requirements of design. Often, one of the two is emphasized at the expense of the other. We feel that one reason for this problem is also one of the most critical issues in recreation planning today; the typical recreation planner is trained in either a technical discipline or a people-oriented discipline, *but not both*. For a recreation design to succeed, it must be functional *and* pleasing to people, and because technical and human needs are at times in conflict with one

another, good design requires compromise. In order to compromise effectively, the planner needs a full appreciation of both aspects of design. Let's examine two case histories to illustrate how inattention to either human or technical considerations can cause problems in parks — problems for users, problems for staff, and problems for the environment.

CASE HISTORY I: INATTENTION TO HUMAN NEEDS

Outdoor recreation came into its own in the 1950's. A number of factors, including the strong post-war economy and urban growth, led to an unprecedented increase in use of

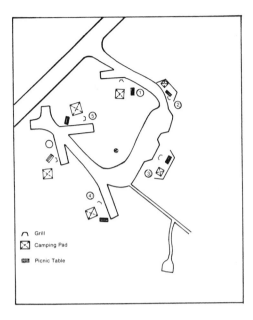

Grill

Camping Pad

Picnic Table

Figure 1.11

natural resources for recreation. The relatively sudden popularity of outdoor recreation caught many federal and state resource management agencies unprepared for such heavy use of their lands and waters. A case in point was the USDA Forest Service. Prior to the passage by Congress of the Multiple Use Act in 1960, provision of opportunities for recreation was not a mandated responsibility of this agency. Even before Congress acted, the Forest Service began taking steps to accommodate growing numbers of campers, hikers, picnickers, and others who, almost overnight, began appearing in ranger districts nationwide. Since this high level of use was a new phenomenon, the first action necessary was to provide facilities for the various types of users. Campgrounds, picnic areas, and boat launches needed to be developed, and someone had to plan and design these areas. Since there were no recreation planners in the agency, the question was, who should get the jobs?

Perhaps, using the logic that building roads and other facilities for recreation should be no different than building roads and other facilities for timber management, the Forest Service assigned the job of recreation planning to engineers. As we'll see in later chapters, engineering skills are critical to recreation design. Alone, however, they are not adequate to meet the needs of the people involved in recreation — users and recreation staff. Figure 1.11 shows a typical Forest Service campground designed by engineers in Arkansas. From a technical standpoint, it works — the road intersection is functional and the turning radii in the curves are adequate. But from a human standpoint, consider the following problems. With only six camp units, most visitors cannot find room to camp. Once these users enter the area, they have to turn around in order to exit; if they have a camping trailer, even a small one, there is no convenient way for them to reverse direction. Given the angles of the parking spurs and the dead-end road, exiting is also a problem for people who are able to find an empty site. From a management standpoint, the size of the area creates administrative problems as well. The campground is too small to cost-justify on-site management. To meet the needs of an increasing number of users, more areas are needed, and numerous small campgrounds are developed. But these areas are expensive to maintain and easy to vandalize. Because this type of design spreads use over a large area, a greater proportion of the environment is affected. From an engineering perspective, this type of design works. From a *recreation* perspective, it does not.

The Forest Service next gave the job of recreation planning to foresters. Overnight they — including one of your authors — became instant "experts" (with little experience and even less technical education). Figure 1.12, a camping area in a National Forest in Mississippi, illustrates a design typical of this group. The area exhibits many

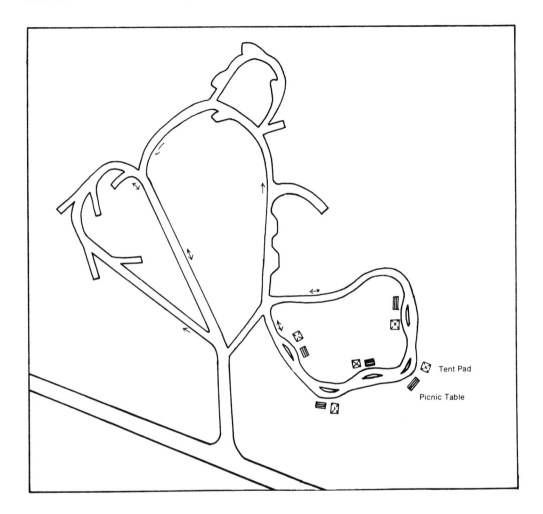

Figure 1.12

of the same problems discussed above: too few units to manage, maintenance and vandalism problems, and environmental damage. Additionally, this design wastes large amounts of potentially usable land in wide, or "fat" camping loop roads with few camp units. The roads themselves are a major mistake. First, there is no sensible system of circulation; the number of intersections and their relative locations are a source of confusion to users. (Remember, what you see in this bird's-eye view is not what confronts the user on the ground.) From a management standpoint, the road system is difficult to sign and, more importantly, is extremely expensive on a per-site basis; that is, the amount of road per campsite is much too high. As in engineering, the technical knowledge foresters have is important to recreation planners. As is the

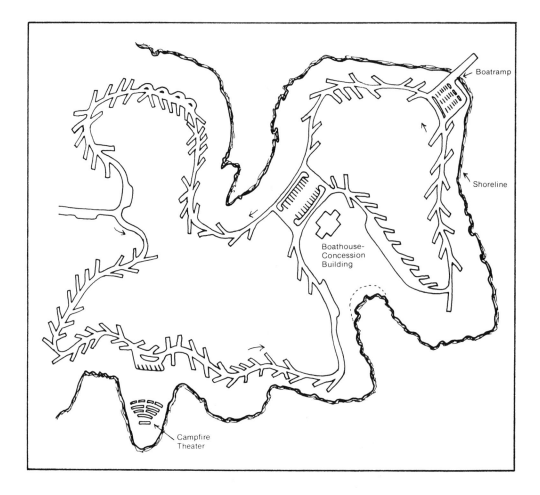

Figure 1.13

case with the engineers, however, this area — planned by foresters — does not take into consideration the needs of people who use and manage the area for recreation.

In the early 1960's, the Forest Service began hiring extensive numbers of landscape architects, and they were the next group to whom the agency assigned the job of recreation planning. Figure 1.13 depicts a National Forest campground in Texas, designed by a landscape architect, which corrects some of

the mistakes made in the previous two plans. More sites are included, so on-site management is feasible. The increased number of sites also reduces the expense of per-site maintenance. Since all sites are centrally located instead of dispersed at several small areas, the potential for environmental damage is limited to one location. There are problems with this design, however. The long, single loop precludes the opportunity to use a large portion of developable land between the upper and lower portions of the road. Also, the boat launch is located improperly. To get to the launch, it is necessary to drive through half the campground since traffic is regulated to a one-way, counterclockwise flow. This arrangement creates problems for management and users. With this design, it is impossible to open the area for boat launching only without allowing users access to the campground. Thus, a planning decision *dictates* how the area has to be managed. From the user's standpoint, regardless of where you choose to camp, every person who launches a boat is required, *by this design,* to drive by your campsite. Disregarding technical considerations for a moment, our goal should be to create a positive recreation experience for users. Routing *all traffic* by each campsite is not an effective means of accomplishing this goal. The major mistake made by the Forest Service was in thinking landscape architects had the expertise and academic park training to provide design excellence — they did not!

In fairness to the Forest Service and their technical staffs who planned these areas, it must be stated that other agencies have made similar and ofttimes greater mistakes. When the designs above were conceived, outdoor recreation itself was a new phenomenon, at least on a large scale. There were no recreation professionals to whom agencies could turn for design assistance. Thus, much of the recreation planning during the 1950's and early 1960's became, by default, the responsibility of technical personnel. As the demand for outdoor recreation continued to grow, more universities began offering curricula in recreation, and graduates of these programs started entering the job market. Some of these new recreation professionals began producing designs for recreation areas, and this brings us to our second case history.

CASE HISTORY 2: INATTENTION TO TECHNICAL REQUIREMENTS

Unlike their predecessors with backgrounds in technical disciplines, the new recreation graduates were trained in "people-oriented" skills. Courses in programming and leadership provided a better grounding in the needs of users; the new recreation professionals had a more complete understanding of management and program staff requirements in operating facilities for visitors. They did not, however, have the technical skills available to engineers, foresters, and landscape architects. Concepts such as road alignment, drainage patterns, and spatial awareness were not, *and generally still aren't,* part of the recreation curricula. Thus, a new generation of individuals developing recreation plans emerged. These individuals were trained in areas where previous planners were weak, but unprepared in areas where their predecessors were partially competent.

In many instances, the new recreation graduates who produced designs had no training as planners. In this sense, they shared a common background with earlier planners, and made some of the same mistakes. Part of the problem has been a matter of economics. Most of the land available for outdoor recreation is owned by either the federal government or the states, and agencies at this level of government are more likely to have the funding capability to staff planning positions. Historically, however, these levels of government have not been heavily involved with intensive recreation development; most advancements have been made by county and municipal governments and by private and commercial concerns. Yet many of these smaller recreation agencies and companies cannot justify the expense of a full-time planner.

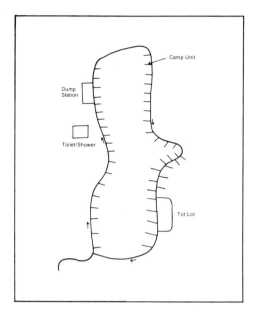

Figure 1.14

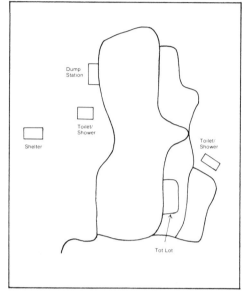

Figure 1.15

Assume for a moment you've just graduated from college with a degree in recreation. Your first job is as the Assistant Director of Parks and Recreation in Median, Ohio (population, 27,500). Your boss has a strong background in programming, so most of your responsibilities seem to fall in the area of park management and maintenance. The annual budget has funds earmarked for the development of a new park, to include a day camp, picnic area, playground, and trails system. You are given the assignment of overseeing the design effort. If you can't afford to hire a consulting firm (and you probably can't) what do you do? In this case, you probably have two choices: design it yourself or go to the city engineer for help. If you can afford a consultant, how do you know his or her plan has merit? Almost all consultants do an excellent job of *packaging* their products with professional drawings and presentations. But at times, the old saying about beauty being only skin deep is worth remembering. An attractive package,

whether developed in-house or by a consultant, *does not guarantee a good design.* In fact, it can often cover up a poor one.

The fact is, none of these solutions is ideal, yet all too often this is how park design evolves; the responsibility for planning falls to the person who is "least unqualified." To illustrate this point, let's examine the evolution of a campground in a city park in Kentucky. The campground was designed by an individual with a background in recreation programming, and this original development is shown in Figure 1.14. At this stage, the only major problem with the design was the failure to take advantage of all of the usable land — with five exceptions, no campsites were built on the outside of the loop. The problems began to compound when a series of additions to the campground was built. The first addition, shown in Figure 1.15, was typical of developments of this type all over the world. The planner erroneously assumed *there was a need to extend from the roads already in place.*

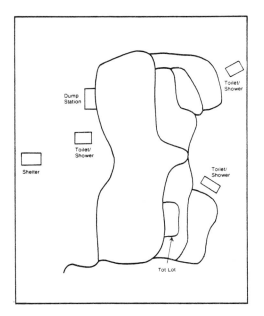

Figure 1.16

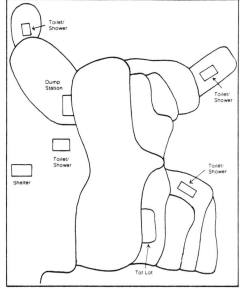

Figure 1.17

The difficulty with such an assumption is this: it takes for granted that the original development was well designed. If the original is bad, extending from it will usually make the situation worse, and whether you are adding to a campground, a trail, a playground, or any other recreation facility, this principle of design applies.

The design in Figure 1.15 begins to create several problems we've already discussed. The number of intersections increases considerably, making the area confusing to users and difficult to administer. The new roads widen the use zone and increase the potential for environmental impact associated with increased use, thus creating additional maintenance problems. These problems are all compounded further with the completion of the next addition, shown in Figure 1.16. Once this type of addition sequence has started, it's difficult to break away from the pattern and salvage a functional design.

One final addition was also completed, and the campground, as it exists today, is shown in Figure 1.17. For a simple example of the type of problem created by this design, consider the small loop in the upper left-hand corner of the design. The administration decided the campground should have an area reserved exclusively for tent camping and designated this loop for that purpose. The question is, how does the on-site manager enforce this regulation? It is possible, through design, to limit an area to tent camping (although, as we'll discuss in Chapter Seven, this may be a poor management decision in developed campgrounds). One way to accomplish this is to provide nearby parking and have users walk to their tent sites. If a road or other circulation system interconnects all areas, it is almost impossible to separate different types of users. This holds true for campsites, trails, play equipment, and most other recreation facilities. It may not be a management or design goal to separate areas, but if it is, they should be zoned without obvious circulation access between them.

From a design standpoint, we've been fairly critical of planners with either a technical or a recreation background. Most of the design problems in these two case histories caused two undesirable consequences. First, they encouraged environmental damage. Second, they created management and maintenance complications. The primary problems for *users* we've discussed to this point have been *confusion* or *inconvenience* resulting from poor road patterns, but the examples in both case studies also omitted the most important aspect of recreation possible. This omission wasn't a facility — it was the philosophy that *recreation should be fun!* Surprisingly, most parks and recreation areas seem to be designed without this idea in mind. None of the areas in either case study had play equipment, ball fields, hike 'n bike trails, or other areas to provide *recreation opportunities* for users. None of the campgrounds in either case study had shelter houses, campfire theaters, or other facilities to provide *program opportunities* for staff to share with users. The first two Forest Service areas we discussed were too small to justify these developments; the other, larger, campgrounds actually neglected to include these facilities.

We can't afford such negligence in recreation. As we suggested at the beginning of this chapter, recreation professionals have a dual responsibility: protecting the environment *and* creating an enjoyable experience for users. Provision of a facility such as a campground doesn't carry with it guarantees of enjoyment, and while recreation programmers shouldn't force their programs on park visitors, they should nevertheless offer opportunities for people to participate in planned activities. Programmers should also provide a pleasing environment — one which has aesthetic appeal and protection from impact built into it. Programmers, managers, and maintenance crews can all contribute to user enjoyment and environmental quality. In our opinion, however, none of these individuals has more potential for benefiting — or harming — these efforts than the recreation planner. To guarantee that the outcome of the planner's work is positive, he or she needs to be familiar with both technical and people-oriented skills. In the following chapter, we'll explore the specific kinds of knowledge planners should have.

2

TOOLS OF THE TRADE

Our aim throughout this book is to weave individual elements of recreation administration — planning, design, programming, maintenance, construction and management — into a complete tapestry. The old saying about "a chain being only as strong as its weakest link" seems appropriate here. If facilities are constructed poorly, maintenance will be difficult. If management is lax, programs may suffer. The three authors agree, however, that the link causing *most* of the problems in parks and recreation areas today can be traced to poor planning and design.

This chapter has two purposes. First, we want to share with you some examples of problems created by inadequate planning. Second, we will examine the types of knowledge recreation planners need to consider in their work. Successful planning may depend on skills as diverse as engineering and political sensitivity, yet no one individual can expect to master all the areas of expertise necessary for planning. Thus, part of the role of the planner should be to gather and synthesize information from various sources. Consider, for example, the recreation complex shown in Figure 2.1. This area has at least thirty planning errors designed into it, ranging from landscaping and engineering to maintenance and programming. We have included a list of errors at the end of this chapter. How many can you find? To provide you with some help, let's explore some of the concerns facing planners.

HYDROLOGY

Water is one of the best friends outdoor recreation professionals have. It provides the major attraction at many parks in the form of boating, fishing, swimming, skiing and other activities. However, water can be one of our worst enemies as well — if we fail to cope with it properly. For example, *water runs downhill,* often causing erosion problems. When water is allowed to run downhill over extended distances, both volume and velocity increase. The results of this are evident around beaches and other waterfront attractions which, since they are at lower elevations than surrounding land, are particular victims of water-caused erosion. One method of coping with this "mysterious" property of water is to place a ditch and berm combination just above the beach, as shown in Figures 2.2 and 2.3. This moves surface runoff water to the side of the beach, preventing the buildup of a large enough volume of water to erode the sand. The velocity of the runoff water is also slowed by reducing the distance of the unchecked downhill flow.

Polluting agents are another problem caused by runoff water around beach and waterfront zones. Parking lots collect gases, oils, and waxes spilled or leaked from vehicles. When these lots are uphill from beaches, rainwater collects the pollutants and carries them to the recreational water below. To avoid this problem, parking lots can be constructed with slightly tilted surfaces (at a

17

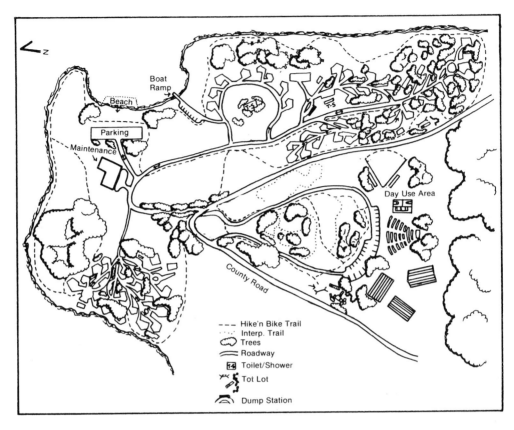

Figure 2.1

County Road Day Use Area

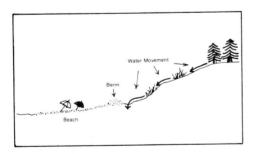

Figure 2.2   Ditch and Berm (Side View)

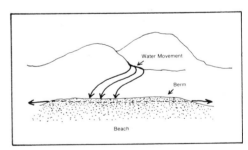

Figure 2.3   Ditch and Berm (Front View)

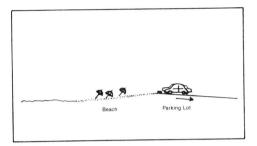

Figure 2.4   Parking Lot Outsloped

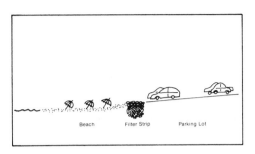

Figure 2.5   Parking Lot with Filter Strip

two- to three-percent grade) away from the beach zone, as shown in Figure 2.4. The tilt directs water away from the recreation area into a sump or rock-filled filter strip. If a parking lot is already installed (and the lower edge of the lot is facing the beach), the same sort of filter strip may be added to the edge of the lot, as shown in Figure 2.5. Such a strip should consist of a ditch two to three feet wide and four feet deep that is filled with septic-tank rock and topped with 1/2″ crushed stone. As water-borne pollutants hit this strip, they percolate through it instead of passing over to reach the shoreline below.

The roofs of buildings in parks — picnic shelters, restrooms, entrance stations, and others — act as mini-watersheds, too. Rainwater will drain to the edge of rooftops and then fall immediately below. Unless the ground surface beneath the eaves of a roof has been protected with crushed stone or other reinforcing materials, erosion will occur here rapidly.

Another "mysterious" property of water is its tendency to seek low places. If a park has them, water will rarely fail to find them, as Figure 2.6 shows. In this instance, the campground in the Cedars of Lebanon State Park in Tennessee received a less-than-corrective form of renovation. Essentially, roads and parking spurs were built up with rock, making the zone around each camping table the lowest point on each site. Planners

forgot water's habit of seeking low places, so every time it rained, each campsite became a built-in swimming pool. Ten years later, the same campground was renovated with attention given to water movement. The result was a highly functional design.

Parking lots, trails, roads, play fields, and play courts are among the other types of areas where water tends to pool. To avoid the problem in facilities such as these that are built on flat ground, crown them in the middle as shown in Figure 2.7. In other words, make the central portion of the surface slightly higher (two to three percent is enough) than the edges. This prevents water from standing, creating a nuisance for users, becoming a potential breeding ground for insects, and causing inconvenience for maintenance crews.

A final "mystery" of water is this: if recreational facilities are geared to waterfronts, they may get flooded, as shown in Figures 2.8 and 2.9. Because so many recreation lands are located next to lakes, streams, and rivers, many parks are partially or entirely situated on flood plains. The possibility of periodic overflow should not necessarily prevent building recreation areas on flood plains. Athletic fields, golf courses, primitive campsites, picnic areas, and similar facilities may not suffer a great deal of damage if they are subject to periodic flooding. Since they are relatively flat, flood

Figure 2.6

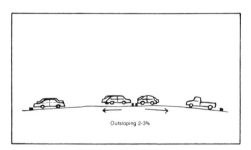

Outsloping 2-3%

Figure 2.7   Center Crowned Parking Lot

plains are also well suited for certain types of recreation facilities.

Caution should be exercised, however, if any of the following conditions are present. *Frequent flooding:* if an area is subject to flooding on a regular, cyclical basis, it may be best to avoid development entirely. *Rapid flooding:* in areas such as the narrow valleys and canyons of mountainous areas, flood waters may rise rapidly enough to create dangerous conditions. Sites where this danger exists should be posted as hazardous or avoided, and facilities such as campgrounds, where people could be caught unaware, should not be located here at all. *Developed sites:* structures with modern facilities such as

Figure 2.8

plumbing and electrical hook-ups should not be built on flood plains. Water damage here can create maintenance headaches as well as potential danger to users.

One of the most difficult tasks in planning is learning to identify potential water problems before developing recreation areas. Drainage patterns, minor changes in elevation, and potential sources of erosion and standing water are not easy to see. Additionally, construction may alter the water movement patterns on the site. If you have questions about preventing or solving water problems, we suggest you contact your local office of the Soil Conservation Service (SCS) for advice.

SOILS

Probably more information is available about soils than any other element of recreation planning. Yet the characteristics of soil — its potentials and limitations — may also be neglected more frequently. There are three basic types of soil: clay, which tends to absorb and hold moisture; sand, which does not; and silt, which covers all the gradations between clay and sand. The basic problem with soil, from a recreation planning perspective, is that certain types of facilities are not compatible with certain types of soil. If a recreation planner fails to incorporate soils information into his or her design, the results can cause a variety of problems.

Figure 2.9

Consider, for example, the garbage cans in Figure 2.10. Aesthetically, it may be a well-conceived plan to bury unsightly garbage cans up to their lids. However, the planner forgot to investigate soil conditions and placed the garbage cans in a pocket of moisture-absorbing clay. As a result, each heavy rain causes the clay to swell and forces the cans to float up out of the ground.

A less humorous mistake caused by in-attention to soil conditions is depicted in Figure 2.11. The plan for a recreation area in Texas called for a septic drain field to be located on a hill overlooking the beach. Effluent from the toilet's septic tank, as usual, moved down grade through the drain field. With proper soil absorption, the effluent should have percolated through the field safely and harmlessly. Since soils

information wasn't gathered prior to construction, planners and engineers weren't aware of a hard pan of non-absorbent soil less than three inches below the bottom of the drain field. This pan sloped gently toward the beach zone and actually came to ground surface above the beach. The effluent hit, ran along the top of the pan, and seeped out on the slope above the beach. As a result, the beach area became unsafe and unusable because engineers and planners didn't take time to gather adequate soils data.

It is not essential for recreation planners to be soils scientists. As with hydrology, your local SCS office can help provide most of the information on soils you need. It is important, however, to understand the *implications* of this information for the design of

Figure 2.10

recreation areas. Recreation planners should avoid placing facilities in areas where soils are inappropriate for them. For example, if you were a planner visiting the construction site in Figure 2.12 (with a heavy clay base), would it surprise you to return a year later and see the finished road looking as it does in Figure 2.13?

A word of caution seems advisable here — based on the authors' extensive experience. As a planner, you must have enough expertise to know when and how to use soils, along with vegetative, hydrologic, and other technical information. Soils scientists are likely to have little or no knowledge of recreation planning and design. Their advice may be helpful in curing the *effects* of problems (such as soil compaction), but may not address the true *causes* of your woes.

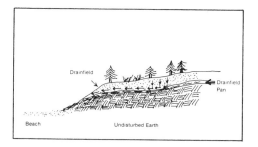

Figure 2.11

Figure 2.12

The same sort of caution should be exercised when dealing with foresters, hydrologists, engineers, and others (including the public).

VEGETATION

There are two basic problems with existing vegetation in recreation areas. One problem is removing too much of it. The other problem is not removing enough. First, let's consider some of the reasons why vegetation should be removed.

Hard surfacing: Some recreational facilities, such as the parking lot in Figure 2.14, are not compatible with existing vegetation. Hard-surfaced lots and deep-earth fills cut off the moisture and air needed for survival by the root systems of trees. Failing to cut

most trees prior to building such facilities will lead to their death and the need to remove them within a relatively short period (one to two years) after construction is complete. This later removal is normally far more costly than a pre-construction cutting, and it leaves stumps which must either be removed or left as eyesores. As the tree dies, rotting limbs may also cause hazards during windy periods. Leaving big trees in new parking lots creates costly maintenance problems worldwide.

Vista cuttings: Parkways and roads within recreation areas often traverse a scenic countryside, particularly in mountainous areas. In many instances, it is possible to enhance the experience of visitors by cutting trees that block vistas. Site-specific conditions dictate the appropriate type and

Figure 2.13

amount of clearing. In addition to aesthetic views, the planner should also consider visitor safety when developing vistas. Safety may be increased by providing parking areas or turn-outs with wide shoulders sufficient for vehicles to pull off the road. If you develop off-road parking facilities, plan and design them for travel trailers and other large recreational vehicles as well as for cars. Where narrow right-of-ways or other factors prohibit off-road viewing areas, safe vista viewing is still a concern. Avoid vista cuts in areas near sharp turns, crests of hills, intersections, or other areas where driver attention should be focused entirely on the road.

Overshading: Particularly in warmer climates, recreation areas and shade go together like hot dogs and baseball.

However, in some instances, thinning vegetation to reduce shade is appropriate. Campsites should be provided with morning sun for drying equipment (and warming campers). Beaches should have afternoon sun. Some areas, such as playgrounds and picnic areas, should have a mixture of shade and open areas. Given this mixture, users can design their own experience, based on their preferences and the current weather conditions.

As a general rule, asking users what their shade preferences are will not provide you with a valid guide for deciding how much vegetation to cut. People tend to overestimate the amount of shade they actually prefer, so your own careful observation and common sense are useful tools when prescribing levels of shade.

Figure 2.14

Susceptibility to impact: Some species of trees are more prone to damage from recreation use than are others. Young, vigorous hardwoods, particularly the deep-rooted species such as hickory, are probably most compatible with recreation use. Species such as Scarlet Oak, American Beech, White Pine, and Aspen are more subject to damage from impact. Knowing your trees has two implications for planning. For some recreation developments, it may be possible to devise planting plans prior to completion of facilities. In these instances, the planner should take steps to insure that the vegetation planted is capable of withstanding impact. In other cases, recreation developments may be planned in areas where vegetation is already established. Here trees likely to be damaged by use (such as large and shallow-rooted ones) should be removed prior to development. Remember, foot traffic creates impact as well as vehicular traffic.

Perhaps it is appropriate to raise an ecological point here. From the perspective of environmental protectionism, it may seem immoral to cut down trees at all. However, recreation professionals are faced with a choice: protect the environment by *prohibiting* recreation use or protect the environment by *conscientiously planning for* recreation use. If we make the choice — both personal and professional — that using our natural resources for recreation is a good thing, then we must accept some alteration of and impact on these resources. However, as we suggested briefly in Chapter One (and as we'll discuss in later chapters) it is possible to minimize the impact of outdoor facilities. Cutting trees subject to impact is an example of this. If, in the name of protecting the environment, a planner chooses not to cut an impact-susceptible tree in the middle of a new playground, he or she has condemned the tree to slow death by moisture and oxygen starvation, created a maintenance problem, and encouraged a potential safety hazard. Trees should not be removed indiscriminately. However, when the situation warrants it, they should be cut.

Tunnel effect: Another instance when it may be desirable, from an aesthetic perspective, to manipulate levels of vegetation is to control a tunnel effect. Vegetation along the sides of roadways and trails may grow up and over these corridors, creating a tunnel-like enclosure. A tunnel effect in itself is not bad; however, the old proverb about too much of a good thing should be invoked here. One key to aesthetically pleasing design is *visual variety*. Long, unbroken sections of road or trail which are enclosed become oppressive. Conversely, long open stretches can be monotonous. Other prescriptions for visual variety are suggested under the *Design Psychology* section later in this chapter.

"Invisible" effects: Some problems that result from failing to cut vegetation may not be readily evident. An excellent example of this is the attraction some species of trees, such as willows, have for water and sewer lines. In an effort to find moisture, the roots of these trees will, in effect, "attack" utility lines. Another often unseen problem with vegetation is dead limbs on otherwise healthy trees. Thus a good motto for planners (as well as maintenance crews and other field personnel) is "learn to look up!"

Although the problem does not arise in as many instances, it is possible to remove too much vegetation. In some circumstances vegetation should be planted, encouraged, or left in place. While it is not directly related to recreation, an excellent example of over-clearing may be found in many housing developments. Often, developers purchase a large tract of land, clear it of vegetation, grade the topsoil, and build homes. Home buyers must then purchase topsoil, seed grass, and plant trees in order to have yards. An appropriate principle to remember when you plan parks is: "cut what must be cut but *only* what must be cut." Vegetation should be left in place or planted to accomplish the following goals:

Screening: Trees with dense, low limbs as well as thick understory vegetation are useful for providing physical and psychological screens between areas you wish to separate. For example, if a design goal is to maximize the number of camp units per acre, vegetative screening around units can provide a sense of privacy for campers while allowing the planner to develop a high-density camping area. A campground with sites carved out of a dense stand of young spruce can average ten to twelve camp units or more per acre without producing a feeling of being crowded.

Screening can also be used effectively to "channel" people from one area to another. For example, if you wish to have people use a reinforced trail between a lodge and a campfire theater, cut only the vegetation necessary to construct the trail. This makes it convenient for the public to use the trail and inconvenient for them to stray from it, meeting users' needs and protecting the environment at the same time. Walking on a trail or camping on a site surrounded by vegetation also tends to create a "natural" atmosphere.

Noise reduction: Leaving vegetation between facilities can also help attenuate, or muffle, obtrusive sounds. If, for example, an area is limited in size, it may be possible to develop a wide variety of facilities and programs that might otherwise conflict with one another by leaving or planting vegetation strategically.

Advance plantings: If an area has been designated for future development in a long-range plan, it is a good idea to consider future levels of vegetation. For instance, if the plan calls for construction of a picnic area in five years, will there be adequate shade? Long-term advance planning of recreation sites is not always available, but if it is, additional plantings should be implemented as needed.

Cover plantings: Development and maintenance of vegetation in parks and recreation areas can benefit users in a variety of ways. Grasses, trees, and understory vegetation help prevent the erosion caused by both water and wind. Many species of shrubs also provide browse and shelter for deer and other wildlife. And shrubs bearing fruit and berries can be planted along the edge of an open field pathway to create a songbird walk.

Mowing: A tragic axiom in far too many parks involves grass — yes, acres and acres of grass. This axiom states that parks are run by grass mowers, a bit facetious sounding, but containing a ring of expensive truth.

When given a choice, most maintenance personnel love to mow, mow, mow. Compared to most other maintenance tasks, mowing is not a difficult job, and as a result, they tend to mow more than is necessary. However, if you want to establish screening around individual camp units, you should instruct maintenance crews to cut *nothing* or *only* one mower width around the perimeter of each unit. This gives a well-kept, groomed look to the site without eliminating desired vegetation before it has a chance to develop into screen. Mowing patterns should be prescribed specifically by administrative personnel with advice from the planner, rather than left to the discretion of maintenance crews.

A final word about vegetation: During the late 1960's, outdoor recreation was enjoying an unprecedented popularity. With increasing numbers of users, many recreation areas began to take on a trampled, overused look. In response to this, government agencies began investing research funds into ways of coping with recreation impact. One federal agency spent considerable time and effort attempting to determine which kinds of grasses grew well in picnic areas receiving high impact. The answer, which, in retrospect, should have been obvious, was that none will. Grasses will withstand impact more readily in sunlight than in shade; however, if the potential for use is fairly consistent, the planner should recognize this and reinforce areas where impact will occur.

There are several sources available to help provide expertise on questions concerning vegetation. Each state has an agricultural extension service. Central extension offices are generally located on the campuses of land grant colleges or universities. Additionally, the extension service maintains branch offices in every county in the United States. Often, help may be available through the various district or regional offices of the US Forest Service. State governments support departments of forestry, and many colleges and universities have schools or departments of forestry or natural resources.

TOPOGRAPHY

Developing recreation plans and designs on a flat piece of paper is quite different than designing facilities in the field. One skill essential for creating plans and assessing the merit of alternative designs is reading and interpreting topographic maps. These maps contain imaginary *contour lines* indicating elevations above sea level. For example, on a topographic map all points on an area elevated 1250 feet above sea level would be connected by the same line. Normally, contour lines are drawn in intervals of two, five, or ten feet, depending upon the scale of the map. Along with the contour interval, this scale, which typically shows that one inch equals fifty, one hundred, or two hundred feet, allows you to determine the percent of slope of the land. Assume the contour interval is five feet and the scale is one inch equals one hundred feet. If there are approximately three contour lines per inch on the map, the slope is $(5x3)/100$ or fifteen percent — too steep for most recreational facilities. Figure 2.15 illustrates contour intervals, scale, and other features commonly found on topographic maps.

While topographic maps are important, they should not be relied upon exclusively to provide information for developing plans. Unlike maps drawn on paper, real topography is not entirely static. Streams may change course and lakes may vary in "pool" (the elevation of the lake surface). Features such as roads or adjacent housing developments may also have been developed after the survey that produced the map was carried out. Actual contours or other features in the field may not be located exactly as shown on the map, either. Your authors (who, of course, *never* make mistakes) once

Scale 1":400'   Contour Interval=2'

Figure 2.15

located a camping loop road adjacent to a tree line shown on a topographic map. Our intent was to provide shade for the camp-sites. While studying the map in the field, we realized that the actual tree line was over one hundred feet away from where it was indi-cated on the map.

Remember, on a scale of one inch equals two hundred feet, a hiking trail six feet from side to side is indicated by a line the width of a pencil mark. As a result, mistakes are not difficult to make, and information drawn from topographic maps should be supple-mented by other, more reliable sources. One such source, particularly if the area to be planned is larger than a few acres, is aerial photography. In some cases, your local soil conservation service office may be able to provide you with aerial photographs of your area. If not, commercial agencies are avail-able to conduct photogrammetric surveys, usually at a reasonable cost. There is no substitute, however, for a hands-on approach. A recreation facility — whether a vest-pocket park or a thousand-acre complex — should *never* be planned without on-site visits. There are too many intangibles which, without "field planning," might be left unconsidered.

One design error we have seen a number of times relates to the inattention planners sometimes give to the interaction of people with topography. A common mistake is to choose a site for a recreation complex based on its proximity to a lake or reservoir, then develop the site on a hill or bluff over-looking the water. From an aesthetic perspective, this may be appealing. However, there are two program-related problems asso-ciated with this approach. First, the lake is probably one of the primary attractions asso-ciated with the facility. If the recreation complex is several hundred yards away from the lake — as well as a few hundred feet in elevation higher — then access to the water becomes a problem.

Second, a design goal may be to provide active play areas such as ballfields and play courts. Generally, when lakes are present,

most of the developable, i.e., flat, land will be immediately adjacent to the shoreline; therefore, access from the main complex, if it is located on an overlooking hill, may again present a problem. The severity of this problem depends on the type of population for which the facility is intended. College students and young adults might find a half-mile walk down a three-hundred-foot hill with an eleven percent grade an incon-venience at most; for other users such a path might present real barriers.

We know of two recreation complexes in Indiana built on bluffs overlooking lakes. One is a university alumni camp catering to senior citizens and families with young children. The other is a resident camp frequently visited by children and adults with severe physical impairments.

There are several sources of information and assistance if you have concerns about topography. In addition to the SCS and photogrammetric services mentioned above, the United States Geological Service (USGS), with regional offices across the country, may provide help for you. Also, many colleges and universities have departments of geography and/or regional planning capable of providing topographic assistance.

PROGRAMMING

Chapter Eight provides a more detailed look at the implications recreation programming has for planning. However, we mention programming briefly here for two reasons. First, let us re-emphasize that programs and the benefits they provide to people should be, but rarely are, the ultimate goals of recreation. Planning, administration, construction, and maintenance should *all* be oriented toward facilitating program delivery. Second, we mention programming because it illustrates, through two simple examples, the need to seek a *balance* in planning. While there are exceptions, a good starting point for planners is to balance "too much" with "too little;" "too expensive" with "too cheap;" and, as illustrated below, "too near" with "too far."

Figure 2.16 shows the design for an activity area in a developed site, a family campground operated by the Tennessee Valley Authority (TVA) in Kentucky. The playcourt, which consists of volleyball and basketball courts, is lighted to permit play after dark. The courts are popular, and normally attract a mix of twenty to fifty children, teenagers, and adults each evening. Another popular campground attraction is the campfire theater. Passive programs, including movies, puppet shows, and sing-alongs are held in the theater four evenings each week. Often, several hundred people attend these programs. As the drawing in Figure 2.16 shows, the theater and play courts are built within one hundred feet of each other with no physical or vegetative screening between the two facilities. As a result of this design, the noise from games on the playcourts makes it impossible to conduct quiet programs in the campfire theater.

The point is: both types of recreation — the passive campfire program and the active court sports — provide enjoyment for campers and are valuable assets to the campground. However, the design provided by the planners creates a situation where it is impossible to take advantage of both facilities at the same time. We'll talk more about concurrent programs in Chapter Eight; however, keep in mind that one goal of design should be to maximize the use of *all* facilities. If one program will conflict with another, the design should allow for this by separating the areas designated for each one. Placing the campfire theater too close to the playcourt is an excellent example of *not* planning parks for people.

Separating use areas by too much can also create problems. Part of Paris Landing State Park in western Tennessee is depicted in Figure 2.17. In this case, the park camp-

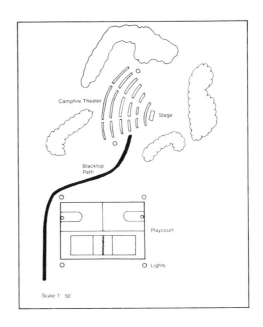

Figure 2.16

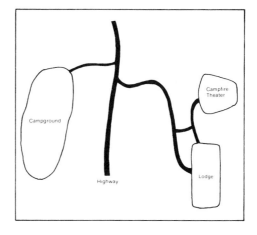

Figure 2.17

ground is on one side of a busy highway. The park lodge and campfire theater are on the opposite side. Along their parkways, the National Park Service, as well as many state systems, make this same mistake. The distance between the campsites and a campfire theater is between one-third and one-half mile. On our visits to the theater, the evening programs were quite entertaining; however, we rarely met people from the campground who attended the programs. Two comments are worth making here. First, program facilities should be relatively close to the areas supporting them. This close proximity should be physical, although, if this is not possible, it may be psychological. Large theme parks such as Disney World, for example, use shuttles in their parking lots: the attraction thus *seems* close because it is easily accessible. Second, program areas function more effectively when they are perceived to be *a part of* the recreation complex people are using. The TVA campfire theater discussed above is in a large campground. Some campsites there are further from the theater than is the case in the complex at Paris Landing, but attendance from these distant TVA campsites is as good as that from campsites near the theater. There is no perception of leaving the campground, and the program area is well-attended. Experience tells us participation at various program facilities *within* a campground is not a function of distance from campsites. This allows you considerable latitude in deciding where you locate such facilities.

A few sources may be able to provide you with advice if you have questions about planning outdoor recreation areas to enhance programming. Most "direct programming" — where agency staff actually interact with users on a face-to-face basis — occurs at the local level in municipal park and recreation departments. As a result, city personnel are probably more familiar with programming than the majority of state and federal recrea-

tion, staff, and may be able to advise you. Likewise, college and university recreation departments *where courses in programming are taught* can provide assistance.

A final means of gathering information about programming needs — and one too frequently neglected — is to develop a working relationship with user groups. Local chapters of the National Campers and Hikers Association, the American Motorcyclist Association, horseback organizations, hunting and fishing clubs, and similar groups can provide you with a wealth of advice about their needs and preferences. In addition to gathering information, the public-relations benefits make working with user groups well worth your time. One word of caution: special-interest groups tend to have a special interest. A bird-watching organization and the local duck-hunting club may not see completely eye to eye on all issues. Ask for and take into account the opinions of user groups, but learn to balance what they tell you with professional judgment and common sense. As we mentioned earlier, programs should be supported by planning. However, other concerns — including those of maintenance crews and administrative personnel — need to be addressed as well.

ADMINISTRATION

Parks can be planned to work *for* or *against* effective management. Conscientious planning can make recreation areas easy to administer. Failure to consider the needs of management personnel can create administrative problems throughout an area or in specific locations. Consider, for example, the design in Figure 2.18. This shows the entrance to a campground within a state Division of Reservoirs Property on Lake Monroe in central Indiana. Immediately across the road from the campground fee station (where campers register), the planner installed a large parking lot. The

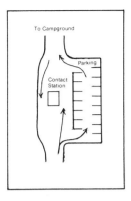

Figure 2.18

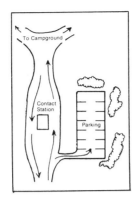

Figure 2.19

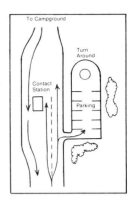

Figure 2.20

problem? The parking lot has two entrances — one on the outside and one on the inside of the fee station. This design makes it possible to drive around, as well as past, the entry point. A parking lot may have been a necessary feature at this location, but the entrance inside the fee station severely limits the ability of management to control traffic flow into the campground.

Interestingly enough, the entrance road to the campground at McCormick's Creek State Park, also in central Indiana, has exactly the opposite design problem — and creates another type of headache for management. As shown in Figure 2.19, the approach to the fee station has only one lane for incoming traffic. The zone has a parking lot for visitors to the campground (a good idea), with a single entry/exit point outside the fee station. The problem? Because of the one-lane entrance, campers who have already registered and who display a registration ticket on their vehicle must wait in line for newly arriving campers to check in. Assume, on the average, it takes one-and-a-half minutes to register; on Friday evenings there may be times when previously registered campers are required to wait in line behind twenty to thirty vehicles just to get back to their campsite after a day of sightseeing. This may not, on the surface, seem like an admini-strative problem, but would *you* like to greet a family of preregistered campers at your fee station after a forty-five-minute delay in central Indiana in July?

Figure 2.20 shows an alternative design which solves this problem. The parking lot is accessible only from outside the entry point, and a dual entrance lane past the fee station lets newly arriving campers check in, using the inner lane, while those who have already registered may enter the area via the right-hand lane. (Note also the turnaround we've added to the parking lot for folks with trailers.) Campgrounds and other use areas with entry stations where only newly arriving vehicles are required to stop should have a minimum two-hundred-foot, double-lane road on the *right-hand* side of the entry station. In addition to this minimum, planners should allow one foot of double-lane road for every potential user group beyond the first one hundred. In other words, if an area has a maximum capacity of three hundred vehicles, the double-lane portion of the entry road should be two hundred feet for the first one hundred vehicles plus two hundred feet for the next two hundred, or a total of four hundred feet.

Poor planning can affect your ability to manage entire recreation complexes as well as specific areas such as entrance zones. This

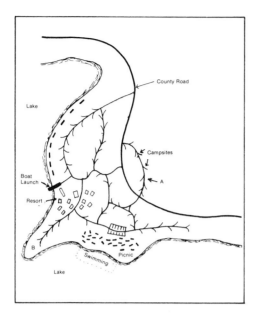

Figure 2.21

is illustrated by the multiple-use area shown in Figure 2.21, which depicts a park built on a broad peninsula of land. Prior to planning and developing the park, the only existing human-made feature on the peninsula was the county road. Consider the following administrative problems resulting from the design of the area.

Traffic control: a good axiom of design is to limit to one the number of entry/exit points in a recreation area. This minimizes user confusion (Where am I? How did I get here?), as well as reducing the number of points which must be controlled by management. If, for example, a design goal were to prohibit entrance to this park after 10:00 p.m., five intersections on the county road would have to be staffed or barricaded.

User safety: once the area between the county road and the shoreline was developed, the only place to install new use areas was on

the other side of the road (area A). In addition to creating a safety hazard for users who want access to the lake front, this area creates other maintenance and administrative problems. Since it is outside the rest of the complex, it may be more difficult to control vandalism and rowdyism in area A. It also requires either the costly installation of additional toilet/shower buildings and utilities or forces users to cross the county road for these facilities.

User convenience: designs such as this one — which are surprisingly common in parks — are extremely disorienting to users. Each road juncture presents a new challenge. (Do I turn here, or go straight?) You could argue that directional and informational signs at each intersection would eliminate confusion; our response to this argument is: Phooey! Extensive numbers of signs are a symptom of poor planning and design; they help cure *effects,* but not *causes!*

Consider also the dead-end camping roads (areas B and C). Once a camper, towing a twenty-two-foot trailer, reaches the end of these roads, how does he or she turn around? Pretend you are the park manager who must tell them what to do. (*We* certainly don't care to.) This suggests another point to remember: build to anticipate your clientele. If you plan on attracting users with large recreational vehicles or boats on trailers or kids in wheelchairs, be sure you *design* for them.

Zone management: When you plan recreation areas, it is important to remember a concept called *simple zoning of use areas.* Design and locate facilities *near* other, similar areas and *away from* dissimilar ones, as with the play courts and campfire theater we examined earlier. The design of the park in Figure 2.21 did not follow this principle. For example, to reach or exit the boat-launch zone, it is necessary to drive through and disturb part of the campground, inconveniencing users. From the manager's point of view, assume you want to close the campground after Labor Day, but keep the boat launch and resort open. How would you route traffic? Don't ask us — we're just planners. Similarly, the swimming and picnic areas — both day-use activities — are zoned near overnight camping areas, but campers and day users may have different recreational goals. We suggest that these types of areas be zoned separately. Use conflicts are thus avoided and management difficulties reduced.

Some areas within recreation complexes should be planned as "neutral zones." For example, the picnic sites (area D) violate this principle. Because of poor planning, a few individuals or groups are able to monopolize an entire section of shoreline which should be open to all park users. Camping or picnicking immediately next to the edge of a lake or river is an enjoyable experience; however, placing use facilities too close to a shoreline may also encourage erosion. Further, it tends to limit maximum use and enjoyment of the resource to the few groups who happen to arrive first. We suggest "primary attractions" such as shorelines, scenic vistas, and overlooks be designed so *all* visitors have an equal opportunity to enjoy them. To accomplish this, individual-use areas — picnic sites, camp units, and the like — should be kept a minimum of seventy-five feet away from such attractions.

One of the most difficult but necessary tasks of developing and assessing plans for recreation areas is to step back and view the "big picture." Most of the design errors in Figure 2.21 were committed because of one *basic mistake* committed early in the design. Can you identify it? Here are some hints: it created safety hazards; it forced dissimilar areas to be zoned together; it placed a severe limit on the opportunity to take advantage of usable land. Remember — look at the entire area.

This park design was doomed before it was ever constructed because planners allowed

the existing county road to *dictate design to them*. Using roads and other support facilities already in place is cost-effective if, and only if, existing facilities serve the needs of the design. In this case, the county road ran through the center of the peninsula, splitting the available land into two marginally usable pieces. Figure 2.22 shows the same peninsula with the obtrusive section of old road replaced by one which allows full development of the peninsula. This redesign also changes the mixture of day use and camping (which is difficult to administer) to a well-zoned single-use family campground with a broad spectrum of desirable amenities.

We'll dig more deeply into the fine points of area design in later chapters. For now, just consider how this new design functions from an administrative standpoint:

— It contains a single entry/exit point for control;
— The administration/maintenance complex is zoned *a part of,* yet *apart from* user-oriented facilities;
— The campground support amenities — boat ramp, beach, interpretive area and campfire theater, hike 'n bike trails, play courts and fields — are zoned away from the camp units;
— The active play zone is separated from the passive zone;
— A series of inexpensive barricades allows the park manager to determine how he or she wants the area to be used based on existing needs. A barricade at point A closes the entire park. The barrier at point B permits access to the boat launch only. Closing point C prevents entrance to the campground. Barricading point D limits camping to one area when demand is low;
— All users have access to the shoreline because lake-front developments on those facilities — the boat launch, beach, and trail — do not encourage "first come, first served" placement.

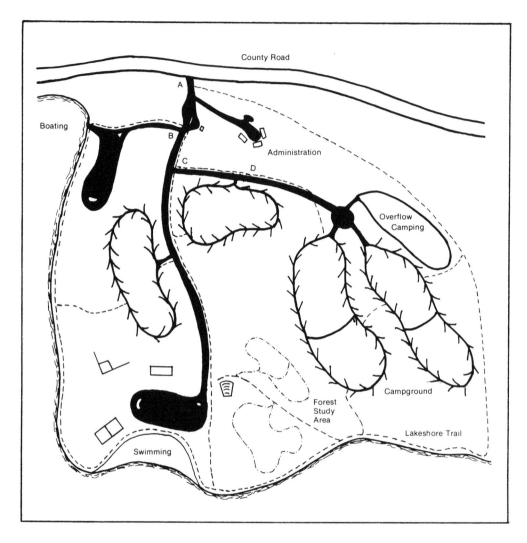

County Road

A

Boating

B

Administration

C

D

Overflow
Camping

Forest
Study
Area

Campground

Lakeshore Trail

Swimming

Figure 2.22   Prototype Stage 3

Sources of assistance for planning the administration of recreation complexes are somewhat limited, but college and university departments of public administration and schools of business are possible ones. Some state and federal resource-oriented agencies also maintain technical assistance programs. If you are developing a private or commercial facility, the Small Business Administration may prove to be a helpful resource, too.

One final word about planning and administration is worth mentioning; include managerial personnel in recreation planning and design. Their opinions need to be considered and their concerns addressed. However, as with other groups with whom the planner works, managers have their own perspective on how the world turns. For example, the on-site manager of a large-use area may hear fifty people complain about "X" brand drinking fountain during a four-month season. After apologizing for "X" fifty times, the manager may be inclined to tell you "X" should be torn down and replaced with "Y" before the end of the week. The only problem is, there may have been 65,000 people who used "X" with only the fifty not liking it, and research might have told you that "Y" has even more detractors. People, human nature being what it is, are much more inclined to complain than to compliment, and managers are more likely to remember and repeat the complaints they hear. After hearing fifty complaints, they are also likely to tell you that *"Everyone* says 'X' drinking fountain is the pits." Thus planners should listen to managerial staff, but keep their comments in perspective. Two more axioms worth remembering are "beware of managers bearing tales" and "learn to lean on applied research data."

MAINTENANCE

There are several types of maintenance involved in parks and recreation areas. Typically, we think of *ongoing,* or *periodic,* work such as mowing, minor repairs, and the like and *long-term tasks* such as planning for new roofs for structures or resurfacing roads. There is another type, however — *preventive* maintenance — which, over time, is more important in terms of money and effort saved or spent. Since the planner can have a positive or a negative effect on all types of maintenance, let's examine how this happens.

On-going maintenance. As with administration, maintenance can be affected by planning on both a large and small scale. To illustrate, think about a basic maintenance task: collecting garbage. Figure 2.23 shows three ways a planner might design garbage-can locations on a portion of a camp-loop road. Design A shows twelve campsites and twelve garbage-collection points. (Remember — maintenance crews are generally paid by the hour.) Design B shows the same campsites, but with the garbage cans *clustered* to permit fewer stops for collection. In terms of benefits to users, there is a trade-off here. On the negative side, campers might have to walk a little farther to deposit garbage. However, with this design cans are available and odors removed from the "living area" of the campsites. Design C consists of the same twelve sites serviced by a single bulk-waste container, or "dumpster." With this design, the number of collection stops is reduced even more, although the average distance from campsite to dumpster has increased. There is no "correct" answer to which of these designs will best suit the needs of a particular area, but both B and C are generally better than A. With clusters of cans, it is normally about right to group between a minimum of three and a maximum of six cans together to balance ease of collection with user convenience. Bulk-waste containers will service, depending on frequency of collection, size of containers, and campsite density, from twenty-five to fifty camping units.

The same type of logic can be applied to on-going maintenance on a larger scale. Continuing with our example of garbage collection, and with hourly paid workers, look at the design shown in Figure 2.24. This design depicts one way of planning camping areas in a large resource area, perhaps a state park or a Forest Service ranger district. (A typical ranger district in the eastern United States might contain 100,000 acres of land.) Figure 2.24 illustrates the way most resource-based recreation areas have been planned historically. The design

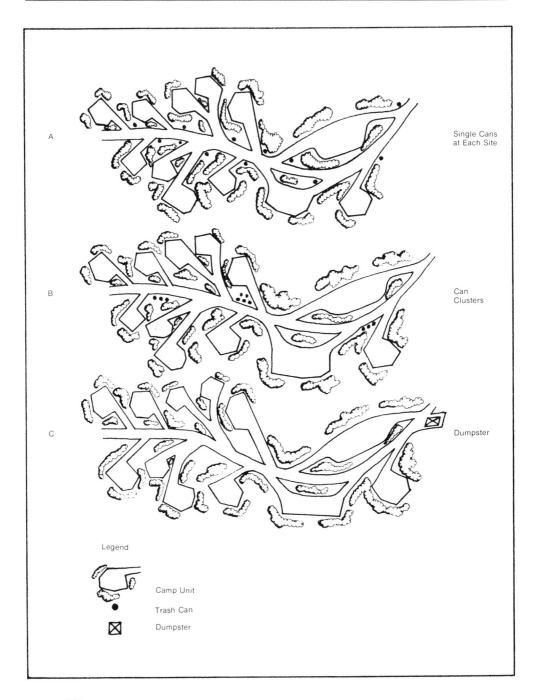

Figure 2.23

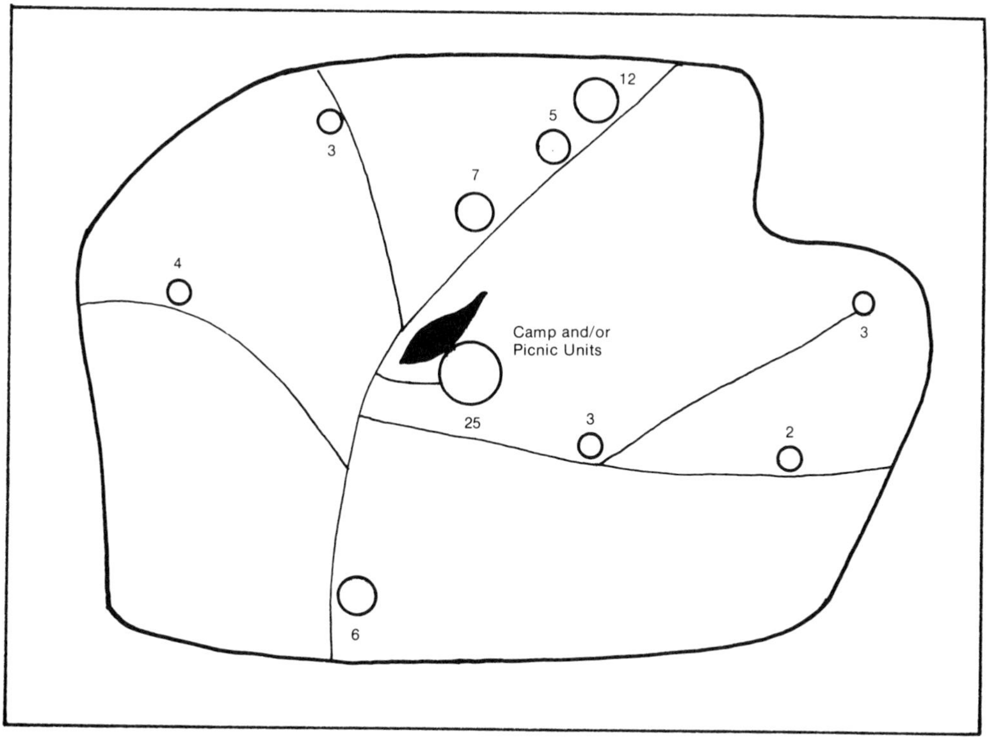

Figure 2.24

F.S. Ranger District
10 Areas—70 Units

contains ten small combination picnic and camping areas with a total of seventy camp units available for use. As you might imagine, the cost-effectiveness of collecting garbage from seventy units at ten sites spread over 100,000 acres is not particularly high.

In addition to being difficult to maintain, this type of planning violates sound principles of resource stewardship and, indeed, people management and protection. By providing small facilities throughout the resource base, the planner has scattered use, including that by vehicles, over the entire area. This error will increase the proportion of the resource subject to impact and consequently environmental damage as well. This type of design thus suggests the need for another planning principle: *areas subject to*

use and potential impact should be localized. Most federal agencies, including the Forest Service, the Corps of Engineers, and the Tennessee Valley Authority, have not approached recreation planning from this perspective. As a result, their recreation areas tend to be laborious to maintain, difficult to program, and hard to manage. For instance, one Corps of Engineers friend of ours who manages a rather small reservoir has a three-hundred-mile drive just to visit the campsites for which he is responsible.

The plan in Figure 2.25 shows how areas can be localized. Here the number of campsites has been increased from seventy to 815, while the number of areas has been reduced from ten to four. There is a small remote area with fifteen dispersed sites for

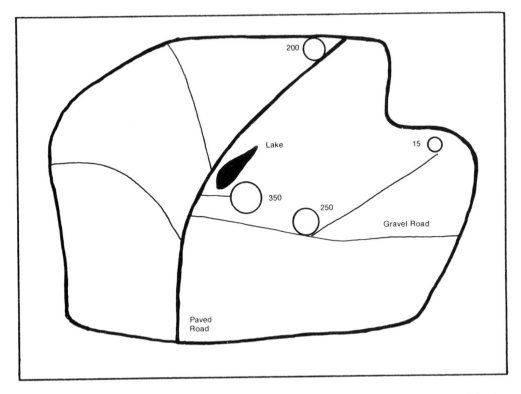

Figure 2.25

F.S. Ranger District
815 Sites—4 Areas

users who desire a backcountry experience. This site can be managed, because of its placement, as an addition to the adjacent area with little increase in effort. The three large areas are big enough to cost-justify on-site management and maintenance crews, so potential for support facilities and programs enhancing the experience of users is increased. The planning principle involved here is: *"Think big, plan big, and build big."* Large areas benefit the manager, the maintenance crew, the program staff, the user *and* the environment. From an ecological stand-point, this type of design allows us to identify where high levels of use will occur and enables management to take steps to *prevent* environmental damage.

Long-term maintenance. One excellent example of how planners can increase or decrease problems of long-term maintenance is in replacing roofs on park cabins. Planners in the environmentally charged 1960's placed countless rental cabins in densely vegetated areas where tree limbs covered and even touched roof tops. This led to rapid rotting of roofs and far too frequent replacement. These cabins needed more sunlight and much less shade.

Preventive maintenance. Perhaps one reason it isn't difficult to find maintenance problems "designed into" recreation areas is the nature of the planner's job. Once an area is planned, designed, and constructed, the planner is finished with it. He or she doesn't have to worry about how well or how poorly the area functions. Trails deteriorate, erosion occurs, campsites are compacted, signs get knocked down — these couldn't be the result of planning! Or could they? Extensive experience at hosting workshops on park design and rehabilitation tells us three unfortunate facts:

— planners and designers rarely attend continuing education courses;
— in far too many public agencies, planners and designers rarely work closely with managers; and
— most planners aren't users of the facilities they plan, and they rarely work with real park visitors.

Let's explore a few results of these planner characteristics. Some trails, because of the volume of use they receive, need to be reinforced with a hard surface. In parts of the country where frost heave is not a factor, hot-mix asphalt is one of the more popular hard surfaces used on trails. Asphalt holds up fairly well with one exception: it tends to crumble along the edges, especially in hot weather, when people step on them. The maintenance "solution" (again, this addresses effects rather than causes) would be to patch the edges with new asphalt on a periodic basis. Yet the *preventive* maintenance solution — the responsibility of the planner — occurs during construction. As the trail is built, a border of crushed rock can be placed along the edge of the asphalt surface and tapered to ground level, as shown in Figure 2.26. This keeps weight along the sides of the trail, which in turn prevents crumbling.

As an added benefit, the gravel border prevents users from stepping off the edge of the trail, which is above ground level, and falling or spraining an ankle. As this example shows, planning techniques aimed at solving one problem will frequently prevent other types of difficulties as well.

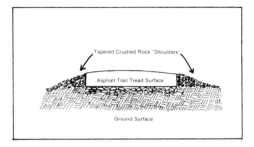

Figure 2.26

Staying with trails for a moment longer, let's continue with preventive maintenance. Figure 2.27 shows a trail head leaving a Forest Service parking lot on the Cherokee National Forest in Tennessee. A few months before this picture was taken, the trail was covered with a three-inch layer of sawdust, which remained there *until* the first big rain. Due to some interesting design, the only outlet on the paved and curbed parking lot fell where the trail began. Water in Tennessee, as in other places, runs downhill. In this case, it ran away with the trails' sawdust surface. As you can see, planning for preventive maintenance requires anticipating what *will happen* as well as knowing what current conditions are. One of your authors, by the way, designed the trail and the parking lot, but the other two of us never make mistakes.

In our discussion of administration, we talked about the need to *localize* potential areas of impact. The question here, from a maintenance standpoint, is rather like catching a cranky bull by the tail: now that we have it, what do we do with it? Once areas subject to impact have been localized and identified, the answer is to take steps to *reinforce* them. To illustrate this point, let's look at three different ways of designing campsites. Because campsites receive impact from recreational vehicles as well as foot traffic, the potential for damaging the

Figure 2.27

environment and creating maintenance problems is among the highest of all park-related facilities. Figure 2.28 shows a campsite with the facilities — the picnic table, grill, tent pad, and garbage can — on the right-hand side of the parking spur as you face the site. We'll discuss campsite design more completely in Chapter Seven; for now, let's concentrate on the area of impact, shown in Figure 2.29, *caused* by designing the site this way.

One of the more unfortunate aspects of this type of design is the tendency for park administrators, as well as some members of environmental "awareness" groups, to blame users for the damage to the site. While campers and other recreationists do cause some problems in the natural environment, there are none that professionals can't

control through conscientious planning and administration, i.e., designing preventive maintenance measures into park plans and enforcing regulations. Also keep in mind that if we didn't have a recreating public using our resources, we wouldn't have jobs either!

Figures 2.30 and 2.31 show why it's easy to blame users for environmental damage, but Figure 2.30 also shows a poor campsite layout at Hungry Mother State Park in Virginia. Vehicles are allowed to drive throughout the camping area, over non-reinforced surfaces, so the ground has been stripped of grass and compacted. The picture in Figure 2.31 was taken from the same vantage point to illustrate what this compaction does to trees. Users "caused" the problems here, but are they at fault or should we blame the planner?

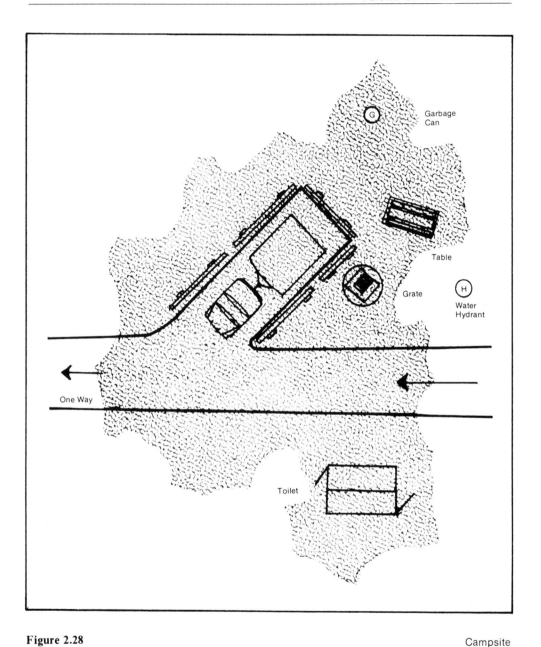

Figure 2.28   Campsite

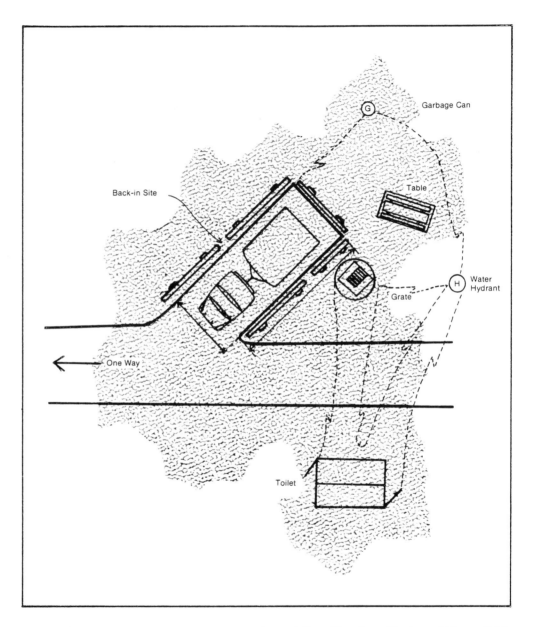

Figure 2.29　　　　　　　　Impact Resulting from Design of Figure 2.28

Figure 2.30

Figure 2.32 illustrates a *somewhat* better campsite design. The shaded area of impact has been reduced by moving facilities to the opposite side of the spur from where they were in Figure 2.29. To understand *why* this reduces impact, it's necessary to know a little about users and their equipment. Recreational vehicles and camping trailers all have doors on the *passenger side* of their body (except pick-up truck shells, which open in the rear). The campsite in Figure 2.32 takes this into account and aligns facilities to accommodate the movement of visitors between the site and their recreation vehicle. Maintenance and environmental concerns aside, isn't this *more convenient for the users* as well? In this illustration, we've also moved the water outlet adjacent to the toilet

building to remove another potential path of impact.

Figure 2.33 shows a campsite designed to reduce impact, cut maintenance costs, and meet user needs even more efficiently. In addition to aligning the facilities on the passenger side of the site, the entire camping area is *defined* and *reinforced*. Unlike those in Figures 2.29 and 2.32, the parking area, or spur, is not barricaded from the "living area" of the site. This allows users the opportunity to decide where to park on the site and thus how to design their own space. Site definition and reinforcement identifies and localizes impact on the area, helping to protect the surrounding environment. Figure 2.34 shows the result of designing sites this way. When this picture was taken, the site had been in

Figure 2.31

use in a popular camping area for nine years. Grass still grows, surrounding trees are still healthy, ongoing maintenance costs are minimal, and users are happy with the site. The principle to remember here is that *operations and maintenance costs of recreation areas, as well as environmental damage, can be reduced significantly by building preventive measures into plans and designs for these areas.*

Before we leave the subject of maintenance, let's look at a few general considerations with implications for both planning and management. First, maintenance areas need to be *a part of* but *apart from* the park or recreation complex they serve. Figures 2.35 and 2.36 show two alternative locations for a maintenance complex in a park. The main-

tenance yard in Figure 2.35 is slightly closer to the areas which need to be maintained. However, with this placement, the maintenance zone is the first thing visitors see upon entering the complex. Generally, maintenance areas are not among the most aesthetic visual features our parks have to offer. Also, they tend to be noisy, particularly early in the morning when many campers enjoy sleeping late, and in some instances hazardous. The design in Figure 2.36 removes the maintenance complex from the viewing area open to visitors as they enter the park. Planting a screen, or, better yet, using existing vegetation to shield the complex makes it even less obtrusive. Note how the angle between the park-entry road and the maintenance-access road at point "A" prevents users from having to decide which is the right road to take as they enter the park.

Other maintenance challenges may result from a lack of familiarity by recreation staff, particularly program-oriented personnel, with maintenance problems; thus an occasional short seminar in the kinds of problems likely to need attention may save maintenance costs and other problems. A program leader or an interpretive specialist may walk past a plugged drainage culvert several times without noticing it (until it rains and his or her program area floods due to the lack of drainage). Encouraging communication among different types of staff can help make everyone's job easier.

One interesting aspect of working with maintenance personnel is their tendency to resist change. If a grass-mowing pattern has been in effect for ten years, it may be difficult to convince maintenance personnel to change the pattern in order to establish screening around the new campfire theater or to make whatever change is in order. Maintenance staff are generally excellent at what they do — their input into planning is, and should be, valued. However, like other groups — managers, programmers, construc-

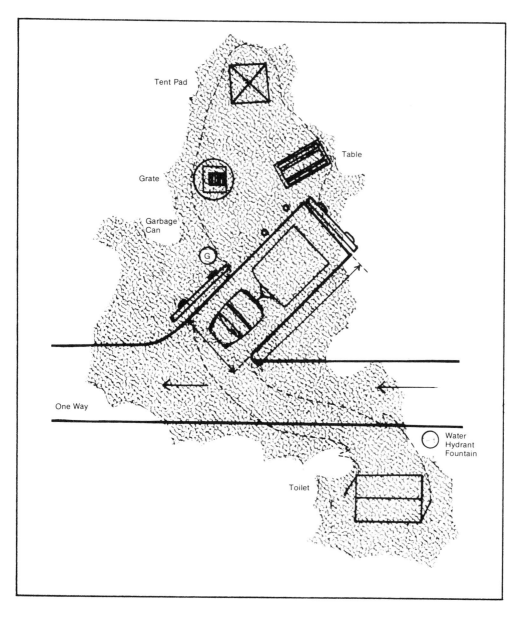

Figure 2.32

Partial Solution to Figure 2.29 Impact

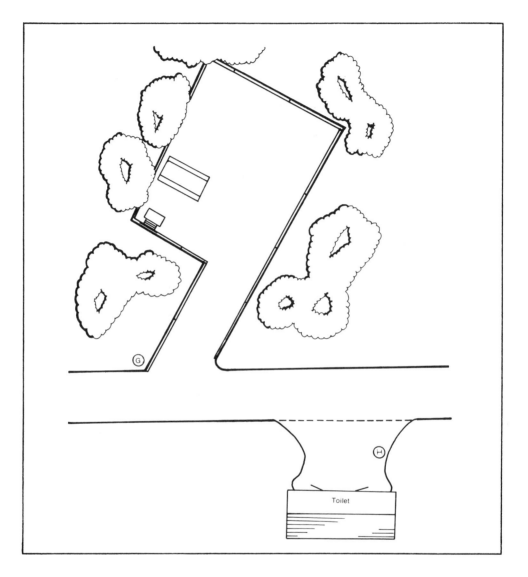

Figure 2.33   Reinforced Unit

Figure 2.34

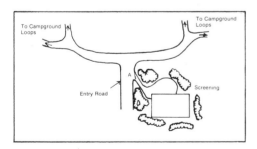

Figure 2.35

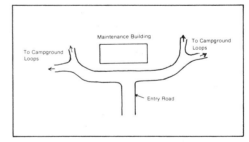

Figure 2.36

tion crews, and users — they tend to see things from a single perspective, one which is often unfavorable toward new ways of doing things. The planner has the responsibility to consider the perspective of maintenance folks *along with* the idea of other consumers of the planning process.

In addition to maintenance personnel, there are sources available to provide advice for building maintenance into park designs and facilities. The journal *Grist,* published quarterly by the National Park Service in cooperation with the National Recreation and Park Association, is a valuable maintenance tool. The United States Forest Service's Equipment Development Center, San Dimas, California, also conducts research on maintenance equipment used in parks. Representatives from maintenance equipment manufacturers may additionally serve as sources of information as long as you remember that they have products to sell, too.

USER PROTECTION AND SAFETY

Not so many years ago, the Tennessee chapter of the National Campers and Hiker's Association voted to "blacklist" a campground in the Cherokee National Forest in eastern Tennessee. In other words, they recommended that their members discontinue using the campground. Could an occurrence such as this possibly have been the fault of the planner? You bet it could! For some time, the Forest Service, along with many other federal and state agencies, followed a formula that provided recreation services based on *access* and *attraction;* that is, if a natural resource had some appealing feature — a lake, a river, or a largely undeveloped tract of timber — it was an attraction. Add to this a system of roads and small, unobtrusive areas for camping (access), and the needs of recreationists would be served. In fact, this approach did and does serve the needs of

some outdoor recreationists — those who prefer an undeveloped, backcountry experience. However, and this is one of the most important statements we'll make in this book, backcountry recreation enthusiasts, although growing in absolute numbers and well publicized, *are but a small minority of the population who use outdoor resources for recreation.*

In order to serve the entire spectrum of users — from the backpacker to the camper in an air-conditioned trailer — access and attraction are not enough. The formula must be expanded to include *administration,* which includes visitor protection. Administration has a number of implications, many of which can be enhanced *or* made difficult by the work of the planner. Ironically, the blacklisted campground had only recently been built, and, for the Forest Service in 1966, it was a large one — one hundred camp units. There were three gated loops which could be opened or closed, a residential area for seasonal or protection personnel, and a single-gated entrance/exit. In its first two years of use it also had a history of excellent visitor protection. Moreover, only campers who had paid the required fees were allowed inside the campground.

However, forest supervisory and ranger district staff changed; day users (non-campers) were allowed in and encouraged to use the beach inside the campground; enthusiastic evening and late-night patrols by rangers and forest supervisory staff became a thing of the past. Instead of shouldering responsibility for visitor protection, the Forest Service, on a national basis, shifted it to the local county sheriff. This policy change and the infusion of day use in an area previously designed for campers only "opened wide the door" for local rowdies. No longer were the campers welcomed and protected by the agency. Thus a once heavily used campground built on the shores of a beautiful one-hundred-acre mountain-framed lake became blacklisted by the nation's largest organized user group.

The takeover by rowdies and subsequent blacklisting was not an isolated event in Tennessee or, for that matter, limited to USDA Forest Service recreation facilities. We believe the missing security can be defined as a need for *agency propriety*. By this, we mean that public agencies which develop and maintain recreation areas must take upon themselves the responsibility for protecting and hosting these areas with their own personnel. Hiring private individuals to collect fees and maintain areas may be less expensive than using agency employees in some instances. Likewise, contracting local law-enforcement agencies to police recreation areas may save hours of work. However, public agencies should go beyond providing physical facilities for park users. It is the authors' opinion that park agencies have a moral obligation to *host and protect* the visitors to their areas!

Part of hosting, just as it would be in your home, involves providing a safe and usable environment for your guests. After all, this is who users really are. Planners can facilitate administrative functions by designing areas large enough to justify on-site management and protection. Recreation areas should be planned for service by road systems built to allow controlled access.

A final aspect of hosting that can be influenced by the planner is recreation programming. We'll discuss this topic in detail in Chapter Eight, so for now we'll make two basic points. First, planners can design programming potential into outdoor recreation areas. By being aware of these opportunities, planners can thus consider *fun* as well as access and attraction to parks. In our view, this has rarely been done in our nation's resource-based public parks. Second, design efforts aimed at providing program opportunities should address both a *broad spectrum of users and a broad spectrum of programs*.

Given the diversity of the recreation interests of people who use parks and resource areas, planners should work to facilitate opportunities for all user groups — from the hunter to the preservationist. Program facilities also need to complement one another; the nature trail should not be developed instead of, but in harmony with, the play court. The issue here is a principle of professionalism; *it is not the planner's role to decide what the needs of the recreating public are.* Too often in the past, planners have developed facilities based on the attitude that "if I like it, it must be right." This is not an appropriate approach to the development and delivery of recreation services. The planning function should support rather than dominate programming and administration.

One of the most comprehensive sources of information on standards to consider when planning for user safety is the American National Standards Institute (ANSI). The Recreation Vehicle Industry Association also maintains standards which may prove useful, particularly in the development of campgrounds, and the National Park Service provides a good model to follow for visitor protection and hosting as well. Their use areas are well-staffed, well-protected, and, with the exception of their campgrounds, generally well-programmed.

ENGINEERING

It would be difficult to imagine developing recreation areas without the expertise of engineers. However, engineers are not trained in the "people" aspect of recreation. As a result, the recreation planner should be responsible for integrating user needs with the technical aspects of design engineers provide. The parking lot in Figure 2.37 illustrates this point. This lot was designed by engineers for a Tennessee Valley Authority group camp in western Tennessee. Use of the camp was restricted to organized groups,

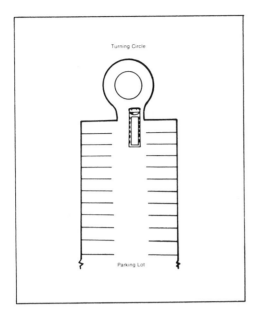

Figure 2.37   Turning Circle Parking Lot at Brandon Spring

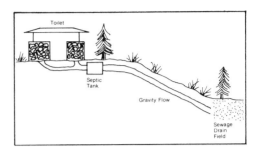

Figure 2.38

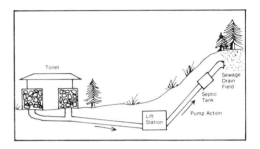

Figure 2.39

many of whom arrived in buses, but the "people need" was neglected in the design of the lot. The center island in the turning circle was too large for buses to maneuver around the island. Thus, in order for the lot to function for the clientele using the camp, the island had to be removed and replaced by one with a smaller diameter, an expensive alteration caused by the engineer's neglect of users.

Like other professionals whose expertise is necessary for the planning process, engineers can increase or reduce the cost of developing parks. To demonstrate this point, consider the alternatives for sewage disposal shown in Figures 2.38 and 2.39. The first alternative shows a sewage line running from a toilet building to a septic drainfield located *at a lower elevation* than the toilet. The effluent flows unaided to the drain field. Conversely, in Figure 2.39, the drain field has been

located at a higher elevation than the toilet. In this case, the sewage must be pumped uphill, via a lift station, to the disposal site. In all instances, site-specific conditions will influence this type of problem. Perhaps the only suitable soils for the drain field are above the toilet buildings so that the expense of lift stations is justified. However, *all other things being equal,* the planner should work to keep the cost of engineered facilities to a minimum.

Another example of how engineered features can increase both development and maintenance costs in recreation areas can be found in several state parks in central Illinois. Designed by the Corps of Engineers, these parks included drainage ditches along road-sides. In flat areas such as central Illinois it is usually not necessary to provide any type of ditching system if roadways, including final surfacing, are built at ground level. If the

Figure 2.40a

land gently tilts downhill, so should the road surface. Yet in addition to the cost of digging the ditches, each road intersection or branch required that a culvert be installed so that ditch water would pass under the adjoining road, a particularly expensive operation if you add a culvert at each parking pad. Not only did these installations create unnecessary construction costs, the ditches had to be mowed by hand because of their slope, and the culverts tended to clog with leaf litter and other debris. Thus maintenance as well as development costs were increased by unneeded engineered facilities.

The planner should take responsibility for limiting engineering to a role that supports recreation services and programs. Engineered features such as waste treatment areas should

not be allowed to dominate the park landscape. While these types of facilities are necessary to support the operation of a park, the planner should work to balance them with the aesthetic appeal of natural resources. Engineered support facilities like maintenance yards should be designed as *a part of* but *apart from* recreation areas.

An example of how engineering expertise can be misdirected is shown in Figure 2.40. The pictures are of campsites at the Edgar Evans State Park in Tennessee. Someone decided to locate a campground on the side of a ridge overlooking a lake. The slope on the ridge was too severe to develop conventional campsites, so the "solution" was to build wooden platforms supported by concrete and steel pilings, cantilevering approxi-

Figure 2.40b

mately one hundred campsites over the side of the ridge. Because the platforms are wooden, the users' evening companion, the campfire, is prohibited. From the standpoint of engineering principles, the sites are sound. But when you consider the need to plan for *people,* they fail to get a passing grade.

As we suggested earlier, use engineers and others with technical expertise, but keep their help in line with the recreation experience. There is an old saying called "the rule of the tool:" "Give a small child a hammer and suddenly everything in sight will need pounding." Perhaps this applies to some who depend too heavily on engineers in recreation resource areas as well.

We suggest the American National Standards Institute as a helpful source of information about concerns regarding engineering standards. Additionally, the USDA Forest Service has, over the years, developed a comprehensive system of manuals dealing with engineering developments related to recreation resource planning.

DESIGN PSYCHOLOGY

On a subconscious level, visitors are turned away from the entrance to a county park in Washington State. In contrast, the entrance to McCormick's Creek State Park in Indiana seems to welcome park users to a comfortable environment. The feelings generated by these two entrance zones are examples of what the planner can accomplish or lose

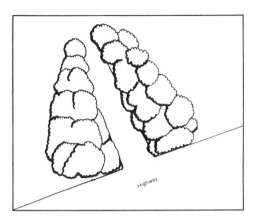

Figure 2.41

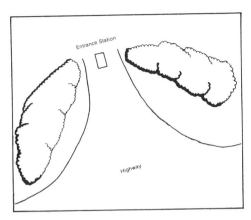

Figure 2.42

through attention to aspects of *design psychology*. The park entrance in Washington, built at a right angle to the main road, consists of a narrow, sixteen-foot roadway completely enclosed within a full canopy of overhanging trees (Figure 2.41). Because of the almost total shade cover, the narrow, constricted entrance is dark and uninviting. Compare this to the entrance to McCormick's Creek, shown in Figure 2.42. Here, the juncture of the park-entrance road and the highway is curved to produce a more natural approach to the park. The entryway is also built in the shape of an inverted "V," with the narrow end facing the interior of the park. Psychologically, this design "pulls" the users' vision into the park. The effect is reinforced by pruned vegetation alongside the entryway, a manipulation designed to repeat the "V" shape of the entrance road.

Design psychology can have a significant impact on park visitors. If used effectively, the results are highly positive, as along the Natchez Trace, through northern Mississippi, northwest Alabama, and southern Tennessee. This parkway, developed by the National Park Service, passes through a part of the country having less than outstanding scenic qualities. A few hundred feet to either side of

the Trace, the land is characterized by open fields and low hills, typical of this part of the South. However, driving along the Parkway itself is one of the most re-creative visual experiences you can find anywhere.

The key to the visual appeal of the Natchez Trace is the way in which the planner employed *visual variety*. The tree canopy over the Parkway alternately opens and closes to produce a sensation of changing environments. Plantings of pines have been employed to create contrasts in color. Variations in topography and sweeping curves are used to prevent long line-of-sight visuals along the right-of-way and to avoid monotonous views. Grass-mowing crews, instead of cutting on straight lines along the edge of the road, create naturally shaped patterns on the shoulders of the Trace. In sum, the Parkway was planned with design psychology in mind. The attention given to interplay of *color, texture, form,* and *line* has resulted in an overall backdrop capable of creating a meaningful recreation experience. Perhaps the most successful aspect of the Natchez Trace is this: the effects created by the design, while refreshing, are *so subtle* that the typical visitor passing along the parkway will rarely perceive the techniques used to enhance the environment. This, in fact, is the key to design psychology: the effects created by park designs are felt by the *subconscious mind.*

Unfortunately, inattention to principles of design psychology can produce negative effects on park users as well. For a number of years, TVA's Land Between the Lakes has operated a nature center as a focal point of its five-thousand-acre environmental education complex. The center contained a small, perhaps thirty-by-sixty foot, interpretive room with both historical and nature exhibits on display. The design mistake made was to try and develop far more interpretive themes than the physical space was capable of supporting. The area's cultural history, iron mining, wildlife management, local environment, and alternative energy sources were all interpreted here, and the staff planned on adding at least twenty percent more to the existing displays. Negative psychology forced visitors to move quickly through narrow aisles from one exhibit to another, tending to minimize both their quest for new knowledge and their enjoyment. Most of the exhibits were well done; however, the quality of the exhibits themselves is not the point — the spatial arrangement of the room created an uncomfortable environment for visitors.

The purpose of design psychology is to make users feel comfortable in the park environment without calling attention to the techniques used. We'll discuss specific applications of design psychology as we talk about different types of recreation facilities in later chapters. There are, however, a few general concepts you can apply in most park plans and designs — techniques aimed at enhancing *visitor receptivity* to the recreational environment.

Curvilinear design. Few straight lines occur in nature. As a complement, our park designs should avoid straight lines also. Curvilinear walkways, trails, and roads not only repeat natural shapes, they create an aura of mystery and anticipation for the user: what new scene waits just out of view around the next curve?

Blending human-made with natural colors. In most instances, our designs should intrude into the natural environment as little as possible. Signing schemes and paint on buildings can take advantage of earth-tone colors. Exceptions to this do exist; some signs, such as those indicating dangerous conditions, should be brightly colored to draw attention to them readily.

Designing to avoid confusion. Circulation patterns inside parks should be kept as simple as possible (KISS!). Consistency can help in this respect as well. A color scheme might be developed for a park in which all trail heads are indicated by signs painted with brown backgrounds, signs for campgrounds with green backgrounds, and so on.

Designing facilities compatible with adjacent uses. This includes the principle we discussed earlier of zoning use areas simply and expands the concept. Adjacent facilities should avoid conflicting with each other's intended uses and should complement one another in terms of anticipated use. A picnic shelter placed next to a nature center may encourage picnicking. A tennis court next to the same nature center will probably not attract many players.

Designing to human scale. The scale, or size, of areas and facilities can have an effect on park users. Some facilities and areas, e.g., the height of bulletin boards and the length of tennis courts, are dictated by intended use and standards. Keep in mind, however, that scale can be psychological as well as physical. Particularly in areas where people stay for long periods of time, scale the design to make them comfortable. For example, a picnic table on top of a small hill with no trees in the middle of a Kansas prairie would not have a high comfort factor.

Lighting aesthetics. Different types of artificial lighting produce different types of effects. Thus your choice of lighting depends upon the intended use of the area to be lighted. For sports and other areas where visual accuracy is needed, high-intensity discharge lamps such as metal halide, mercury vapor, or high-pressure sodium are appropriate. However, color *rendition* — the accurate reproduction of shades of color — is probably more important for producing human comfort in outdoor recreation areas where the natural environment is dominant. On pathways and other unstructured sites, incandescent lighting produces the best color rendition.

The number of sources to enlist for help and advice on design psychology is somewhat limited. College and university departments of landscape architecture often include a staff member with an interest in park planning and design. The Forest Service, particularly in the western regions of the country, has also developed guidelines for the visual management of resources. Their emphasis, however, is limited to designing extensive areas rather than fine-tuning site-specific resources that beckon visitors into and through small parks and facilities. The best guidelines for developing parks according to the principles of design psychology are common sense and practice. Questions such as "Does it fit the environment?" "Is it a functional design?" and "Does it invite rather than repulse?" should be answered affirmatively before construction begins.

LANDSCAPING

Closely related to design psychology, landscaping fundamentals are helpful to the recreation planner. More important, however, the planner must understand the *implications* of landscaping *for recreation* rather than know the fine points of the discipline. To make the point clear, consider the example of a National Park Service use area below Boulder Dam in Arizona. Here the designer used a plant called oleander to provide a screen between campsites. As we have discussed before, it is desirable to provide intersite screening in campgrounds. Armed with a knowledge of landscaping and plant growth patterns, the designer *knew* oleander was capable of developing this screening and *knew* oleander is an especially attractive plant. However, the designer did not know, or didn't consider, the *implications* for recreation; campers like to roast hot dogs on sticks they can find around the campsite. Oleander is dense (for screening), attractive (for aesthetics), and *poisonous* (for campers).

Landscaping can be an effective tool for the park planner. It can enhance the natural attractiveness of an area, channel people along reinforced pathways, and help disguise maintenance areas and other human-made structures. But the planner also needs to remember the relationship between landscaping and recreation planning. Unless the design goal is to create a formal, landscaped area, landscaping should *support* rather than *dictate* planning efforts. We know of a small city in western Tennessee where exotic plants, species not naturally occuring in the area, were used to landscape a riverside community park. The results make the park look out of place with the surroundings. To remain consistent with the natural environment, use indigenous plants, species which naturally occur in the area, for landscaping.

There are other human needs besides aesthetics which should be considered when you landscape. Design decisions should not focus exclusively on the *form* of the area; the *function* is your primary concern. You should address the effect landscaping has on user safety and convenience. For instance, tall, dense shrubs along quiet walkways may create dangerous conditions, particularly in some urban areas; poisonous plants or those with thorns are inappropriate in most use areas; some plants, such as the female Ginkgo, bear fruit which emits offensive odors. Factors such as these do not always preclude the use of certain plant materials. The planner, however, should either know or take the responsibility for determining the potential effects plants may have on areas.

As with other topics discussed in this chapter, landscaping decisions should incorporate not only recreationists but other "users" of the park: the managers, programmers, and maintenance staff. We know of a park which has a shower building completely surrounded with attractive shade trees and low understory vegetation. At the end of each summer, a maintenance crew must spend several days scraping mold from the interior walls and repainting the inside of the building. The reason? Shade from the attractive trees prevents the walls from drying, allowing mold to grow throughout the summer. Managers may also need to keep some areas free of vegetation in order to lessen the amount of time it takes to patrol for vandals or muggers. And programmers may require a mixture of sunny and shaded areas for various activities.

Generally, the planner will have to compromise to address the needs of all concerned. The important point to remember is *how* landscaping will affect all these groups both immediately and some time after newly introduced plants reach maturity. The planner's role is to ensure that landscaping in parks and recreation areas remains a *means* to an end rather than an end in itself. University departments of landscape architecture may prove helpful to you in this decision-making process.

USER INVOLVEMENT

A planner can develop an excellent design for a recreation area and watch it fail miserably if the public, for whatever reason, doesn't use the area. Fortunately, there is a way to help insure that people will take an interest in and accept areas for recreation use. The key is to *involve users in the planning process.* This action has several benefits: it provides a needed *source of information* since nobody can tell you more about a group's needs than group members themselves; it is an excellent *public relations tool,* particularly for public agencies which are frequently seen as insensitive bureaucracies; and, perhaps most importantly, it gives users a sense of having a *vested interest* in the area being planned.

When the Hillman Heritage Trail was developed into a campground in TVA's Land Between the Lakes, the local chapter of the National Camper's and Hiker's Association was invited to help, both in planning and construction. The local press was notified, and it became something of an "event" for the club. The trail was later designated as a National Recreation Trail, and more publicity (and positive public relations for the agency) ensued. The approach taken encouraged benefits beyond physical development. Since a local group had a high degree of interest in the project, programming opportunities emerged. Group-hike weekends could be organized, with the hikers using campgrounds and thus adding to program potential. Maintenance costs were even minimized because one program during the weekend was centered around periodic trail maintenance — with assistance by the hikers. The single act of inviting users to become *truly* involved, rather than simply holding a required public meeting, can benefit management and program staff, maintenance crews, and, most importantly, visitors.

When involving users, planners should also try to draw operations and maintenance crews into the planning process. These people are responsible for managing recreation areas on a day-to-day basis, so they can have a strong influence on successful facilities. In the real world, there are two ways operations and maintenance crews do their jobs. They can accomplish tasks assigned to them at a minimal level of performance, or they can do the same tasks more efficiently and effectively. A number of factors, from salary to length of coffee breaks, influences their level of performance. Many of these factors are beyond the control of the planner; however, if operations and maintenance crews are made to feel a sense *of responsibility* for parks and recreation areas, they may be more concerned about their upkeep. One way to instill this sense of responsibility is to involve these individuals in the planning process. Their opinions are important — let them know it.

One problem we have encountered on numerous occasions concerns the renovation of old established areas. If a campground, picnic site, or other use area has been in service for some time, it likely needs extensive rehabilitation. We can guarantee that some users, particularly those who have frequented the old area on a regular basis, will be opposed to this renovation. Frequently, they protest strongly. Sometimes a patient explanation of the need to protect the environment will help, and sometimes not, but it should at least be offered. Ultimately the planner has the responsibility of protecting the environment, and one means of accomplishing this is to rehabilitate deteriorating sites. In our experience, most users don't stay away permanently. A few do, but if you hope to please everyone all of the time, we suggest you look for work outside recreation.

planning for one person to master. We feel it is time for the role of the planner to evolve one step further: planners should be recognized (and recognize themselves) as fulfilling a *service function.* Far too often, we have seen instances in which a planner produces a single design for an area, oversees the construction, and then turns over the finished product to managers, programmers, and maintenance staff. In effect, this says "here's the design for this area, now bend your programs and policies to fit it!" In fact, there is no single "right" design for a recreation facility. There are always *alternatives.* Functioning in a service role, the planner should (with input from those who will work and recreate in the area) develop several alternative plans for a given facility. Given these alternatives, staff responsible for managing, maintaining, and programming the facility can choose the best possible combination of components to meet *their* needs.

Speaking of alternatives, we hope you were able to find some poor ones in the recreation complex shown in Figure 2.1. We've reproduced the complex in Figure 2.43, with a listing of mistakes keyed to the numbers on next page. We purposely designed in thirty errors; if you find additional ones, no one said we were perfect!

CONCLUSIONS

Traditionally, the role of the recreation planner has been to develop plans and designs. In recent years there has been a move to expand the role of the planner to one in which the synthesis of information is of importance as well. This is a step in the right direction. As we've tried to illustrate in this chapter, there are simply too many substantive areas of knowledge involved in

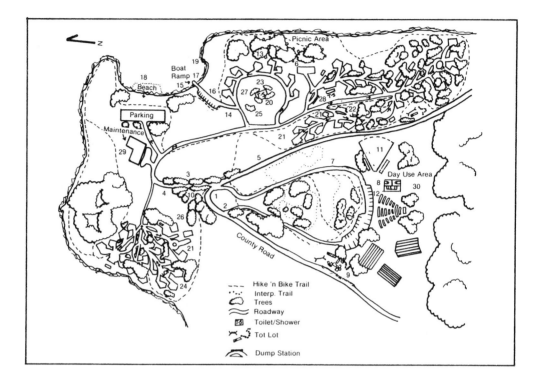

Figure 2.43

Entrance Zone

1. Three entrances (loss of administrative control)
2. Entrance zones placed too near a curve (safety hazard)
3. Full tree canopy over one entrance (too much tunnel effect)
4. Long straightaway on entrance instead of curvilinear layout

Road Design

5. Existing road dictates design
6. Requires driving through campground to get to picnic area
7. Too much road in day-use area

Program

8. Passive and active areas zoned together instead of apart
9. Tot lots located immediately adjacent to main road (safety hazard)
10. Hike 'n bike trail crosses main park road at entrance (safety hazard)
11. Baseball field aligned on an east-west axis (Should be north-south to keep sun from batter's and pitcher's eyes)
12. The parking lot adjacent to the campfire theater is aligned so headlights will shine on the theater stage
13. All picnic sites are located in heavy shade (some sun needed for cooler weather)

Water-related Facilities

14. Need to drive through camping loop to reach boat ramp

15. Boat ramp is adjacent to beach (pollutants and possible safety hazard)
16. Parking slots in area serving boat ramp are not designed for boat trailers
17. Boat ramp is single-lane only (Most boating ends just before darkness arrives — a "rush hour" results)
18. Swimming area on east-facing beach (south- or west-facing preferred)
19. Boating area in base of a cove (Needs to be located so wind and wave action won't fill launch area with silt)

Camping Area (see Chapter Seven)

20. Toilet/shower located in center of loop (increased impact)
21. Pull-in campsite
22. Pull-through campsite on wrong side of road
23. Too much shade surrounding toilet/shower (poor ventilation)
24. Living space on wrong side of parking spur
25. Camping loop too fat (wasted space)
26. Parking spur detached from living area of site
27. No campsites on inside of loop (wasted space)

Support Facilities

28. Sewage dumping station on camping loop (inconvenience for campers on other loops)
29. Maintenance building placed near entrance of complex
30. No comfort facilities in day-use area

3

TRAILS:
PATHWAYS FOR PEOPLE

INTRODUCTION

This is the first of several chapters discussing specific types of recreation facilities, and we'd like to start by asking you a question: what do you think *makes a good trail?* Before giving you our answer, we'll provide you with a hint. The correct response to this question would be the *same* for the subjects of the remaining chapters as well: what makes a good Day Use Area? Play Area? Camping Area? If this is beginning to sound like a trick question, that's because it is. It's also an important one since it emphasizes the point implied by the title of this chapter. Trails are, or should be, pathways for people.

The answer to our question — what makes a good trail? — is actually two more questions. To determine if a trail is well planned, you must first ask: *what kind of a trail is it?* What's "good" design for an interpretive nature trail is often poor, poor planning for a hiking trail. As we'll see shortly, some principles of planning and design remain the same, regardless of the type of trail involved. For example, measures to prevent erosion should always be considered when developing trails. However, different types of trails may require different techniques to accomplish the same goal. Trails for dirt bikes and trails for wheelchairs would not always fight erosion with the same methods. Further, the nature, or intended use, of a particular kind of trail may require some design strategies unnecessary or undesirable on other types of trails.

To illustrate this, consider a short interpretive trail paralleling a Confederate Army line of defense at Shiloh National Battlefield, maintained by the National Park Service. The purpose, or design goal, of this sort of trail should be to take users back in time for a firsthand perspective of an era in our history when families were divided on two sides of an issue that tore the nation apart. This is clearly *not* the design goal a planner would have in mind when developing a jogging path in a city park. Both are examples of trails, but each needs a different planning approach to function effectively. Gertrude Stein said, "A rose is a rose is a rose." We say, "A trail is not a trail is not a trail." In part, the *type* of trail determines how it must be planned and designed.

Trail type, however, is not the only criterion for determining whether a trail is well planned or not. The second part of the answer to our question "what makes a good trail?" is this: "who's going to use the trail?" Designing trails would be easier if trails with similar uses had similar users. This is not, however, always the case. For example, hiking trails may be found both inside and outside of developed recreation facilities. Those inside of areas such as group camps and family campgrounds need one set of design goals, strategies, and characteristics. Hiking trails outside of developed areas, such as the Appalachian and Pacific Crest Trails, require a different planning approach. Even two trails with the same design goal in the same area may differ, depending on the intended users. A group camp visited by a variety of user groups might have two interpretive trails: one accessible by groups with members in wheelchairs and the other for groups whose members are all ambulatory.

As you might expect, the types of people we need to consider when designing trails are not limited to the recreating public. As with other kinds of facilities, the planner can make trails easy or difficult to administer. Preventive maintenance measures built into the trail or neglected during construction can have a positive or negative impact on the expense and difficulty of on-going maintenance. The potential for recreation programming can be designed *into* or *out of* trails by the attention the planner gives to his or her work. Many of the skills we discussed in Chapter Two — user protection and safety, design psychology, programming, and others — have specific applications in making trails "pathways for people." As we suggested in Chapter One, however, recreation planners who design facilities have a dual responsibility. The trails we develop must consider *resource protection* as well as provision of positive experiences for people who use them.

More often than any other type of recreation facility, trails seem to be designed by persons with few skills in planning or resource stewardship. On the surface, designing a trail appears simple. From the standpoint of meeting program requirements, it isn't difficult to provide a *minimally effective* one. Disregarding standards for special populations for a moment, all you really need to do to construct a trail is clear a path wide enough for people to travel on. Unfortunately, there is a considerable difference between *clearing* a trail — which anyone can do — and *designing* a trail that minimizes environmental damage. Even more unfortunate, it seems this distinction has not been made frequently enough, particularly among recreation programmers and interpretive specialists. Too often, these individuals take it upon themselves to

develop trails because they think they understand what needs to be done from a programming perspective. When this happens, environment and visitors both suffer.

As we've stressed before, it takes more than one type of expertise to plan facilities which are both usable and environmentally sound. This holds true for trails, too. Shortly we'll discuss the types of general concerns you need to consider when developing trails. We'll also explore how and how not to design several specific types. Before getting into these topics, however, we'd like to share a "mistrake" with you. Starting with trails, each of the next six chapters deals with a specific type of recreation development. We'll include in each of these chapters a description of one or more actual areas or facilities which have been poorly planned and/or designed.

There are two reasons for taking this approach. First, we feel the recreation profession has a tendency to perpetuate design errors. Planning mistakes made in the 1950's are still being made *commonly* today. This may be a result, in part, of the service orientation of our profession. The mission of recreation is to improve the quality of life. Thus everything we do must be well intended. Unfortunately, there is often a wide gap between good intentions and good results. Recreation professionals need to be idealistic and enthusiastic. However, these qualities must be combined with pragmatism. Our resources are too limited to continue making errors we should have stopped committing twenty years ago. The second reason for providing what we intend as constructive criticism is to demonstrate the need to ask *why*. Most of the mistakes we'll share with you in this and later chapters didn't have to happen. They occurred because no one held the planner accountable for his or her designs. Much of our criticism in these "mistakes" sections will be directed at planners for what we feel are flawed designs.

However, much of the blame for these designs actually being implemented lies with the programmers and administrators who deferred to the "expertise" of the planners.

THE BLUE-GREY COMPLEX

The Setting. Near the southern end of TVA's Land Between the Lakes (LBL), recreation staff developed a complex of hiking trails called the Fort Henry Trails System. The trails were named for a Confederate defense installation constructed on the banks of the Tennessee River. When Kentucky Lake was built nearly eighty years after the Civil War, Fort Henry was completely flooded, except for portions of three sets of trenches, or earthworks. The trail head for the hiking complex was located at a mid-point between these sets. (Figure 3.1 shows how the trail head and support facilities were designed.)

There are several positive aspects of trail design shown in Figure 3.1, including those keyed to the following legend:

A) a single entry/exit parking lot for ease of administration;

B) a turning circle on the upper end of the parking lot to facilitate use by large recreational vehicles and buses;

C) toilets located inside a "pocket" of screening where they are both unobtrusive and easy to locate;

D) a wide trail head narrowing toward the interior of the trail to attract users' vision;

E) vegetative screening cut to reinforce the shape of the trail head;

F) an enclave containing a bulletin board with a map of the trail system and other information for hikers (Note how the enclave is set back from the trail entrance and screened from the parking lot. Both of these tactics are aimed at minimizing visual contact from the parking lot and, as a result, reducing vandalism.);

G) the trail head, the enclave, and the first few hundred feet of each trail (where use will be heaviest) reinforced with crushed stone to reduce impact;

H) signs bearing the names of the two paths leading from the trail head located at the point where hikers need to choose which route to take (Each sign is number- and color-coded to the map on the bulletin board to reduce confusion and placed slightly to the sides of the intersection to screen them from the parking lot.);

I) screening between the trails and the remaining Fort Henry trenches maintained to minimize impact on the trenches (The vegetation provides a psychological barrier between hiking trails and possible interpretive zones.)

Recreation staff planned the historical hiking system with the help of National Park Service personnel, making certain the three sets of earthworks (interpretive zones) wouldn't be penetrated by hiking trails. This approach was taken to allow later development of the interpretive zones to fit a functional, overall planning scheme. Several years after the hiking complex was built, interpretive services staff at Land Between the Lakes decided to develop one of the three potential interpretive zones — the one with earthworks leading down a narrow ridge and terminating at the lake edge. To develop this, they built an interpretive trail, named the Blue-Grey Trail, as shown in Figure 3.2. The on-the-ground results of their planning have given your authors a host of major and minor mistake illustrations to share with you. Since Land Between the Lakes is designated as a demonstration area in outdoor recreation, including interpretation, part of its original mission was to share mistakes with other professionals and students when they occurred. Unfortunately, neither interpretive staff nor their supervisors had the planning background to recognize or understand the errors committed during development of the

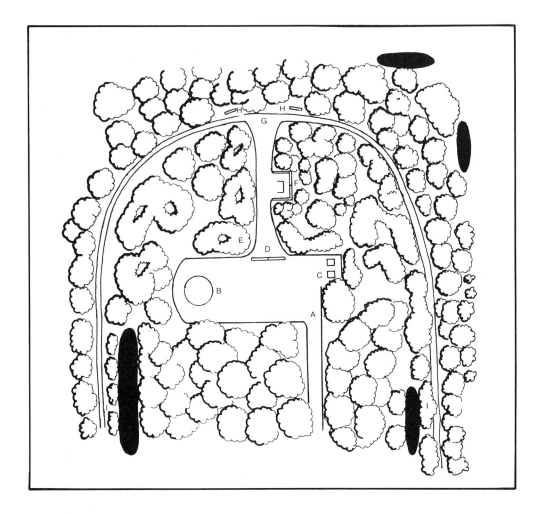

Figure 3.1

Blue-Grey trail. In fact, they were quite pleased with what were, from a planning perspective, negative results. (In later chapters, you'll read more about the lack of *outdoor recreation* expertise in many public agencies, particularly at the federal level.)

The Blue-Grey Trail was initially intended to be an adventure in historical interpretation. Unfortunately, the results of poor planning gave management, and you, the taxpayers, an extremely costly collection of

errors in design, design psychology, interpretive messages and maps, and architectural features. The new trail also eliminated previously completed work aimed at helping to prevent vandalism. However, these errors were minor compared to four major planning mistakes. These included the following:

1. Borrowing some excellent National Park Service trail construction ideas, but using them in the wrong place;

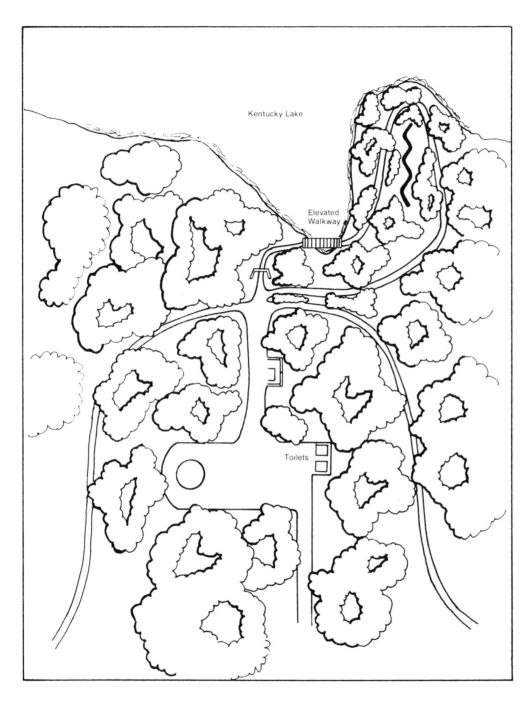

Figure 3.2

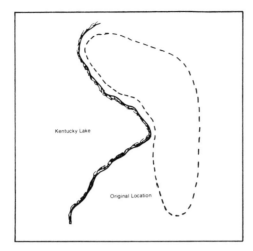

Figure 3.3a

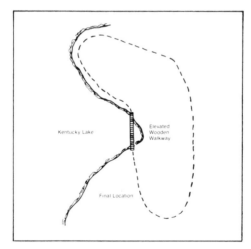

Figure 3.3b

2. Building an expensive facility with electronic gadgetry in an isolated, unprotected area;

3. Creating an outstanding short-distance hiking trail rather than meeting the objective of developing a quality, history-flavored interpretive experience; and

4. Failing to coordinate the interpretive development with previous planning efforts.

Let's explore these mistakes in detail.

1. Misplaced ideas. During the planning phase of the Blue-Grey Trail, LBL's interpretive staff borrowed an idea from South Florida's Everglades National Park. This idea involved the outstanding Anhinga Trail located just behind a staffed and thus protected visitor center. The Anhinga Trail moves gently through a low, freshwater marsh. Since the area is naturally wet, visitors ofttimes travel on elevated wooden walkways. You can be quite close to the freshwater marsh environment with its bounty of unusual plant and animal life, including snakes, water birds and alligators, as you enjoy a relatively safe and dry experience on the walkways. The more important natural features along the trail are even interpreted by small signs located on upper safety rails.

Unfortunately, LBL's interpretive staff decided this idea was just the thing for the Blue-Grey Trail. So instead of developing the loop on an inexpensive, solid-ground location, TVA built over one hundred feet of costly, elevated walkway across a wooded low area of a Kentucky lake embayment even though there was no water under the walkway for much of the year. The original location for the trail before the discovery of the walkway idea and the "as built" location are shown in Figures 3.3a and 3.3b. While the walkway added considerable spice to the hiking experience, it provided no *relevant* interpretive features and no views of open water. It did offer some opportunities for environmental interpretation; however, these couldn't be used since the focus of the trail was the *historical* interpretation of the Battle of Fort Henry.

Management — including budget personnel — shared some of the "credit" for this expensive mistake: no one thought to ask *why* — why the elevated boardwalk was needed; how it would enhance the trail's historical interpretation objective; and, most obvious, how it re-created the aura of the history being interpreted. Was such a walkway used by the soldiers in 1862? *The moral* (and a good planning axiom): borrowing planning ideas from others ofttimes enhances your facility or program. Make sure, though, that what you borrow accomplishes this. Does the idea — successful elsewhere — *enhance* your facility or program, or does it — in your setting, with your objectives — *detract* from it?

2. Unprotected facilities. Most of the interpretive messages for the Blue-Grey Trail were on cassette recordings activated by pressure-sensitive rubber pads hidden a few inches under the trail surface. The recordings were sequential, meaning the information at each station built on the message from the previous station. We believe this sort of interpretation can be an excellent technique in *highly protected, carefully monitored* areas. *However,* the Blue-Grey Trail was in an isolated area over twenty miles from interpretive personnel. The cassette installations were subject to vandalism *and* tended to malfunction due to moisture accumulation in their below-ground boxes. Since the interpretive messages were sequential, malfunctioning stations caused visitors to miss important parts of the story. *The moral* (and another good planning axiom): don't locate expensive facilities, particularly those requiring constant care, in remote areas.

3. Mixing incompatible uses. The authors believe the most common of all trail-related errors made by recreation planners, interpretive specialists, and others is the *mixing* of types of trails such as those for hiking, those built to link facilities, or those leading around or to scenic vistas. This mixing, whether intentional or not, causes the same drastic results all across America. Adding the unneeded elevated wooden walkway which provided lakeside access for viewing and fishing at the western end of the loop helped make the Blue-Grey "interpretive" trail the best short distance *hiking* experience in Land Between the Lakes.

The basic difficulty in mixing hiking and interpretation lies in the inherent conflict between the two types of use. The primary functions of a simple hiking or walking trail are to cover distance on the ground, to move from one point to another, or to move by foot to points of interest such as scenic vistas or observation towers. The *motivation* may differ from person to person and include exercise, being out-of-doors, and viewing wildlife or scenery, but the common denominator is *the hike itself.* Conversely, with interpretive trails the opportunity to gain new knowledge is the primary reason to participate. As a result, visitor interests, their pace or speed, and their moods are different on hiking and interpretive trails. Mixing hiking and interpretation also increases vandalism by those who simply aren't interested in the trail's educational aspects. Most naturalists, as well as planners who *should* know better, get an evangelical gleam in their eyes when they see visitors walking pathways to scenic points, strolling along lake or stream sides, or moving from camp-grounds and picnic areas to other features such as beaches. Far too often, these professional folks decide to make sure that *all* visitors get to enjoy and learn from interpretive messages whether or not some give a hoot. We never learn, it seems, that this is poor planning and can lead to recurrent replacement of interpretive installations due to excessive vandalism caused by trail users disinterested in such force-fed education.

Back to TVA's Blue-Grey Trail: had one of the other two woodland-based earthworks been selected for a simple historical interpretation experience, the trail would have been void of water views, beckoning fishing sites, and fun-to-walk-on elevated wooden walkways. Thus, the *primary* reason for walking through the earthworks would have been to learn a bit from the interpretive messages. Use of simple inexpensive signs, or numbered posts and a self-guiding brochure, rather than electronic devices in a remote area would have meant minimal vandalism. *The moral* (and yet another good planning axiom): *please, please*, resist the temptation to mix extensive interpretation with hiking or other types of trails!

4. Coordinating efforts. The fourth major mistake involved the issue of coordination with other staff who had a stake in the planning and management of the Fort Henry trails complex. At no time during the development of the Blue-Grey Trail did the interpretive staff request to review or discuss the potential impact of the interpretive trail on the existing facilities. TVA recreation staff who managed the hiking complex were faced with new maintenance challenges. As a result of a failure to communicate, management-maintenance problems were amplified and, perhaps even worse, from the visitor's standpoint, opportunities to maximize the benefits of both interpretive and recreation programs were missed. Unfortunately, this failure to communicate happens all too frequently in most agencies. It seems to us this represents one of the many missing elements in the training of recreation personnel and, indeed, those in natural resource and related disciplines. We feel what's missing is an academic emphasis on the need for inter- and intra-agency *coor-*

dination. The moral (and a — for now — final axiom of good planning): keep others abreast of your current and planned actions, be mindful of the possible impacts, both positive *and* negative, that these actions may have on staff in related disciplines and agencies, and expect and ask for the same courtesy in return.

As we suggested earlier, there were other errors associated with the planning and programming of the Blue-Grey Trail. Refer to the numbered locations on Figure 3.4 and consider the following problems. During construction, the vegetation at point 1 was removed. This provided a direct line of sight from the parking lot to the bulletin board and the entrance zone of the trails, so the rate of vandalism in these areas increased shortly after the new trail was opened. Expensive, easy-to-vandalize facilities such as bulletin boards and sign installations near trail heads should be easy to find *once people leave their vehicles*. However, they should also be screened from the sight of vehicles passing through the parking lot whenever possible. People who stop their cars, get out, and walk into a trail zone tend to be interested in enjoying the experience on the trail. People who are inclined to vandalize may not go to the trouble of stopping if they don't see something worth breaking while still in their car.

The entrance zone of the Blue-Grey Trail had several design problems. All of them were created because one human factor was neglected in the design: *people, when given a choice of directions, tend to move to the right instead of to the left.* This phenomenon occurs in movie theaters, on sidewalks, in hallways, and *on interpretive trails* and should be reinforced by the planner. If at all possible, loop trails with a single entry-exit should be designed with a *counterclockwise* traffic flow. The Blue-Grey Trail was not designed this way. Instead, interpretive messages were sequenced to have users walk the trail clockwise (2), so they had to enter

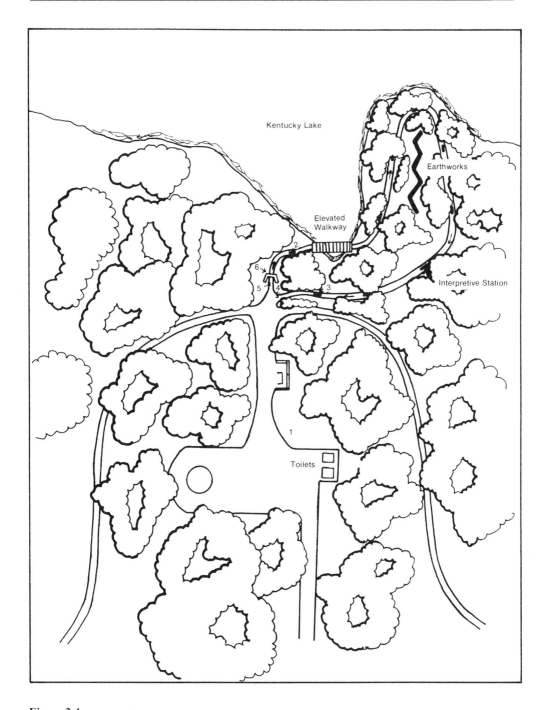

Figure 3.4

the trail to their left instead of to the right, against their natural tendency.

In some instances — because of topography or other constraints — it may be necessary to encourage people to move to the left. When this is the case, there are design techniques available to reinforce the movement. However, on the Blue-Grey Trail there were no such physical constraints, and some additional factors compounded the confusion for trail users at the entrance zone. The last audio pad in the sequence (3) was relatively close to the entry-exit point. When it was activated, people just entering the trail could hear the recording, although it was far enough away that the words could not be understood. The message, which was fairly long-playing, tended to "beckon" users to the right out of curiosity to find the source of the sound, reinforcing their tendency to enter the trail where the planner intended for them to exit. Unfortunately, the last audio station tended to malfunction and come on even though no one was there to activate it, so the beckoning problem was even further compounded.

Turning right was further encouraged by the wide throat and open angle (4) at which the *exit* was built. Neither discouraged users from moving in this direction. To compound the problem, the intended entrance to the trail (5) was designed to move users through a narrow *constriction*, a poor planning technique. The trail, which at this point was not widened, passed through a metal frame (6) shaped like an inverted "U". Similar in design to an airport metal detector, the frame contained background information about Fort Henry's role in the Civil War. This and other interpretive installations had several problems associated with them. From the manager's perspective, the metal frame was an attractive target for vandalism. It could be seen from the parking lot and was defaced soon after the trail was completed. It could also be seen from the rustic bulletin board describing the Fort Henry Hiking Trail

complex, causing a serious and clearly visible conflict in architectural styles.

From the user's standpoint, the metal frame added to the confusion over which direction to take upon entering the interpretive trail head. Only as wide as the trail itself, the frame added to the feeling of constriction brought on by the narrow entrance to the trail.

A final error does not relate to design, but mentioning it helps raise an important point. Some of the interpretive information on the trail was incorrect. A map showed the city of Nashville located on the Tennessee River (which it isn't). One of the interpretive messages referred to the Union forces who attacked Fort Henry as being under the command of "Admiral Foote," a rank which, at the time of the battle of Fort Henry, was non-existent in the Union Navy.

The point is this: the planner neglected to pay attention to detail when designing the trail. None of the errors made created safety hazards for users. In fact, most people who walked the trail were probably not aware, beyond a vague feeling of confusion, of its problems. The question, then, is: "So what? A few minor mistakes were made, but no one was hurt by them." The answer to this question is a matter of professionalism. One of the major challenges facing those of us who work in recreation today is *to be accepted as professionals by the public.* To provide anything less than the best possible programs and facilities we know how to develop detracts from our professional image. If only one person in one hundred notices a mistake we make, our stock as professionals goes down in the public eye. If we make an avoidable error and no one notices, it still diminishes our standing as professionals — perhaps even more so.

Some solutions. There are ways the Fort Henry complex could have been changed to function as an effective interpretive zone. As we discussed earlier, the Blue-Grey Trail, as built, was a better hiking trail than an interpretive one, but Figure 3.5 shows an alternative concept which makes this type of trail viable. With this design, there is nothing to compete with the interpretive function. Further, the flat topography and nearness of the earthworks to the parking lot would allow the planner to design a barrier-free pathway.

This solution was fairly simple, but let's assume for a moment that the design in Figure 3.5 wouldn't work; perhaps the new area isn't flat enough for an interpretive trail. If we should want to use the same entrance zone for both hiking and interpretation, can we improve the design in Figure 3.2? Let's further assume that the program staff needs traffic on the interpretive trail to flow clockwise (to the left). This may not be a good idea from a design standpoint, but perhaps the story being told or the history being interpreted "fits" a left-hand entrance. In this case, as always, the program needs should take precedence over the general rule of design.

Figure 3.6 shows some design techniques aimed at simplifying the original entrance for users and reducing vandalism problems for management. Here, we've left the vegetation (1) to help screen both the bulletin board and the trail head from the parking lot. A *small* directional sign (2) perpendicular to the parking lot, and thus less obtrusive, points to the interpretive trail. The metal frame (3) has been moved around the corner from its original position, also out of sight of the parking lot. The point (4) where the exit rejoins the trail has been designed as a *reverse curve*. This technique involves a very sharp right turn adjacent to a gentle curve moving to the left, making it psychologically easier for people to take the path to the left. It may necessitate a sign (5) pointing to the exit to avoid confusing users who have completed the loop. The last audio pad (6) has been moved further toward the interior

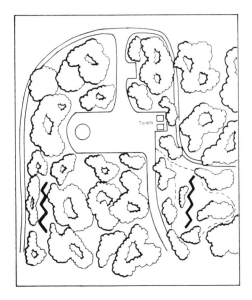

Figure 3.5

of the trail to reduce the chance of hearing the recording from point 4. (An unsophisticated, but effective design technique when faced with situations such as this: before the trail is built, have one person stand at point 4. Have another person walk toward point 6, stopping every few yards and speaking loudly. When his or her voice can no longer be heard from point 4, it's safe to place the audio pad there.) Finally, the section of the interpretive trail at point 7 has been moved away from the parallel section of the hiking trail to prevent potential contact between users.

Interestingly, none of the solutions to the original problems required more effort, more expense, or more technical knowledge. The needs of the programmers were still met, management problems were reduced, and user convenience was enhanced. The only element added to the original design was *attention to detail* — a necessity for conscientious planning. The greatest tragedy in the Blue-Grey Trail adventure was this:

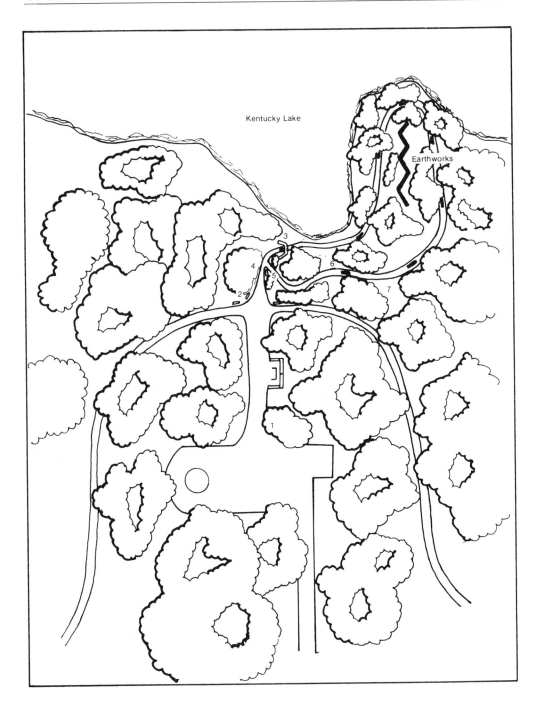

Figure 3.6

neither the interpretive staff nor the TVA managers recognized any of the "major" or "minor" mistakes. Further, when the problems were described and explained, there was no attempt to correct them. At the time this was being written — Fall, 1985 — the Blue-Grey Trail was weed-grown and closed, a $40,000 mistake.

BASICS AND STANDARDS

It's difficult to talk about basic concepts and design standards for trails because of the diversity of trail types and users. There are, however, some general guidelines we can apply to trail planning and development. The *methods* used to implement these guidelines may vary depending on the intended use of the trail. For example, a general guideline might be to "reduce impact on the trail surface." The method — type of surfacing material — might depend on trail type, intended clientele, and expected level of use. In our discussion of different types of trails a little later in the chapter, we'll focus on specific kinds of concerns for each. For now, let's consider some general guidelines for a variety of trail settings. You should keep four topics in mind, and, although there will be some overlap, their general order is: *zoning, design psychology, field design and construction, and administration.*

Zoning
A trail can be superbly designed, built, and managed and still fail to function effectively if it is not properly zoned. Three areas of concern must be addressed during the zoning phase of trail development. The first is to *determine the function or functions* to be served by the trail. Will the trail be devoted to a *primary function,* such as hiking, interpretation, or horseback riding? If so, which use or combination of uses will the trail serve? Who will use it? If the trail is not

intended for primary use, it can serve a *secondary function* such as *access* to an area, *connection* between two areas, or *circulation* within an area. For example, we might design an access trail from a roadside parking lot to a scenic overlook, connect a play area to a picnic shelter, or develop a circulation system within a campground. Knowing how a trail is supposed to function allows us to make informed judgments on how to implement later phases of trail development. As with other types of facilities, the decision regarding intended trail function should not be the responsibility of the planner; administrators and program staff should take the lead in this phase of trail design. Figure 3.7 shows a tree diagram you may find helpful in determining trail function. Remember that planning decisions are too site-specific for any diagram to be all-inclusive; this is only a guideline.

Don't let the diagram in Figure 3.7 lead you to think that determining trail function is a complex process. Remember, KISS! If you're a programmer and you know you need a hike 'n bike trail in your campground, for example, a diagram isn't necessary. The point is this: consider all the options (Is a hike 'n bike trail better *in this setting* than just a hiking trail?) and make a decision regarding function based on your needs and those of your users. Don't leave the decision regarding function to a planner or you may end up with a trail he or she wants to see developed.

Once the trail's function has been determined, the second zoning consideration is *how does this trail relate to other trails in the area?* As we suggested earlier, some types of trails (hiking/interpretive, horseback/off-road vehicle) conflict with each other. Other trail functions (hiking/biking, dirt bike/four wheel) may, in some instances, compliment each other enough to permit combined usage. Even if there are no other trails in the area, the issue of conflicting or complimentary use must be addressed if future developments are

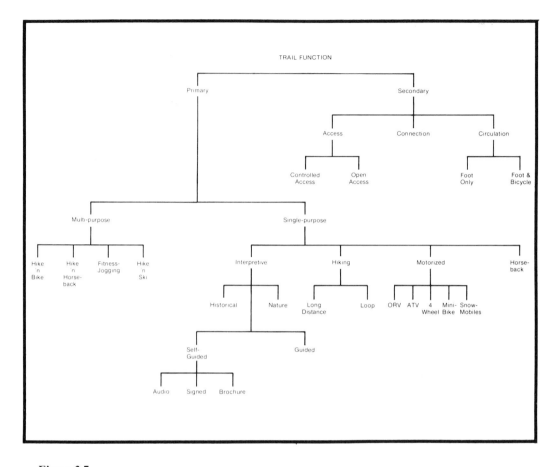

Figure 3.7

anticipated. Consider, for instance, the trail development complex in a national forest in Colorado shown in Figure 3.8. Initially, the trail had four uses: access to the trout stream; hikes to the scenic vista and lake; short walks from the parking lot toward the lake for photographing, and hiking and horseback riding into a designated wilderness area. While this created a considerable volume of use on the trail, these functions were not in serious conflict with each other. The conflict occurred when staff decided to add interpretive stations around the trail, figuring again to provide *all* users with

opportunities for environmental education. Vandalism on the interpretive facilities was excessive, and people seeking different experiences began getting in each other's way. Figure 3.9 shows an alternative to the original design with more attention given to zoning of uses. With this design, people interested in fishing can have access to the stream via the hiking trail, while those interested in a short picture-taking walk can use the entry-exit section of the lake-shore trail and those wanting an interpretive experience can use a trail designed solely for this purpose.

Figure 3.8

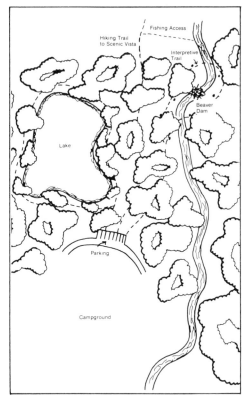

Figure 3.9

The final zoning consideration to address is *how does the trail relate to other facilities?* As with many types of trails, some use facilities are compatible with pathways and others are not. "Quiet" facilities such as campsites and campfire theaters should be far enough away from motorized trails to avoid conflict. Even hiking and other trails which don't normally generate high noise levels can disturb certain areas such as popular fishing and bird watching locations. On the other hand, some types of facilities and trails complement each other. Campers who use recreational vehicles often carry bicycles with them to provide transportation within the campground. By providing a hike

'n bike trail system, you may be able to offer: (1) safer routes for bicycle circulation; (2) less congestion on roads (we've seen campgrounds with as many as five hundred bicycles on busy weekends); (3) a host of program opportunities; and (4) an increase in the number of campers who bring bicycles with them. All of these options provide more program participants for you and more fun and exercise for campers. *Programmable facilities, such as trails, tend to create "snowball" effects if they are designed and managed properly.* More facilities means more uses; more uses means more users; more users means more facilities.

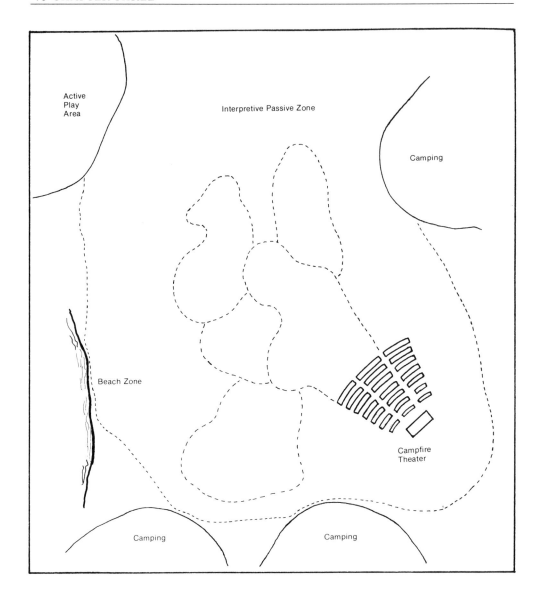

Figure 3.10

Another example of a trail-compatible facility is a campfire theater. Since the theater requires a passive, quiet zone, it can be surrounded by an interpretive trail system as in Figure 3.10. These trails provide a buffer zone for reducing noise which would otherwise reach the theater. In addition, the theater can serve as a focal point for interpretive programs; for example, a naturalist might meet a group at the theater to talk about "night sounds in the forest" and then lead a walk on the trail to listen for them. Remember these two critical elements when thinking about zoning: first *look at the big picture* and don't limit your planning to the trail itself — think about how the trail fits into the entire surrounding area; second, learn to think *program, program, program* — how can the trail be used to provide fun experiences for users? Trails aren't merely cleared strips of land, but vehicles for your creative programming ideas.

Design Psychology

Once the function of a trail is set, it's time to think about how to enhance the experience of the users. While this depends upon the type of trail, certain elements of design psychology apply to most situations. The ultimate goal of design psychology is to *make the user feel comfortable in the natural environment.* When utilized correctly, design techniques should be subtle enough so trail users aren't aware that the environment is being manipulated for their benefit. For example, with the exception of secondary use trails and long-distance hiking trails such as the Appalachian Trail, a loop design is almost always preferable to a linear one. Even long-distance trails can be improved by the addition of loops as you can see in the section on hiking trails below. A loop eliminates the need for backtracking and seeing the same scenery twice, it reduces the number of other people the user is likely to see on the trail, and, from a management perspective, decreases trail wear since people walk around the circuit once instead of out and back as they would on a linear trail. Unless the planner makes the loop design obvious by "forcing" corners and turns when they aren't necessary, users may be pleasantly surprised to find the trail ends where it began.

Loop design also lends itself to supporting another good rule of trail planning: whenever possible, use a single entry-exit point.

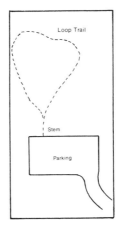

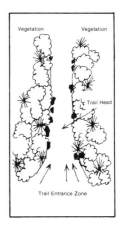

Figure 3.11   **Figure 3.12**

Single entry-exits, as we discussed earlier, are easier to administer and control — whether the facility is a trail or a state park. From a design psychology perspective, they benefit the users as well. Many people, especially those who only use trails on an occasional basis, may become disoriented in natural environments. If you design a loop with a single entry-exit, as in Figure 3.11, visitors finish the trail where they started it. At times, difficult terrain or other factors may keep you from developing a single entry-exit point. As an alternative, try to place the exit within sight of the parking lot, picnic shelter, or other facility from which the trail started. If this is not possible, and there is any chance trail users may become disoriented upon leaving the trail, signing may be necessary.

Before moving away from the entry-exit zone, let's discuss three other techniques of design psychology that you may find useful. First, as we suggested earlier, you can focus a person's vision on your trail head by designing it in the shape of an inverted "V" as in Figure 3.12. Be careful, however, that you do not reduce the width of the trail too much with this type of entrance zone. If this

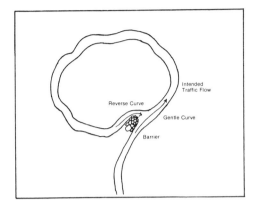

Figure 3.13

happens, the user may sense a feeling of being constricted — a sensation you want to avoid. Again, the planner must balance between "too much" and "too little." A second design technique aimed at making the user more comfortable with your trail entrance is to *try to avoid starting a trail on an adverse grade.* This is a technical way of saying "don't start trails by going uphill." In some situations, uphill entrance zones are impossible to avoid. The problem with uphill starts is again psychological; if users see a climb waiting for them at the entrance, they may decide that the trail isn't going to be worth the effort and avoid it entirely.

A final point on entrance zone psychology: earlier, we mentioned the tendency people have to move to the right when a choice is available. When developing a loop trail with a single entry-exit, you can reinforce this tendency through design. By moving people in the direction they prefer to go naturally, you can eliminate any vague feelings of anxiety they may have and reduce the chances of them entering what you designed as the trail exit. As shown in Figure 3.13, three aspects of design are used in conjunction with one another to move users to the right on the trail. First, a *gentle curve* extends from the "stem" of the trail through

the right-hand entrance. This encourages a natural continuation of the direction users were going while on the trail stem. Second, a *reverse curve* connects the left-hand trail exit to the stem. To enter the loop via this reverse curve, users would need to turn nearly 180 degrees, a very unnatural movement, particularly with the gentle curve as an alternative. Finally, the trail is designed with a *barrier*, a pile of rocks, a large tree, or a bush, between the trail stem and the left-hand exit. The barrier and reverse curve are not intended to prevent users *physically* from turning left at this point; they do, however, serve as effective psychological blockades to move people onto your trail in the direction you want them to go.

Once users enter the trail, it is generally a good idea to reduce the number of encounters they have with other people. On most trails *not* designed for motorized use — hiking, interpretive, bicycling, skiing — the planner should try to create a mood of being in a secluded natural environment. Ways of reducing the potential for contact with others on trails include *curvilinear design,* which decreases the linear distance people can see. A trail that avoids long tangents, or straightaways, and "snakes" through the woods will also increase user anticipation of what lies ahead. In flat areas, trail loops can be designed with a *"fat"* or *broad layout* to increase the distance between parallel points on the trail. If a trail is developed in an area with ridges and valleys, a narrow loop can be created by *placing the trail below and on both sides of a ridge top* as in Figure 3.14. In this case, the elevation of the ridge top provides a screen between parallel sections of the trail. In some environments, *existing vegetation* can be used as screening between sections of trail where people might otherwise see each other. Keep in mind, however, that deciduous trees and plants lose their leaves and will not provide a screen throughout the entire year. For this reason, and for ease of design, it is often a good idea to

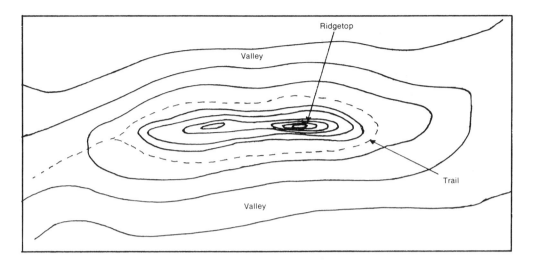

Figure 3.14

work on the trail layout in these environments during the months when trees and
shrubs have lost their foliage.

· To sum up, design psychology should be
used to *invite users onto trails* by providing
appealing entrance zones to *reduce confusion*
on the trail and at the exit by removing the
choice between directional options, and to
eliminate contacts with as many other users
as possible by manipulating loop design,
topography, and vegetation. A final aim of
design psychology should be to create as
much *visual variety* as possible, particularly
on trails where foot travel is used. Remember,
people move at a fairly slow pace on foot
trails. As a result, scenery can become
monotonous rather quickly. Moving in and
out of forests and meadows, using frequent
and gradual curves, and taking advantage of
interesting scenery can all enhance the user's
experience. And that's what design psychology is all about.

Field Design and Construction
In practice, the actual laying out and
construction of a trail can't be separated

from design psychology. In the last section,
we talked about what techniques to consider
for enhancing the user's experience. The
construction phase of trail development is
where these techniques are actually implemented. For example, if a loop trail is being
designed in hilly country, the planner should
try to construct the first half of the loop on
an uphill slope (excluding the entrance zone).
With this layout, users who exert themselves
will have an easier trip on the second half of
the loop. While this is really a technique of
design psychology, it is actually implemented
during the construction phase. In-the-field
design of trails is also the time at which to
apply techniques of resource stewardship. We
could ask another trick question at this
point: when, during the life of a trail, is
maintenance most critical? The answer is
during the design and construction phase.
The level of attention we give to building
preventive maintenance into our trail will
determine the ease or difficulty we have
maintaining it after it is completed.

Let's consider some of the preventive
measures the planner can take during design

Figure 3.15

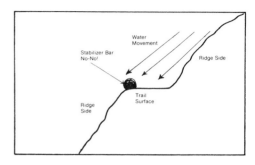

Figure 3.16

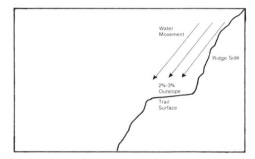

Figure 3.17

and construction. Problems caused by water depend on whether trails are built on flat ground or on slopes, and the measures you can take to prevent water-related damage are fairly simple but important. In flat areas, the sides of the trail should be designed with *drainage escape channels.* These are simply "gutters," or mini-ditches, which provide a path for run-off water to take. In order to move water to these escape channels, trails built in flat areas should be *center crowned* — two to three percent higher in the middle than along the edges. If possible, although this will increase costs of construction, trails should be *built slightly above natural grade.* These techniques prevent water from pooling on trails in flat areas.

When trails are built on hills and along the sides of ridges, the challenge is to minimize damage from water movement. In moving downhill, water seeks the path of least resistance. Clearing and grading a trail down the side of a ridge is an invitation for water to use your path as its own, as shown in Figure 3.15. The solution is to move water *off* the trail surface as soon as possible to prevent the buildup of volume and velocity. One trail construction technique used frequently that actually encourages erosion is the installation of stabilizer bars (Figure 3.16) along the lower side of the trail tread. As water moves down the ridge side and across the width of the trail, it strikes the stabilizer bar, usually long sections of log or railroad tie. Instead of continuing down the ridge side, the water is forced by the bar to remain *on* the trail surface, where it encourages erosion.

While stabilizer bars should be avoided, you can use several other methods for moving water from the trail surface. One of the most effective ways of removing water from ridge side trails is shown in Figure 3.17. By constructing your trail so the downhill side is slightly (two to three percent) *lower* than the uphill side, the natural tendency for water to move across the trail is increased. This is called outsloping. Conversely, if the trail were constructed on the level or, even worse, insloped, water would tend to pool on its surface.

Another means of preventing water buildup on trail surfaces is shown in Figure 3.18. Water bars may be made with a log six to eight inches in diameter laid on the trail at a thirty-degree angle and fastened with heavy stakes, posts, or steel pins. The trail surface downhill from the water bar should be level with the top of the log, and the outslope should be slightly increased immediately above the water bar to permit water release. If your trail must make a slow, steady climb, it may be advisable to install a *grade dip* (Figure 3.19). These are sections of trail where a short segment (not over five to six feet) has been built with a grade slightly *adverse* to the prevaling one. As with other techniques used when changes of topography are present, grade dips are employed to *slow* the downhill flow of water and *remove* the water from the trail surface at suitable intervals before it builds up an erosive force. A combination of all these methods usually provides the best erosion control.

Occasionally, you may find it necessary to construct your trail across the path of a major natural drainage. Often dry except during rainstorms, these drainage courses and pathways can cause major damage to trail surfaces during short periods of wet weather. The best solution is to *armour plate*

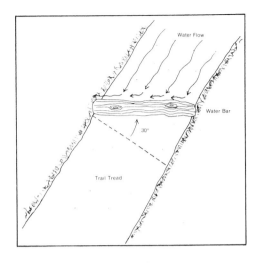

Figure 3.18

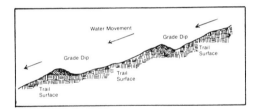

Figure 3.19

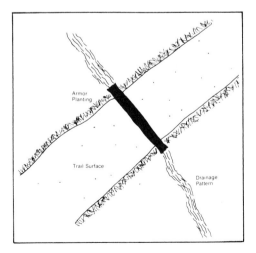

Figure 3.20

DESIGN SPECIFICATIONS

Trail Type	Clearing Width	Clearing Height	Tread Width	Surfacing[2] Material	Maximum Grade
Hiking - Backcountry - Distance	6 Feet	8 Feet	New tread 24 in. Existing tread (old road) variable	Natural with rock added in wet areas.	Variable - Can have steps and steep grades for short distances.
Hiking - Internally within a campground or other facility.	Single lane 6-10' Double lane 10' (Traffic both ways)	8 Feet	Single lane 3' Double lane 6' 10"	Natural if possible, gravel woodchips, or a combination of all three.	12% with 6% being general grade.
Horse[1] - Including pack animals	8 Feet	10 Feet	New tread 24" unless a wider tread is required for administrative vehicles.	Natural if possible, gravel in wet areas.	10% broken at short intervals by "rest" grades.
Bicycle[1]	8 Feet	8 Feet	Single lane 3' Double lane 6' 10"	Paved if possible Limestone Fines acceptable.	10% for short distances.
Interpretive	Single lane 6' Double lane 8'	8 Feet	Variable Single lane 2'-6'	Dependent on use - Blacktop, woodchips, sawdust. (Gravel not acceptable.)	8% with 5% or less preferred.
Handicapped	Variable but generous	8 Feet	Loop - 3' (single lane) Double lane 5' minimum.	Blacktop almost a necessity	5% - Trail should be as flat as possible.
Off-road Motorcycles	Single lane 6'	7 Feet	12"-18"	Natural	Variable

[1] If the trail is other than a single-purpose trail (multi-purpose) the design requirements should be geared to the most demanding specification within the planned uses.
[2] If asphalt paving is used, be sure to provide a gravel border along each side to keep the edge from crumbling.

Figure 3.21

such drainage areas with asphalt, stone, or tile, as shown in Figure 3.20. Except for the need to place a hard surface across major drainage paths, the material used for surfacing trails depends on the type of trail and the anticipated amount of use. Preferred surfacing materials, along with other design specifications, are shown for various types of trails in Figure 3.21.

Although vandalism would seem to be more the problem of the administrator, there are steps the planner can take to reduce damage to trails. In our experience, we've found that vandalism seems to occur most frequently within five hundred feet of the trail entrance. (Perhaps people who enter a trail intending to vandalize it don't feel it's "worth the trouble" to walk the entire trail.) As a result, you may be able to reduce damage to more expensive facilities, such as

benches, by placing them more than five hundred feet into the trail. One of the most common forms of vandalism is initial carving in smooth-barked trees — usually aspen in the West and American Beech in the East. By developing trails immediately adjacent to such trees, the planner invites such scarring. Trails should be kept at least fifteen to twenty feet from smooth-barked trees, and understory vegetation between these trees and the trail should be encouraged. If people are really intent on defacing trees, they will leave the trail and do so; the design goal here is to create a *psychological barrier* of distance and screening.

At times, people may cause damage to trail-side signs without meaning to vandalize them. Part of human nature is curiosity, and curiosity is satisfied by touching objects. While on trails, people may reach out and touch, hold, or hit posts simply because they are there. Thus planners should consider such quirks of human nature and place sign installations too far from the trail to reach. This won't stop vandals from damaging signs, but it will prevent casual users from loosening sign posts over time.

One feature sometimes encountered on trails is the switchback (Figure 3.22). The purpose of a switchback is to reduce the percent slope, or grade, of the trail by increasing the linear distance traveled relative to the change in elevation. (Remember, slope is a function of rise over run, or elevation/ distance.) In general, *switchbacks should be avoided whenever possible* because if the slope is steep enough to require one, it may be too steep to develop a trail. Severe grades discourage people and encourage erosion, but if switchbacks *must* be used, they should have a four foot minimum turning radius on walking trails and an eight foot minimum turning radius on multipurpose or motorized-use trails. The area where turning radii are placed should be graded nearly level, with enough slope to prevent water from being retained.

When stream crossings are necessary, the planner has several options. Whenever possible, a *ford* is the method preferred because of minimal construction and main-tenance costs. At times, some improvement in the stream channel may be necessary to improve footing at a ford, like placing large rocks in a straight line on the *downstream* edge of the crossing. Large rocks should be removed from the actual trail crossing. If a stream is too deep for fording, footlogs are the next best alternative for walking trails. When a footlog is used, its top surface should be planed flat and a safety handrail or cable provided. Each end of the log can be secured by cable to the stream banks. For bridges on walking trails, two or three foot-logs making a twenty-four inch width are usually adequate. Larger bridges and those

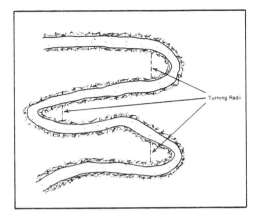

Figure 3.22

for multipurpose or motorized use require individual design.

When users approach the end of a trail, they may be tired or ready to leave. As a result, the planner should avoid designing it so they can see the end of the trail from the interior. If users can spot the parking lot or whatever facility is at the exit point from the interior, they may be inclined to cut across country to reach it. Remember, we want to localize impact through design. Giving users visual encouragement to leave the trail before reaching the exit *spreads* impact rather than containing it.

Although we've reached "the end of the trail," the planner's job isn't over. There are several aspects of administration yet to consider, and the planner is at least partly responsible for these.

Administration
Generally, trails require less active, on-site management than many other recreation facilities. Less active, however, doesn't mean trails should be given less conscientious attention than other types of areas. Policies for use must be set and enforced, periodic maintenance schedules devised, and program opportunities developed. One of the first

administrative tasks should be naming the trail, and the planner can advise management regarding appropriate names since he or she should be familiar with the pathway. The name should meet two objectives. First, it should provide a *description* of the character of the trail. Second, it should be something users will remember. Both these objectives can be met by using a little creativity. One excellent technique is *alliteration* — using words which all begin with the same letter or sound: "Shoreline Stroll;" "Tulip Tree Trail;" "Paw-paw Path."

Part of administration is keeping the user informed and oriented while on the trail through the use of signing. Because of their familiarity with the trail, planners should serve in advisory roles when these decisions are made. As a general rule, signing should be kept to a minimum, though it must be adequate to *warn, restrict,* or *inform* trail users. The following suggestions may prove helpful when considering how to sign trail systems. *Schematic signs,* which incorporate maps of the area the trail traverses, should be placed at major termini and intersections. These may be metal photo, painted, routed, Scotchlite, or laminated paper. A sign with the *trail name and a matching symbol* should be located at all trail termini, trail intersections, and road intersections; the symbol alone can be used at other points along the route. (The symbol should be easy to associate with the trail name; for example, "Telegraph Trail" might use "T" as a symbol. See *Blazing,* below).

Information on distances to shelters, water, campsites, and other important features should be provided on termini and intersection signs, trail brochures, or both. When necessary, termini and road crossing points on foot, bike, and horse trails should be marked with a sign prohibiting all motorized use (except administrative). Other prohibitions, as required by the type of trail or local conditions, e.g., no open fires, should be posted at these points as well. Gates, steps,

stiles, posts, or fences may also be required in some places to limit misuse, and markers with slogans like "Pack it in, Pack it out," along with adequate garbage disposal facilities, should be located at the termini and major road crossings. These types of signs may be located one hundred feet or more from intersections to minimize sign pollution and vandalism. All springs located on or near the trail should, if possible, be boxed in and signed "safe only after suitable treatment." If they cannot be boxed in, they should be signed "unsafe without treatment." Too much signing can produce a negative experience for trail users, so when signs are necessary, mount them on posts as low as possible to avoid a high profile.

Often, signing, or at least verbiage, can be avoided by *blazing* or painting symbol stencils on trees. When you use this type of marking, be sure the blazes are *intervisible;* from each tree marked, you should be able to see one blaze in either direction. In some instances, it may be necessary to place a blaze on opposite sides of a tree so it can be seen from either direction. The planner should walk the trail *in both directions* to determine appropriate locations for them. The interval between blazes will vary with terrain, type and density of vegetation, and trail alignment. The bottom of each blaze should be located about five feet above ground level. The frequency of blazes should increase as the trail approaches intersections, particularly those with other trails or logging roads. Blazes should also be used more frequently near trail termini and road crossings. If trees are not available at critical trail junctions or in sections of trail crossing extensive open areas, blazes may be marked on four-by-four posts. These should be visible above tall grass or weeds.

Trees must be prepared for blaze stencils carefully. Smooth-barked species such as beech, aspen, and yellow poplar require little or no preparation, but the bark of other species should be scraped or smoothed lightly to provide a flat, clean surface for the marking template. The *cambium,* or thin layer just beneath the tree bark, must *not* be exposed, and the template should be made of flexible material to conform to the rounded shape of the tree. Marking paint should be applied with a one-and-a-half- or two-inch brush, and the paint should be color coded so each trail is designated by a different color. A five- to ten-year forestry *boundary* paint should be used to ensure long life.

Zoning, design psychology, construction, and administration are all critical elements of trail development, regardless of the type of trail being discussed. We now need to shift our focus and briefly consider some aspects of design pertaining to specific *kinds* of trails commonly developed in parks and recreation areas. In the following sections, we'll look at trail-design strategies for hiking, hike 'n bike, interpretation, mini-bikes, and special populations.

Hiking Trails

There are two basic types of hiking trails. One is the *linear corridor,* the best examples of which include the Appalachian and Pacific Crest Trails. The purpose of this type of trail is to make a backcountry hiking experience fairly accessible to a large number of people. Being avid recreationists, we think this purpose is commendable. As planning critics, however, we feel the design of these trails could be improved and use extended to a wider variety of clients than those who currently hike them. Remember that *access to* an area doesn't insure widespread *use of* the attraction.

Figure 3.23 shows a typical section of a linear corridor trail. The distance between the two access points on the roads might be twenty or twenty-five miles, thus the design of the trail has, in essence, *limited* use to serious, long-distance hikers. These people may leave one access point, hike all day to the shelter, stay the night, and hike to the next access point the following day. But the

design in Figure 3.23 creates logistical problems for even this type of user. They have the option of bringing two vehicles to shuttle between their beginning and end points, or hiking back the way they came. As we discussed earlier, doubling back has its disadvantages: an increased potential for contact with more people; twice the impact on the trail; and seeing the same scenery over again. Shuttling is not an ideal solution either because of difficult logistics and double the expense of fuel. Also, parking

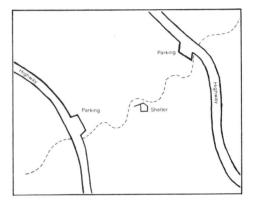

Figure 3.23

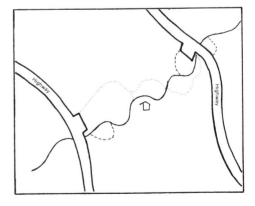

Figure 3.24

your two vehicles in a safe spot is ofttimes a problem.

The key to improving the type of design shown in Figure 3.23 is the key to successful planning of *any* type of recreation facility: *understanding and accommodating the needs of users, including potential users.* There are really two types of people who use linear corridor trails: the serious, long-distance hikers described above who are both willing *and physically able* to use these trails as their designers intended and the "typical tourist," perhaps on a family vacation, who stops at an access point, walks in one-quarter of a mile or so and then returns. Planners generally don't understand this second phenomenon: the Appalachian and similar trails, because of their nature, have an aura of adventure about them. The average person may want to experience this briefly just to be able to say "I was on it."

How can we, as planners, take the needs of these two groups and develop a better approach to linear-corridor trail planning? One solution is shown in Figure 3.24. In this design, the linear experience is left intact for those people who want to use two vehicles and hike in one direction only. The design also meets the needs of the casual user by providing a series of short connector loops (dashed lines). Now, instead of walking in one-quarter mile and returning back the same way, this group can walk a loop trail tailored to fit their preferences for short distances. The planner might develop one very short loop (one-quarter to one-third mile) on one side of the road where the main trail crosses. On the other side, a longer loop — perhaps one to two miles — could be constructed. This approach would be aimed at *expanding as much as possible* the potential types of users.

The longer loops, shown by dotted lines, create an opportunity for a third type of hiking experience. These loops may be used by the long-distance hiker who can't, or prefers not to, use a shuttle system. With

long connector loops, it's possible to leave your car at a parking lot, hike in, stay the night, and hike back without retracing your steps. In the southern United States, where linear trails pass through national forests, the existence of old logging roads gives the planner some real help.

The type of development shown in Figure 3.24 is important for two reasons. First, it creates the potential for additional types of hikes on a linear corridor trail. Second, *it begins to present the opportunity for users to design the type of experience they want.* This is an important point. Instead of the planner saying, "Here's a linear trail — take a long walk or don't use it," we begin to say, "Here are some *choices;* pick the one meeting *your* needs and preferences" (planning parks for people again). This type of design, with the user in mind, becomes even easier to achieve with another kind of hiking trail.

The Trail System

A system or complex of hiking trails such as the one shown in Figure 3.25 has certain advantages over a linear-corridor system. From the standpoint of trail management, these include the following: *Right of way;* linear-corridor trails may be difficult to develop because they require long, narrow tracts of land. Corridors adequate for trails may alternate between public and private ownership, making it difficult for public agencies to acquire title or easements and even harder for private concerns to attempt linear-trail development. Conversely, a hiking system incorporating a fairly large number of miles of trail can be developed on a relatively small plot of land. *Control;* because hiking systems can be contained on single-ownership properties such as state parks, it is easier to manage access to and use of the trails. Systems may be designed with fewer entry-access points and road intersections than linear trails, and, in most instances, on-site management need not be as far removed from the system. *Maintenance;* linear

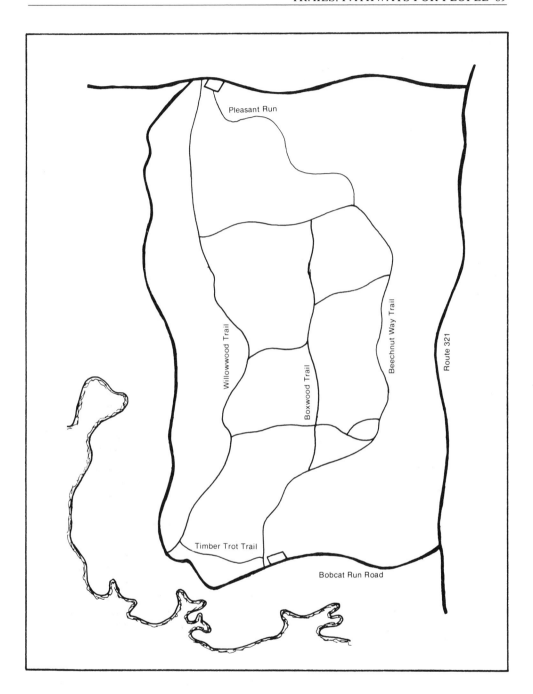

Figure 3.25

corridors, because of their length, have to rely on several different maintenance operations. Hiking systems can be maintained from a single point, permitting more uniform maintenance and less need for coordination among crews and supervisors.

Users and management may both benefit from the opportunity to *program* trail systems. Since the trail system is geographically contained in one area, it is likely to receive more repeat use by local hikers as well as the transient use from out-of-area visitors. *A local base of support* gives any facility, including trails, an advantage in terms of program development. With area hiking clubs and branches of conservation-oriented societies drawn into cooperative relationships with the agency or organization managing the trail system, hike days, litter-collection walks, and overnights with Scout troops can be planned. The chief advantage of trail systems is *the opportunity for users to design their own experiences.* As shown in Figure 3.25, the trail system, with its honeycomb of short, intermediate, and long loops, can accommodate walks lasting from several minutes to several days. Accessible

Figure 3.26

from connectors to the nearby campground, linear trail, and park-entry station, as well as the trail head, the system "invites" users from a variety of sources. In Northern climates, the complex can double as a cross-country ski system.

The management key to making trail systems convenient for users is adequate signing. One challenge with signing a hiking complex is to reduce cost, and the method we suggest is shown in Figure 3.26. As we discussed earlier, locational signs need to be provided at each trail intersection. Instead of producing a separate map for each of the numerous intersections on a hiking complex, the signing system shown in Figure 3.26 uses a master map with numbered locations. Corresponding numbers are then placed *on the sign post,* eliminating the need for thirty or forty original maps, each with a "you are here" indicator on it.

Hike 'n Bike Trails
Inside of developed recreation areas such as state parks, and particularly campgrounds, there is an excellent opportunity to design a system of walking and bicycling trails. These systems, if designed carefully, can serve a dual function; providing *circulation* among the various facilities within the area — campsites, play courts and fields, beaches, campfire theater, and the like — and increasing *program* opportunities as well. The actual design and use of hike 'n bike systems are site-specific. Such factors as type of other facilities and physical characteristics of the site will help determine what you can and can't do with the system. There are, however, some general guidelines to consider.

Trails with more than one purpose need to be planned for the use with the most demanding requirements. For example, hiking trails need only a four-foot turning radius on curves and, unless use is heavy, can function with a natural ground surface. When bicycling is added, however, the turning radius should be eight feet and a surfacing material should be added. Ideally, an asphalt surface is best but also quite expensive — several dollars for each linear foot of trail. Depending on the situation, there may be an alternative. In some parks and campgrounds, users bring bicycles with them for internal transportation. For instance, recreational vehicles (RV) campers often bring one- or three-speed bikes as opposed to ten-speed models with narrow gauge tires. If this type of user predominates in your area, we have found that finely crushed limestone works well, at a considerably lower cost than asphalt.

Hike 'n bike trails should be designed to connect major use zones with each other. Since circulation is one aspect of this, it may be possible to take advantage of part of the road system within the park or campground. There are two ways of developing hike 'n bike trails, both of which should be used in most instances. Portions of the system can follow roads connecting areas by developing signing schemes and painting bike lanes, though additional paths for circulation may be necessary to supplement those using the road system. In designing the circulation function into a hike 'n bike system, it's important to remember that motorized vehicles will be using the roads and crossing the paths. Keep in mind that *speed* is a design requirement which must be considered from the standpoint of safety. A cyclist needs more advance warning of an impending intersection than a hiker requires. Departing slightly from our need for curvilinear design, an occasional straightaway safe for passing should be included for faster bikers.

There are several aspects of trail design useful in enhancing program opportunities on hike 'n bike systems. *Variety* should be included in the system as much as possible. Design the trail so it moves in and out of stands of timber, through open meadows, along lake shores — whatever resources are available in your area. *Varied length loops* are important to hike 'n bike systems. A loop

taking two hours to walk leisurely may take an industrious ten-year-old less than half an hour to bicycle. *Organized bike hikes* can be planned by program staff if the trail design takes this need into account. Developing the trail near scenic views, abandoned cabins, or interesting geologic features will create opportunities for program staff. Programs can also take advantage of the connector function of hike 'n bike trails. The program areas connected by the trails can serve as bases for starting and completing hikes and bicycle tours.

Mini-bike Trails
During the mid-1970's, mini-bikes became popular additions to the recreational equipment users brought to parks and campgrounds. Adults used them for transportation and children and teens used them (when they were permitted) for recreation. We include a section on planning trails for mini-bikes for two reasons. First, people still use them, although the proportion of users has declined. Second, a new trend, the use of three-wheelers, seems to be emerging. The type of trail system discussed below functions well for mini-bikes and three-wheelers. Mini-bike trails are easy to develop, inexpensive to build and maintain, and — like hike 'n bike systems — add another program element to outdoor recreation areas. This fits well with our philosophy of planning and designing areas with *all* users in mind.

Mini-bike areas and other recreational facilities that may be a nuisance to some users require the same zoning given to maintenance yards. They should be *a part of, but apart from* the rest of the recreation complex. They should be far enough away from other types of areas so the noise created will not be noticeable. Sound-level tests should be conducted to determine how great this distance needs to be, given local topography and levels of vegetation. (You may be surprised at how close they can be located to other uses). If a mini-bike or

Figure 3.27

three-wheeler isn't available for testing how far noise will carry, you can borrow a chain saw from your maintenance crew.

To reduce development costs, the ideal setting for a mini-bike area is in an open field surrounded by timber. Once the appropriate zoning and distance factors have been determined, all that remains is to develop the trail complex. We suggest a design similar to the one shown in Figure 3.27. This complex, which can literally be built in one day, requires only minimal development. A parking area large enough for five or six vehicles serves as an entrance zone. Vegetative screening should be left here to help minimize the visual effect of the area. Using a bush hog, clear a long trail stem

from the parking area to the mini-bike zone. This stem should be made as level as possible, and fairly straight. The goal here is to provide *access into* the area rather than to create a zone where people will ride recreationally. Past the entrance, the design shown provides three areas for use. A staging area where riders can view the field and make minor repairs leads to a circular trail with gentle curves, which can be used by novices and as a warm-up area. A trail of intermediate difficulty and an advanced trail are also included here, and a sign at the juncture of the three trails informs riders about the difficulty level of each trail.

The trails themselves require little more preparation than cutting a swath width with a bush hog, assuming a suitable open field is available for development. The trail should be walked and inspected before use, for any woody plants, such as sumac, cut by the bush hog will leave protruding stumps that should be dug out at ground level. All vegetation between the trails should be left to discourage users from cutting across between trails, and periodic mowing is normally the only maintenance the area will require. Mini-bike areas are easy to design, develop, and maintain. If an area has a suitable zone and the potential for use, they can add another dimension to program opportunities.

Interpretive Trails

Developing a successful interpretive trail depends on several factors. The most obvious criterion for judging a trail is the quality of its historical, cultural, or natural elements. However, this judgment must be made in light of the question: "who is the intended audience?" *An interpretive trail in a camp-ground should not be expected to function the same way as one outside a nature center.* People go to visitor centers at national parks, museums at Civil War battlefields, and nature centers at state parks for the same reason: they are interested in them. People go to campgrounds to relax and enjoy them-selves. Campers, then, generally don't have the same level of motivation to take advantage of interpretive services. This is not suggesting that people who camp aren't interested in interpretation; only that inter-pretation is the primary reason people go to these centers. *Camping* is the primary reason people go to campgrounds, thus the key to developing successful interpretive facilities, including trails, is *introspection*. Think about who your users are and develop displays and trails with them in mind. Interpretive messages wouldn't be designed the same way for children as they would be for adults. Likewise, they should allow for different adult motivations *in different settings.*

Once an audience has been targeted, design of interpretive trails is not difficult. For best results, we suggest that an interpretive specialist and a planner develop the trail *together* to insure that both program *and* planning requirements are considered. The first step in the field planning process is to locate the two types of *control points.* The first is the set of features to be interpreted — specimen trees, geologic features, gunnery sites from a battle, and the like. The second relates to physical layout; the trail needs to start gaining elevation here, cross the stream just ahead, rejoin the loop over there. Once these points have been identified, the layout becomes rather like a game of connect the dots. How can we best design a pathway from the first to the last point?

Interpretation should be the primary focus of an interpretive trail. Walking it can be a good source of exercise, but you should *avoid building excessive physical challenge* into interpretive trails. Grades should not be overly steep and routes should not be too long. Depending on the audience and the features to be interpreted, one-quarter mile is probably a good length for most interpretive trails. The experience should be educational, but also enjoyable, and too much walking can spoil the mood you want to create for interpretation. Another way of detracting from this mood is to surface interpretive trails with gravel. When people walk on gravel, it crunches underfoot, and the noise can detract from the experience you want users to have.

Interpretive trails, to enhance the quality of the experience, should be as convenient as possible. *Turnouts* for people reading messages, such as those shown in Figure 3.28, should be provided at stations. If signs are used, place posts just out of reach to reduce casual damage. This will require using a larger typeface or print. Messages printed on signs or brochures should also be kept relatively short and non-technical. People

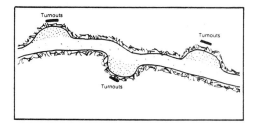

Figure 3.28

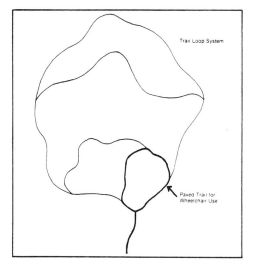

Figure 3.29

may remember that the wood of the Osage Orange is used to make bows if you tell them the tree is also known as a bowdock. They probably won't remember *Maclura pomifera.* One effective technique when using interpretive signs is to spray a paint spot on the sign and a corresponding spot on the object being interpreted. This is helpful if there is any chance that the user might not be able to distinguish between the object being interpreted and other nearby features. For example, a person not familiar with nature might read an excellent message about

poison ivy and then look knowingly at a nearby grape vine. If a paint spot is used, we recommend white; some bright colors look out of place in a natural environment, and others — reds and greens — are difficult for color-blind individuals to discern.

Trails for Handicapped Persons
Whenever possible, avoid building trails "for handicapped people." Designing specifically for those who happen to be blind or in wheelchairs reinforces the perception that these individuals are somehow "different." We feel a better approach is to plan trails for interpretation, hiking, circulation, or some other purpose, and then design them so they can be used by as many people as possible — including those with disabilities. The only difference between an accessible trail and one with barriers is careful attention to standards. Trails designed to accommodate wheelchairs should not exceed a five percent grade[1] and should be hard-surfaced. Bridges on these trails should have railings. (We suspect that a trail built to these specifications wouldn't be recognized by most people as being for the "disabled.") Accessible trails should be marked with the international barrier-free symbol, but planning trails specifically for the disabled is demeaning.

Attempting to design trails for disabled people can also limit the potential for trail use. Braille trails may be well-intended, but only a small proportion of visually impaired persons use Braille. Designing a trail with Braille symbols and regular-sized typeface for sighted people may actually hamper use by most of the visually impaired, but large type-face and audio cassettes can be enjoyed by all users, regardless of their visual capabili-

---

[1] Students with expertise in therapeutic recreation are quick to point out trail-grade standards for wheelchair users; however, in testing the same students the authors found that most of them had no idea of what a five percent grade looked like or how to attain it.

ties. At times, it seems that planning for people with disabilities stops with good intentions. There are numerous instances of trails built "for the handicapped" where the planner apparently *thought of* but didn't *plan for* the expected clientele. We've seen Braille trails with major hazards removed but a four-inch drop off along the edges of the paved trail; trails surfaced for wheelchairs without a curb cut in the adjacent parking lot; trails three miles long for people with ambulatory problems. When possible, trails designed to accommodate handicapped persons should be developed to allow them to choose the extent of their own experience. Building hard-surfaced loop trails with connectors, like the one shown in Figure 3.29, is a way of accomplishing this for individuals in wheelchairs. Our experience indicates the *shortest* trail can be about one-eighth mile long. Longer loops provide a variety of options.

Synthesis

Regardless of the type of trail you need to develop, the critical aspects of planning are to fit the design to the needs of users, protect the environment, minimize management and maintenance problems, and enhance program opportunities. At times, some of these goals may conflict with each other. When this happens, the best solution is to compromise on the basis of common sense. Ask yourself, or your planner, *why* the trail is designed as it is, and make sure the answer is satisfactory. Be sure a trail is needed before you build it. Consider, for example, the trend in building jogging paths with fitness stations at intervals along the trail. We don't suggest these shouldn't be built, yet they are relatively expensive. We see people jogging on them fairly frequently, but in some locations the number of people using the exercise stations seems to be low. Do enough people use these trails for exercise to justify the

expense, or would the jogging function alone meet the needs of most users? Do fitness trails need to stand alone, or could exercise stations be combined with trails designed for multiple purposes? We don't know how to respond to these questions, other than to say the answers probably depend to some extent on the location and other available opportunities. The point is twofold: first, we shouldn't *assume* that demand for a new type of trail or any other facility exists just because other parks or communities are beginning to install them; second, to determine demand it is first necessary to *assess need.* When we suggest ways to help design trails, we assume you have already justified development.

Trail Design Exercise

At the end of each of the next few chapters, you'll find an opportunity to design an area or facility similar to the one discussed in the preceding pages. Here's your challenge for trails.

The setting. Haunted Hill Campground (Figure 3.30) is located in a large state park in the midwest. The area is built on the shoreline of a Corps of Engineers project, Veronica Lake. There are three hundred campsites, two hundred of which have electrical hook-ups. Users are mostly families with children ranging in age from a few months old to high-school age, although retirees use the area regularly. The nearest community has active Scout troops and a chapter of the National Audubon Society. As an experienced consultant or team of consultants with a background in planning, management, and programming, your job is to develop a conceptual plan for a comprehensive system of campground trails.

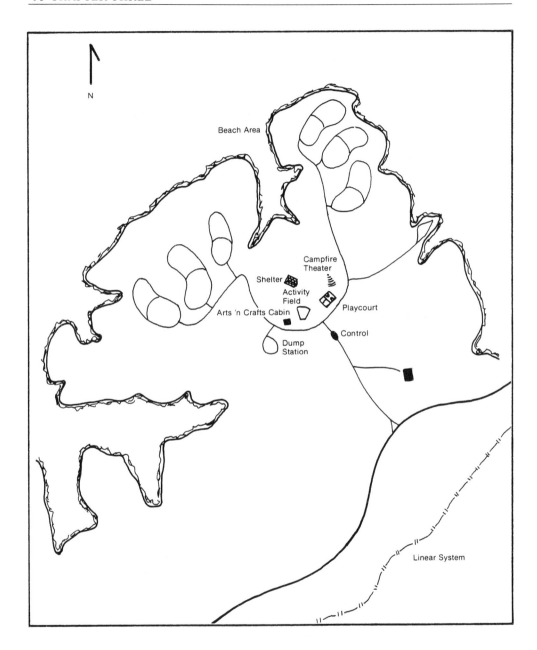

Figure 3.30

Givens:
1. Topography slightly rolling and sloping toward lakeshore. Land suitable for facility location anywhere.
2. Soils excellent. No problems with heavy clay content and frost heave not a concern.
3. Vegetation:
   — Overstory already thinned to a fifty percent shade factor with a mixture of high-quality, young vigorous hardwoods.
   — Understory ten-to-fifteen-foot dogwood, redbud, and other young hardwoods; three-to-fifteen-foot material in shrubs and small trees adequate for good screening.
4. Land ownership: all public. Boundary line as shown on Figure 3.30.
5. Features: no outstanding cultural, environmental, or historical features located on on the land base. South side of southernmost bay of lake has interesting limestone bluffs, but no developable land between bluffs and shoreline. Bluffs are visible from northern shore.
6. Other park features outside campground: linear corridor hiking trail one-and-a-half miles beyond campground entrance and fee station.

Your conceptual plan should include:
1. Connections between camping areas and program areas, including the beach zone;
2. Recreational trails for *all* types of users, including hikers, bicyclists, three-wheelers, and nature enthusiasts (Indicate proposed surfacing materials.);
3. Locations where directional and information signs should be installed;
4. Any necessary support facilities (There's at least one we haven't discussed yet — here's your chance to apply some common sense.);

5. Something innovative — a special program using the trail system, an additional use for a conventional trail, a type of trail use we haven't discussed (*Be creative!*);
6. Names and any necessary regulations for your trails; and
7. A map legend distinguishing among the various types of trails you develop.

Obviously, there is no "right" answer to this exercise. We have included one solution in Appendix A, but since we've told you everything we know about trails, you should do better than we did. Good luck!

APPENDIX A

Solution to Chapter Three Trails Exercise

As we suggested at the end of Chapter Three, there is no single correct solution to planning a comprehensive system of trails for the campground shown in Figure 3.30. A good solution should address circulation, access, and recreation needs, should include at least one innovative concept (we added a water-oriented interpretive trail to take advantage of the otherwise inaccessible limestone bluffs), and should provide support facilities as needed (did you think to include bicycle racks at program areas?). As a follow-up to this design exercise, you might try to "sell" your plan to others in your class. What would be your reaction to aspects of the plan they don't accept?

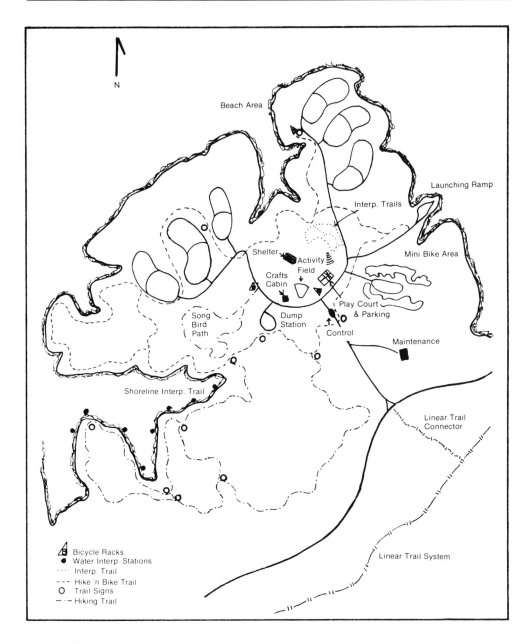

Appendix A

4

DAY USE AREAS:
HOSTING THROUGH DESIGN

INTRODUCTION

This is the first of several chapters wherein we briefly discuss planning several special recreation areas. Chapters and even entire texts have been or could be written about these special areas, e.g., visitor centers. However, our challenge in a text like this is to give you as much guidance as possible within a reasonable number of pages and chapters. *Your* challenge is to learn the basics of planning parks for people and then use them to help solve most of your park-design problems. This means determining as many facts as possible about potential users and their program needs — and, indeed, any special park areas; then based on analysis of these facts you *must* plan facilities to meet the needs of users, managers, and *programs*. In the real world it rarely has been done this way; thus we again emphasize that histori-cally most of our parks have been poorly designed!

Day-use areas, the focus of this chapter, include boat ramps, beaches, picnic areas, visitor centers, and day camps. In previous chapters, we've tried to stress the importance of program, program, program. This is still an excellent philosophy: never miss a chance to design or manage for the *enjoyment* of your users. Keep in mind, however, that the opportunity for programming won't always be present — at least not to the same extent for all types of facilities. How, for example, would you program a boat ramp? Actually, there are several ways. The main problem is

a lack of creativity on the part of the planner. Ask yourself what a boat ramp is. If you conjure up a mental image of a broad slab of concrete sloping down into a lake, river, or bay, you're at least as creative as most planners.

Instead of imagining what a boat ramp or other facility is *technically,* train yourself to think *creatively* about what potential it has. A boat ramp is a slab of concrete, but it is also a use zone for people. And whenever you have people, there's an opportunity to program. Given a few extra dollars, perhaps you have room for a fishing pier next to the ramp; a little care taken in design and the pier is barrier-free. Anchor a number of old tires near one side of the parking lot and your program staff can teach bait-casting techniques. Suddenly your lonely slab of concrete is hosting, through design, seventy-five children — plus their parents — for an all-day fishing rodeo. Add some simple props such as gunny sacks and spoons for relays and egg races, and you have a full-fledged recreation program!

There are two points to make here: first, the scenario we've just described doesn't happen on its own. It requires a commit-ment to programming on the part of management, a creative planner, an enthusi-astic program person, marketing and organizational strategies, and a willingness to work with local media and user groups. We'll never tell you successful programming is easy. Secondly, programming — as important

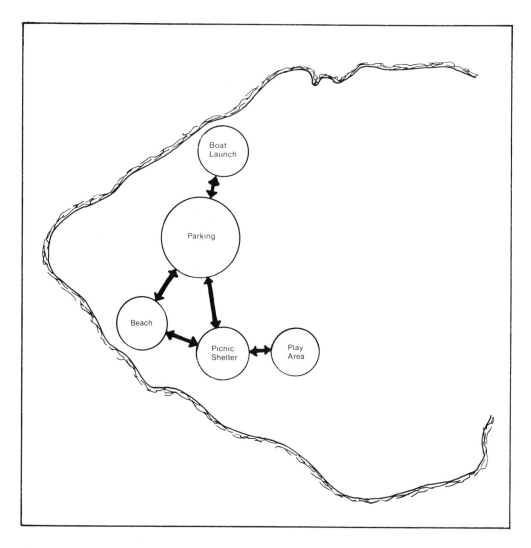

Figure 4.1a

as it is — isn't always appropriate. If the boat ramp or other type of facility isn't convenient to reach, or if physical-site conditions dictate "a slab of concrete and nothing else," you shouldn't try to force a program on the facility. Remember, our recipe for successful planning includes common sense as well as creativity. This brings us back to the point in the chapter title: hosting through design.

Whether programs are feasible or not, the primary purpose of day-use areas is to provide enjoyment for those who use them. One way to *increase* people's enjoyment is to *decrease* the potential for hassles within the area. This is a function of design. If an area,

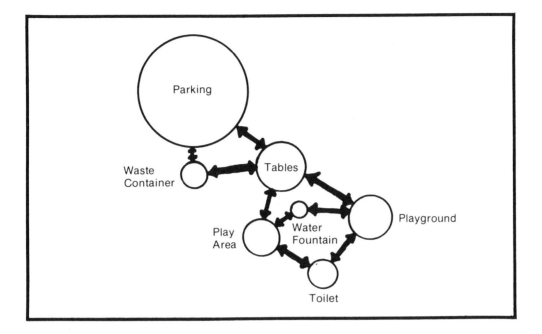

Figure 4.1b

whether boat ramp or day camp, is well-designed, it will be convenient, safe, and easy to use. On the other hand, if you often see visitors who appear frustrated or who violate regulations (such as driving the wrong way on a one-way road), or if facilities are heavily vandalized, much of the blame can be traced to the person who planned the area. Before discussing specific types of day-use areas, it may be helpful to consider these types of issues from the perspective of zoning.

Earlier, we discussed the topic of simple zoning of use areas — how they relate to each other. There are really two types of considerations to keep in mind when you focus on zoning, and the first of these is *inter-area* zoning. In other words, how well (or how poorly) does the area in question "fit" with other use areas within the same complex? For example, a large lakeside park might have a picnic area, a beach, a boat-

launching ramp, ball fields, play courts, and playgrounds. The concern of inter-area zoning is the relationship between two or more of these areas: do the locations of the picnic area and the playground complement one another? Are the beach and boating site zoned so they don't conflict with each other? The second type of zoning to consider is *intra-area*. For intra-area zoning, we want to ensure that major and support facilities *within a given use zone* relate to one another in a reasonable manner. Within the area designated for play equipment, are the swings and the drinking fountain on the same side of the road? At the picnic shelter, are the garbage containers a part of, but apart from the eating area?

Note how one concept was repeated in both inter- and intra-area contexts: *relationships*. Relationships between use areas and among facilities within a single area are a

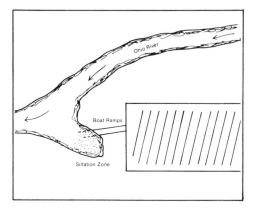

Figure 4.2

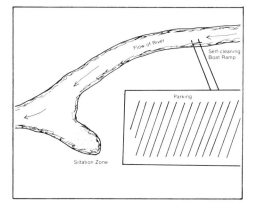

Figure 4.3

crucial element in conceptual planning. A helpful tool for determining the sensibility of alternative ways of fitting use areas together is the *relationship diagram*. Examples of these diagrams are shown in Figure 4.1. The purpose of the relationship diagram is to help you conceptualize how "pieces" of an area can best be joined to each other. When placed on a base map of the site to be planned, these simple drawings are easier to interpret than formal plans. Indeed, relationship diagrams can often help form the basis

for more sophisticated designs. For example, if the "fit" of facilities in Figure 4.1a seems to be the most logical of several alternatives from the standpoint of relationships, you might next consider the feasibility of various park-entry points. If you have a firm idea of where the parking lot will be, you can "work backwards" to plan alternative road alignments and, ultimately, the best possible entrance zone. "Best" implies a compromise of several elements, including user safety, aesthetics, cost of development, and resource protection.

A final point to remember concerning relationship diagrams is this: "relationship" doesn't always imply proximity between areas. A passive sitting area and a tot lot may be placed adjacent to each other if the purpose of the seating area is to provide a vantage point to supervise children playing. If the purpose of the seating area, however, is to provide a quiet enclave for contemplation, it should accommodate the tot lot by being well removed from it.

BOAT RAMPS

In keeping with the theme of sharing mistakes with you, consider the facility shown in Figure 4.2. This drawing depicts a boat ramp built by the Corps of Engineers near Louisville, Kentucky. The ramp provided access to the Ohio River, which flows in the direction indicated by the arrows. The mistake resulted from the planning decision to place the ramp in a small inlet which was not in the path of the current. The lack of current in the inlet meant water moved slowly there, creating a siltation zone at the boat ramp. In other words, the natural flow of water moved silt into, but not out of, the inlet. As the silt settled, the inlet quickly filled in, and before long boats could no longer be launched. The initial solution to this problem, incidentally, illustrates a point we discussed earlier. After recognizing the problem, staff attempted to solve it by dredging the silt out of the inlet. As you know by now, however, such action would for a short time cure the *effects* of the problem rather than the *cause* of it. The final — and correct — solution, shown in Figure 4.3, was to close the original ramp and replace it with one where water movement provided a "self-cleaning" action.

You should note that there are some instances in which the solution in Figure 4.3 could create hazards to users. If the current is particularly swift, or if the boat ramp is for human-powered boats, a put-in point exposed to direct current might be unsafe. You can still avoid siltation zones in these situations by providing a breakwater immediately upstream from the launch point, as shown in Figure 4.4. The point to remember is this: a critical aspect of boat ramps is their *slope*. To maintain the degree of slope needed, you must keep the base area free of silt deposits. Allowing natural water movement to wash these deposits away is the most effective (and efficient) maintenance solution we know.

Although the above example discussed a situation on a river, lakes are also subject to siltation. If you build a ramp at the base of a sheltered cove with a predominately incoming wind, as in Figure 4.5, siltation may occur fairly rapidly. Ignoring soils studies, along with a lack of attention to erosion control measures above the lake shore, can also contribute to siltation. Soil washed down to a sheltered inlet may remain near where it enters the lake if wind and wave action aren't sufficient to remove it. Thus boat ramps on lakes should be built along the main shoreline (safety permitting) where the self-cleaning movement of water can be permitted to keep siltation in check.

Features of Boat Ramps. Finding a location naturally suited for a boat-launching ramp can often be quite challenging. The desirable

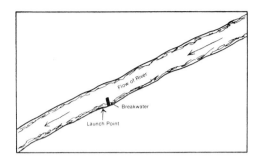

Figure 4.4

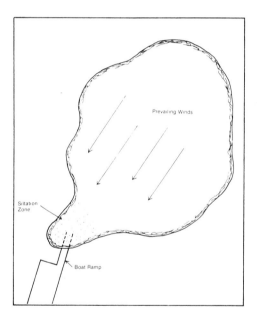

Figure 4.5

slope, or grade, for a ramp is twelve to fourteen percent. This slope is needed both above and below water level. The length of the ramp is also a concern if the surface elevation of the water is subject to change. Reservoirs may drop or rise several yards (or both) during the course of a season. The length of the ramp is not especially critical during a launch as long as there is room to back the boat or craft to the water. With a fourteen percent grade, users should be able to launch most boats when the rear wheels of the tow vehicle reach the water's edge. The ramp should be long enough, however, to extend several feet below the lowest expected lake elevation, permitting launching when water levels are low. A few COE and TVA Lakes have elevational changes of one hundred feet or more. Obviously planners can't realistically provide access at all ramp sites throughout the year.

During most hours of the day, you can drive through the parking lot serving a boat ramp and not experience heavy launching traffic, even if the lot is nearly full. People tend to launch their boats at different times of the day depending on their type of recreation use. Fishing parties tend to launch their boats early in the morning and/or late in the afternoon. Pleasure craft and power boats usually launch later in the morning and earlier in the afternoon. However, many people, both pleasure boaters and fishing parties, want to stay on the water as long as possible, leaving just before dark. As a result, many boat ramps suffer through a late afternoon/early evening "rush hour." If you expect this phenomenon to occur, you should plan a ramp wide enough for two boats or more, depending on the expected amount of use, to be taken out at one time. Minimizing the time users have to wait in line to get their boats put ashore will reduce their aggravation. Reducing hassles should be a goal of planning parks for people!

The problems users encounter on and around boat ramps can be decreased considerably through careful attention to detail. Since wet ramps can be slippery, the surface of paved ramps should be grooved perpendicular to the direction of the ramp to provide better traction. When building a ramp, you may want to include a series of iron rings three to four inches in diameter anchored along either side. This provides a convenient spot for boaters to moor tem-

porarily while they drive their vehicle from the ramp to the parking lot upon launching and back again when they land.

The parking lot should be as close to the launch area as possible for convenience, but also should be located with environmental protection in mind. If the parking lot is built too close to the shoreline, construction may alter the site environment and make the shoreline more susceptible to erosion. When you design or build a new parking lot, remember to tilt it two to three percent *away* from the launch. If rainwater is carrying pollutants from an existing lot to the launch area, you may also need to add a rock filter strip, as discussed in Chapter Two. Regardless of the placement of the parking lot, the increase in wave action and vehicle and foot traffic around the launch area can create shoreline impact. Areas subject to traffic should be reinforced. If the shoreline has a steep pitch or lacks vegetative cover, "rip-rap" may be needed. Rip-rap is large rock (six inches or larger in diameter) laid along the slope of the bank. The rip-rap receives the energy or force of wave action and thus helps prevent soil erosion.

When designing the parking lot to serve the boating site, remember the flow of traffic to and from the ramp as well as into and out of the area. Local conditions will have a bearing on what you can and can't do, but in all circumstances try to make the parking and launching maneuvers as simple as possible. Individual parking slips must be long enough to park vehicles towing boat trailers. Given the conditions existing on a particular site, try to design the parking lot and launch area to eliminate as much backing up as possible. Figure 4.6 shows one excellent method for reducing backing between the parking lot and the ramp. (We'd love to claim credit for this, but we saw it at a Corps of Engineers campground on Barren River Lake, Kentucky). With this type of a turnout system, vehicles can drive two-thirds of the distance between the parking lot and

the launch point in a forward gear. They
need only back a short distance and, if
you've ever backed a trailer, you can appreciate the convenience of this design.

If site conditions permit, another
convenient addition to a launch zone is a
small loading dock adjacent to the ramp.
This allows boaters to load and unload
equipment — as well as themselves — from
their craft without having to wade alongside
it, another example of hosting through
design, particularly for senior citizens and
handicapped users. The dock should be close
enough to the ramp to reach by paddling,
but far away enough to avoid interfering
with the actual launch. If a dock is provided
and the water elevation is subject to fluctua-
tion, the dock should be hinged where it
joins the shore. If the lake frequently rises
above normal elevation, a dock can be
designed to glide up and down on steel poles.
These designs will permit the dock to change
elevation with the water level.

As with all recreation areas, user safety
and security should be incorporated into the
design of launch-ramp areas. Swimming near
the ramp should be prohibited, and signs
indicating unusual safety problems, e.g.,
snags, should be posted. Regulations such as
no wake speeds near the ramp should be
clearly signed and enforced. Since boaters are
often away from their vehicles for several
hours at a time, Parking lots should also be
as secure as possible. Area lights may be
needed if the lot will be used after dark.
Underbrush and other areas for vandals and
thieves to hide in should be eliminated.

Developing a recreation area or facility
such as a launch ramp is a *minimum* level of
service provision. As a professional, you
should make every effort to *maximize* the use
of resources allocated to recreation. There
are at least two reasons for this. From a
practical standpoint, recreation budgets are
usually tied to quantitative measures: more
users mean more dollars. From a somewhat

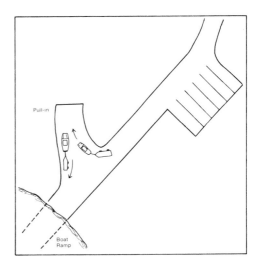

Figure 4.6

more idealistic perspective, spreading the
qualitative benefits of recreation to as many
people as possible is a worthwhile goal. The
point is, don't stop with building a boat
ramp. *Imagine* ways of increasing the use of
the facility. For example, if fishing is one use
of your water resource, work with a state or
federal fisheries agency to provide fish
attractors. A pile of brush or several old tires
held together with bailing wire makes an
excellent environment for game fish. By
sinking a number of these and making their
locations available to fishing parties, you will
enhance the recreation experience, and word
of mouth will enhance your use figures.
People who fish also appreciate the availability of depth charts, or underwater
contour maps, as aids in locating game fish.
If you can provide these, do so. *Anything
you can do to improve the recreation
experience means a better hosting job.* One
result of quality hosting can be a wealth of
public good will for your organization. If this
isn't one of your management goals, it
should be!

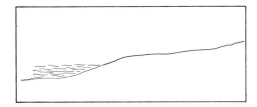

Figure 4.7a

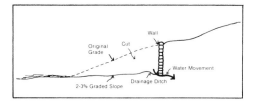

Figure 4.7b

BEACHES

Each spring, the maintenance crew of a parish park we know in Louisiana has a dredging job. During the year, rain water runs downhill, picks up the sand on the beach, and deposits it in the swimming area. So before the beach opens, the crew has to dredge the sand out of the lake and "put the beach back on the beach," another case of fighting effects rather than causes. Instead of an annual *corrective* action, a better solution would be to employ a one-time *preventive* measure. How simple it would be to provide a ditch and berm combination above the beach and route the runoff surface water away from the area where it causes damage!

The problem facing the parish park maintenance crew wasn't highly technical — they simply didn't look beyond the surface (effects) to see the real problem (causes). In addition to the phenomenon of water running downhill, beaches are subject to damage because of the erosive potential of sand. Sand will not stay by itself on a slope

greater than two to three percent. If you need to develop a sand-surfaced beach, or already have one on a steeper slope, a little preventive maintenance is in order. Figure 4.7a shows an existing grade leading to the water line. (We've exaggerated the slope somewhat for the sake of the figure; as drawn, the slope is too severe for a beach.) Figure 4.7b shows a solution to this problem; a *cut* has been employed. Using a bulldozer or other earth-moving equipment, the original slope (dashed line) has been cut down to a grade of two to three percent, acceptable for a beach. Just above the beach zone, the angle of the cut has been increased and a low vertical wall installed.

Earlier in discussing boat ramps we suggested that the parking lot be tilted away from the boat ramp to eliminate the flow of pollutants from the lot to the ramp zone. This is particularly important with parking lots at beaches. The USDA Forest Service, Tennessee Valley Authority, and a host of other park providers, including the private sector, have designed countless parking lots which act as collection areas for gases, oils, and waxes from automobiles and allowed these pollutants to flow directly into their beach areas. In most instances their designers didn't realize this was a potential problem.

Often, recreation planners tend to equate a beach with an expanse of sand, bordered on one side by water and the other side by a road or parking lot. This is unfortunate, because designing an area like this limits the potential for user enjoyment. In the first place, you should ask yourself, as always, *why;* why do people go to beaches? Many go to swim, but others go to sunbathe, socialize, read, play, and pursue a variety of other recreation activities that aren't necessarily water-related. Designs for beaches should encourage multiple uses of the waterfront zone. Ideally a beach should consist of a strip of sand between the water and an expanse of grass since people who don't care to swim may find it more convenient to sit on grass than sand. To protect the sand from erosion, placing a low wall or ditch-and-berm combination between the sand and grass is good practice. A portion of the seating area should be shaded so users have the option of sunbathing or not. The design should also include benches for seating as well as open areas where people can sit on the ground on towels or blankets.

This topic — designing a beach for "landlubbers" as well as for swimmers — brings up an important point: *the use of a given recreation facility is not necessarily limited to people who actually use it.* This sounds like a contradiction, but it's really just an extension of what we suggested earlier. There are *at least* three types of people who go to a beach: those who go primarily to play in the water; those who go primarily to play on the beach; *and* those who go primarily because the person or group *with them* wants to go to the beach. Young children, who really want to enjoy the water and sand, may have parents who find little pleasure in sitting in hot sand under a hotter sun. Providing a few benches and a little shade may enhance the experience for these "unwilling users." When recreation planners develop formal or structured use areas, they generally attend to the needs of non-participants. Providing bleachers at a ball field is an example of this. The same consideration, however, is rarely extended to informal, non-structured areas and facilities such as beaches. As you develop plans and designs for recreation areas, stretch your thought process to incorporate the needs of all people who may frequent the area, whether they are typical "users" or not. Ah, yes, we are *again* asking you to plan parks for people!

Design of a beach zone shouldn't stop at the water's edge. The planner needs to consider swimmer safety. Questions to ask should include: How deep is the water? How steep is the slope? (Around six percent is ideal.) Are there any ledges or holes in the area? Are there large submerged rocks a swimmer might strike? Is the bottom free of broken glass and other debris? Are there dangerous currents, undertows, or unusual temperature changes due to underwater springs? Physical conditions in the water should be made as safe as possible. Other issues, such as how to define the beach, e.g., buoy lines, lifeguards, and necessary signing, should be made in accordance with state regulations or standards. We also recommend that you seek the advice of your legal counsel.

On a happier note, design in the water should also provide opportunities for play. Two old tires, each filled with concrete and a metal post, make an inexpensive, hard-to-vandalize set of water volleyball standards. You can purchase floating basketball standards as well, although these should be limited to areas with on-site supervision to prevent theft. We've seen the addition of a few simple water play amenities increase both the amount of use at beaches and the fun people have there. Play equipment, however, doesn't need to be limited to the water. Generally beaches mean children, and children enjoy play equipment. Zoning a play area adjacent to a beach can multiply the opportunities for creative use of both zones.

Speaking of zones, there are several factors to consider when determining where to locate a new beach. The first of these is the availability of land and water suitable for the beach zone. It is, as Figure 4.7 shows, possible to "create" one next to good water by making a cut with construction equipment. This approach, however, is comparatively expensive if another, more suitable piece of land is available. A second criterion for locating a beach is the set of nearby site conditions. Ideally, a beach should have a western exposure for afternoon sun and should not be located directly in the path of incoming wind. As a general rule, beaches developed on lakes will be less subject to erosion and collection of stagnant

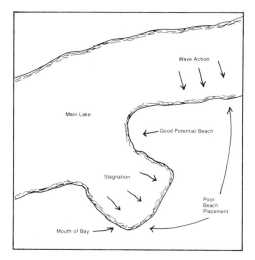

Figure 4.8

waters if they are placed as shown in Figure 4.8. Beaches exposed to the main channel of a lake are more subject to wave action and incoming wind, both of which contribute to erosion. Conversely, the mouth, or upper end of a bay or inlet, may not get enough wind and water motion to provide cleansing action. Trash and pollutants may thus tend to collect here, creating unpleasant conditions for swimming.

The potential for placement of other use areas also plays a part in determining where beaches should be located. As with other facilities, a beach should be zoned to complement nearby areas. Beaches fit together well with other active use zones such as play areas and picnic grounds. Swimming and other beach activities may conflict, however, with passive recreation pursuits such as a nature center or interpretive trail, and these areas should be zoned apart from one another. Thus the potential various sites have for a nature area may have a significant impact on where to locate a beach.

Recreation planning doesn't have to be difficult, but it is often quite complex. The "perfect spot" for a beach may be less than ideal once you consider the other pieces of the design puzzle needed to make up a functional area.

PICNIC AREAS

One of the other pieces of the design puzzle you may be challenged with is the picnic area. Picnic areas are almost as popular as fast food restaurants — they seem to be everywhere. But in our opinion, more of them are planned incorrectly than any other type of recreation facility. A picnic area can be designed perfectly from a technical standpoint and still fail to serve user needs from a functional perspective. Remember: *form follows function,* or at least it should. The problem with most picnic areas is...well, let's look at one and see if you're beginning to get a more critical eye for creativity in design. Figure 4.9 shows the layout of a typical picnic area. This one happens to be in a small town in western Kentucky, but there are literally hundreds of areas similar to this all over the world. Federal agencies have them; cities, counties, and states have them; quasi-public, commercial, and private concerns have them; almost everyone has them and most are poorly designed. A quote from Anatole France seems appropriate here: "If fifty million people say a foolish thing, it is still a foolish thing." Continuing to build picnic areas such as the one shown in Figure 4.9 doesn't make the design any better — it just perpetuates the error.

What's wrong with the design shown in Figure 4.9? Here are some hints for you. First, a basic planning error doesn't always have to be something *committed* — a mistake can just as easily be something *omitted.* This is the case here. Second, it's an error in planning, in your author's opinion, to miss an opportunity to *maximize the types of use* you have the chance to develop.

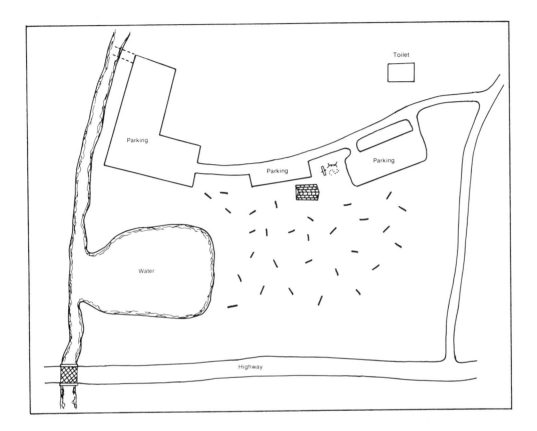

Figure 4.9

Finally, and here's the kicker, how would you program an area like this? If you haven't solved this little puzzle yet, the problem with this site, like most others is this; *it is just a picnic area.* Technically it may not violate any principles of design, but the layout fails to encourage other uses complementary to picnicking. Moreover, the design discourages any picnics except those by individual families or small groups. Let's consider these two problems in a little more detail.

First, let's think about the kinds of things people might enjoy doing while on a picnic. Cooking and eating are normally the focal points, and almost all designs provide

facilities — grills and tables — to support this site, like most others, is this; *it is just a picnic area.* Technically it may not violate any principles of design, but the layout fails to encourage other uses complementary to picnicking. Moreover, the design discourages you don't have a pool or a beach to offer them. But this logic hasn't been extended to many of our picnic areas. If the only amenities available at a picnic ground are grills and tables, users probably won't do much there besides cook and eat. Some users may bring a frisbee to toss and some may have access to a volleyball and net, but most won't.

There are really only three directions a picnic area designed with tables and grills alone can take, and none of them is positive. At best, people may continue to use the area as it was designed, improvising their own recreation experiences. The problem here is simply one of *missed opportunities*. Never ignore the chance to enhance the user's experience, whether through design, management, or programming. A second possible consequence of such areas is for people to stay away in droves. In this case, the issue is boredom. People can cook and eat out in their backyard or balcony, at least those fortunate enough to have a backyard or balcony. If your picnic area has nothing else to offer, why should they bother with it? If we had a dollar for every empty picnic table we've seen, we wouldn't have asked for an advance on this book.

A final possibility in "cook and eat only" designed picnic areas is negative user behavior. If Dick and Jane are bored, Dick and Jane may carve their initials on the picnic table. If positive recreation behavior — ballgames and the like — aren't occuring, negative patterns may set in to fill the void. An unused picnic area invites vandalism.

The second kind of problem you should consider in the picnic-area design in Figure 4.9 concerns types of user groups. Depending on its construction, a picnic table will normally seat either six or eight people. When a larger group wants to picnic together, there may be problems. If your tables aren't permanently installed, made of concrete, or chained in place, large user groups will simply try to move them to suit their needs. This may be difficult for some, such as those with a few adults and a lot of young children; it may encourage arguments between separate user groups wanting the same table; it may create a confrontation between users and management if moving tables is against your policy; and it certainly won't be popular with your maintenance crew as they repeatedly put the tables back where they

belong. If your single picnic tables are permanently anchored in place and separated from each other, large groups simply can't picnic together as a group, an excellent example of negative hosting and not planning parks for people.

Look again at the design in Figure 4.9. Pretend for a moment you're the recreation director in Gerrymander, Oklahoma, and this is your picnic area. The president of the local chapter of the Young Republicans Club calls you on Monday to reserve the area for a get-together on Saturday afternoon. With the area designed as it is, you really can't control access (people need to get to the boat ramp), so you can only suggest that the club get to the park early. Meanwhile, the Democrats are planning an open-air fund raiser to begin at noon — at the picnic area, of course. Have you created a confrontation? No, you're saved because Inez Independent and her 87 relatives descend on the site at 10 am for their annual family reunion. Of course there isn't any room left (or right) for individual families to picnic now, either.

There is a design solution to this problem and, happily, with a little rehabilitation, it will work for many *existing* areas as well as for new ones. The key is to design picnic areas using a *pod concept*. Figure 4.10 shows the same road layout, parking, boat launch, and toilets as Figure 4.9. The difference is the addition of four pods suitable for *group use*. Each of these can be reserved in advance for large parties or managed on a first-come-first-served basis. The point is that because of the design, management now can control how the area will be used. Let's explore some other features of this new set-up in a little more detail. First, note how each pod is *buffered* from the others by play zones, vegetative screening, and/or the road. Some groups, as in our example, may tend to conflict with each other. By separating use areas — even though they serve the same function — potential conflicts can be avoided by allowing managers to assign who goes

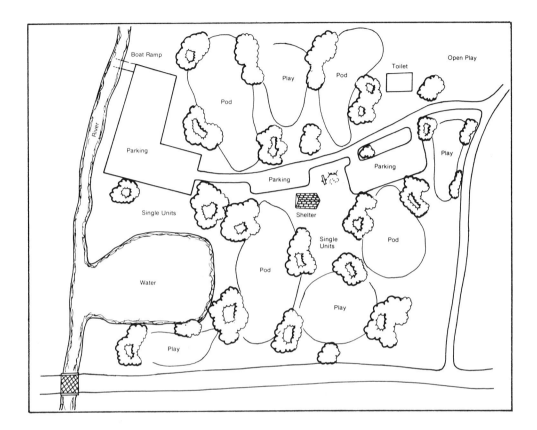

Figure 4.10

where. Buffer zones perform another function as well. By providing play equipment or open play fields next to each pod, we've given users something to do besides cook and eat and created opportunities for organized programs. Note also how this new design has kept a sprinkling of individual units for single families or small groups. If a pod is not being used by a large group, families can picnic there as well.

A bit of imagination in developing pods can create a host of opportunities for maximizing area use. Before building, or renovating, a picnic area, find out who potential visitors might be and design for their needs. Each pod can also be designed with a different *theme* in mind. One might stress competitive games for adults with a volleyball area, horseshoe pits, and badminton courts. Another might be oriented toward team activities and be built adjacent to an open play area with a backstop and goals for softball and soccer. A third might be planned for passive recreation, with space for board games, bingo tournaments, and musical events. A fourth might emphasize outdoor skills such as archery, fishing, and campcraft. Other ideas should come to your mind once you identify your clientele. Industry, civic clubs, schools (from elementary through college), scout groups, military groups, churches, special-interest organizations, and others are *all* potential picnickers. All you need to do is to plan areas suited to their needs, making sure you don't forget those with special design requirements.

You should also consider a few other characteristics of picnickers and picnic areas. Since young children will frequently be present, each pod, even those designed for adult sports, should have at least a minimal collection of play amenities nearby. Often groups appreciate the opportunity to cook large amounts of food as well, so some or all of your pods should contain large fire pits or grills, or perhaps you should offer portable grills for rent. If possible, it's a good idea for some pods to be lighted for evening use, unless, for administrative reasons, your area will close at dusk. Adding a shelter building to a pod, while increasing the development cost, can also both salvage a rainy-day picnic and increase potential for use. The floor of a shelter building is an excellent surface for square dancing. If you have the means to check out recreation equipment, try painting a shuffleboard court on the surface — you may be surprised how popular this game can be.

Regardless of what program amenities are available, distance between the parking and picnic areas is still a critical factor in design, since users will need to carry drink coolers, ice chests and other supplies from their vehicle to the site. Experience suggests that a distance of about 250 feet is as far as most folks will want to walk. Remember also that large groups may come in buses, so design parking areas accordingly. Ideally, each pod should have its own parking for the convenience of the users. Picnic areas with a large central parking lot rarely meet the needs of either visitors or managers.

In addition to orienting pods to the needs of users, on-site potential may help you decide on an appropriate theme for picnic sites. If the area is adjacent to a water attraction, such as a lake, one or more pods may be planned with water activities in mind.

Remember, however, to allow for water access by users whose picnic sites are not as near the shoreline. Walking trails along an adjacent stream or radiating out into a nearby wooded area can further increase use potential. The amount of space you have available, terrain and vegetation, and budgeting factors will all have an impact. The important thing to keep in mind (and this is true for *all* types of recreation areas) is to look at a site in terms of its *potential for creative development* instead of the possible limitations associated with it.

VISITOR CENTERS

Visitor centers should be designed with their namesakes kept carefully in mind. By developing one conscientiously, you can create a positive experience for users *and* a wealth of good feelings for your agency or company. Visitor centers are often the initial contact point for people coming into your area. Whether it's their first stop or not, users often base much of their opinion of an area on their reaction to the center. A clean restroom, an easy-to-interpret wall map, a friendly greeting — paying attention to seemingly minor details like these can result in more *good will* than an expensive display or audio-visual presentation.

Failure to attend to "minor details" can leave a lasting impression as well. Not too long ago, we visited a National Park Service visitor center in northern Indiana. The building had been altered to make it accessible to persons in wheelchairs, and barrier-free signs were prevalent. Inside, one prominent display employed magnifying glasses to show the contrast between two local soil types. The display had one pair of magnifying glasses set at a height suitable for an average adult, and another set at a height appropriate for small children. Most adults in wheelchairs would not have been able to use either display.

Ask yourself two questions: If you visited this center in a wheelchair, would you find it barrier-free? Would you leave with positive feelings toward the center? Attention to detail is a *critical* aspect of design.

Before you reach the stage of designing displays, however, you should consider some more basic concepts. The first to address is developing a visitor center with *one central function* in mind; you and your staff should determine what this will be well before the center is designed. Also, the need for *form to follow function* is especially important. Amount of space needed, location of permanent interior walls, and circulation patterns all depend on the function of the center. Generally, most will be designed around one of three purposes: *geographical and activity orientation* in the area the center serves; *environmental education* conducted inside and near the center; or *historical interpretation* of the area surrounding the center.

To a certain extent, visitor centers often play more than a single role. One might, for example, contain an excellent display on local history. But users could enjoy this considerably and still leave with a sense of frustration if information on nearby campgrounds was not available or out-of-date. Focusing on one central purpose doesn't mean *ignoring* all others. Certainly *every* visitor center should serve a "hosting" function; personnel, displays, and facilities should all be oriented toward making the user feel welcome and comfortable. Further, visitor centers will normally provide a number of secondary services as well — comfort stations, a place to meet friends travelling in another vehicle, a spot to refill a thermos of water. The point is, you should determine which *major* function best suits your particular situation and make this your central focus. A common planning mistake is to attempt to develop an "all things to all people" visitor center. Generally, focusing on a number of major attractions will result in failing to achieve *any* purpose with successful

results except for confusion and lack of consistency in displays.

Determining which of several alternatives should be your central focus depends upon two factors. On one hand, the *needs of your clientele* will influence what function you develop. If most anticipated use will originate from a long distance, orientation to the area and to local recreation opportunities may need to be the primary focus. Also, the *potential of the site* affects your decision. Theoretically, any site can be interpreted from historical or environmental perspectives. However, planners and programmers shouldn't try to force, for example, a major set of historical interpretive displays on a center where nothing of particular historical interest has occurred. This is an excellent reason for determining function *before* designing the site for the center. If you and your staff agree, prior to development, that an environmental orientation is what your center needs, you have some basis for proceeding with design: you know you need to look for an area where nature trails can be incorporated into the plan; you can anticipate — and design for — the type of display space and circulation patterns best suited to environmental education.

Another common error in designing visitor centers is the "too much of a good thing" syndrome. This affliction seems especially likely to attack educational and interpretive staff, and the symptoms sound something like this: "If it's a good thing to teach people something, it must be better to teach them a whole lot more." Unfortunately this logic breaks down beyond a certain point for two reasons. First, people can only absorb so much information before calling a halt to the process. Second, attempts to provide as many displays as possible can create a cluttered, "busy" look. From a design-psychology standpoint, such a look should be avoided when you provide a recreational experience. For instance, we know of a visitor center in central Pennsylvania with an

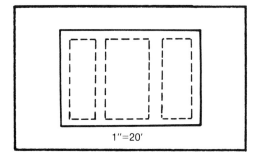

1"=20'

Figure 4.11

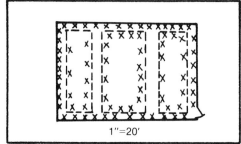

1"=20'

Figure 4.12

environmental orientation. The main room of the center measures approximately twenty by thirty feet for an area of six hundred square feet. Figure 4.11 shows a scale drawing of this room, with the circulation aisles indicated by dashed lines. The problem isn't the room or the circulation pattern; it's the displays. On the day we visited, the room contained seventy-eight, all environmentally oriented. Figure 4.12 illustrates the visual effect that seventy-eight displays have on a six-hundred-square-foot room. Too much of anything, including a good thing, is simply too much.

Keep in mind that the primary function of *any* recreation-related facility, including visitor centers, is to provide enjoyment for users. A crowded, claustrophobic appearance resulting from attempts to fit too many displays into a limited amount of space is not a good means of accomplishing this. Regardless of the subject of your displays — orientation, history, or the environment — you can use a few "tricks" to maximize the benefits of your efforts for visitors. One important concept is to *limit your displays*. Take a critical look both at the amount of space you have available and at potential circulation patterns within the center. Circulation patterns for interior spaces should use the same principle as for outdoor areas. Relationship diagrams, traffic flow, and

alternative layouts should all be employed to make an informed decision on locating displays. Avoid the temptation to add too many — let common sense tell you when enough is enough.

If you are building a new center, it's probably a good idea to exclude any permanent walls from the display space except those around the outside of the room. This allows you considerably more flexibility both initially and after you decide to make alterations later. If you're renovating an existing space, you may want to consider removing an interior wall or cutting in doorways if it creates a barrier to your circulation needs. Before altering an interior wall, make sure it isn't load-bearing (supporting the weight of the building). And remember the suggestion from Chapter Two regarding existing features in an area or building: incorporate existing features or structures into your design when it makes sense to do so, but don't allow these to dictate design.

Movable displays, including floor-to-ceiling panels, tables, and cases, are useful for directing circulation patterns within a display area. Tall panels tend to create a feeling of enclosure, but you can counteract this by using wide aisles and by alternating panels with lower displays. Some of the techniques applicable to moving people on trails will

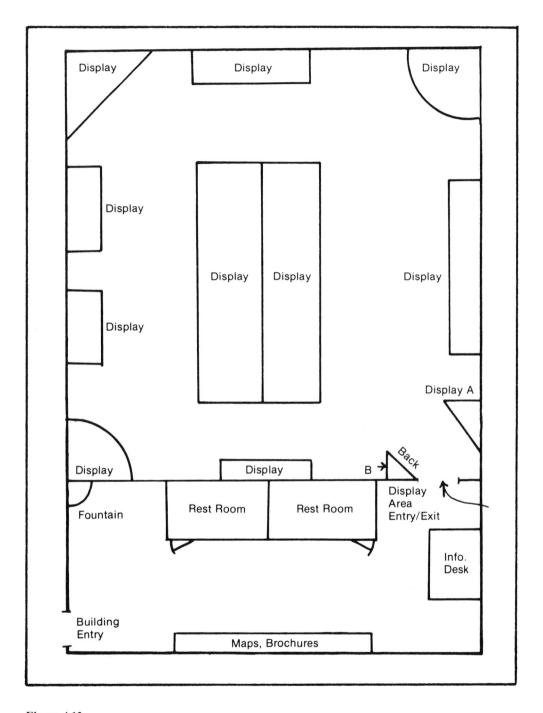

Figure 4.13

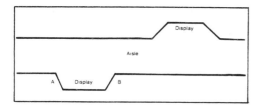

Figure 4.14

work in display areas as well. Figure 4.13 illustrates how they can be used to create a functional traffic flow within a room. In this instance, a display (A) to the right of the entry/exit has been angled toward the path people will take coming into the room. This display, coupled with the tendency people have to move to the right, will "pull" visitors in the direction of the arrow. Such movement is reinforced by orienting a panel display (B) so that people entering the room see the back of the panel rather than a display which might move them to the left. By encouraging a single-direction traffic flow like this one, you can reduce the perception of crowding.

Another way to create a feeling of spaciousness is by designing some display areas as alcoves off the main aisles, as in Figure 4.14. With alcoves, people viewing a display must move out of the aisle; however, this technique will require more space since the areas at points A and B are not functional. Whether you use alcoves or not, aisles should be wide enough for viewing *and* for circulation. If you plan to use both sides of an aisle for displays, it may help to "stagger" the panels, cases, or tables so two exhibits aren't directly across the aisle from one another. This may help prevent "traffic jams" as people move from one to the next.

Traffic problems can also be reduced by developing displays with *simplicity* and *clarity of meaning*. Pictures with brief captions, artifacts like a soldier's pack, naturally occurring items like a hornet's nest,

and three-dimensional displays like a paper-mache relief map are all effective. Long, wordy explanations emphasizing scientific names and "seventy-three uses for the wood of the American Beech" are less than effective. The best way we know to teach people something is to *entertain* them: make them smile at the close-up color picture of the "cute little beaver" and then tell them *briefly* why beavers build dams. This approach will help visitors retain more information *and* enjoy your displays, as well as keep traffic from getting congested. The subject matter and the number of exhibits your available space can support will help determine content. As a rule of thumb, visitors should be able to absorb the information in a single display in twenty seconds or less without hurrying.

Visitor centers, because they are often an initial stop for people entering your area, are excellent locations for policies regulating use. However, remember that visitors are your *guests* and that as such they should be made to feel welcome in as many ways as possible. You should avoid emphasizing things people shouldn't do, or at least avoid telling them in a negative way. Given a little thought, it's usually easy to provide information in a manner users will find *helpful* instead of restraining. For example, you may want people to keep pets away from the entrance to the center. Instead of posting a "No Pets Allowed Here" sign, post one reading "Pet Area Is Located at End of Parking Lot." If you must prohibit a particular act, such as building fires during dry seasons, it often helps to *explain* the problem and *request users' cooperation* in abiding by your policies. Users should be informed, but you should avoid overwhelming them with negative wording.

Visitor centers, in addition to focusing on a major function like historical interpretation, are usually more successful if they are designed around a central *theme*. While the purpose lets visitors know *why* the center exists, the central theme explains *what* it is for. If, for example, you are developing a Corps of Engineers visitor center on a reservoir, the central theme might be the water resource. A center in a state forest, on the other hand, may concentrate on forest resources.

A central theme can be oriented to any of several major functions, including education, interpretation, or information. To support the Corps example from above — with its central theme of water — you might provide information on recreation facilities and activities surrounding the reservoir; education relating to the objectives met by the reservoir (power, fisheries management, recreation); or interpretation relating to the history or environment surrounding the reservoir.

The point is that a central theme provides an "umbrella" for the center functions. An excellent example of this concept is the visitor center at Blanchard Caverns in the Ozark National Forest in Arkansas. Here managers and planners started with a theme — the caverns — and *then* built a center to compliment it. Unfortunately this process is often reversed: someone builds a visitor center and then administrators must try to figure out what to do with it. The structure you build should be designed to accommodate the exhibits and the needs of the clientele you anticipate. By anticipating uses *and* users in advance, you can make a center responsive to yours and your users' aims. Too often, for example, in areas where camping is popular, we've seen visitor centers built with dead-end parking lots. What does this design "say" to visitors with camping trailers about consideration of their needs? Have you ever tried to back a trailer out of a dead-end lot?

This raises a final point about the purpose of visitor centers. In addition to whatever you want your center to accomplish for users, ask yourself: "What do we want the center to accomplish for *us* — the management?" A visitor center, by design and administration, serves a *quasi-political purpose*. It reflects what you think of users and helps determine what users will think of you. Whether you intend it to be or not, a visitor center is a public-relations medium. Presumably, you want people to leave your area with positive feelings about what a good job is being done there. You should encourage them to feel that their money, whether tax dollars or admission fees, is being well-spent. Unfortunately this does not happen frequently enough, particularly in the public sector, for three reasons. First, visitor centers are often poorly designed in terms of user needs. Second, some centers tend to leave visitors confused because there is no central theme and/or major function. Finally, management frequently ignores the public-relations potential of a visitor center.

In general, the lay public — people who visit parks and recreation areas — are for some reason quite naive about the management of these areas. Try asking people in a state or national forest, at a Corps of Engineers area, or at a state game preserve where they are. You may be surprised by how many people tell you they are in a national park. Perhaps this is because they associate the Park Service with the provision of outdoor recreation opportunities, but whatever the reason, there seems to be a wasted opportunity here. We aren't suggesting that the Park Service shouldn't get credit for doing a good job. We do suggest that you're missing the public-relations boat if they get credit for your good work and you happen to be employed by someone else. Visitor centers should be a focal point for generating good public relations. The opportunity for public contact with your personnel is high, as is the chance for you to impress the public with the quality of your facilities and displays. Creativity, conscientious design, attention to detail, and a sensitivity to the needs of people can have a lasting, positive effect. Visitor centers, by their nature, attract people; it's up to you to attract their favorable impressions.

DAY CAMPS

Those of us who work in outdoor recreation fight a seemingly continuous battle between *quality* and *quantity.* On one hand, our mission is (or should be) to provide a meaningful experience for as broad a range of potential clients as possible. Yet when it comes time to account for this year's expenditure and justify next year's budget requests, the bottom line is numbers. How many picnickers? What percentage of the campsites were occupied? Did visitation rates increase or decrease? Sometimes philosophical debates over the quality-versus-quantity issue miss the point. *Both* are legitimate concerns and both can be addressed by the same strategies. Let's consider another scenario.

You're the manager of Possum Paw State Park in northeastern Arkansas. The park is typical in terms of resources — a mix of forest and open land, flat fields and a low ridge system, and a small lake and facilities — a campground, picnic area, boating site, nature center, play fields and courts, trails, and open space. Your location is excellent — fifty miles from Memphis, near an Interstate highway, and close to five or six small towns ranging in size from 2,000 to 15,000 residents. There are several issues hidden in this brief description which, if addressed in combination with one another, can change the complexion of your park completely. First, if Possum Paw is a "typical" state park, the chances are good that visitation figures are less than earth-shaking. Holidays and pleasant-weather weekends may fill the park, but during the week it often seems as if staff outnumber visitors. Consider also the surrounding population. Many small towns simply don't have the financial or other resources needed to maintain a diversified parks and recreation program. Memphis, like many cities, maintains urban parks and has a broad spectrum of recreation opportunities but lacks the natural environment of a large, rural park.

One final aspect of this scenario needs to be considered. Most large parks and resource-based recreation areas have a tendency to orient their facilities and programs toward individual visitors and families. These users should be a concern, but not at the expense of *organized groups.* The development of a well-conceived day-camping program for organized groups at Possum Paw could increase use, particularly during traditionally low visitation periods such as summer weekdays, and meet a need left unfulfilled by local communities. If the five towns near Possum Paw average only 7,500 residents each, a potential clientele of over 37,000 people exists, not counting the urban center less than an hour away. A brief listing of the types of organized groups you might find in these small communities could include Scouts, 4-H clubs, youth and adult groups from perhaps a dozen religious organizations, school parties, senior citizens clubs, fraternal organizations such as Elks and Moose, civic clubs such as Lions and Rotary, employee organizations, handicapped groups, the YWCA and YMCA, and special-interest groups such as garden clubs and local chapters of national societies. A successful day-camping program may also be developed in conjunction with an *assembly area* for special events such as arts-and-crafts fairs, large family reunions, industrial picnics, and the like.

There are several ways of designing day camping areas, but they all have one requirement in common — the need for a *thorough* knowledge of programming and marketing skills. Organized groups may not seek you out; it's possible to develop excellent facilities for a day-camping program and have them sit idle because of a lack of initiative on your part. You should be prepared and able to approach local group leaders and "sell" your facilities and programs, so both design and management of day-camping areas require you to understand and provide for the different needs of boy scouts and the League of Women Voters; the Kiwanas Club and Ms. Pinbug's tenth-grade biology class; the local chapters of the Audubon society and a trade union. If you work in a resource-based agency like a state division of forestry or the Department of Natural Resources, you may not be blessed with large numbers of staff possessing recreation programming skills. When this is the case, one solution is to develop cooperative ventures with municipal agencies. Local park and recreation systems are typically program-oriented. Quasi-public agencies such as "Y's" also fit this description as well. Local-level professionals often have a good sense of community — they may know where and how to market a day-camping program to local groups most effectively.

There are three basic ways to go about designing a day camping area, but the ideal solution is probably to develop a site specifically for group-oriented day use. Types of recreation at campgrounds and those facilities intended for single-family day-use, such as trails systems and small picnic areas, may not be compatible with large-group needs. Just as potentially conflicting *facilities* should be separated by design, *types of recreationists* whose use patterns may be in conflict should be separated if possible.

If you lack an available resource base or are limited by funding constraints, an alternative to developing a site specifically for day camping is to *superimpose* day use on an existing facility such as a campground or picnic area. A word of caution is in order here: in many cases, trying to alter an existing area will result in creating more problems than it solves since existing use may be heavy enough to interfere with attempts to program for day-camping groups. Other areas may be designed in such a way to prevent effective programming for large groups. Figure 4.15 shows the design for Piney Campground, a TVA facility in western Tennessee. The area is poorly designed from the standpoint of campground

administration and user circulation. It is, however, zoned to function well if management decided to superimpose day use on the site. The primary program zone is located near the entrance; thus, day campers need not penetrate the camping zone and conflict with campers in order to reach facilities. The central program site contains a variety of active and passive program zones, including a campfire theater, play courts and field, a shelter building, and a crafts cabin, and a network of trails radiates out from this central complex. The primary advantage of this type of design is its ability to function in a dual role. The facility can be devoted to the overnight camping clientele if demand justifies it. When camping use is low, groups of day users can be brought in on an advance-schedule basis.

A third alternative for developing a day camp is to design the necessary facilities *adjacent to* an existing site such as a picnic area or campground. Some, indeed, far too many, existing areas have been built without adequate programming facilities. For these, it may help to justify development of the facility needed for day camping by arguing in favor of benefits added to the existing site. As with a superimposed day-camping experience, the addition of a day camp adjacent to an existing facility must be carefully planned. A poorly designed addition can compound problems already in existence, such as the mistake shown in Figures 4.16 and 4.17. Both of these drawings are taken from the *Recreation Carrying Capacity Handbook,* published by the US Corps of Engineers and showing an area where day use and overnight camping have been combined. According to the *Handbook,* the design of Figure 4.16 creates problems. Indeed it does! Such a design

— makes poor use of land;
— allows the primary road to divide the property into difficult-to-use sections;

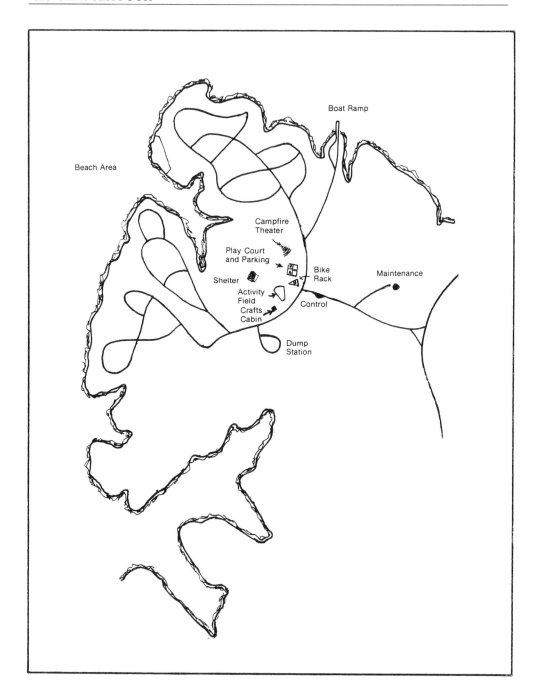

Figure 4.15

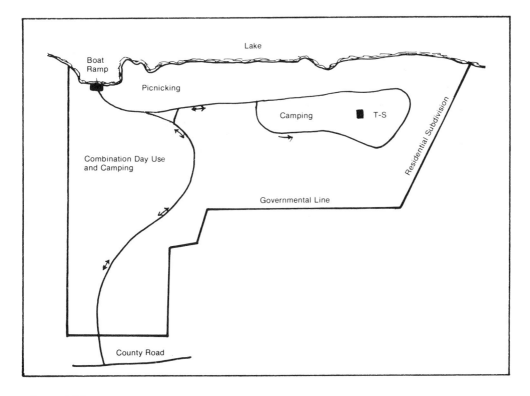

Figure 4.16

— commits a large expenditure if development dollars to an area with too few
  campsites to justify the cost;
— mixes day use and camping through
  improper zoning; and
— invites the opportunity to blame degradation of the environment on "overuse" by
  the visiting public.

However, the plan shown in Figure 4.17
(which the *Handbook* suggests as a design
solution for the area) is, in many ways, worse
than the original. The amount of road has
been increased without a significant gain in
potential use, and more developable land has
been used up by these additional roadways.
The traffic pattern is more complex for users
and more difficult to administer for manage-

ment. The day-use and overnight camping
areas are zoned to conflict with instead of
complement one another, and the camping
area contains a number of design errors.
Perhaps most importantly, though, the
design eliminates the opportunity to provide
a diversity of programs. We'll suggest a
possible solution shortly — one aimed at
combining day use and overnight camping
while increasing carrying capacity and
decreasing impact, user problems, and
management headaches. However, you
should have an opportunity to try your hand
at improving upon the designs shown in
Figures 4.16 and 4.17 as well. To give you
some guidelines, we'll describe for you what
could potentially go into an area designed for
day camping.

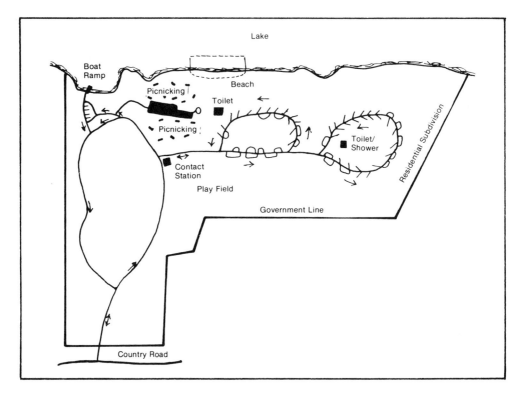

Figure 4.17

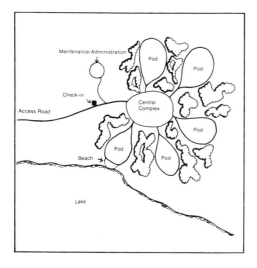

Figure 4.18

A good day-camping area should simultaneously accommodate a number of groups with different interests. In your authors' opinion, the best way to achieve this objective and separate conflicting uses is to fashion a *pod system* similar to the one we discussed for picnic areas. Picture a flower such as a daisy with a central stem and a circular arrangement of petals. This type of pattern lends itself quite well to day camping from the standpoint of both managers and users, and Figure 4.18 shows a pod design in schematic fashion.

Obviously, not all areas will lend themselves to this type of layout. The need to include a large, overnight camping area on the property shown in Figures 4.16 and 4.17 would, for example, limit the amount of space available for day camping. Addition-

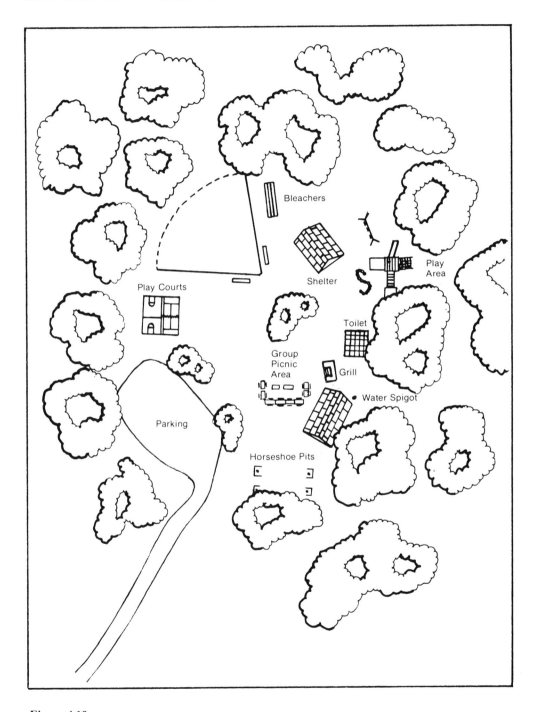

Figure 4.19

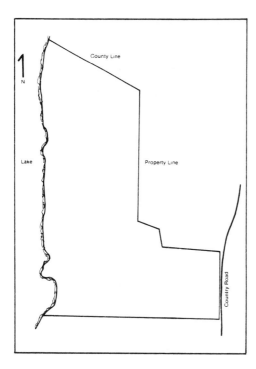

Figure 4.20   COE Resource Base for
Chapter Design Exercise

ally, when day use and overnight camping are combined, program ammenities need to be placed so users from both zones can take advantage of them.

When the pod system is feasible, however, it works well. The primary advantage of this type of design is the option for programmatic *themes* within separate pods or enclaves. For example, a master plan might be developed with pods for waterfront activities, nature arts and crafts, outdoor skills, active sports, environmental education, and passive programs. Specific themes should, of course, depend on your potential clientele groups, and all pods should be constructed with basic facilities to make them self-contained. Parking, sanitary facilities, small shelters, a fire circle, picnic tables,

water, electricity, barbecue pits, play space and equipment, and access to an encircling system of trails might be considered. Figure 4.19 shows the layout of a sample sports-oriented pod. A central complex, or commons area, near the center of the development may serve larger groups or drop-in day users. The pods themselves, designed to accommodate thirty to three hundred people, can also be opened for informal occupancy when demand by organized groups is low. The central complex might contain a nature and/or crafts center, a shelter space for large groups, a campfire theater or assembly area, large playfields, and equipment storage space. Remember that these are simply possibilities. Decisions on what to include in a day-camping area depend on local conditions: possible user groups, available resource base, opportunities available at other area sites you wish to serve. This last consideration is one planners overlook all too often. It's possible to get so involved with designing our own little project that we forget to look at the "big picture" and fail to see the forest for the trees.

Now you should have some ideas for creating day-use opportunities. Figure 4.20 shows the resource base depicted in Figure 4.16. Your design challenge is to develop the area for a combination of overnight use, organized day camping, and informal day use. You can assume all land is suitable for development. The shoreline is also usable all along the property, and vegetation is good, with shade increasing as you move from south to north. There are only two constraints you need to consider. First, any program facilities you install must serve both overnight and day users. Second, the only access to the property is from the county road, as shown. Since we haven't discussed overnight camping facilities yet, you may want to limit your efforts to a simple zoning of this portion of the area. You should, however, consider circulation, separation of use areas, administration, and program potential in your design. We've shown one possible solution in Appendix B — no doubt you can improve on it.

APPENDIX B

Solution to Chapter Four Recreation Complex Exercise

The primary constraints you faced in this exercise were to develop program facilities to serve both overnight and day uses and to access the property from the county road shown in Figure 4.20. These "limitations" should give you two hints; first, that program amenities need to be centrally located, which actually works to your advantage since you can use these facilities as a buffer between overnight and day use; second, that for administrative control, you should separate campers and day users as soon after they enter the complex as possible. Compare your solution (and ours) to the ones shown in Figure 4.16 and 4.17 and think about how yours and the one shown here address the problems with the COE designs shown in Chapter Four.

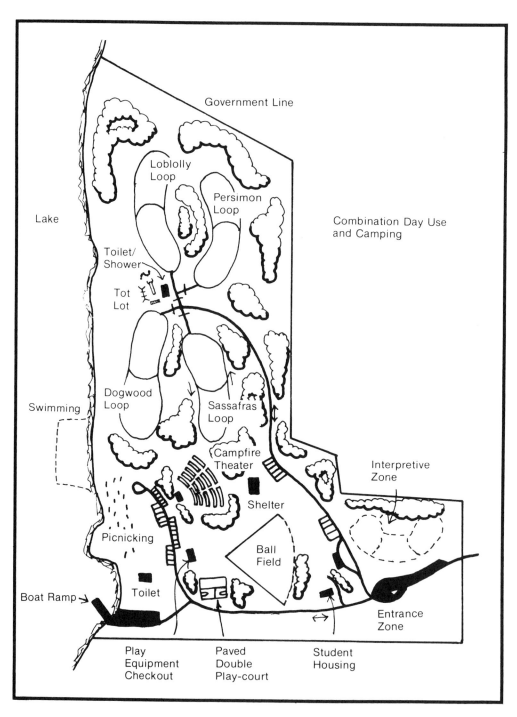

Appendix B

5

SPECIAL USES FOR SPECIAL USERS

In this chapter, we'll consider five types of use areas: living-history complexes; off-road-vehicle areas; wrangler's camps; group camps; and military recreation complexes. The term "special use area" may be a bit inappropriate in one sense since these types of facilities aren't any more "special" than others. They're only different because they provide opportunities for people who share something of a common interest or background. For example, folks who use military recreation complexes are similar in most respects to visitors to "civilian" parks — except for an affiliation with the Armed Services. Additionally, after reading this chapter and the discussion of campsite design in Chapter Seven, you'll find that there aren't many differences between "mainstream" campers and those who visit wrangler's camps, except that the latter group enjoys combining camping with horseback riding. Because of the children, bicycles, and heavier traffic in large family campgrounds, it may be somewhat unsafe to allow horseback riding to coexist here, and the same is true for off-road vehicles. However, both horseback and off-road riding are legitimate uses of outdoor recreation resources. Recreation professionals — because they are professionals — have a *duty* to provide opportunities for *all* types of uses.

The solution to meeting the needs of users whose recreation preferences are specific or may conflict with one another rests in the development of special-use areas. The principle behind this solution isn't complex;

in fact, it's one you've heard before. Just as incompatible program areas such as a lighted playcourt and a campfire theater should be separated, conflicting *facilities* should be zoned apart as well. As Chapter Four suggested, day-use and overnight camping may both function more effectively (for users *and* management) if separate areas are designated specifically for these functions. The same logic applies to horseback and off-road enthusiasts, organized group and individual family campers, and certain other combinations of outdoor recreationists.

When you first begin to consider special-use areas, the idea of providing separate resources for different groups may seem prohibitively expensive. However, most individuals who visit special-use facilities such as wrangler's camps or off-road riding areas are more concerned about pursuing their particular interest than expensive program amenities contained in a developed, family campground or day-use area. Organized group camps may be developed in a number of ways, from rustic to highly modernized, depending on the needs of potential clients and your budgetary considerations. The point is, special-use areas for off-road riders, horseback enthusiasts, and organized groups *can* be developed with a relatively small expenditure of capital dollars. The only high-cost requirement is an adequate land base, though other expenses like developing campsites, support facilities, and trails, will also be incurred. Often some of these costs can be offset by enlisting the help of user groups during the early stages of planning and development.

Further, unless you happen to ride off-road bikes for leisure, it's not likely you'll know as much about the needs of bikers as someone who does ride them. Local riding clubs and interested individuals can provide a wealth of information about design needs, as long as you remember theirs is only one of several perspectives to consider. These groups may, in some instances, also be willing and able to help with construction and on-going maintenance of areas. It's been our experience that special-interest groups are quite responsive when asked to cooperate in these ways. More often than not they are willing to help because they aren't used to being asked or to having recreation folks, especially those in the public sector, pay attention to their needs.

LIVING HISTORY COMPLEXES

Living-history complexes haven't been included in our discussion to this point, because they are somewhat different from other special-use areas ("special" special areas, so to speak). Here development costs will generally be greater than the other types of areas discussed above, with the possible exceptions of highly modernized group camps and military recreation complexes. Living-history resources also differ because they don't include overnight use, as do the others considered in this chapter. This characteristic in particular has implications for the planner and designer. Entrance zones, parking, circulation, visitor-contact points, and other facilities need special attention. As with others, living history areas should serve a hosting function; they should make visitors feel *welcome* both explicitly and implicitly. Explicit forms include the attitude of the staff, including the historical characters.

Implicit forms include carefully managing and maintaining the area and designing the complex to balance *the needs of the user with the need for historical accuracy.* This point is important enough to elaborate on through an example of another of our mistakes.

The 1850's Homeplace

Located in TVA's Land Between the Lakes, the Homeplace-1850 is a living-history area developed to portray farm life in the early 19th century. Figure 5.1 shows a schematic of the development complex. The interpretive function, as is usually the case in living history areas, was developed conscientiously here. Buildings are authentic, having either been moved from nearby locations or reconstructed from portions of original structures. The history of the area was also researched thoroughly and in detail. For example, individuals who settled here originally, according to all available records, did not build outhouses, which were characteristic in other areas from the same period. Thus the Homeplace-1850 omitted outhouses as well. The interpretive staff, both those in period costume and others, are competent and personable. So what's the problem?

The problem with the Homeplace-1850 is a matter of design psychology. Several factors combine to reduce its potential to make a highly positive impression on users. People *are* favorably impressed by the experience they have here; the fact is, most may not even be aware that it could be improved. *But* — and this is important — whether the public will notice the difference or not, we should make every effort to do the job "as right as we are able." As we've suggested before, interpretive staff generally are good at interpretation, but this quality does not speak to designing for people.

For instance, early in the planning of the Homeplace, some staff suggested using the existing entrance to the valley where the complex was to be located (the site of the old

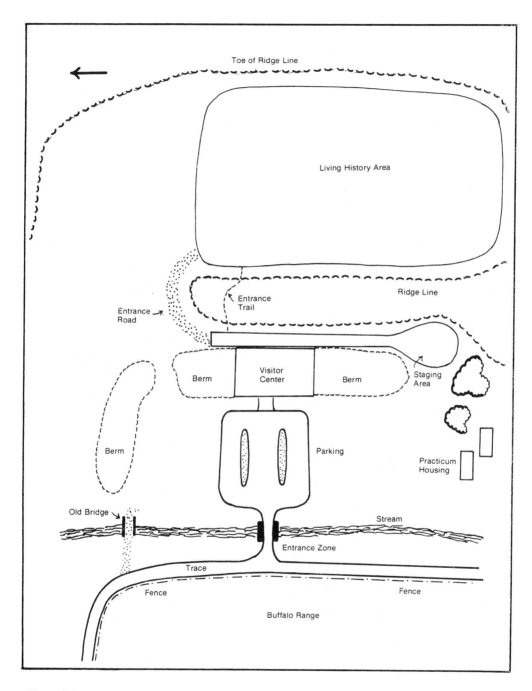

Figure 5.1

bridge in Figure 5.1). This entrance was located in a sharp bend in the Trace, the main north-south road running the length of Land Between the Lakes, and the potential hazard of developing an entrance in the curve was complicated by two factors. First, southbound traffic on the Trace entered the curve at the base of a long hill and tended to be moving rapidly. Additionally, a large field along the west side of the Trace contained a herd of about fifty buffalo, which would have attracted the attention of drivers away from the proposed intersection leading to the Homeplace. Fortunately this entrance zone was rejected and an alternative site located in the middle of a long straightaway was selected. Obviously, no one on the interpretive staff would have advocated developing a hazardous intersection, but neglecting to consider the potential *effects* of the design would have produced a dangerous situation all the same.

Unfortunately other design problems did find their way into the final construction plan. While these problems didn't create hazards, they reduced the potential for maximizing the experience of visitors. Take another look at Figure 5.1 and try to develop a mental image of what visitors would experience as they move into and through the area. As you penetrate the entrance zone, several features may capture your attention. One is a large, earthen berm, constructed to serve as a buffer between the initial contact area, the parking lot for the visitor center, and the interpretive zone, the living-history area. On the right are two house trailers for practicum student housing, and a modern visitor center stands in the center. These are the features meeting your eyes, but from the standpoint of design psychology, what do you *see*?

We see several things. First, the earthen berm is an excellent design tool. Once visitors enter the Homeplace itself — the living history area — you want them to experience a step back to the past with as

few intrusions from modern times as possible. The berm helps to limit these intrusions and, since it is made of natural material (earth and sod), it is not intrusive itself. The rest of the initial contact zone, however, contains several errors — some of omission and others of commission. Consider the practicum student housing. Two white house trailers are in plain view of the entry point. These are necessary components of the complex, but there is no reason to place them where visitors entering the area have clear views of them. Since every design decision should have a justifiable reason behind it, this argument goes beyond our current example. Two questions should have been asked and answered here: Why are the trailers located where they are? And why couldn't they be placed someplace less obtrusive?

From the first moment visitors enter a living-history complex, they should begin a transition that takes them from the present back to the period being interpreted. A split-rail fence or perhaps a rustic welcome sign mounted on a period-piece wagon or other artifact can begin to set an appropriate mood just inside the entrance. In addition to having visitors begin to "enter" the past, you should gradually draw them out of the present through design psychology. One way of accomplishing this is to physically separate the parking area from the visitor center. This technique gets users out of their automobiles and continues their transition back in time. The distance from the parking area to the visitor center shouldn't be too great, and it may be well to provide an alternative to walking — perhaps a mule- or oxen-driven wagon to aid the transition even further. At the Homeplace-1850, the parking lot is immediately adjacent to the visitor center, which, as suggested earlier, is a modern structure. This point is worth emphasizing: the initial contact point of a living-history complex, often a visitor center or interpretive building, should *complete the transition* back to the period in time being interpreted. The visitor center at the Homeplace-1850, both inside and outside, is completely out of character with the aura of the early 19th century. Thus instead of "easing into" another culture, visitors are thrust there.

Figure 5.2 focuses on the portion of the facility between the visitor center and the living history area. After users have completed touring the visitor center, which contains displays and a brief orientation program, they exit to the rear of the building into a staging zone. This paved area is used primarily for organizing the formal groups, particularly school groups, who often tour. Form this point two entrances, a road and a trail, lead into the interpretive zone, but both have design errors. As shown in Figure 5.2, the staging area is between the visitor center and a low ridge. The ridge tapers into level ground to the left of the staging area, where the entrance road curves into the interpretive zone. As with the earthen berm discussed above, the ridge helps to buffer the living-history area from the present; however, consider the trail confronting the users. As we discussed in Chapter Three, you should avoid starting trails on an adverse (uphill) grade. The trail leaving the staging area climbs steeply, and presents at the least a psychological challenge. To some individuals, the trail is inaccessible.

Visitors who do not take the trail by choice or otherwise enter the living-history facility via the road as shown. To understand the design error here, you need to consider the layout of the interpretive zone itself, shown in Figure 5.3. According to the history of the area, as told in the interpretation, the Homeplace evolved as follows. About 1830, a family settles the valley and builds a home at site 1. A generation later the children of the original family, now grown, build the house at site 2. By 1850, the period being interpreted, the family spans three generations; the original settlers at site 1 and their children and grandchildren at

site 2. Other structures like the stable and tobacco barn are typical of the period.

Can you identify the design problem hidden in this narrative? The *story* doesn't evolve in the same sequence as the *design* does. Instead of following a physical trail of the family history, the visitor follows a reversed version of it. He or she first learns about the way of life in 1850 from the point of view of the children of the original settlers. Then, by moving toward the interior of the interpretive zone, the story from twenty years earlier unfolds. Wouldn't it be a more effective experience if the design matched the chronology?

There are several design considerations left to discuss about living history areas, but this mistake serves to focus on the most important one and points out a good axiom of planning, regardless of the facility type. Prior to developing any facilties, managers, planners, and program staff should come to agreement on a *master plan* for the area that incorporates several elements. The first should be a conception of what you and other staff responsible for the living history area *want to accomplish*. From a programming perspective, how do you want the area to function for users? Ask yourself and other staff what *themes* will be involved in the area — agriculture, family life, energy, community, recreation, education, and others. While the focus shouldn't be too narrow, it's usually a good idea to select a central issue and arrange complementary ideas around it. In the case of the Homeplace-1850, the program goal, or theme, was to show the evolution of a mid-19th century farm from generation to generation. Yet the *physical design* of the area conflicted with this program. Design elements should be developed to *complement* program considerations.

Once a tentative program goal has been determined, take the *physical capabilities and limitations* of the site into account. If you refer to Figure 5.1, you'll see that the inter-

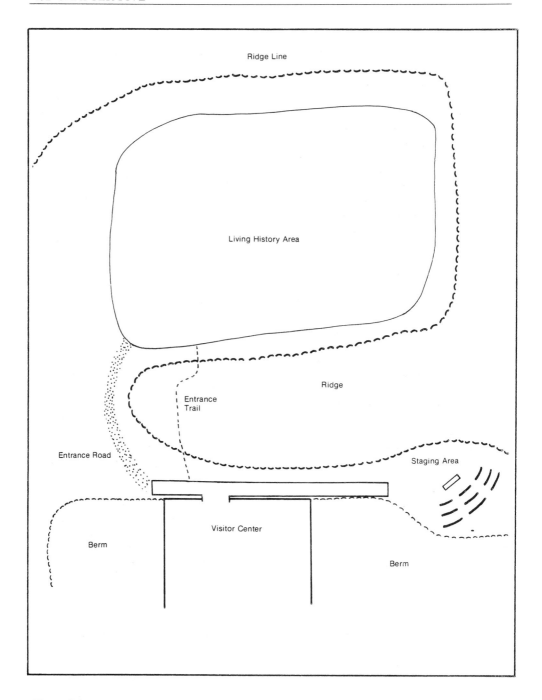

Figure 5.2

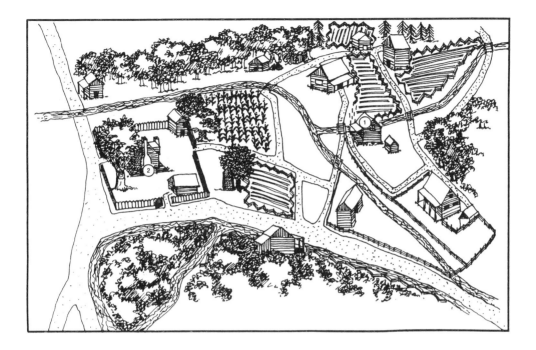

Figure 5.3

pretive zone of the Homeplace-1850 is in a broad valley surrounded by ridges. The only logical entrance to the historical area was used; however, the physical limitation of being surrounded by ridges with only one usable entry point should have suggested placing the original homestead at the mouth of the valley (near the entrance) instead of in the center of the developed complex.

Figure 5.4 shows a graphic depiction of these last two points. Concurrent determinations of program goals and on-site conditions should lead you to a beginning idea of the development to follow, a process that should be followed regardless of the type of area being designed. Once you have addressed these preliminary aspects, design can become more specific. Also, a concern for anticipated types of users must permeate the entire design process. The needs of organized groups of school children will

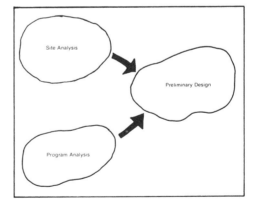

Figure 5.4

differ from those of smaller, family-oriented parties. In working toward a final design, visitor movement to and from the living history complex and circulation within the interpretive zone are important. Consider *concurrently* the paths people should take — from the standpoint of design psychology — and the locations of specific features — houses, barns, and the like. In other words, you shouldn't attempt to develop a circulation pattern and then add facilities. On the other hand, it's not a good idea to determine building locations and then try to work out a circulation pattern.

While the internal elements of a living-history complex and their interrelationships are critical, it's important to remember support facilities as well. The master plan should account for the relationship of the historical zone to administration, parking, the initial visitor-contact point, where the transition to your historical period begins, and other support facilities. Depending on projected use, the addition of a group picnic area (see Chapter Four) may also be a good idea. Regardless of what support facilities are involved, all need to relate in some way to the historical complex *and* to each other. They should additionally be *convenient to but not intrusive on* the interpretive zone. Living-history areas normally represent a major investment. They can also be enormously popular attractions. Both of these considerations are strong arguments for a conscientious and combined design effort on the part of planners, programmers, and managers.

OFF-ROAD VEHICLE (ORV) AREAS

In two respects, ORV areas represent the opposite end of the design spectrum from living-history complexes. In the first place, developing an off-road complex requires a relatively small investment of capital dollars. The facilities necessary for off-road riding are minimal, and the required ones are not particularly expensive to build *or* to maintain. A reasonably large resource base of several hundred acres is desirable, but not absolutely necessary, especially if variable terrain such as a ridge and valley system is available. The major challenge in generating an ORV area lies in the political realm, and this is the second difference between ORV and living-history areas. Unlike the latter, ORV developments can be enormously unpopular — at least with individuals and organized groups who are opposed to off-road riding in principle. Off-road riding can and has caused environmental damage in some areas; however, the activity itself is a valid form of outdoor recreation. As professionals, you should thus be sensitive to the needs of ORV enthusiasts to the same degree as you are to the needs of other groups.

The key to the successful provision of off-road opportunities is one you've heard before. Most of the damage (and therefore the controversy) caused by off-road riding is the result of poor planning, design, and management. (Remember the discussion of "over-use.") Shortly we'll discuss some design techniques aimed at minimizing the potentially harmful effects of ORV use and enhancing the experience of riders. First, however, let's examine some of the concerns raised by environmentalists and others, perhaps including you, who are critical of off-road riding opportunities. These concerns cover damage to the environment, impact on wildlife, and — probably the greatest misconception — the difference between the *perceived* and *actual* profile of off-road enthusiasts.

The Off-Road Rider. People who enjoy all-terrain vehicles, 4-wheel-drive trucks and jeeps, snowmobiles, and especially dirt bikes have an image problem. Mention the term "biker" to people unfamiliar with off-road riding, and chances are the image they conjure up will be a black-leather-jacketed hoodlum. Some bikers fit this impression; fortunately most don't. Too often the image is applied to *all* people who like to ride off the road — mostly by opponents of ORV areas. In our experience, and we've spent a fair amount of time working with rider groups, these folks are just about like everyone else, barring their fondness for the challenge of their chosen activity. A profile of riding groups at TVA's Turkey Bay in Kentucky, the nation's first federally designated ORV area, showed that most riders participate as members of family or multi-family groups. The old saying about "one bad apple spoiling the barrel" is especially appropriate when applied to ORV enthusiasts. If you visit an off-road area, you may see black leather jackets, but you might not understand why riders wear them unless you've had the pleasure of turning a bike on its side on a stretch of gravel.

Environmental Impact. One distinction you should keep in mind is the difference between environmental *impact* and environmental *damage.* Camping in a designated wilderness area, regardless of how careful you are, affects the environment. The trick is for recreation participants and professionals to cooperate in ways designed to nullify, or at least minimize, the incidence of damage created by bike use. Most ORV enthusiasts are conscious of their image problem. As a result they will generally make efforts to pursue their activity in an ecologically sound manner. As we'll discuss below, there are ways the professional, through design and management, can address this problem as well. For the moment, let's consider one example of how much damage stems from ORV use.

Harm to the environment was a major concern of management after TVA opened Turkey Bay in the early 1970's. Consequently, when TVA personnel developed the area,

they implemented a plan to assess future impact. Staff conducted a baseline survey of the 2300-acre area and then repeated the survey bi-annually to monitor impact. After six years of use, approximately five percent of the area showed evidence of riding — about 115 acres. Impact, however, is not the same as damage. Trails were evident, but erosion was not prevalent and surrounding vegetation did not exhibit particular stress. We'd be shading the story unfairly if you weren't told the reason for this: the impact was minimal and the damage even less because the soil type in Turkey Bay was predominantly chert. Cherty soil has a high rock content and isn't particularly subject to wheel-to-ground injury. This may sound as if we're drawing an unfair conclusion, *but one reason Turkey Bay was selected in the first place was the low potential for damage because of the soil type!* Here a conscious planning decision led to a situation in which user needs were met with minimal problems for the environment. Our dual responsibility, remember, is to enhance the experience of users while providing resource stewardship.

Impact on Wildlife. As with soil and vegetative concerns, the issue of off-road riding and wildlife needs to be viewed in the context of impact versus damage. ORV's are relatively noisy and as such probably disturb wildlife. Damage, however, is another matter. We aren't aware of any studies which have shown that off-road riding has injured wildlife. Soon after the Turkey Bay area was opened, TVA conducted a test using a volunteer rider and a technique called bio-telemetry. This procedure involved capturing a mature wild turkey, a male, and fitting it with a small radio transmitter, then mounting the receiving unit on the handlebars of an off-road bike. The rider followed the signal (and the bird) for a two-hour period. To avoid the noise, the bird led the rider on quite a chase, but ended the test period only a few hundred yards from where it began. It's possible the turkey suffered some trauma from its experience, such as a disruption of its reproductive cycle. However, the wildlife biologist involved found no outward signs of damage (at least on the bird — the rider was beaten up from the ride through the underbrush).

The Turkey Bay area, which is managed as a wildlife unit by TVA, is also opened seasonally for deer hunting, and the deer harvest there has been comparable to surrounding units where ORV use is prohibited. These arguments aren't intended to suggest ORV use *isn't* in some way harmful to wildlife. They simply fail to prove that damage *is* associated with riding. If someone tells you that off-road riding is harming wildlife, ask him or her to show you the proof, preferably in the form of an article in a scientific journal. We'd like to see it too.

Impact on People. There are two types of people who may be affected by ORV use: those who don't ride and those who do. Controlling the impact on individuals who don't ride is simple — simply zone use areas. As with other activities and facilities, ORV areas need to be separated from areas with which conflict may occur. If you're working with a relatively large area like a state forest, this should not be a problem. The major "people impact" of ORV is noise, which doesn't always carry over long distances, especially in a wooded environment. Terrain, atmospheric conditions, ground cover, and number of vehicles all affect noise levels. One way of reducing the potential for a problem here is to provide a *buffer zone* as shown in Figure 5.5. By containing ORV use within a bordered area and buffering this area from other uses, noise and user conflicts are both reduced. If your resource space is limited, you may have to choose between ORV's and one or more other forms of recreation. This decision, however, should be based upon (1) the needs of the people in your area and (2) the opportunities available through other

agencies and private/commercial concerns nearby. The decision should *not* be based on your personal preferences, biases, or opinions of what people want. You will be called upon periodically to make professional judgments, but these should be just what the term implies: professional.

Off-road riding can also have quite an impact, literally speaking, on the participant. Therefore one legitimate concern of management should be the potential danger of this and other forms of recreation and the possible legal liability involved. Not being lawyers, we won't pretend to give you a definitive answer to this one. We do, however, have our opinions and a couple of comments. First, be careful and conscientious in your approaches to planning and management. ORV enthusiasts seem to appreciate the opportunity for *challenge*, but this doesn't suggest that you create or maintain hazardous conditions. Second, we've found off-road riders to be fairly stoic about injuries. If a biker "hits the dirt," he or she tends to get up, brush off, and keep on going. Again, this should not encourage lax management on your part. Safety and challenge are not mutually exclusive.

Getting Help. It's probably a good idea to get legal advice during the process of developing an ORV area. Another source of help you should not fail to seek is the rider. There are two levels of aid available here, and you should use them both. First, solicit help from riding clubs, if they exist, and from individuals. As with other activities, participants tend to know their own needs, and many of the design techniques discussed below grew out of meetings and conversations we've had with riders. On a broader level, you can and should contact the American Motorcyclist Association. Located in Westerville, Ohio, this national organization encourages conscientious use of resources and can provide technical advice, literature, contacts within your area, and

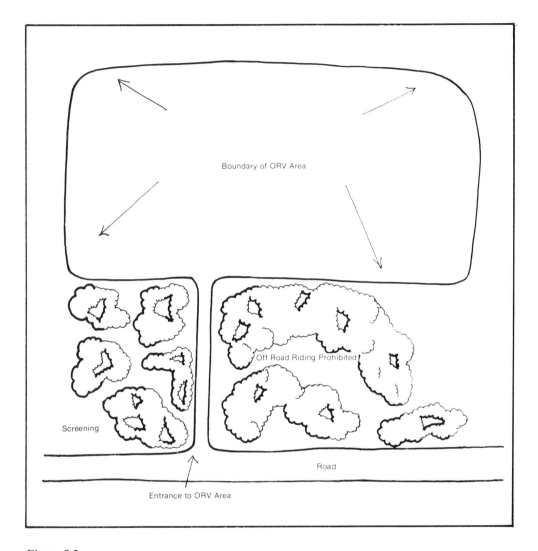

Boundary of ORV Area

Off Road Riding Prohibited

Screening

Road

Entrance to ORV Area

Figure 5.5

other valuable assistance. Let's turn our attention now to what to do once you've made the decision to develop an ORV area.

Designing off the Road. It's not difficult to provide the types of facilities ORV enthusiasts need to pursue their riding. It would only be a slight oversimplification to suggest

that the only amenities they need are places to camp, warm up, and ride. Like most other recreation areas, however, designing facilities is a bit more complex than just listing them. For example, one of your authors was involved in designing the area shown in Figure 5.6. This plan called for the development of a warm-up area, a broad, flat area

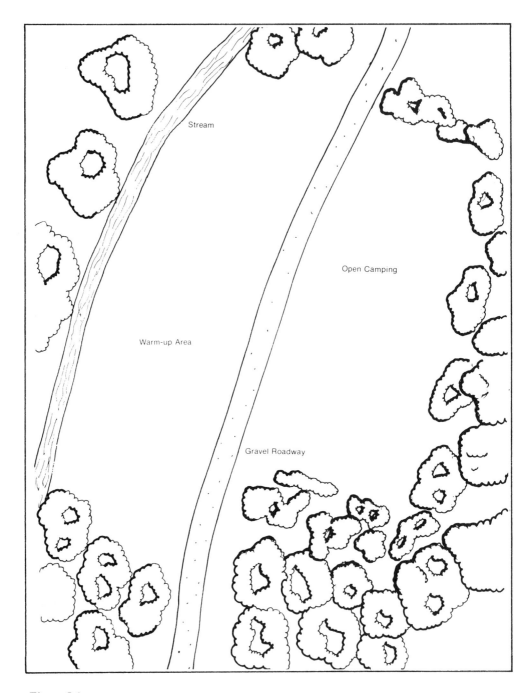

Stream

Open Camping

Warm-up Area

Gravel Roadway

Figure 5.6

for riders to check out their equipment before taking to the trails, associated with several campsites for other groups. Users had indicated they needed both these facilities, so the design challenge seemed straightforward. It turned out to be another of our mistakes. Given an audience — the people at the campsites — riders began using the warm-up area as an arena for showing off. After a few near-accidents, it was necessary to relocate the campsites in order to create a safe riding environment. The problem wasn't *design* — the warm-up area and campsites were developed correctly from a technical stand-point. The error was one in *planning*. A lack of understanding of the psychology involved created a problem for users and management.

As it turns out, you need to know a little about the organization of off-road riding groups in order to develop camping facilities for them. You may find local clubs in your area, but this doesn't always provide an indication of how riders utilize an area. In our experience, ORV user groups tend to consist of fewer than ten individuals, and a typical group might include two families. This suggests a need to develop camping facilities with some opportunity for separation of user groups built into the design. A "pod system" similar to that suggested for picnic areas also functions well in ORV areas, and Figure 5.7 shows such a design. Note how, in this design, the camping area has been developed with a series of pods or enclaves. Each unit is separated from the others by vegetative screening for privacy, and the camping zone is removed from the warm-up area. With this design, a club can request use of the entire camping area if your management plan includes a reservation system. Conversely, individual user groups — whether they belong to a riding organization or not — can use an enclave and retain a sense of privacy.

Individual camping units should be designed with attention given to both environment and type of user group you anticipate.

You'll find a more complete discussion of camp unit design in Chapter Seven that covers issues such as coping with topography. For now let's consider some basics. Since natural ground cover won't hold up under vehicular impact, each campsite should be reinforced with gravel and defined along the borders with railroad ties or similar material. The defined borders seem to function as "property lines" for users and help to provide an indication of where management expects vehicles to be parked. The sites themselves should be relatively spacious, perhaps thirty feet wide by fifty feet long, since use parties tend to be large. It's been our experience that most ORV groups camp in vans, pick-up campers, small recreation vehicles, or tents. Large camping trailers and motor homes are rare. Small, two-wheel trailers for off-road bikes, however, will be used frequently and should be anticipated. For example, the "mouth" of camping pods should be broad enough to permit easy access when backing a trailer.

On-site facilities can be minimal — a picnic table, fire pit/grill, and lantern-hanging device (see Chapter Seven) — should suffice. Your expected volume of use and the amount of space you have available will help determine the number of campsites you need. A cluster of six to ten pods should be enough in all but heavy-use areas, since many riders may come for the day without plans to camp. You should also provide toilet facilities and potable water. The physical characteristics of the site and probable use patterns (the number of day users versus campers) will help determine whether toilets should be in the camping zone, warm-up area, or both.

The warm-up or staging area for ORV's is quite simple to develop. The critical aspect of this portion of the complex is zoning. In addition to being separated from the camping zone, you should develop the staging area in conjunction with the entrance to the system of riding trails you provide.

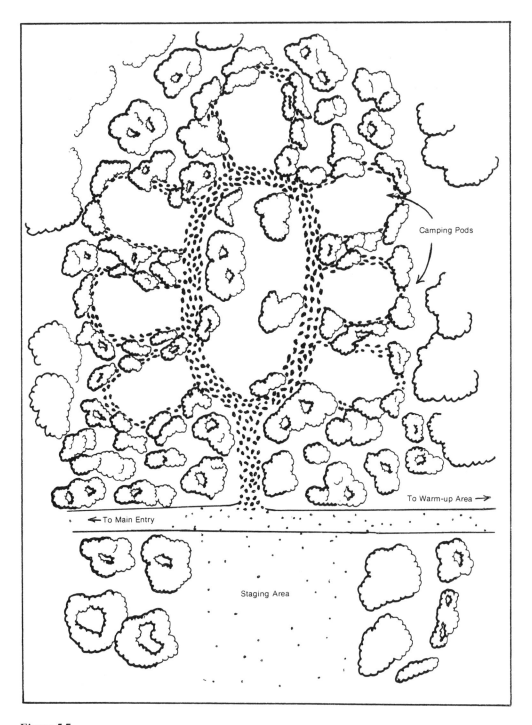

Figure 5.7

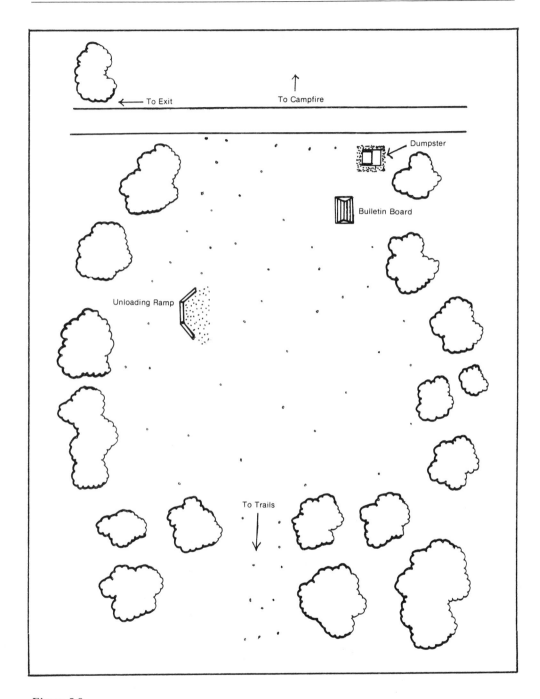

Figure 5.8

SAMPLE RULES AND REGULATIONS
GOVERNING MOTORIZED VEHICLE USE

- All properly licensed motor vehicles may be operated on paved, gravelled, and graded roads unless otherwise posted.

- Driving in woods, fields, utility right-of-ways, or trails is prohibited except in areas specifically designated for off-road use.

- All vehicles must be equipped with properly functioning mufflers.

- All motorbikes must have a properly functioning spark arrester.

- Drivers must hold a valid drivers license to drive on improved roads, although neither vehicle nor operator's license is required for off-road riding in designated areas.

- Motorbike riders are required to wear safety helmets and protective eyewear.

- In areas provided specifically for off-road riding:

Riders must operate within posted boundaries;

Use is allowed only during daylight hours;

One-way trails must be traveled in the direction indicated;

All garbage and debris must be placed in the containers provided;

Users must refrain from harassing people or wildlife;

Riders should observe the safety practices recommended by the American Motorcyclist Association.

Figure 5.9

Other than the trail head, the only facilities needed in the warm-up area include a loading/unloading ramp, a garbage collection point, toilets, and an information-posting station or bulletin board.

Figure 5.8 shows a possible layout for a staging area. While design requirements are minimal, they deserve careful attention. Consider the following details which are given attention in this figure. The entrance to the staging area is quite broad, making the zone easy to locate and enhancing safety. Off-road vehicles, trail bikes, and motorcycles also accelerate quickly, so your plan should avoid narrow constrictions and blind corners where a bike might meet a four-wheel drive vehicle or a truck transporting other bikes into the warm-up zone. The road leading to the staging area is an exception to the curvilinear design need; a fairly long straight section of road approaching the warm-up zone may help prevent accidents.

The trash collection point is near the entrance to the area. This is convenient for users and reduces the distance travelled by trash collection crews. Also note the placement of the dumpster on the side of the staging area *opposite* the direction of incoming traffic. This should further reduce the chance of accidents.

Next to safety for users, probably the most important management consideration for ORV areas is controlling use. Off-road riding has received a good deal of "bad press" and the activity does have the potential to damage the environment. Both managers and planners, however, can take steps to minimize physical impact and prevent negative feelings toward off-road riding. Posting *and enforcing* clear and reasonable regulations is one preventive measure. Figure 5.9 shows a possible set of rules for ORV use. Note the wording; the rules prohibit several kinds of behavior, but negative language ("do not . . .") is minimal. These regulations emphasize the provision of an exclusive area for ORV use and safety practices recommended by the American Motorcyclist Association. Remember to check wording and specific regulations with legal counsel.

The role of the planner in controlling use lies in his or her ability to develop facilities which can be managed effectively. In Figure 5.8, the bulletin board where rules, area maps, and other information are posted is in clear sight of the entrance to the staging area. The unloading ramp is near enough to the entrance to be convenient, but is located off to one side of the staging area. To build this ramp, use a three-sided border of railroad ties, stacked two high and filled with gravel. Taper the gravel to ground level behind the ramp. Figure 5.10 shows two views of this construction, a profile (A) and a top view (B). Users soon discover the ramp works nicely as a jump as well as for loading and unloading; thus it must be located out of the main flow of traffic. The planner should also place clearly marked boundary signs around the perimeter of the ORV area that *face into* the riding area so riders can see them. Locations for signs must be inter-visible as well. (You should be able to see one sign from both directions.)

The development of a trails system for an ORV area depends on site-specific condi-tions, and the help of a soils scientist is critical in choosing one. Avoid ecologically sensitive areas and sites subject to erosion; soils with a high gravel content are generally good choices. From the rider's perspective, there are several other factors to consider in design. Build ORV trails with attention to *variety* in degree of difficulty. While the staging area provides a flat area for warm-up and for novices, the trails should offer differing challenges for more advanced riders. The key here is to avoid designing diverse obstacles into adjacent sections of trail. In other words, don't follow a broad, gentle curve with a tight, hairpin turn, but do plan hill climbs, dips, and other changes in eleva-tion. Avoid having the trail cross stream beds

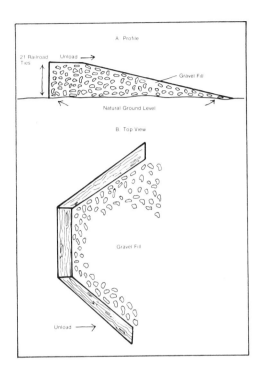

Figure 5.10

and narrow ravines if at all possible. These abrupt changes in elevation can be dan-gerous, and such zones are particularly subject to erosion. Solicit help from off-road clubs and individuals who pursue the activity whenever you can. In some instances you may find them willing to help with layout and construction. In all instances you should find that asking user groups for help and providing facilities for them to use will buy you a major dose of positive public relations.

WRANGLER'S CAMPS

Planning facilities for recreational horseback riding, as with other types of activities, requires you to become familiar with your clientele. As it turns out, the main thing you

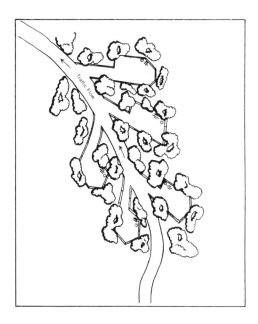

Figure 5.11

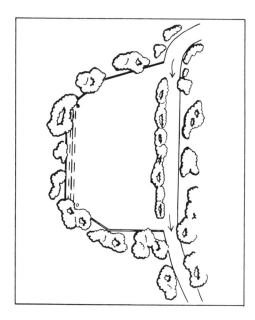

Figure 5.12

need to know about horseback riding is where it occurs; the primary distinction in riding is a geographical, or, more specifically, a *sectional* one. In general, riding in the western portion of the U.S., from the Rocky Mountains west, is a wilderness-oriented, long-distance, linear activity, and the basic trail design can be similar to that for linear hiking discussed in Chapter Three. It's a good idea to provide connector trails, as shown in Figure 3.24, so users have the option of shorter rides that begin and end at the same point. Other features discussed in the section on long-distance hiking — parking, signing, trail marking, and the like — apply to this type of riding experience as well.

The topic of this section is the wrangler's camp, an experience more aligned with the recreational preferences of horseback riders in the East and South. A wrangler's camp is a *destination facility*. By this we mean it's a location where users plan to stay for a period of time, unlike "way stations" or overnight camping spots on a linear trail. A destination facility, like ORV areas and developed campgrounds, is characterized by a central complex. In the case of the wrangler's camp, this must include facilities for camping, keeping horses, and riding.

Camping. The number of campsites you need to provide in a wrangler's camp depends on a wonderful acronym, popular in recreation literature, that we've been waiting to use: PAOT. In English, this means *persons at one time*. The more popular riding is in your locale, the more PAOT you should expect, but we'll leave it to you to determine PAOT and limit our discussion to the types of camping facilities (TOCF?) you may need to consider. People seem to arrive at wrangler's camps in one of two types of groups: small, as in a family or a group of friends; and large, as in an organized group of several families. Since you may find some of each wanting to use your facilities at the same time, it's a good idea to design your camping area accordingly. To avoid re-inventing the wheel, we'll refer you to the section on campsite design in Chapter Seven for site-specific information (construction materials, topographic challenges, and similar considerations). For now, let's consider campsite design from the standpoint of layout for wrangler's camps.

There are three ways to develop campsites for wrangler's camps. Since groups consisting of one family or a few friends may visit your area, some of the campsites you build should be *individual units*. These are smaller sites, perhaps thirty by thirty feet of reinforced living space plus attached parking large enough for a vehicle and a horse trailer, along with a single picnic table, grill, and lantern-hanging device. (See Chapter Seven.) You should build these sites *together* to localize impact but *apart* to provide a sense of privacy for users at each site. Figure 5.11 shows a section of a camping area devoted to individual use, and three aspects of this design contribute to a psychological sense of privacy: the screening between sites, the "staggered" spur-to-road junctures, and the "property lines" created by edging the sites with a defined border.

A second type of campsite design, shown in Figure 5.12, functions for larger groups. This type of site is distinguished by its larger living and parking space and by a collection of several tables and grills. (A single, large fire pit is also an alternative here.) Note how unit furniture has been "tucked" into a corner of the living space. This allows users to arrange the remaining space to suit their own particular needs.

Figure 5.13 shows a compromise between the types of sites shown in the previous two figures. Here they are built adjacent to one another to allow groups of several families to congregate if the families make up a larger party. Since they are individual, these sites will function for separate parties of users as well. Though you may not know what type

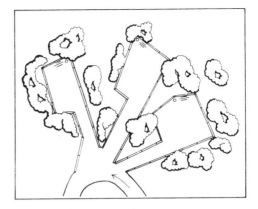

Figure 5.13

of user groups to expect in advance, they are a good hedge against uncertainty.

Figure 5.14 shows a possible layout for the camping zone of a wrangler's camp. Here, the three types of campsites have been combined, and the impact from camping (vehicles, campfires, and the like) has been localized. Also, the sites are zoned into a single area so that potentially conflicting activities, in the program zone, for example, need not interfere. (Intensive programming may not be a design goal at all special-use areas. However, we advocate a philosophy of never passing up an opportunity. By adding a program zone, you may *create* opportunities for programs — horseshoe pitching, group barbecues . . .)

Designing Space for Horses. We promise not to stoop to any comments about horse sense, but there are a few things you need to consider in planning space for these animals. First, *common* sense tells us to *avoid common space* — the corral — which functions quite well in the western dude ranch environment. At a wrangler's camp, most of the animals won't know each other. Unlike people, for whom recreation is a social experience, horses need their private space. Providing a corral may create a situa-

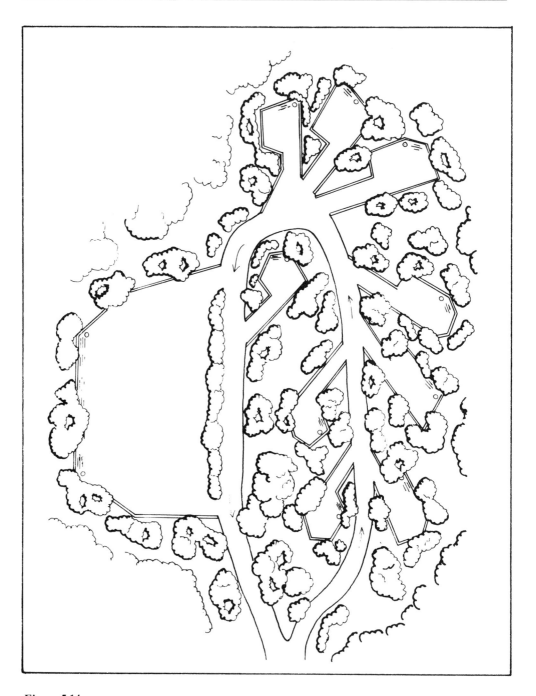

Figure 5.14

tion in which one or more horses could be injured, so this leaves you with a couple of alternatives. First, if you have the budget for it, stables with individual stalls are a possibility. A second less costly alternative is to provide facilities for riders to tether their horses near their campsites.

Our old friend "attention to detail" comes into play here. Particularly in the warmer months of the year, horses will need shade when tethered outside. The KISS principle by itself would tell us to use the straight-forward solution and let users tie their horses to trees. There's a problem with this, however; horses will quite happily eat the bark off the trees to which they're tied, so you'll need an alternative. The best one we know is to use a series of four by six inch posts anchored in the ground fifteen feet apart with rope attached between them. You can place these tethering posts near trees to provide shade but far enough away to keep your bark intact. The fifteen-foot spacing of posts also allows enough room for horses to be kept separate from one another.

Riding. The wrangler's camp experience seems to consist of two main components. Riding is obviously one reason people are attracted to these types of facilities. The other — and this is important to know from a design standpoint — is the *social component.* Riders seem to enjoy meeting and being with other riders, and this tendency has implications for the develop-ment of camping areas, as we discussed above. It should also influence how you design trails for wrangler's camps. Since most of the socializing occurs at the camp, rather than on the trail, users will want to begin and end their rides at camp. In fact, this "out and back" preference is what makes the wrangler's camp a distinctive recreational experience.

The best way to design trails to meet this need seems to be with a series of loop trails radiating out from the central complex, as

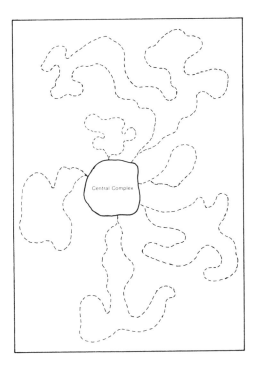

Figure 5.15

shown in Figure 5.15. The important point to consider about the trails shown here is their *varied length.* As loop trails, they allow users to begin and end at the central camp. With varied lengths, as well as information about riding times and distances posted, riders can also design the length of their experience to meet their needs. Trail-riding times might vary from two or three hours to all day, and some riders might even appreciate a loop trail long enough to offer the opportunity for an overnight excursion.

As with other types of recreation, you should make it a point to get to know local user groups and work *with* them to design facilities to meet their needs. For example, you might have an active interest in square dancing among members of a local riding group. Therefore, perhaps you can find enough budget dollars to build an open-sided shelter building with a concrete slab floor to add another dimension to their recreation experience. More importantly, through provision of facilities *and* program opportunities, you can demonstrate to user groups your responsiveness to their needs.

GROUP CAMPS

In the preceding sections on wrangler's camps and ORV areas, you've already been introduced to group camps. We now need to generalize a bit and discuss some basic concepts — ones you should consider regardless of the type of group you're planning for. These concepts aren't new — you've heard them before. They also involve nothing more than plain old common sense, but they ofttimes get ignored in the planning process.

When you begin to plan for a group-oriented facility, you need to ask yourself three questions: *Who* is the camp for? How do you want it to *function*? And what are your *program goals*? Group camps can be developed along a continuum from the very primitive to the highly modernized, but we'll limit our discussion of design techniques to a few general considerations since we don't have the space to consider all types of group camping. First, however, let's consider two examples to illustrate the importance of our three questions.

For twenty years, a girl scout council in northern Georgia had saved its money to develop a camp. Finally they raised enough to buy a piece of property. The council commissioned a plan for the area and found a committee to review the plan. The property featured a fairly large flat field and several surrounding steep wooded slopes. The plan called for a stream running through the field to be dammed to create a lake, with facilities for the camp itself to be built on the lake's slopes. Total development cost would have been approximately two million dollars —

half for the property, dam and lake and half for the facilities to be built.

As good fortune would have it, the review committee vetoed the plan and our story has a happy ending. The council ultimately bought another property with a preexisting camp and lake, then modified them to meet their needs. The important point is this: the decision to veto the new development was not made on the basis of how well the plan was packaged, but rather on our three questions. The camp was to be for girl scouts, it was to function as a resident camp, and program goals included developing space for a variety of activities. The lake planned for the original property would have flooded the *only developable land* available for both activity areas and "bedroom" space. Also, while this body of water was desirable from a programming perspective, creating it would not have been worth the trade-off in opportunities lost for building other types of areas. The decision to move the camp was the correct one since the committee made it on the basis of *users, function,* and *programs.*

The second example we'll share with you is a boy scout High Adventure Base in Kentucky. The function of this camp differed from the previous example in that the High Adventure site was a *base camp.* The program called for scout groups to arrive at the site on Monday for orientation and then camp overnight at the base. The next morning, the group would leave for a several day trek, either sailing or hiking. At the end of the week, the group would return, spend one night at the camp, during which preparations to leave were made, and depart the following day. As with our other illustration, the program provided the information necessary to design and administer the High Adventure Base Camp. Since groups did not use the facility in residence, there was no need for a major programming zone. Thus it was possible to develop the site on a relatively small, and fairly marginal, piece of land.

Major considerations from a planning perspective included administration space, office, departure points, and equipment storage; a staging area for arriving groups; and a "departure camp" for groups spending their last night at the base. This arrangement — and the considerations for planning that accompany it — exemplify the potential diversity of group camp experiences. In one small area, three types of camping needs were met — the first night orientation, the extended trek, and the checking-out camp. The approach used to meet these needs at the High Adventure Base was excellent in its simplicity. Upon arrival, groups checked out an appropriate number of small, two-person tents. They then set up camp for the night in the staging area and made final preparations for the upcoming outing. The next morning, the group would break camp, *keeping the tents to use during the trek.* Upon their return to the base several days later, they would bivouac at the departure camp, which consisted of larger tents set on raised wooden platforms. With this arrangement, there was no need for the group to spend time setting up camp their final night or breaking camp the morning of their departure. Instead, this time could be devoted to making any necessary equipment repairs, cleaning gear, and recreating. Figure 5.16 shows a schematic of the base arrangement. Again a knowledge of user needs, camp function, and program dictated appropriate development.

In creating a group camp the most basic consideration, and the test of how successful the camp will be, is the program. In order to function effectively, a group camp must feature appropriate activities and zoning. Figure 5.17 illustrates the layout of a group camp designed to function for user groups and for management. Our old friend, separation of use areas, plays a primary role here. The central complex that houses administrative functions such as group check-in and the dining area is immediately adjacent to the arrival point. Bedroom areas

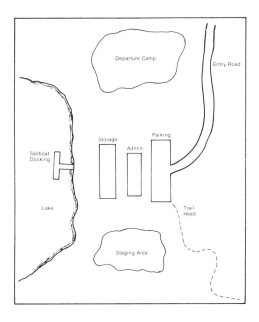

Figure 5.16

are zoned next to the central complex to simplify maintenance and clean-up, as well as camper set-up and departure. This example shows a dormitory system, although camping pods for a more rustic experience could be developed with the same spatial arrangement.

The central complex and bedroom zone serve another function as well; they provide a *buffer* between active and passive program zones. With this arrangement, it is possible to program, for example, an interpretive hike and a basketball game at the same time. The design, in other words, encourages program flexibility. If the size and capacity of the camp are large enough, it is also possible to open the camp to two or more groups at the same time. If this possibility exists, you will need to consider one management issue — some groups may be incompatible with others. We recall one instance (although we'd prefer to forget it) in which this concern wasn't given enough attention. While working in the federal sector, we reserved

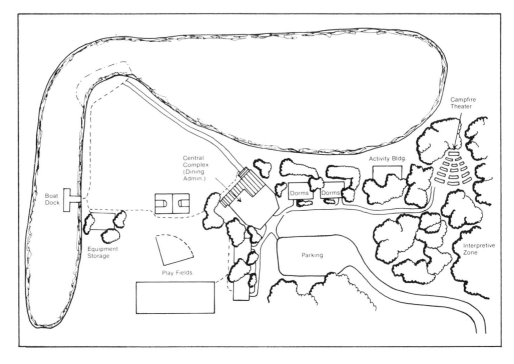

Figure 5.17

space in a group camp for two sets of teenagers from different religious denominations. Although the camp was well zoned, there were opportunities — such as in the dining hall — for the groups to interact. Before their stay was finished, they were literally throwing rocks at each other.

This story reminds us of one final point about group camps since many such camps are owned and operated by religious organizations. All too often, group camps are poorly maintained, unprotected, subject to vandalism, and unoccupied for much of the year. In the case of camps operated by religious organizations, there are probably two reasons for this. First is an inadequate operations and maintenance budget. Capital investment fund drives to buy or build camps are often quite successful, but can neglect the need to operate and maintain a camp once it

is built. A second problem involves comprehensive program planning. Building a camp so a youth group can have an annual two-week retreat is a commendable purpose, but what about the other fifty weeks of the year?

It really doesn't matter whether the camp is owned privately or operated by a public, quasi-public, or commercial concern. What does matter is *maximum use* through as much of the year as possible. Ideally, maximum use means more opportunities for recreation; pragmatically, we're talking return on investment. We wish there were a simple, straightforward solution to this problem for you, but if there is, we aren't aware of it. One possible answer might be cooperative ventures in which several groups combine forces and resources to develop a single facility to be shared by all. This approach can create a few extra hassles — sharing property titles, scheduling, accounting, and the like. However, these problems are preferable to an underused, poorly funded, heavily vandalized facility.

MILITARY RECREATION COMPLEXES

As we suggested in Chapter One, outdoor recreation entered a period of unprecedented growth and popularity during the 1950's. Public agencies at all levels of government — and later in the commercial sector — witnessed increases in staff, funding, areas, and programs in response to new demands. Generally speaking, this trend has reversed itself in the public sector during recent years. Particularly at the federal level, recreation agencies have experienced hiring freezes, cutbacks in funding, and, in cases such as the Heritage, Conservation, and Recreation Service, dissolution of programs altogether.

One exception to this reductionist trend has been the provision of outdoor recreation opportunities by the Armed Forces. Recreation services for military personnel are not, in themselves, new phenomena. In fact, histories tracing the growth of recreation in general often point to the emphasis on physical fitness in the Armed Forces as one of the major causes that increased recreation services during the first quarter of the twentieth century. *Outdoor* recreation, however, is something of a "new kid on the block" as far as the military is concerned, and the 1970's were its "early days." Somewhat surprisingly, outdoor recreation in the military has not followed the same pattern of program provision — or lack of it — that we discussed in reference to other federal agencies. From the beginning, the military has made excellent strides in providing outdoor recreation programs and facilities.

In fact, we suggest (and we're pretty stingy with our compliments) that the Armed Forces are unique among federal agencies in their approach to recreation services: *they plan parks for people.* It seems to us there are three reasons for this. First, Armed Services recreation personnel are *people-oriented.* Below a top echelon of military personnel, a large proportion of the people involved are trained in the profession. The Armed Forces hire graduates of recreation curricula, and, as we've suggested before, these folks tend to have good backgrounds in people-related skills — administration and programming. Thus recreation staff in the military tend to be sensitive to the needs of users.

A second factor contributing to the success of Armed Forces recreation programs and facilities is their *mission.* Their very reason for existence is to meet the recreational needs of the clientele they serve, and although each branch of the military has its own recreation arm, the professional staff involved use this mission as a guiding force. It's been our experience that various branches of the military are relatively efficient in holding their recreation staffs *accountable;* recreation service is their function, and they are expected to perform effectively.

A final and related factor leading to effective recreation services for the military is the *spectrum of users* for whom professional staff provide areas and facilities. Consider for a moment the population at a typical military base. This may consist of retired service personnel and their spouses, career servicemen and women who have served several tours of duty and their families (including teenagers), young married personnel with smaller children, and single officers and enlisted men and women ranging in age from teens to sixties. In other words, the recreation clientele at a military base — whether in the US or overseas — resembles a *microcosm* of society. With such a diverse population, military recreation staff have a need (remember their mission) to provide a *broad spectrum* of programs and facilities in order to meet the demands of all users.

As we've noted, military recreation personnel are quite successful when it comes to providing programs and facilities because of two factors. The first is something we feel is *essential* in a professional: if you're doing a good job, accept the fact and the praise accompanying it. Second, *never be complacent* about your work. It's one thing to perform a task well; it's quite another to assume you can't do any better. We feel that part of being a professional involves never being entirely satisfied, and while this does *not* imply you should downgrade yourself, it *does* suggest that you should always ask yourself how you can do even better next time.

In the case of military recreation services, one of the strong points contributing to their success is also a hindrance to improved performance: the background of many of their personnel. The programming and administrative expertise of Armed Services recreation staff does not often translate into effective planning and design skills. As a result, many recreation facilities at military installations are laid out ineffectively. Another way of looking at this problem is to suggest that all the pieces of the puzzle are present, but that the "assembly" doesn't fit together as it should. To illustrate this point let's consider the evolution of a military recreation complex in Europe we've seen. This particular complex happens to be operated by the Army, but branch affiliation is incidental.

First, we need a brief "history lesson." As early as the mid-1970's, Army recreation services became involved — particularly in Europe — with providing facilities called "travel camps." These were high-density campgrounds, some of which now contain up to thirty-five campsites per acre. (In comparison, a Forest Service campground might have three to four units per acre, a National Park Service area ten to twelve.) As outdoor recreation services in the military became more sophisticated, these travel camps underwent an evolution of sorts. Today an Army recreation complex has become known as a "community park," which offers a wider variety of program opportunities and facilities, one of which may be a campground. Other facilities are also oriented toward day use and might include play fields and courts, picnic areas and pavilions, playgrounds, game areas, a recreation building, and similar developments you might expect to find in a typical municipal park.

Figure 5.18 shows the area allocated to recreation development at the European army base we mentioned above. Before recreation development began, portion 1 of the site had been fenced in and used to park tanks. Since a road and parking spurs were already in place here, the planner decided to add a trailer campground, the first stage of development. Proposed facilities — to be built later — included an indoor lounge area (2), a picnic area and pavilion (3), a miniature golf course (4), a multipurpose building (5), a tent-camping zone (6), a playground (7) and two softball fields (8). The design also called for a toilet/shower building at the entrance to the trailer camping area.

There are several problems with this design. First, the various facilities don't fit together in a cohesive fashion; the tent-camping area seems more a part of the day-use zone than of the overnight use development; the playground doesn't relate to day-use facilities and, indeed, is in a rather dangerous location. A second problem occurs in circulation and use of space. Aside from the one parking lot and the campground, all movement within the area would require walking, and the areas above and below the softball complex are wasted. A third problem concerns administration and support facilities. Since the campground is reached via a separate entrance, control problems exist.

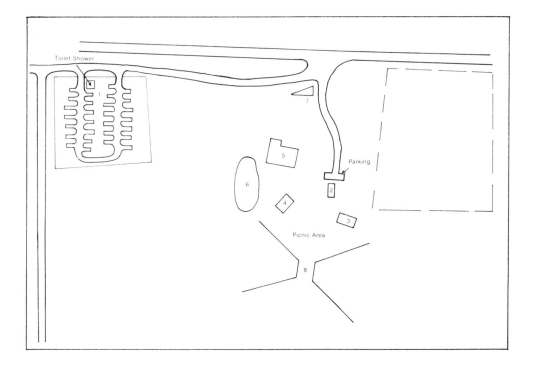

Figure 5.18

The location of the toilet/shower keeps you from taking full advantage of this facility — as placed, it won't serve any area except the trailer campground.

Let's try to redesign this area so it functions more effectively for users and management. Since it's quite easy to design just about anything on a flat piece of paper, let's also put some real-life *constraints* on our design: (a) area 1 must be used for camping, since the parking spurs are already in place; (b) the road leading to and beyond this zone must be kept open to traffic; and (c) the lounge (2), miniature golf area (4), multipurpose building (5), and softball fields (8) must be built as shown in Figure 5.18. Our design goals should be to improve circulation, to provide better zoning of use areas, to build in ease of administration, to allow for

an expansion of the campground, and to use space more effectively. It turns out that these constraints don't force us into a more complex design solution; as is so often the case, the KISS principle can serve as a guide to improving the design.

Figure 5.19 shows one alternative solution to our problem, though other approaches could accomplish the same goals as well. This design meets the constraints we imposed. Area 1 is used for camping and the road past it has been kept open while the two former entrances to the campground have been sealed off, allowing us to use a single entry-exit to the entire area and control use with the addition of a small entrance station (2). We've also provided both vehicle circulation and parking at the lounge, multipurpose building, miniature golf

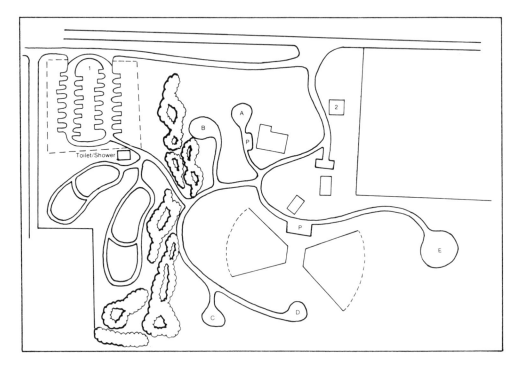

Figure 5.19

course, and softball complex. The screen planting shown separates day-use facilities from the camping zone, which has been expanded. Note how the new location of the toilet/shower serves both the "old" camping area and the new loops added to the design. Within the camping and day-use zones, more of the previously "dead" space is now devoted to functional use areas.

Probably the most important feature of the design shown in Figure 5.19 is the addition of *theme pods* for day use. We've talked about pod design before, and the principle works as well in military recreation complexes as it does in civilian parks. Notice how the new design has eliminated the poorly placed playground and the original picnic area and pavilion. In their place, we've added a series of day-use pods (A through E). These pods function as group-use areas.

Depending on the needs at a particular military base, each of these can be devoted to a specific theme. One might be designed for group picnics, including unit parties; another might be planned around a playground for younger children; still another could be built for adult play space, tennis, volleyball, and the like; and so on. The contents or themes of the pods might vary from one military base to another, but the *logic* is the same: the design follows the principle of zoning of use areas.

Overnight use is separated from day use as well. Note how the original text camping area — point 6 in Figure 5.18 — has been removed. (In general, trying to separate tent and trailer camping creates a management problem; however, if this separation is a management objective, one of the camping loops in Figure 5.19 could also be designated for tents only.) Further, within the day-use zones, potentially conflicting uses are kept separated by the development of pods.

In military recreation complexes, as in civilian parks, *form should follow function.* Providing a broad spectrum of recreation opportunities is the ultimate program goal, and careful application of design techniques is, as always, a means to an end. By attending to the basic principle of zoning of use areas, military recreation personnel can improve what is already a good example of planning parks for people.

For the last ten years and more, we have been involved in dozens of park planning and design workshops, some of which we've hosted and others for which we've been resource speakers for various groups. Wherever and whenever we've had the opportunity, we've espoused the need for programming and its companion, truly planning parks for people. Having program-oriented military recreation professionals in our "student" groups has been a real joy. These folks *know why* they need to develop park facilities (remember their people-flavored mission!). While some military recreation professionals are inexperienced in the basics of planning and design, they are eager participants in the learning process, probably as a result of recognizing programs as a goal and planning as a support function. Those who aren't trained in the program realm — foresters, landscape architects, wildlife biologists, and other "rascals" — are ofttimes quite reluctant to embrace or even believe in the need to consider people and programs in the planning process. Unfortunately, their designs litter our parkscapes worldwide!

SPECIAL USE AREAS:
AN EXERCISE

The problems at the end of the previous chapters have been design oriented. You've been given a set of guidelines and asked to plan a recreation area to meet a specified use. For a change of pace, this exercise takes a somewhat different approach. This chapter has considered the development of recreation areas for special uses. Since the spectrum of "special uses" entails a broader range of groups than those discussed here, we'll leave it to you to determine the type of group and thus the type of area for whom you're planning. Your plan should consist of several steps. First, identify a special-use group in your area in need of a recreation facility. To do this, you need to consider what types of recreation opportunities already exist within reasonable proximity to your location. (Hint: what's "reasonable"?) Avoid duplicating services; your challenge is to meet a currently unfulfilled need.

Once you've determined that the need for a particular type of use area exists, your second task is to specify how you would go about getting the information necessary to make planning decisions, i.e., what do the users want in the area? The questions for you to address are: how would you *collect* the information? Would you meet with individuals? Use a questionnaire? Meet with the special-interest group together? Hold a public meeting? You should be able to justify your approach.

A parallel task you need to tackle in addition to assessing user needs is considering potential resources for the development of the area. You'll need *physical resources* in the form of a land base suitable for the area, and *fiscal resources* in the form of development funds. Finally, after taking needs and resources into consideration, you should develop two or preferably three alternative concept plans for the area.

Here's a final note to consider before you approach this as just another sterile textbook exercise: *Do it.* We believe strongly in applying information, in receiving firsthand, real-world experience, and in getting recreation facilities built. Make this assignment a class exercise. Find a real user group with a need and a local agency or corporation willing to cooperate with you and make something happen. You don't need a lot of funding or a large piece of land; a passive sitting area at a retirement home can be a real design challenge if you're conscientious about meeting user needs. You may be surprised how much you can learn by doing. You may also be surprised at how challenging it can be to translate a plan into a reality. We never claimed design was easy, just enjoyable and rewarding. Try it and see for yourself.

6

GETTING SERIOUS
ABOUT PLAY AREAS

INTRODUCTION

Some theorists have suggested that play is the "business" of children. It would seem that a bigger problem for the recreation professional is the tendency for these roles to be reversed in too many adults who make business their play. We'll leave this concern for the leisure educator, however, and confine the discussion in this chapter to another serious aspect of play: design of areas and facilities devoted to the pursuit of fun. We'll consider a variety of types of play areas in the next few pages, some of which you may be surprised to find. We'll also discuss play areas for adults as well as for children.

Since most people (grown-ups, anyway) tend to think of play in terms of youngsters, let's start by thinking about the traditional playground. At several points in this book, we've tried to stress the dual responsibility recreation professionals have: the need to develop and maintain spaces which function for people *and* protect the environment. Nowhere is this need more evident, and perhaps more frequently forgotten, than in play areas. Consider for a moment the area shown in Figure 6.1. The designer, a friend of ours, was working with a series of knowns. He *knew,* for example, children were going to use the play equipment he provided. He *knew* he wanted to maintain a stand of grass in the area surrounding the play space. He *knew* the average annual rainfall in Boulder, Colorado, the location of this playground,

was only fourteen inches per year — not enough to grow grass on land subject to the impact associated with play. He *knew,* therefore, that he had to *recognize* and *reinforce* the area of impact, which he did. As a result of this careful planning, the children and the grass both thrived.

The twist in our story is that the designer of the Boulder site wasn't a recreation professional at all. He worked in a factory, and the play space was his family's back yard.

The play space shown in Figure 6.2, however, *is* in a public park, *does* suffer from a lack of attention to people and environmental needs, and *was* designed by a "professional." The planner responsible for the area shown in Figure 6.2 had access to the same set of knowns available to our friend in Boulder, yet failed to attend to the potential problems associated with the intensive use inherent in a play area and likely blamed its later appearance on users!

It may seem that our constant nagging about impact is akin to beating a dead horse, but you should consider ways to reduce impact associated with play areas as well as how to make play spaces functional from the standpoint of people. In fact, an excellent starting point for designing play areas and facilities is the topic of *function.*

The Question of Purpose. As with other types of recreational developments, play areas should be considered from the basic perspective of *why:* Why is the area designed as it is and what is the function to be served?

Figure 6.1

Play areas can — although they don't have to — be planned for a *primary use.* In other words, provision of a play space may be the main reason for the development of a given resource base. If this is the case, one set of design questions and considerations needs to be addressed. In some instances, however, play areas may serve a *secondary use.* Perhaps the best example of this is the development of play space as a *support area.* Consider the construction of play equipment at fast-food restaurants. Here play is only used to draw people into the eating establishment. This same logic is often ignored in parks where play areas could be developed to support other types of recreation facilities.

Family-oriented recreation areas like picnic sites and campgrounds can be enhanced — for all family members — if planners give careful consideration to play areas in a supportive role. Drive-in theater operators recognize this secondary function when they provide space and apparatus for children to use during parent-oriented movies. However, we frequently see *parks* where this isn't considered, where adult play spaces are often designed without attention to the needs of children. What is there, for example, for a six-year-old to do at a softball complex during adult league play? We don't advocate putting a swing set in the third-base coach's box, but we do suggest that you consider zoning use areas with the relationship between areas for adults and children in mind. If a play space is to serve a secondary function, design questions and considerations may not be exactly the same as those for play spaces intended as primary-use areas.

Another concern you'll need to address is the question of *who:* play areas and equip-

Figure 6.2

ment for tots need to be designed differently than those for older children. Twelve-year-olds have a different degree of motor control than six-year olds. Levels of imagination also change as children mature, and, more obviously, children grow as they age. Therefore the age range for which you develop a play area means considering *safety, creativity,* and *scale* in design. Too often, we limit our concept of play to children. All of us play, but in varying degrees and in different ways. Recreation professionals often *react* to the recognized need for children's play by providing children's play equipment. We should take the next step, however, and create opportunities for players of all ages by being *proactive:* a bench in a city park

provides a place for adults to sit. A bench in a city park with an adjacent checkerboard table provides a place for adults to *play.*

A Mistake

The play area we'll discuss as an example of flawed design is truly a comedy of errors. In fact, the mistake serves to illustrate two problems, for once the initial difficulty was recognized, the "solution" compounded the original problem. Figure 6.3 shows the design of a playground complex built in a small town in central Pennsylvania. As indicated in the drawing, the original plan primarily

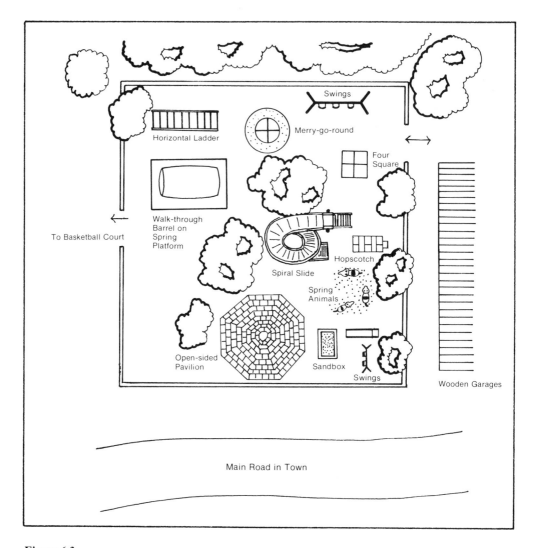

Figure 6.3

provided a number of pieces of traditional or conventional play equipment spread over a roughly rectangular area. If you're beginning to get a "feel" for design and for the need to think in terms of total concept planning, you should recognize one problem immediately. The play area in Figure 6.3 is rather sterile.

There is little or no continuity in the relationship of one piece of apparatus to another. Thus the opportunity for creative play tends to be discouraged. Given the imaginative abilities of children, however, let's assume they can outsmart the planner and create enjoyable play scenarios here.

From the standpoint of the user, the playground is the proverbial "accident waiting to happen." Note where the two sets of swings are located. In theory, it is a good idea to tuck equipment with motion involved into corners of play space because of the potential for collisions with people passing by. However, one entrance to the playground is located so that the circulation pattern into the area forces users to cross dangerously close to the larger set of swings. If we wanted to be sarcastic, we'd suggest that children in the swings "bail out" in the direction opposite the playground entrance if they anticipate a collision with a pedestrian. However, this probably wouldn't work too well since both sets of swings are quite near the fence surrounding the playground. Did we mention the fence just happens to be topped with barbed wire? Believe it or not, it is.

As if user safety weren't enough of a problem, the agency responsible for this playground has to contend with a resource concern as well. As Chapter Two suggested, planners often fail to borrow expertise from disciplines related to recreation. In this case, the forgotten element was soils information. The playground was built on soil with a heavy clay content. Using the area compacts the soil, and the point was soon reached where moisture was not being absorbed into the ground. Since, during the planning and construction phases, no one provided for drainage, like center crowning the area, water began to pool after every rain. The plot now thickens, for someone eventually realized that water standing in a playground was a problem in need of a solution.

The solution? Pave the playground. No more standing water? Right. No more hassles with compacted soil? Right. No more concerns? Wrong. Let's look at the problems *created by* this solution:

— First, by paving over the entire area planners sealed the fate of the trees,

though chances are that the impact from play would have killed them eventually anyway since they weren't protected from impact in the initial design. However, paving over the entire root system cut off their supply of water and oxygen, condemned them to an early death, and removed the only source of shade in the playground.

— Perhaps in an attempt to seek revenge, the trees struck back, creating costly short- and long-term maintenance headaches. Soon after the playground was surfaced, root systems began to break through the asphalt, creating mounds and humps in the pavement. As trees began to die, dead limbs also became a hazard, and ultimately removing entire trees tended to leave rather obvious holes in the pavement. It really doesn't pay to mess around with Mother Nature.

— In addition to destroying the resource base, paving created a new hazard for children using the area; underneath existing play equipment, it increased the potential for serious injuries severalfold. The spiral slide in the center of the playground, for example, was over fifteen feet high. If a child fell from this height onto natural ground, or onto a padded surface, the chances of him or her sustaining a serious injury would be high. Falling from this height to a paved surface would make the odds even higher.

— Putting an asphalt covering on the playground created another potential hazard where none had existed before. Hard surfaces permit you to paint permanent lines for courts and games, and a four-square court was added after the playground was surfaced. (See Figure 6.3.) We applaud the attempt to create new program opportunities, but balls roll under the swing set if the player fails to catch them because of the placement of the court. Since four-square is aimed at very young children (remember the motor development issue mentioned earlier), the chance of missing a catch is considerable. Younger children are also the least likely to be conscious of potential hazards, so the problem is compounded further.

As with the mistakes discussed in previous chapters, the real tragedy associated with the "playground problem" described above is simple error. It doesn't require a technical degree to question the wisdom of placing a swing set next to a barbed wire fence. You don't need twenty years of experience to understand why water won't drain from a concave surface. All you need in order to plan safe and environmentally sound areas is common sense, an open mind, a willingness to pay attention to detail, and some knowledge of a few facts pertinent to the type of area being considered. If you've never thought much about the basic considerations necessary for developing play spaces, the following section should provide you with a few starting points.

SOME BASIC CONSIDERATIONS

Types of Play Equipment and Their Inter-relationships. In an earlier chapter, we introduced the concept of relationship diagrams because area interrelationships must be considered relative to user circulation. While circulation is an important aspect of how play areas fit together, two other concerns need to be raised as well. First, play spaces should provide users, especially children, the opportunity to *create creativity*. Fantasy is an important element of play, and play areas can either encourage or discourage it, so pieces of play apparatus should relate to each other in a *fluid* rather than in a *static* sense. In other words, the positioning of play equipment should encourage *flow* throughout the play space. As with other types of areas,

play-space planning can benefit by input from potential users. Successful playgrounds have been developed by giving children scale models of play equipment and asking them to position the pieces as they would like to see them installed. Remember, however, if you ask children for design help they won't think of safety requirements.

A second consideration of equipment relationships should be balanced against the need for creativity. In play areas for children, *safety* is a primary concern, and to balance this need with convenience and creativity you need to consider the various *types* of play equipment. Generally speaking, there are three types available for children: *stationary; manipulated;* and *motion.*

Stationary play equipment includes apparatus and environmental features like climbers, horizontal ladders, balance beams, tunnels, hills, and pathways. With this type of play opportunity, the child interacts with the structure or equipment. The play experience doesn't require or rely on any motion of the apparatus. Playground design should encourage movement among stationary features. For example, a tunnel might "connect" a horizontal ladder with a hill, as in Figure 6.4. Since stationary equipment by itself is static, play movements depend on the child *and* on the way the pieces relate to one another. The primary safety consideration for stationary play apparatus is how the child will move on and through the environment.

Manipulated equipment, not surprisingly, means wagons, tricycles, bicycles, scooters, balls, toys, and the like. Because of the potential for vandalism and theft, most play areas will normally not provide manipulated equipment as such. This should not, however, imply that children don't need it since this type of play aids in developing fine motor skills. Sharing toys and similar manipulated equipment with other children may also help to generate a sense of cooperation and other social skills.

Planners developing a play area should compromise between offering opportunities for manipulative play and avoiding equipment damage or loss. This can be accomplished by designating spaces exclusively for manipulated equipment. The old playground standby, the sandbox, serves as an excellent example of this type of environment. Interestingly, many of the newer "creative play" developments seem to be built without sandboxes, raising a question about playground planning and design: have children passed an evolutionary turning point beyond which they no longer need the simple pleasures of traditional playgrounds? Perhaps, just perhaps, the proliferation of expensive, modern playgrounds could be partly a function of the need some park professionals have to "keep up with the Joneses." In other words, if our neighboring city builds a creative playground, will we be viewed as non-progressive if we don't follow suit? It is important to develop new and exciting play opportunities for children. However, remember that playgrounds are there for youngsters to enjoy; they aren't vehicles to enhance our professional reputations.

As is so often the case, the appropriate planning response to this question would seem to be a compromise. We don't know of any rules preventing you from mixing traditional and creative play apparatus in the same playground. You should provide opportunities for *all* types of play experiences, but for some types of manipulated equipment like tricycles, the best design is no design at all.

Motion equipment includes play apparatus which a child moves or rides on. Swings, merry-go-rounds, slides, teeter-totters, and spring-mounted balancing boards and animals are examples of this. In terms of safety considerations, these types of apparatus require the most conscientious planning for two reasons. First, the child and the equipment both may be in motion (with the

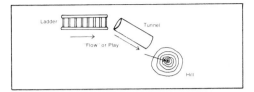

Figure 6.4

exception of slides), so the potential for injury increases. Second, the possibility exists for motion equipment to injure a child who does not interact with it. A "neutral zone" can solve these problems by defining the area devoted to motion equipment. Traffic patterns into the play area and among various pieces of motion equipment should be developed outside of these defined zones.

Manufacturers of play equipment should provide you with safety standards that tell you how much "neutral space" is required around each piece of equipment. Standards for neutral space, however, will not tell you how children move in and among apparatus. Traffic flow depends on how your design connects each piece of play apparatus to others and where your entry/exit points are, so this aspect must be considered in the planning stage of playground development. If, for example, you installed a swing set with a recommended amount of neutral space directly in front of the entrance to a playground, you'd be asking for an accident.

Before moving on to specific types of safety measures you can take when building playgrounds, consider one more general point about design. Integrating safety features into play facilities shouldn't be equated with building sterile environments. Learn to think of play areas as miniature adventure worlds. Rather than merely installing several pieces of play equipment, try to create a *complete experience* in which, as the saying goes, the whole is greater than the sum of its parts. Also build on a *scale* appropriate for the age group for whom you're planning. Use changes in elevation. Mix openings and enclosures. Suggest alternative routes (up and down as well as forward or sideways). Be creative. Let the child in you be the parent to your design.

Creating Play Environments. It's unfortunate to start a new section of this chapter on a pessimistic note, but the issue of playground surfacing materials refuses to go away. When trying to decide on an appropriate one, you need to consider safety, wearability, and cost. Natural turf is somewhat resilient, at least compared to asphalt, and is certainly inexpensive, but it doesn't hold up well under impact. In fact, it can become quite hard as extended use compacts it, so you need to consider alternatives.

When balancing safety, wearability, and cost factors, you should always put safety first, and there are some general guides to follow when you assess surfacing needs. As a rule of thumb, some type of safety surfacing should be used under apparatus where children are elevated to a height greater than their own, and areas receiving constant impact need durable surfaces. For example, the perimeter of merry-go-rounds, the bases of slides (front and rear), and the areas beneath swings need firm but cushioned surfaces. These kinds of areas should also provide good footing surfaces. Rubberized mats meet our criteria for safety and durability, but are extremely costly. Shredded tires are cheaper, but individual pieces tend to spread out, leaving piles in some places and exposed ground in others. Reinforced surfaces are durable and fairly cost-effective, but are too dangerous under elevated apparatus. If you're wondering what the point is, it's this: there is no good surfacing material, to our knowledge, capable of meeting *all* of the criteria outlined above. In our estimation sand surfacing or a fifty-fifty mixture of sand and sawdust may be the best compromise. We stress again the need to put safety first. If you can't afford to buy a

cushioned surface to put beneath a piece of equipment you know needs one, you may want to consider an alternative type of apparatus.

Putting aside the issue of surfacing material, there are other aspects of design and construction you should consider in the interest of creating safe play environments. Although it seems almost unnecessary to say, you should avoid sharp edges on and around play equipment. Most manufacturers of play apparatus will "design out" potentially sharp corners and surfaces before the equipment reaches the playground; however, you should always check before you buy. Some potential locations for sharp edges do not involve equipment, either, and these are the sites you should check during construction. If, for example, you build a railroad-tie border or use ties to create a series of steps, you should be sure the edges are beveled as in Figure 6.5. This is especially critical at the ends of ties where front, top, and side surfaces come together to form a point as in Figure 6.6. However, *all* exposed edges where two surfaces join should be beveled for maximum safety.

Other safety features can be designed into play areas as well. You can avoid bolt protrusions by countersinking as shown in Figure 6.7. Remember to *think ahead* in your design as well — nails hammered flush with a wooden surface may eventually work loose and become exposed, and should be countersunk also. If you use chains on swings or climbing equipment, make sure the links are fused to adjacent links rather than wrapped together. It may even be advisable to encase chains in metal tubes to avoid the possibility of pinching. Flat metal surfaces can grow extremely hot when exposed to sunlight, and fiberglass or other "soft" surfaces can circumvent this problem. Most importantly, remember that equipment wears out. Periodic checks for wear and tear, particularly at stress points, are a necessity.

The issue of building versus buying playground equipment is a difficult one. In many instances, it may be less costly to construct certain types of equipment than it is to purchase them. The problem with building apparatus in-house is mainly one of legal liability. Given the prevalence of lawsuits over playground injuries, it may be cheaper in the long run (and possibly safer for users as well) to buy equipment from a reputable manufacturer. Generally, play-equipment manufacturers do a good job with construction and design safety. This does not guarantee, however, that purchased equipment will always meet the play needs of children. Sometimes, it seems that the apparatus chosen for a playground depends more on the selling ability of the manufacturer's representative than on the needs of the park or the children.

Creating an enjoyable play experience is in part a function of the kinds of equipment you buy, but the primary ingredient for a successful playground is design, which should attend to several factors. The first consideration is not to plan in a vacuum. Think about uses of surrounding areas. The relationship (for circulation) between a picnic area and a playground shouldn't be the same as the connection between a playground and campsites. Campsites, for the sake of campers, need to be *screened* from adjacent uses. Picnickers may prefer to have a direct and easily accessible link between the playground and their table so they can keep an eye on their children.

We've discussed the use of the pod concept in relation to campsites in off-road vehicle areas and picnic sites. This also applies to playgrounds in two respects. First, a playground may be considered as one type of pod in a larger development that can relate to others in different ways, depending on their purpose. Second, you can view a playground as a *collection* of pods with different uses. One section within a playground might be devoted to gross motor skills; another for

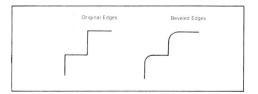

Figure 6.5

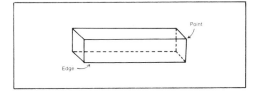

Figure 6.6

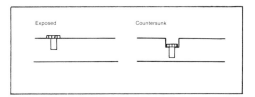

Figure 6.7

passive play; a third for cooperative and/or competitive play; another for individual use. The key is to *understand the needs of your users* and plan for them.

Children aren't the only "users" you need to think about when designing play areas. Particularly when you provide play equipment for younger ones, you should understand that adults may accompany them. If a play area is comfortable for adults, e.g., well-formed benches with shade as opposed to a torture rack placed in the sun, you may find more youngsters using the equipment. Including some types of adult-play facilities such as tennis courts may also increase the use of both the playground and adult area. Just remember to place them near enough together for parents to watch their children and play at the same time. It's difficult to generalize too much about support facilities for playgrounds since areas vary so widely with respect to type and location. Children should have access to drinking water and toilet facilities, but it's pointless to install these in a neighborhood tot lot where none of the users will be more than a block from home or a friend's house. As usual, common sense is an excellent guide.

One last aspect of playground design needs to be considered: challenge. While safety is always a primary concern, you should keep in mind that children need to be drawn to play areas and the equipment they contain. One excellent way to attract them is by challenging them with creative design and equipment. This is not the same as creating hazards. A challenge can come in the form of inviting a child to find different ways of moving through an area. Hills, tunnels, passageways, and climbing opportunities can all be used with imagination. Varied colors and forms can also stimulate vision and movement, alternating textures the tactile sense. Playgrounds should arouse as many of a child's senses as possible, in keeping with safe design. If you take an entirely business-like approach to designing play spaces, you may defeat the purpose of the play experience.

TYPES OF PLAY AREAS

Tot Lots. Play areas or tot lots for smaller children should be planned with both the capabilities and the limitations of this age group in mind. Young children need to develop basic motor skills like coordination, balance, and agility. In general, younger children also have shorter attention spans, so playgrounds using a variety of colors and equipment may be more successful in creating and maintaining play opportunities for them. By the time children are old

enough to visit a tot lot, they have begun to reach the stage in their development where they can establish *secondary relationships.* That is, they can supplement the relationships they have with their parents by interacting with other individuals, particularly those their own age. Tot lots can encourage this type of social development if you include some space and equipment encouraging *common use.* Sand boxes, tunnels, areas for four-square, and similar facilities present situations for these social encounters. While some "group spaces" should stimulate competitive play, others should stress cooperation as well.

Most of our discussion about safety in playgrounds to this point has focused on areas and equipment that children can use without undue risk of injury. It's an unfortunate commentary on our society, but there is another type of safety you need to consider in designing play areas also. Play spaces, especially those for young children, need to be *secure.* Since this isn't a text on social psychology, we won't enter into a discussion of deviant behavior except to point out it does exist. Areas to which children are attracted can also serve as magnets for disturbed individuals who may take advantage of the innocence and natural curiosity of children. Recreation professionals can't solve all the world's ills, but we can at least try to design and maintain safe areas by planning play spaces so they can be supervised. This may mean sacrificing some visual variety and landscaping, but as you've heard before, *form follows function,* and safety is a functional consideration.

Planning play areas with supervision in mind is not difficult — it just takes a little foresight. Benches for adults are helpful, and you should place these where the play area can be scanned. Remember that when you "site" benches (determine where to put them), you need to consider the view an adult will have *when seated* rather than when standing. If you're planning an area where safety may be a problem, it may also help to allot a buffer zone of open space around the perimeter of the playground. In other words, avoid having the play area border immediately, for example, on a tree line that might afford hiding places. In some instances, it may be safer to fence a play space and provide a single entry-exit point. By gating, you may decrease opportunities for vandalism as well. Lighting may also help in these respects.

Playgrounds for Older Children. As is the case with tot lots, playgrounds for older children need to be designed with the question "who's it for?" in mind. Obviously the scale of equipment should be larger to match the size of the children involved, but at times space limitations or cost constraints may preclude the opportunity to develop separate play areas for tots and older children. If this is the case, the principle of zoning use areas should be applied. A play area is no different from any other recreation space in zoning potential. If a single space is all you have at your disposal, it's appropriate to allocate some of the area for tots and another portion for older children. It may not be possible to physically "force" different age groups to stay in separate areas within a playground. However, it is quite feasible to use techniques of design psychology to encourage segregation by age. For example, the flow or circulation from the entrance to a play area for children of all ages can move older children and tots in separate directions.

Figure 6.8 demonstrates this concept. Just inside the entrance to a play area, you can place two pieces of play equipment, one of which is obviously designed — in terms of scale and function — for tots; let this apparatus "pull" younger children to it and "push" older kids away from it. Repeat this logic in the opposite direction with an apparatus for older children, perhaps a horizontal ladder with rungs too high for tots to reach. Each piece can then serve, in effect,

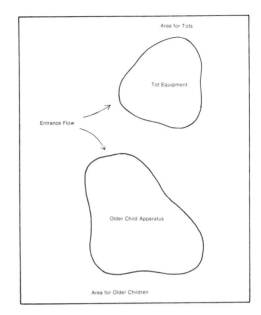

Figure 6.8

as a secondary entranceway to two separate areas of the playground.

Playgrounds, or the portions of them, devoted to older children can stress finer motor skills than areas designed for tots since older children are better coordinated and stronger. Safety features for injury prevention are still an overriding concern, but the need for challenge increases. It may in fact be safer to provide equipment that encourages this. Given the "recklessness of youth," children at times seek some risk in their play. If they take risks on equipment not designed for this type of behavior, they are more likely to injure themselves than if they try difficult maneuvers on equipment designed to accommodate some element of *perceived* danger.

As with tot lots, some portions of play areas for older children should be free of equipment and devoted to open play. These spaces can be larger than their counterparts in tot lots to accommodate increased size, strength, and speed. Playgrounds for older children should also include space for passive use — game areas and resting spots — but these quiet areas in particular should be visible from supervisory points. If you visit any playground containing secluded passive zones, we bet a month's salary (which really isn't much of a risk on our part) that you'll find cigarette butts, beer cans, or other signs of behavior we'd prefer to see avoided in playgrounds.

Although older children have longer attention spans, it may take more creativity on your part as a designer to attract and hold their interest in play equipment. With age comes sophistication, or at least the perception of it, so apparatus for older children may require more imaginative *options*. To some extent, manufacturers have addressed this problem for you in creative designs. It's still up to you, however, to buy the right equipment and then site individual pieces in such a way that encourages a *total* play experience.

You won't find a section in this chapter on playgrounds for children with disabilities. As mentioned in our discussion of trails for the handicapped in Chapter Three, we prefer to incorporate play opportunities for all children in all playgrounds. You should consult someone with training in therapeutic recreation before attempting barrier-free design in playgrounds, but don't make a point of isolating children with differing abilities. Common sense can help too. We once bought a "wheelchair sandbox" designed so children could pull their wheelchairs under an elevated, circular bin filled with sand. It worked fine until the first rain, at which point it became an excellent beach for birds. When we drilled holes in the bottom to drain the water, the sand ran out, so the sandbox is now in an equipment graveyard serving as a monument to our lack of foresight.

Play Areas For Adults. Our society seems to have the idea that play, in the traditional sense, is only for children. When recreation plans and designs consider the need for adult play space at all, the focus is generally on either competitive sports or passive areas for social experience, game tables and the like. Yet some play opportunities are as appropriate for adults as they are for children; it's simply a matter of designing to accommodate adult play. Children have wading pools; we don't typically encourage adults to use them, at least through design. Therefore adults — if they want to wade — either do so in fountains or, more likely, forego the experience. Children also have swings in parks, but adults are usually relegated to porch swings at home. An exception to this is Columbian Park in Lafayette, Indiana. Here, someone thought of adult play and built a number of porch-type swings suspended from A-frames. They get frequent use.

In general, we feel that play areas should encourage people of all ages and not exclude individuals just because they happen to be adults. Some types of areas, such as the field archery course we'll discuss under the "skills areas" below, can be designed primarily with adults in mind. Because of the need for safety, certain sites may not be appropriate for children to use without adults present; thus, you may want to consider adult recreation needs beyond simply providing them with a place to sit. In fact, designing play areas for children with adjacent adult-use options nearby may help encourage families to pursue play together.

Playcourts and Playfields. Most textbooks dealing with recreation planning and design include a section on playcourts and playfields — sites for tennis, basketball, softball, and the like. We'd like to address these issues as well, but from a slightly different perspective. Let's start with an example of an "un-mistake" — a departure from the typical approach to planning. Generally, planners develop designs for recreation areas by considering the "total area," looking at the entire resource base and trying to fit a variety of areas and facilities to it. This approach seems to make sense, but sometimes rules need to be broken.

Consider the case of Beech Lake Resort, a private family campground currently on the drawing board near Lexington, Tennessee. When this area was being planned, the developers had plenty of land — about seventy acres — but not much of it was flat. In fact, there was only one spot suitable for a ball field that wouldn't require extensive grading and leveling. The planning solution in this case was to "design the area in reverse." Instead of considering the entire area, the designer, in effect, said. "We've got one logical spot for a ball field, so let's assume it's going to go there and use that as the focal point of the plan." The approach worked. Instead of forcing a ball field on a spot to complement activities that didn't require flat land, the field was located first and the other uses added around it. To put it another way, the existing resource base *suggested* the only sensible approach to design, an offshoot of our principle of balancing resource needs with people needs. In retrospect, it sounds rather simplistic to say that it makes sense to put a ball field on flat ground. However, we've seen a lot of designers spend money unnecessarily trying to fit land to their plans rather than taking the reverse approach. This approach may be something of a departure from the traditional view of shaping the land to your needs, but it makes sense to us.

There are other instances when design of play courts and playfields should depart from the norm. Here, we're going to be really blasphemous and suggest that not all courts

and fields must conform to traditional standards and basic design principles. If you're charged with developing a softball complex where regulation or league play will occur, then by all means plan regulation fields. If, on the other hand, you're planning a softball field in a campground (and we'll try to convince you to do so in Chapter Eight), standards may not be quite so critical. In a campground setting, you might observe a pick-up softball game with players ranging in age from six to sixty. We've seen games with twenty-five players on the field for the same team at one time. These folks don't need ninety-foot baselines — they need a place to have fun. We once saw a softball diamond on a piece of land about one hundred feet too short with a five percent slope. The designer, probably not "trained" in recreation, put home plate at the low end of the field. Ground balls — hit uphill — didn't roll as far, the field worked, and the campers played. Sometimes, common sense is a better guide than a book on standards.

Play courts in some environments can depart from standards as well. If you build an asphalt basketball court a bit wider than suggested in the rule book, you may be able to put two sets of volleyball standards across it and create a second use. Adding a couple of area lights and an electrical outlet can transform it into a square dance surface. Or you can paint a four-square surface on one end of a play court and add another dimension. The point is this: in some types of recreation areas, a departure from basics and standards can encourage new uses by increasing the variety of activities available. "Skinning" an infield for baseball or softball can enhance league play, but it may detract from soccer or football in areas where the real need is for a multipurpose playfield.

One of the most frequent comments we hear from resource-oriented recreation staff is, "We'd like to provide play space, but we

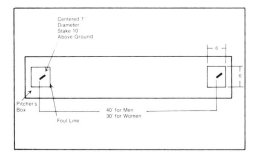

Figure 6.9

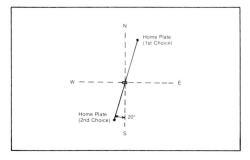

Figure 6.10

don't have the room or the money." Our response to this is "piffle!" In most parks and recreation areas, the resource necessary for play courts is already there in the form of the parking lot someone designed at double the capacity it ever receives. Putting a basketball standard at one end of a parking lot doesn't decrease the parking space, it just increases the opportunity for taking full advantage of your resources. Volleyball standards consisting of the old tires, some cement, and two posts can also be rolled onto a parking lot in no time. This kind of design doesn't require a large investment of funds, just a commitment to enhancing user experience and a little creativity.

In some instances there are "exceptions to our exceptions." If you provide horseshoe pits, it's a good idea to build to recommended size. Since these areas require a minimum amount of space (see Figure 6.9), there's no reason to miss the opportunity for regulation play by trying to save a few feet. If you're designing a field where baseball or softball will be played, you should consider orientation to sun. In general, regardless of the sport, the principle line of play should be perpendicular to the direction of the setting sun. The best choice for a line connecting home plate to the pitcher's mound is about twenty degrees east of south. (See Figure 6.10.) If the field is for multiple-use play, you may want to avoid a permanent home plate and pitcher's mound or rubber and instead "suggest" direction of play by placing a small backstop behind the point you intend for home plate.

If the site for a playfield or play court does require grading and leveling, you can increase playability by center-crowning the land base to aid drainage during wet periods. Similarly, opportunities for using the space can be increased — funds permitting — by providing area lighting. If you do add lighting to a play area, remember the following: first, be sure the play space is zoned so it won't cause conflicts as a result of night use. Don't, for example, site a lighted play court adjacent to a camping loop. (If you do, don't be surprised if campers complain about the "noisy kids" ruining the camping experience. The children get blamed, but *you* know who's really at fault.) Be sure posts used for mounting lights are far enough removed from the play space that they don't cause a safety hazard during the heat of play. Recessed posts for basketball backboards are a good idea, too.

As we've suggested before, design is a matter of *balance*. The need for light posts far enough away for safety has to be balanced with the need for adequate light for after-dark play. Lighting a play area for evening use, by the way, shouldn't stop there. People need to be able to find their way safely to and from these after-dark areas, and pathways connecting play spaces with other zones should be lighted. Yet another "balancing act" needs to be applied here, at least in campgrounds. Pedestrians need lighted walkways, but you want to avoid lighting the entire area so it looks like downtown Manhattan. One solution is to use waist-high pathside lights with downward-directed beams, as in Figure 6.11 (a planning version of having your cake and eating it too).

Shelter Buildings. The primary concern in designing shelter buildings is to make them *programmable.* Any construction crew worth their salt can, if you ask them, build a shelter for you. Your job as a planner is to serve as the link between program staff and the people responsible for the actual builders. Construction crews may know how to build and programmers may know how they want to use the shelter, but these two sets of knowns won't always fit together without a little attention to planning concerns. As a case in point, consider the portion of a TVA campground in Kentucky shown in Figure 6.12a.

The challenge for the planner here was one of potentially conflicting uses. Management and program staff decided there was a demand for an inexpensive, open-sided shelter building in the campground. From a zoning perspective, the logical location for the shelter was in the open field near the existing campfire theater. The problem concerned one *anticipated use.* The staff was familiar enough with the clientele in this campground to know that bluegrass music would be a popular program. Since this produces fairly high sound levels, and since the shelter was to be open-sided, a potential problem arose. Careless design and placement could preclude the opportunity to program the shelter and the campfire theater simultaneously.

The planners' solution (which adhered to the KISS principle) had two components.

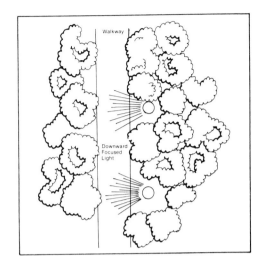

Figure 6.11

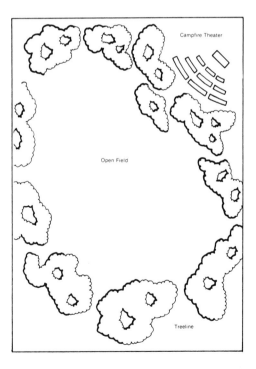

Figure 6.12a

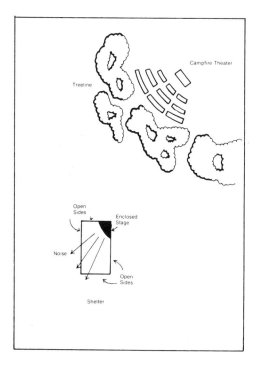

Figure 6.12b

First, since there was a dense stand of trees and understory vegetation surrounding the theater, they were able to use this screening and physical distance to help attenuate, or muffle, the noise from the shelter. The "shouting and walking" technique described in Chapter Three worked here — one person stood at the campfire theater and shouted while another walked across the open field. When the walker could no longer hear the shouts, the planner determined the site for the shelter. KISS. The second part of the solution was also simple. Program staff wanted the shelter to include a stage for the bluegrass band and other programs. The planners' response accommodated this need and reduced the noise problem further by orienting the stage as shown in Figure 6.12b. By placing the stage in the corner of the

shelter *nearest* the theater, the planner "pointed" the noise *away from* the theater. Enclosing the portions of the walls immediately behind the stage also contained sound.

The point is this: the shelter design itself was simple, but it took careful consideration and attention to detail on the part of the planner to make the zone *functional* from a programming standpoint. Shelter buildings don't need to be expensive, highly modernized facilities in order to work for you. They do, however, need to be incorporated, like other facilities, into the total design picture. Depending on intended uses, you can add other features like a barbecue pit or shuffleboard surfaces to encourage other program possibilities.

A shelter building can function as a focal point for programming. If zoning and other on-site conditions are favorable, it may be a good idea to locate it near the center of the program zone or near the point where most users will enter the program area. With these locations, an enclosed room at one end of the shelter can serve as an equipment-storage and check-out room for a variety of programs. We'll address this point further in Chapter Eight.

Skills Courses

Although the "how" of this book centers around planning, the real focus, the "why," is on programming of recreation areas. One of the most successful types of program we've seen in outdoor recreation areas, both in numbers of participants and enjoyment derived from activities, is skills enhancement. Think for a moment about what people *do* in developed recreation areas. Camping, fishing, hunting, bicycling, hiking, and swimming are among the most popular forms of outdoor recreation. While all of these activities may not lend themselves to successful skills

enhancement programs, several do —
particularly bicycling, bow hunting, and
fishing. The logic, or justification, for skills
programs is simple. People who use outdoor
recreation areas already have an interest in
the types of activities available in the out-of-
doors, so you may have a "built-in" audience
receptive to learning more about a given
activity. Further, a broad spectrum of recreational programs can both enhance the visitor's
experience *and* increase your use figures. (See
Chapter Eight.) Finally, the cost associated
with skills development programs can be
minimal.

Nothing in this world is easy, however.
Providing programs of *any* type requires
commitment, investment of time and energy,
creativity, enthusiasm, positive attitude, and
the right "mind set" from staff and administration. These tend to be lacking in many
public-resource management agencies, particularly on the state and federal levels, but no
one says that people like you can't be agents
for positive change if you put your mind to
it. We seem to be on our soapbox again, so
let's step down and consider some specific
types of skills development areas.

Bicycle Skills. Bike-skills courses provide a
good starting point for this discussion
because they can function effectively in
urban, suburban, or resource-based areas. It
seems that wherever children are, bikes will
be along as well. We once polled campers
exiting a developed campground in Kentucky
after a busy weekend and found that one out
of every five individuals (adults included) had
a bicycle with them. This figure may not
sound too impressive, but there were 2500
campers using the campground. Even we
could figure out the potential for programming here.

One of the biggest advantages of a bike-
skills course is the low cost involved. If you
have an existing hard surface like a multipurpose play court or parking lot, you can
superimpose a course by adding a few
painted lines and buying or borrowing a
small number of orange plastic highway
safety cones. If a suitable surface isn't
available, the potential for programming
associated with bicycle skills may help
provide justification for adding a multipurpose court to your area. And if a court-
type layout won't function effectively in your
setting, you can design a bike-skills zone like
a miniature golf course, with progressive
stations. Although this approach will
probably require a bit more land, it does
allow you to incorporate changes in elevation
into your course for added challenge if
rolling topography is available. Figure 6.13
shows one design of a bike-skills course.
Since this concept may be new to you, we've
included, in the following section, an outline
of how this particular course can be used.
The parenthetical numbers after each skills
test in the narrative correspond to the circled
numbers in Figure 6.13. (Our thanks go to
Kathy Howard Cuddebeck, who developed
this program a few years ago.)

Figure 6.14 shows a score sheet for the
course described above. You can use this
design "as is" or modify it to meet your
needs or creative urges. The only additional
comments we have are these: 1) stress the *fun*
aspect of the program along with the safety
and instructional elements of the activity —
don't make it too much like school, or your
audience will stay away in droves; 2) you
may increase participation and enhance
enjoyment by providing some type of *incen-
tive* with programs of this type. An inexpensive "certificate of completion" will find its
way to many a child's bedroom wall,
especially if it's signed (stamped signature) by
someone in authority, e.g., the director of
parks and the staff person or practicum
student conducting the program. If this
certificate has your agency or organization
name and logo on it, we're also talking
positive PR here.

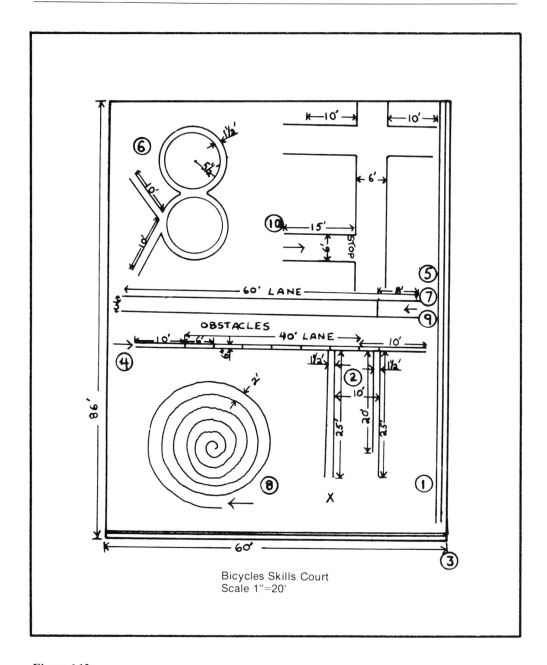

Bicycles Skills Court
Scale 1"=20'

Figure 6.13

BICYCLE SKILLS COURSE

I. OBJECTIVE: to test the riding skills, road knowledge and safety attitudes of cyclists of all ages while developing skills in bike handling and traffic awareness. This skills course is designed to teach cyclists the following:

A. How to recognize unsafe mechanical conditions in his/her bicycle;

B. The types of basic bicycle maneuvers, changes of speed and direction, obstacles, emergency stops, etc. that occur when cycling;

C. The handling characteristics, capabilities, and limitations of the rider's bike;

D. An awareness of the actions of other road users;

E. The self-confidence developed from knowledge and practice;

F. The rules of safe cycling.

II. PROGRAM

A. Introduction and instruction
  1. Explain objectives of the program
  2. Course instructions:
      a. With bicyclists lined up on the outside of the course, one leader will demonstrate each skill while another leader explains the rules and scoring procedure.
      b. Participants must go through each skill one at a time with a leader at each station.
  3. Mechanical inspection
      Leaders will help bicyclists inspect their bikes to score points for the following:
      a. Size — test seat for weight, level, tightness, frame size. Can the rider straddle the frame with both feet flat on the ground? (3)
      b. Frame — frame should be in line, bearings adjusted; no looseness or binding in rotation (3)
      c. Pedals — intact and tight; treads intact and tight (3)
      d. Handlebars — in line with wheel, tightly fitted; grips tight, ends plugged (3)
      e. Front Wheel — runs true, side to side, and round; check air, spokes, rim, tread (3)
      f. Rear Wheel — runs true and round; check air, spokes, rim, tire tread (3)
      g. Brakes (3)
      h. Chain — tension; 1/2" play (3)
      i. Lights and reflectors (3)
      j. Cleanliness — no rust, excessive build-up (3)
  4. Scoring — Total Possible Points (30)

III. SKILLS

A. Balance test (1)
Purpose: To test the rider's primary sense of balance while showing the rider how a slight movement of the wheel can reinstitute balance
1. Rider must coast 45' on a straight line not more than 6" wide with the right foot pushing the ground on the left side of the bicycle.
2. Rider must stand erect with both hands on the handlebars and not sitting on the saddle.
3. Rider is allowed a 20' starting and a 15' stopping distance.
4. Scoring — Total Possible Points (30)
   a. Completion of test (10)
   b. Followed all verbal instructions capably (Take from 1-9 points off if the rider followed some instructions and not others.) (10)
   c. Rider stays in balance without letting wheels touch or go over line (5)
   d. Rider in balance; both feet not on the ground at one time (5)

B. Short Radius Turn (2)
Purpose: To test the rider's ability to turn a bicycle around smoothly within a limited area such as a narrow street
1. Rider must travel 25' down a lane 1 1/2' wide and turn within a 10' wide area into another 1 1/2' wide lane, 25' long.
2. An obstacle is placed 4' away from the turning area as turning marker.
3. Scoring — Total Possible Points (35)
   a. Completion of test (10)
   b. Follows all verbal instructions (10)
   c. Touches neither foot to the ground (5)
   d. Touches neither borderline with wheel (5)
   e. Makes smooth turn with no excessive braking (5)

C. Riding a Straight Line (3)
Purpose: To establish the ability to ride in a straight unwavering line in the street adjacent to a road edge
1. Riders must travel down a 40' straight line 6" wide with a 15' start and finish, making the appropriate hand signal as they exit the lane.
2. Riders must stay within the lane using their right hand and then their left hand only for steering.
3. Scoring — Total Possible Points (45)
   a. Completion of test (10)
   b. Follows all verbal commands (10)
   c. Straight line and hand signal;
      touches neither foot to ground (3)
      touches neither borderline with wheel (5)
      makes correct hand signal smoothly (3)
   d. Straight line and right-hand steering;
      touches neither foot to ground (2)
      touches neither borderline with wheel (5)

  e. Straight line and left-hand steering;
   touches neither foot to ground (2)
   touches neither borderline with wheel (5)

D. Avoiding Obstacles (4)
 Purpose: To establish the ability to avoid objects in the riding path
 1. Rider must ride 40' within a 6" space flanked at 6' intervals on alternate sides with cans or flat stones.
 2. Rider is allowed a 10' starting and 8' stopping distance.
 3. Scoring — Total Possible Points (35)
  a. Completion of test (10)
  b. Follows all verbal commands (10)
  c. Touches neither foot to ground (5)
  d. Touches neither borderline with wheel (5)
  e. Touches none of the obstacles (5)

E. Emergency Stop (5)
 Purpose: To learn change in balance and capability of bicycle for stopping in an emergency while testing visual reactions in relation to momentum
 1. Rider must ride 60 feet, stopping within 10"-14" of finish line or obstacle such as a board.
 2. Leader will measure distance from front tip of the tire to the obstacle.
 3. Scoring — Total Possible Points (30)
  a. Completion of test (10)
  b. Follows all verbal directions (10)
  c. Stops within 10"-14" of the obstacle (10)
  d. Stops within 14"-18" of the obstacle (5)
  e. Stops within 18"-20" of the obstacle (3)
  f. Stops within 20"-22" of the obstacle (2)
  g. Stops within 22"-24" of the obstacle (1)

F. Figure Eight (6)
 Purpose: To test the rider's balance and sense of momentum as well as the changes in balance required by changes in direction (Frequently a cyclist must swerve, shift, and balance to avoid a pedestrian or obstacles in his path.)
 1. Riders must ride around a figure eight, keeping their front tire within a lane 1 1/2" wide circling in both directions.
 2. Scoring — Total Possible Points (45)
  a. Completion of test (10)
  b. Follows instructions (10)
  c. Completes test without touching a foot to the ground (Take 2 points off each time foot touches the ground.) (10)
  d. Completes test without letting front tire go over either line (Take 2 points off each time tire goes over line.) (10)
  e. Keeps control of bicycle at all times (5)

G. Weaving Around Obstacles (7)

Purpose: To test the rider's ability to change direction quickly which requires balance and judgment (A rider often hits an object in his path because he/she is watching it. This test teaches the rider to focus on the clear path rather than obstacles.)

1. Rider must ride 60' at normal speed between obstacles placed 6' apart, going to the right and left alternately.
2. Scoring — Total Possible Points (35)
   a. Completion of test (10)
   b. Follows instructions (10)
   c. Rider completes the course without touching a foot to the ground (Take 1-2 points off each time.) (5)
   d. Rider does not touch obstacles (Contestant is scored down 1-2 points each time a cone is touched.) (5)
   e. Rider completes the test without missing an obstacle or making a wrong turn (Take 1-2 points off each time.) (5)

H. Spiral (8)

Purpose: To determine the rider's ability to balance a bicycle while changing speed and operating brakes (Cyclists often have to change directions quickly and sharply to avoid an obstacle while controlling the bicycle to avoid skidding.)

1. Rider must begin at the wide circle, following the lane until the circle gets so small the rider can go no further. At this point the rider must turn his/her bicycle around and head out of the circle, keeping within the travel lane.
2. Riders must keep their front tire within the 2' riding lane.
3. Scoring — Total Possible Points (55)
   a. Completion of test (10)
   b. Follows instructions (10)
   c. Completes test without touching foot to ground (Take 2 points off each time.) (10)
   d. Completes test without letting front tire touch either boundary line (Take 2 points off each time.) (10)
   e. Rider completes spiral all the way into the center circle (10)
      — Rider stops within second circle (5)
      — Rider stops within third circle (3)
      — Rider stops within fourth circle (2)
   f. Rider keeps control of bicycle at all times (5)

I. Slow Speed (9)

Purpose: To have the rider demonstrate a skill in proper pedaling and braking motion at slow speeds, keeping the bicycle under control at all times (A bicyclist, while riding along a street in heavy traffic conditions, will need to pedal slowly and brake often.)

1. Riders must travel down a lane 3' wide and 60' long within 30 seconds or more.
2. Rider must keep feet parallel to the pavement while pedaling, using brakes when necessary.
3. Leaders must time each rider and record.
4. Scoring — Total Possible Points (45)
   a. Completion of test (10)
   b. Follows instructions (10)
   c. Rider keeps balls of feet on pedals and pedals are kept parallel to the ground (5)
   d. Rider completes test without touching either foot to ground (5)
   e. Rider stays within 3' boundary without touching wheels to the line (5)
   f. Rider completes test within 30 seconds or more (10)
      25-30 seconds time (5)
      20-25 seconds time (3)
      15-20 seconds time (2)
      10-15 seconds time (1)

J. Road Test (10)

Purpose: To establish control of the bicycle with one hand on the handlebars and demonstrate knowledge of traffic signals and the ability to turn rapidly at intersections (Other vehicles and pedestrians need to know in advance what a bicycle rider intends to do. It is very important that proper hand signals are used and that the rider has control of his/her bicycle at all times.)

1. Rider must come to a complete stop at the first intersection, using the stop signal. Turning left with left-hand signal, the rider approaches the leader, who signals for the bicyclist to turn right or left at the second intersection using the appropriate hand signal.
2. Rider must demonstrate all hand signals plainly before each movement.
3. Scoring — Total Possible Points (40)
   a. Completion of test (10)
   b. Follows all instructions (10)
   c. Rider makes all hand signals plainly before each movement (10)
   d. Rider keeps bicycle under control at all times (5)
   e. Rider touches neither wheel to line (5)

Figure 6.14

BICYCLE SKILLS SCORE SHEET

Rider _____ Number _____ Age _____ Score 430 _____

1. Inspection   30 points _____

   Size   3 _____
   Frame   3 _____
   Pedals   3 _____
   Handle Bars   3 _____
   Front Wheel   3 _____
   Rear Wheel   3 _____
   Brakes   3 _____
   Chain   3 _____
   Lights   3 _____
   Cleanliness   3 _____

2. Balance Test   30 points _____

   Test   10 _____
   Instructions   10 _____
   Wheels   5 _____
   Feet   5 _____

3. Short Radius Turn   35 points _____

   Test   10 _____
   Instructions   10 _____
   Feet   5 _____
   Wheels   5 _____
   Smoothness   5 _____

4. Straight Line   45 points _____

   Test   10 _____
   Instructions   10 _____

   Straight Line & Hand Signal

   Feet   3 _____
   Wheels   5 _____
   Hand Signal   3 _____

   Straight Line & Right Hand

   Feet   2 _____
   Wheels   5 _____

   Straight Line & Left Hand

   Feet   2 _____
   Wheels   5 _____

5. Obstacles   35 points _____

   Test   10 _____
   Instructions   10 _____
   Feet   5 _____
   Wheels   5 _____
   Obstacles   5 _____

6. Emergency Stop   30 points _____

   Test   10 _____
   Instructions   10 _____
   Stopped w/in 10"-14"   10 _____
   Stopped w/in 14"-18"   5 _____
   Stopped w/in 18"-20"   3 _____
   Stopped w/in 20"-22"   2 _____
   Stopped w/in 22"-24"   1 _____

7. Figure Eight   45 points _____

   Test   10 _____
   Instructions   10 _____
   Feet   10 _____
   Front Wheel   10 _____
   Control   5 _____

8. Weaving   35 points _____

   Test   10 _____
   Instructions   10 _____
   Feet   5 _____
   Obstacles   5 _____
   Correct Direction   5 _____

9. Spiral   55 points _____

   Test   10 _____
   Instructions   10 _____
   Feet   10 _____
   Front Wheel   10 _____
   Completes Spiral   10 _____
   Second Circle   5 _____
   Third Circle   3 _____
   Fourth Circle   2 _____
   Control   5 _____

10. Slow Speed   45 points _____

   Test   10 _____
   Instructions   10 _____
   Pedals   5 _____
   Feet   5 _____
   Wheels   5 _____
   30 seconds   10 _____
   25-30 sec.   5 _____
   20-25 sec.   3 _____
   15-20 sec.   2 _____
   10-15 sec.   1 _____

11. Road Test   40 points _____

   Test   10 _____
   Instructions   10 _____
   Hand Signals   10 _____
   Control   5 _____
   Wheels   5 _____

Archery Skills. The key question to consider when you think of designing an archery-skills course is *safety.* If there are any concerns about adequate space, relationship of the course to other use areas, or circulation adjacent to the course, it's better to avoid development altogether. If safety issues can be addressed, an archery-skills area can add a new dimension to your program for youths and adults alike. While it's possible to teach archery in a flat, open space, the program can be enhanced by designing a field archery course. You'll need, depending on topography, three to six acres for this approach. Figure 6.15 shows the basic components and target requirements for a fourteen-target field range. The archery skills program itself needs close supervision. However, with adequate regulations and safety requirements posted, such as not permitting broadhead hunting points, the course may be opened for independent target practice as well.

You need to consider a variety of factors, both for safety and programming, when designing a field-archery course. The target sequence should be laid out in a loop, with internal circulation on the *inside* and targets to the *outside* as in Figure 6.16. The order of the shooting lanes can vary, but for skill enhancement alternate among short, long, and intermediate distances with adjacent lanes. Target butts (arrow stops) should not be placed where paths or roads pass behind them at unsafe distances. The minimum distance between shooting lanes should be fifty feet, unless topography provides a barrier between lanes. For shorter lanes, allow fifteen degrees as a safety distance on either side of the target butt, and increase this arc to thirty degrees on longer lanes. Use topography to your advantage, but avoid

---

FIELD ARCHERY COURSE REQUIREMENTS

1. Practice targets
2. Garbage cans
3. Access road or path
4. 1 Entrance sign
5. 1 Regulations sign
6. 25-30 Boundary signs
7. Bulletin board

Requirements for each 14-target unit follow:

Distance	Target Size
20-25-30-35 feet	6″ (four-position target)
15 yards	12″
20 yards	12″
25 yards	12″
30 yards	12″
35-35-35-35 yards	18″ (four-position target)
40 yards	18″
45 yards	18″
45-40-35-30 yards	18″ (four-position target)
50 yards	18″
55 yards	24″
60 yards	24″
65 yards	24″
80-70-60-50 yards	24″ (four-position target)

Figure 6.15

placing targets on hilltops. The clearing width of a shooting lane should be eight feet minimum. The clearing height should be eight to ten feet, increasing for longer lanes to protect against arrow deflections from limbs. An area equal to one-quarter the shooting distance squared should be cleared in front of the target butt, with twice this space cleared behind the target.

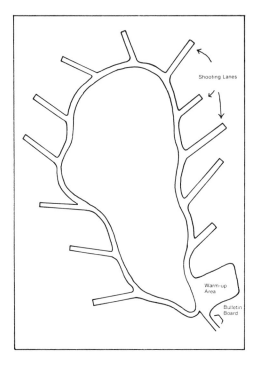

Figure 6.16

Targets themselves can consist of bales of straw or excelsior. On twenty-to-twenty-five-foot targets, two bales will suffice, while longer distances will require bales stacked three high. The bottom bale should rest on used tires to prevent moisture damage, and two wooden posts set behind the target will provide support. A sheet of fiber or rubber attached to the back of the bales will keep arrows from passing completely through. These attach to bales with heavy wire. Polyethylene plastic tied over the upper portion of the top bale will extend the life of the target by affording some protection from rain.

Shooting stations should have markers indicating target distances. Each station can be accompanied by a six-foot post for target numbers and a bow hanger. The National Field Archery Association, Redlands, California, can provide you with additional information on designing and building archery ranges.

Fishing Skills. Often, part of the challenge of recreation planning and design is in developing a type of area or facility you haven't tackled before. We wouldn't want you to miss such an opportunity, so instead of telling you how we might design a fishing-skills course (and program), we'll let you try it as this chapter's exercise. First, identify a suitable area — you'll have to have a program in mind, of course — and consider design needs. It would be nice to have a body of water to incorporate, but it really isn't necessary.

The challenge of this exercise is determining what skills to develop, and then designing an area for practice. We suggest you use a "course" approach similar to the bike-skills area. You might design your stations by starting with simple casts, and move on to more difficult ones, such as placing a plug under a barrier representing overhanging bush. Old tires make excellent targets, too. The key element in this exercise is to fit your design to the site you select *and* to the program you develop. Try this project with a team approach; let one team member be a planner/designer, another a programmer, a third an administrator. Each of these positions has different responsibilities, so each member of your team should act accordingly. How, for example, would you as a programmer justify the purchase of a number of fishing rods to your administrator? What would you as an administrator require in the way of design alternatives? What would you as a planner ask of your programmer in terms of providing design sideboards or guidelines? We could provide you with more questions to ask each other about fishing skills areas, but we'd prefer to let you flounder.

7

THE MANY CAMPGROUNDS
WE REALLY HAVE

INTRODUCTION

This chapter, as you'll see shortly, could have appropriately been called "The *mini-* campgrounds we really have." Since such a title might have implied that the discussion was going to focus on scale models of camp-grounds, however, "mini" doesn't appear in the chapter heading. Even so, the reference to smallness would have been a true — and unfortunate — one. As Chapter One suggested, recreation planners, managers, and designers need to *think* big, *plan* big, and *build* big. For no other type of facility is this guideline more important than campgrounds. While there are some exceptions, which we'll discuss below, in general campgrounds must be large for three important reasons: management, users, and environment.

Management. Several management-oriented concerns can be addressed by building large campgrounds, and perhaps the most impor-tant among these is *cost-effectiveness*. Private campgrounds need to make a profit. Public campgrounds should not have to be subsi-dized by tax dollars any more than necessary. In either case, more campsites mean more campers, and more campers mean a lower *per capita* expenditure for facilities. For example, let's assume we build an inexpensive shelter inside our campground for 15,000 dollars. If the area has thirty campsites, the per-site share of the shelter is five hundred dollars. If our campground has three hundred units, the per-site cost drops to fifty

dollars, *plus* we now have the opportunity to attract enough campers to justify the expense of building a shelter in the first place. Add in the cost of paved roads, play areas, toilet/ showers, trails, and other amenities and the rationale becomes evident.

A second advantage of larger campgrounds for managerial folks is *maintenance*. We've said this before, but it bears repeating. If you plan and build 250 campsites at a lake, you'll have to operate and maintain 250 campsites. You can spread these units out over ten or twelve areas and force garbage collectors, maintenance crews, management personnel, and program staff to drive up to several hundred miles to perform their tasks, *or* you can build one 250-unit campground and have all personnel work in one location. Again, the private sector must make a profit; the public sector, which usually charges smaller fees, should at least break even in terms of operations and maintenance. In other words, the cost of operation and maintenance should be offset by camper fees charged. In the public sector — depending on agency policy, fee structure, and development costs — this break-even strategy requires *at least two hundred campsites* per campground.

Another important size-related manage-ment concern is *control*. Most campgrounds tend to be "out in the boonies," particularly those developed by resource-oriented public agencies at the state and federal levels. If an agency can't afford or justify on-site manage-ment, the area will quite likely become a target for vandalism and camper harassment, a hangout for rowdies, or both. While this may sound rather harsh and perhaps opinionated, we've seen and experienced these phenomena too many times to ignore them. Small campgrounds make it difficult to justify on-site management. Often the presence of official personnel is enough to deter most depreciative behavior, but a ranger-type driving through a small, otherwise unprotected area twice an evening is not a meaningful substitute for on-site staff.

One more often ignored management advantage of large campgrounds is the potential for *programming*. In the first place, it's difficult to justify spending development dollars on program facilities for small areas. If your campground has a maximum capacity of sixty people (fifteen sites by four users per site), it's rather pointless to build a two-hundred-seat campfire theater. In the second place, programs require staff to run them. Even if you take a low-cost approach, such as using practicum students to develop and conduct programs, which we advocate, it just isn't worth the effort for a fifteen-unit campground. We wish campground size were the greatest impediment to provision of programs. Unfortunately this typically isn't the case, as you'll see below.

Users. If you've completed or are working to complete a degree in recreation, parks, or leisure studies, chances are good you'll have some background in programming. With this in mind, think about the campgrounds you've visited. If these are operated by a state Division of Natural Resources or state parks, you may have found a moderate number of programs. (Some state park systems have a strong interest in these; others have very little.) If you've visited campgrounds developed and maintained by federal agencies, we'll bet you haven't seen much, if any, *recreation* programming. Note the choice of words — the National Park Service and, to a lesser extent, a few other agencies have some natural and historical interpretive

programs, *but* rarely is the emphasis on recreation.

Chapter Eight will explore this problem in some depth, but for now consider this question: Where is it written that campgrounds shouldn't provide opportunities for *fun*? The Forest Service, Corps of Engineers, TVA, and other federal and state agencies provide recreation *facilities* but not *programs*. When asked why, they often respond that "it's not in our policy." This is a valid answer as far as it goes, but it's also somewhat analogous to saying that the turkey doesn't have stuffing in it because we didn't put it there. Those of us in the business of providing recreation opportunities have a professional obligation to maximize the experience of all users, campers included. Building large campgrounds provides the *opportunity* to provide programs, and doing so requires an *attitude favorable to* and an *interest in* recreation.

Moving to campground size, let's consider another user need — safety. There's no need to belabor the point about control that we made above, but you should consider it from the user's standpoint as well; campgrounds should be *protected environments* for the sake of the campers. If I set up camp and then spend the day fishing on your lake, I have the right to expect my untouched camping equipment to be waiting for me when I return. Yet in recreation journals you'll find a host of studies and reports dealing with theft, vandalism, and other negative behavior in campgrounds. Often these writings focus on the social and personal causes of such behavior, but more often than not most of them could be avoided if on-site supervision were provided. Again on-site supervision becomes easier to justify as campgrounds increase in size.

A final user-oriented consideration of campground size is *convenience*. Some individuals who participate in wilderness camping prefer to rough it. Others, those who prefer camping trailers and recreational vehicles (RV's), have different tastes in camping. Hot showers, indoor toilets, and other convenience-oriented facilities cost money, but if there weren't a demand for these types of amenities, there wouldn't be a multi-million dollar RV industry. What you think of this kind of camping experience *personally* shouldn't have any bearing on the kinds of camping opportunities you provide as a professional. In order to provide convenience facilities in family campgrounds, the areas you build must simply be large enough to justify the expense. Running utility lines to a twenty-unit campground is unprofessional, and so is building twenty-unit campgrounds in order to avoid providing the amenities RV campers want and deserve.

Environment. If it weren't such a major concern, we'd suggest that the development of small campgrounds was one of life's minor ironies. Consider campground size and design from this perspective: there exist few professions other than recreation and parks for which the environment is such a critical issue. We may build swimming pools, central-city playgrounds, and vest-pocket parks without too much concern for natural resources, but beyond these, the environment is our bread and butter. One of the basic purposes of parks is to offer a natural setting for people to escape the constraints of a highly technological society. Yet in many cases the very areas park professionals develop to provide access to the natural environment end up becoming so severely degraded that the benefit of the experience is lost.

One factor contributing to this degradation is our continuing tendency to build small areas. Because campgrounds are *impact-intensive,* from both vehicular and pedestrian standpoints, they are among the most likely areas to suffer environmental harm. Cost-effectiveness again enters the picture here since it costs money to reinforce areas of known impact. An environmentally protected

camp unit, depending on who is building it and local site conditions, can cost upwards of three thousand dollars. Add in the expense of maintaining the surrounding environment through design psychology and preventive maintenance, and the cost of ecologically safe small areas becomes prohibitive. Further, as we discussed in Chapter Two, the best way to *minimize* impact is to *localize* it. A 250-unit campground may not take up any less space than ten areas with twenty-five units each, but think about *access:* how many acres of land or miles of road does it take to provide the ingress/egress for one area versus ten? Think about *use patterns.* Will one well-designed, reinforced trail system radiating out from a large campground cause the same impact as unplanned "user-designed" pathways surrounding ten small areas? We could go on, but if you don't see our point by now, you're probably on your way to becoming either a bureaucrat or bankrupt, instead of a public servant or successful businessperson.

TYPES OF CAMPGROUNDS

Up to this point, it may sound as if all campgrounds should be the same, and the bigger the better, but neither of these statements is entirely accurate. Most of the topics we'll consider in the following sections are concerned with modernized, developed-site campgrounds because the types of facilities and amenities found here are the types desired by the *majority* of people who camp. Wilderness camping may have a more romantic appeal and receive more "press" in both the public and professional literature, but it is simply *not* the experience sought by most campers.

Perhaps the best way to consider the point is to think of camping as existing on a continuum. At one end are the "purists," who consider equipment purchases by comparing the relative weight of two camp stoves in ounces. At the other end is the family with three kids or the retired couple, who consider equipment purchases by comparing how many electrical outlets the RVs have and how close the four-burner stove is to the fold-down dining table. There's no point in trying to argue the relative merits of either camping preference. Professionally, we'll continue to stress the need to provide opportunities for all users, though if ninety percent of the people who camp want developed sites and convenience, it seems reasonable to channel ninety percent of your energy and resources into facilities for these folks. Similarly, we'll direct the bulk of our discussion toward these types of experiences.

Several hundred years ago, when we wrote the chapter on trails, we asked you to determine what makes a good one. We suggested that the answer depended on two more questions: What kind of a trail is it, and who's it for? The same logic applies to campgrounds. *Purpose* and *clientele* determine planning criteria and design considerations. For example, one way of distinguishing campgrounds, regardless of the level of development or the tastes of the campers, is the *intended length of stay*. Some campgrounds should be developed for *transient use*, like an area along a parkway or an interstate highway where users simply stay for the night and move on, as they would in a motel. These campgrounds need basic amenities like toilet/showers, sewage dumping stations, and high-density reinforced camp units. A heavy emphasis on "program support" facilities, such as a comprehensive trails system or sports fields, isn't necessary since most group-oriented recreation seems to occur when campers spend enough time in an area to "get to know their neighbors." This doesn't imply, however, that program opportunities should be ignored in transient campgrounds. Small group activity areas, e.g., horseshoe pits, beaches, and basketball

goals, can work to your advantage. Also, program areas where activities don't require knowing a lot of other users can function well in transient campgrounds. Campfire-theater programs, for example, may be successful even if you experience a seventy-five percent turnover in clientele each night.

If you do a good enough job of programming you may find your transient camp turning into a second general type of area: the *destination* camp. The destination camp is just what it sounds like, a place where users go to make camp and stay for a period of time — a weekend or a few days or weeks. Developed destination camps are really the focus of our discussion throughout the latter portions of this chapter, so we'll put these on hold temporarily. Let's turn our attention first to other types of campgrounds, beginning at the other end of our camping continuum with the wilderness experience.

The Backcountry Camp

Does the planner/designer really need to enter the picture when the camping experience is wilderness oriented? As it turns out, we can apply the transient/destination distinction to the wilderness experience as well as to the developed camp. Inadequate planning and management in the backcountry can cause problems you wouldn't believe unless you'd seen them.

Transient Backcountry Use: The Backpacking Experience. There tends to be a strong positive relationship between the desire for a wilderness experience and environmental fervor. Preservationists who want to "rough it" are often the most critical of developed-site, modern campgrounds. These individuals sometimes think that hot showers, flush toilets, and recreation programs belong only in the city, that they ruin the out-of-doors for others who "really know how to enjoy nature," and that they degrade the environment. Many — probably most — developed campgrounds you'll see *are* environmentally unsound. As we'll see later in this chapter, however, modernized camping facilities don't have to damage the environment, and, as we've said before, are in demand by the majority of folks who camp.

Ironically, some of the most environmentally degraded and aesthetically unappealing camping areas we've seen are those used and misused by backcountry enthusiasts. In Chapter One, we discussed the concept of *overuse,* suggesting that much of the blame for site impact is erroneously leveled at users when the real fault lies with planners, designers, and managers. This concept holds true in the backcountry as well as in developed areas. We aren't suggesting that environmentally conscious backpackers have an impact on the wilderness. We do propose, however, that a considerable amount of harm has been done. Hike the Appalachian Trail or equally popular backcountry in your area and look for damage. Pay particular attention to sites near overnight shelters where users tend to camp on a regular basis. You'll see compacted soils and erosion. You *won't* see much dead and rotting wood providing needed nutrients for the soil because of the popularity of campfires. While we don't blame backpackers for poor planning and mismanagement, we do get a bit miffed when these users harp on the damage caused by developed campgrounds and remain oblivious to their own impact.

There may be no universal solutions to damage caused by wilderness camping, but you may consider some partial ones. The major source of impact in the backcountry seems to us to be management's designation of *camping zones.* In many wilderness areas, camping is prohibited except in specified areas, often spaced about a day's hike apart. These areas tend to receive the bulk of the use and, of course, the impact. In some areas, particularly where free-flowing streams are scarce, camping zones and shelters are adjacent to springs or other water points.

Obviously we have a problem. Campers need to replenish their water supplies, and in bear country shelters are a good idea. Further, we've advocated the concept of localizing impact throughout this book. Now, it seems we're standing on shaky ground by suggesting that shelters be erected for users and that zoned areas harm the environment. However, if water points are plentiful and bears aren't a real concern, we suggest avoiding zones for camping. Most wilderness users are environmentally conscious, and if their overnight stays are spread along the length of a trail system, the impact they do have may tend to heal itself (particularly in the East and South) before it becomes a problem. If water points are limited, management may need to localize camping to a few designated sites. In these cases, we suggest reinforcing the spots designated for camping with wood chips or bark mulch to minimize impact, as in other areas where use is intensified by design.

One other impact problem associated with the backcountry experience is worth mentioning here. If shelters for campers are provided, they should *not* be accessible by vehicles other than those used by management and maintenance personnel. It may be necessary to provide vehicular access to shelters for periodic cleaning and repairs, but access roads should always be physically and administratively closed. A few people who hunt and ride off-road may misuse or vandalize shelters if they can reach them by vehicle, so shelter access roads need to be controlled. Damage to these facilities can be further minimized by placing them at least a mile into the interior from points where trails cross roadways.

Destination Backcountry Use: An Oft-missed Opportunity. When is backcountry camping *not* backcountry camping, at least not in the traditional sense? Too often, recreation

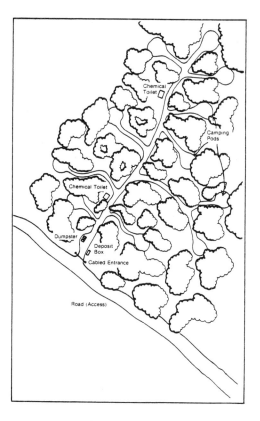

Figure 7.1

planners and managers seem to view camping as a *dichotomous* experience, a situation in which either all amenities and facilities are provided or all are absent. As we suggested earlier in this chapter, camping can be viewed as a continuum. Some users, for example, may want the isolation of a backcountry experience without the exertion of backpacking. With a little foresight and planning, it's possible to provide a facility for these individuals and add a new dimension to recreation opportunities. The backcountry destination camp fills this niche, and Figure 7.1 shows a potential layout for this type of area.

While the design for an area like this should be simple, you need to consider some aspects of development. The key to managing a functional backcountry camp is *administration*. One potential problem with this type of facility is misuse, allowing the site to become a "party spot" for local youth. Our recommendation is to use a *reservation system* in which camping parties call ahead to register for a campsite for a particular time period. Drop-in use can be accepted for sites not reserved in advance as long as there is some controlled use. The best system we've seen involves a locked cable at the entrance to the camp. When users enter the park or recreation area, they go to an administration office or staffed recreation site nearby, register, and pick up a key to the cable lock. They then drive to the backcountry camp, unlock the cable and lock it behind them. Upon departure, they deposit their key in a locked drop box at the cabled entry/exit point.

It isn't necessary to provide backcountry users with a host of amenities. One chemical toilet for every six to eight campsites and a trash dumpster near the entry/exit point are really the only facilities needed. If racoons aren't a problem, it may be a good idea to issue a few plastic trash bags to camping parties when they register, preventing users from having to take their garbage to the dumpster until they are ready to leave the area for the last time. (We assume one of the criteria for renting a site is complete site clean-up by users.) One aspect that users of this type of area will appreciate is privacy, probably the primary reason people are attracted to a backcountry camp. For a large acreage-to-site ratio, allow a ratio of twenty to twenty-five acres per campsite. This amount can be reduced somewhat if steep topography and dense vegetation separate sites psychologically.

The need for privacy raises another point. Land for recreation is at a premium, yet the use rate at backcountry camps will not be intensive and fees should be minimal. Since management's dilemma is to provide a wilderness experience without excessive capital expenditures, the number of camp units at a backcountry camp should be kept low, both to provide a sense of wilderness and to hold down development costs. The major potential expense for this type of facility is a road system, so we also suggest that as you review alternative sites you look for an area where roads are already in place. A defunct logging operation, or perhaps abandoned camps or summer-home sites, can provide you with ready-made road systems.

Another concern associated with back-country camps, as always, is impact. We recommend gravel roads into campsites to reduce vehicular impact at a cost less than paving. Once you decide the locations for the campsites, it's a good idea not to build a reinforced camping pad for this type of user. Rather, we suggest open, grassy sites for tents. Thin overstory vegetation somewhat to allow a good measure of sunlight to reach the ground. Campers will want the sun to dry their equipment after camping on natural ground, and grass can withstand more pedestrian impact if sunlight penetrates the tree canopy.

The backcountry camping experience — whether transient or destination — is a recreation activity planners and managers need to accommodate. To some extent the type of backcountry experience users desire is a function of geography. Transient use is probably more popular in the North, West, and East, while destination camps may receive more use if provided in the South and Midwest. As a professional, you should make an effort to determine what needs exist in your area and act accordingly, remembering that backcountry is only one type of camping experience people seek.

The Boatel

Water-based recreation areas, particularly those on lakes large enough for fishing and other motorized boats, are among the most popular outdoor areas available. In keeping with our concept of developing facilities for a broad spectrum of users, we think it's a good idea to consider the inclusion of "boatels," or boat-camping areas, in recreation management plans. The purpose of a boatel is to provide a camping opportunity for people who like to combine camping and boating but who don't need or want all the amenities associated with a developed campground (and the intensive use associated with these areas). It isn't necessary, or desirable, to develop a large number of boatels on a lake. Depending on the size of the lake and the amount of use, one to four boatels will probably suffice in most instances. Each should be small, with ten to fifteen campsites, and of relatively low density, with three to four campsites per acre. Since boatels are not built with wilderness users in mind, they should be constructed as developed facilities, with defined campsites and basic amenities including tables and grills. (See the section on camp-unit design later in this chapter.)

Figure 7.2 shows a schematic layout for a boatel. Basically, the area consists of a series of individual camp units, each with a water orientation. The distinguishing characteristic of a boatel is inherent in its name, and its design for use by campers who arrive in boats raises two points. First, provision of a boatel (or a wrangler's camp or an ORV area) speaks to your professional commitment to provide facilities for a diversity of users. It's quite easy to *avoid* becoming involved in this type of venture, but being a professional means you should avoid avoiding involvement. Second, developing a

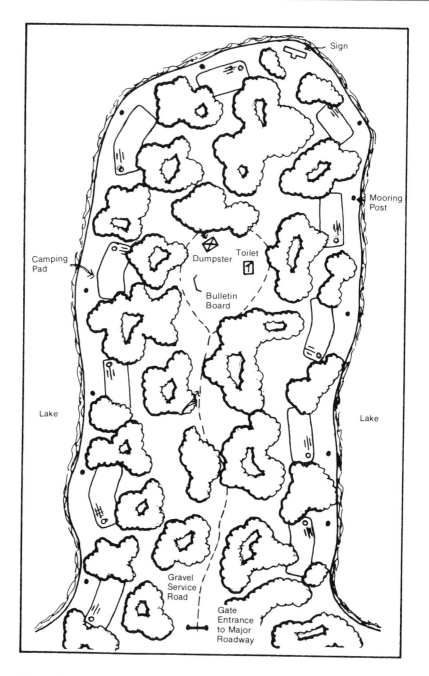

Figure 7.2

special-use facility doesn't guarantee that the area will be *used*. This is particularly true for boatels, which may go mostly unnoticed if you don't let folks know they exist. *Part of recreation management is marketing.* If you hide your light under the proverbial basket, your life may be somewhat easier, but we'll never accuse you of behaving professionally, either. Planning and developing facilities *must* be coupled with concerted efforts to help people find out about them.

How should you go about developing a boatel? Since, by definition, use must be limited to those who arrive by boat, internal circulation is not really a design factor. Road access should be provided, but confined by a cable-and-post system to administrative use only. Aspects of design you should consider include location, physical site characteristics, and ease of on-site development.

When possible boatels should be located near other existing facilities. By placing a boatel close to a developed campground or day-use area you can minimize operation costs like collecting garbage. You can also consider uses of adjacent stretches of water when choosing a location for a boatel. Heavily fished areas may attract people to a boatel if the two are located near each other, so it may be helpful to contact and work in cooperation with fisheries when considering alternative locations.

Since water access is the only real requirement, it's possible to develop boatels on a variety of resource bases. Some shorelines, however, are more favorable than others. In surveying potential locations, look for narrow peninsulas like the one depicted in Figure 7.2. These land forms allow you to maximize shoreline use because you get double the water frontage and space for a double row of camp units. You should also look for sites where the vertical difference between the lake pool and the maximum elevation of developable land is minimized, an academic way of telling you to avoid steep shorelines. This criterion needs to be balanced, though, with the need for sites adjacent to water deep enough for craft with deep drafts, such as sailboats.

Once you select an area for a boatel, consider how to lay out camp units. Along with the general guidelines provided in the section on camp unit design, there are a few other specific requirements. First, provide a *mooring post* for each campsite at the water's edge to allow users a convenient spot for tying their craft. Since boat campers may seek out a boatel partly because of the privacy afforded by the area, *screening* between camp units and *well-spaced sites* (150 to 200 feet between units) should also be design criteria. Place a sign that designates the area as a boatel (and names it) in a prominent spot facing the water. A dumpster, a chemical toilet, and perhaps a bulletin board for posting regulations and announcements about nearby recreation opportunities are the only additional facilities you need. It's a good idea to post a welcoming message here, too. This lets them know who you are as an agency *and* that you are pleased to have the opportunity to host them. After all, hosting and getting a bit of goodwill for it is what providing recreation facilities is all about.

Sporting Camps

Hunting and fishing are two of the more popular forms of outdoor recreation. Apparently these activities are *so* popular that some agencies, and not a few private concerns, seem to develop sporting camps to the exclusion of others. Which agencies? The Corps of Engineers, the Forest Service, the Tennessee Valley Authority, the U.S. Fish and Wildlife Service, the Bureau of Land Management, most state forests, and many state parks. What many of these agencies call family campgrounds sometimes even fit our description of the sporting camp: a small

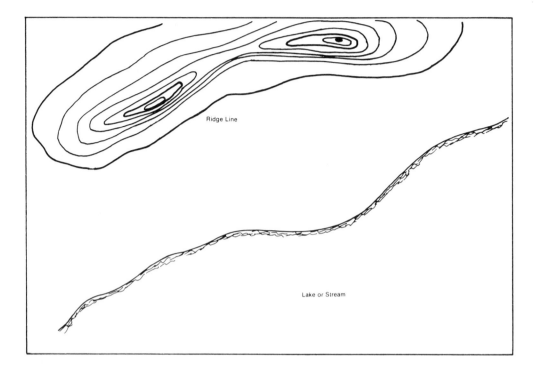

Ridge Line

Lake or Stream

Figure 7.3

fifteen- to thirty-unit camping area; no on-site management; minimal user protection; and maximum impact both locally, since sites are often not reinforced, and regionally, since a dozen or more of these areas are often developed on a given resource base.

In other words, we don't advocate building large, large numbers of small, small areas! Because of the environmental degradation often associated with these sites and the lack of cost-effectiveness in trying to manage and program them, small campgrounds *do not beckon family groups,* although you'll often find families camped here because they have no place else to go. Consider a typical camping family. Let's say we have two parents, a teen-ager, and a five-year-old. Too many times we've seen situations where Pop goes off to fish or hunt and everyone else is left at the campsite with nothing to do! We

say provide camping and other recreation areas for *all* people to enjoy the out-of-doors. Given the scenario described above, most folks probably enjoy about all of the out-of-doors they can stand in an hour or two.

Our basic reason for advocating large family-oriented developed campgrounds is that they provide a "base camp" for people who want to hunt, fish, and enjoy boating *plus activity alternatives* for people who don't! Again, this approach requires program provision that, unfortunately, many agencies have historically been unwilling to give. If we had written this book several decades ago, when public and private sectors were just beginning to provide camping facilities, our advice would have been "don't build 'em small!" Unfortunately, hindsight is usually better than foresight, and we now have a host of small campgrounds to deal with.

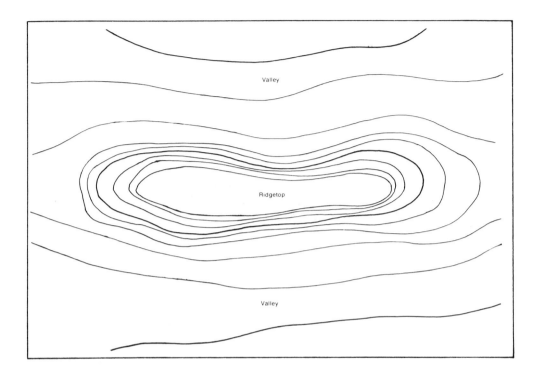

Figure 7.4

Many are in poor condition and most are difficult to manage and impossible to program. As a result, our advice is threefold. First, avoid repeating mistakes by adding new areas too small to maintain. Second, when possible, phase some small areas out of existence. If, for example, you find yourself responsible for ten areas with twenty units each, select one with potential for expansion. Over a period of several years, redesign it by adding units and support facilities gradually. (We'll tell you how to develop large areas below.) As the one area is expanded, gradually close the other small areas and work to attract users to the newly enlarged campground. This will, by the way, likely meet with considerable resistance from some users, and perhaps some of your own staff, but remember your responsibility to protect the environment.

Finally, for those small areas you simply can't close, practice *rehabilitation measures*. Develop new, impact-resistant campsites, realign roads when necessary, identify and reinforce areas of known impact, and try to cut your losses by managing these areas as effectively as you can.

We'll take up the topic of rehabilitation in greater depth in a later section of this chapter. For now, we'd like to move on to another topic. Regardless of the *size* of the campground (number of camp units) you're building or renovating, or the *purpose* of the area, you need to give careful consideration to the potential and limitations of the resource base with which you're working. As with trails, almost anyone with a roll of flagging tape can lay out a camping loop. The challenge, however, is to do it well, and this requires a *thoughtful* examination of the

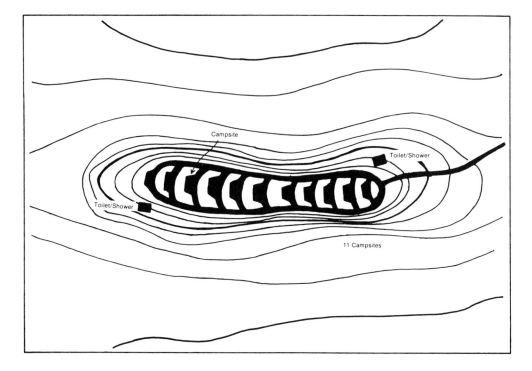

Campsite

Toilet/Shower

Toilet/Shower

11 Campsites

Figure 7.5

chosen site. This topic is so important, in fact, that we're going to devote the next section of this chapter to a discussion of camp-loop design and different types of resource bases.

CAMP LOOP LAYOUT

In the section on camp-unit design below, we'll consider how to develop individual campsites. First, however, let's discuss a slightly broader question: What's the best way to fit a *group* of camp units onto a specific piece of land? To address this question, you need to think about camp *loop* design. Since situation-specific aspects of individual areas like topography, soils, and vegetation should influence each design

differently, there is no single "right" solution to the problem of loop design. Fortunately there are a few guidelines to help you. Generally speaking, you may encounter two basic types of resource bases when planning a group of camp units: the narrow site and the broad, generous site. Since each of these calls for different approaches to design, let's consider each type separately, looking at both mistakes and functional solutions.

The Narrow Site

Often, you may be faced with a situation in which the piece of land you want to develop is long and narrow. Two examples of this situation are shown in Figures 7.3 and 7.4. The area in Figure 7.3 represents a site

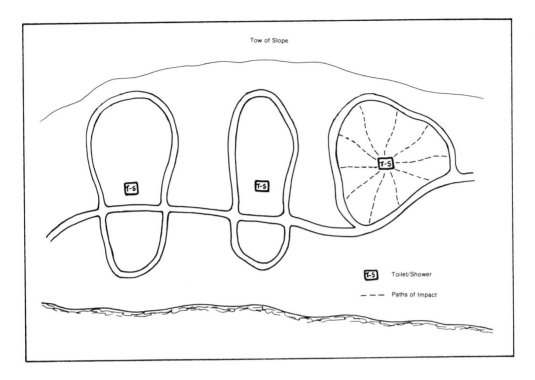

Figure 7.6

between the edge of a ridge and a lake or stream, and Figure 7.4 shows a similar potential development site along the top of a narrow ridge bordered by steeply sloping land on either side. Figure 7.5 illustrates our first "solution" to this design challenge. This approach seems to be popular with a number of recreation consultants we've met.* However, the basic problem with the design in Figure 7.5 is the amount of road involved. In the first place, roads are expensive. In the second place, they tend to gobble up what

*These folks can help you if they're good. When working with consultants, remember two things: first, a nicely packaged and presented design does *not* guarantee a good design since beauty is only skin deep; second, consultants don't have to *manage* the products of their designs — you do. Make sure you get what you need rather than what they tell you you need.

little space you have available on the narrow site. The solution here contains eleven campsites.

Now look at the design shown in Figure 7.6. Both the public and private sectors use this solution frequently, but from the manager's standpoint, it's poor practice to move traffic through one loop into another one, and from the user's perspective, this creates unsafe encounters of the pedestrian-vehicular kind. By the way, this design also shows one of the causes of what we've referred to as "over-use." Can you see it?*

*Putting the toilet/shower buildings in the center of the loops creates as many pathways to these buildings as there are camp units. How would you solve this?

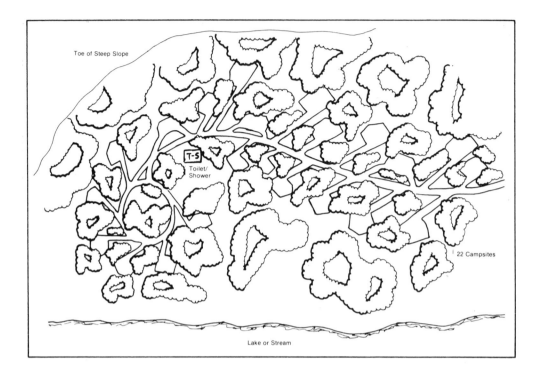

Toe of Steep Slope

T-S
Toilet/
Shower

22 Campsites

Lake or Stream

Figure 7.7

Figure 7.7 shows a functional solution to building camp units on a narrow site. Consider the following features. First, this design uses much less road access than either of the previous plans. By aligning the main road with the portion of the site at the top of the drawing, you can route traffic away from the shoreline, freeing this area for other uses. The camp units themselves are also laid out in an "up and back" sequence that utilizes both sides of the road and takes full advantage of the limited space available. You can fit twenty-two camp units here — double the number shown in Figure 7.5 with considerably less road access. Note, too, how the placement of the toilet/shower building, plus a little judicious screening, moves people psychologically to and from the building on the reinforced road surface. Thus, even with

the increase in camp units, you improve *use* and discourage *overuse*.

Let's look at the problem of developing camp loops on a narrow site to demonstrate another good design technique. Figure 7.8 shows a narrow site, in this case a peninsula of land jutting out into a lake. The challenge would *seem* to be how to provide access to the camp units we want to build here. Simple enough. Figure 7.9 shows one way of doing this. The road generally follows a single contour line, so we don't have to worry about elevation changes. In fact, this is how most folks would tackle such a design problem. Most folks, however, use *too much road* in their designs. Determining road locations first and *then* deciding where to put camp units is the way it's typically done, but it's also a mistake similar to letting

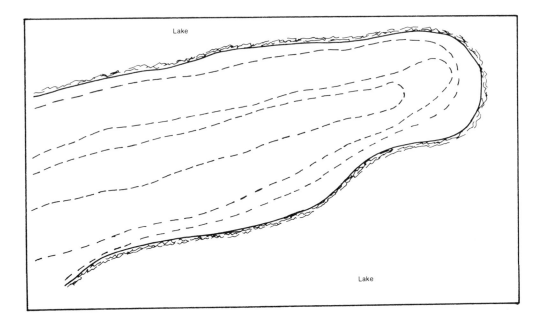

Figure 7.8

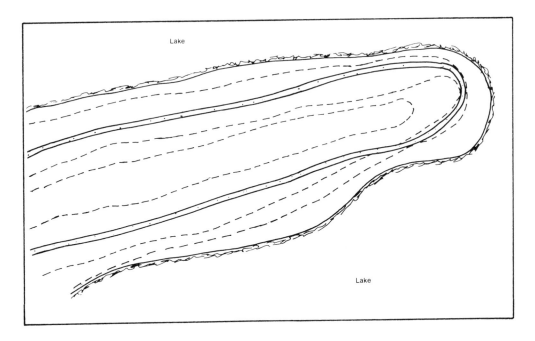

Figure 7.9

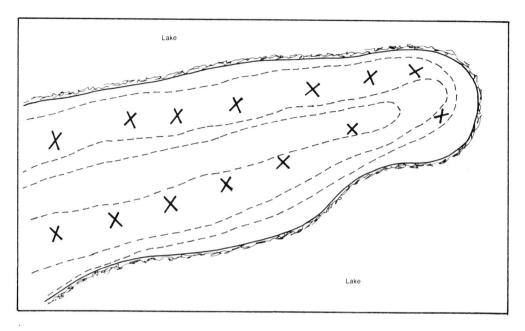

Figure 7.10

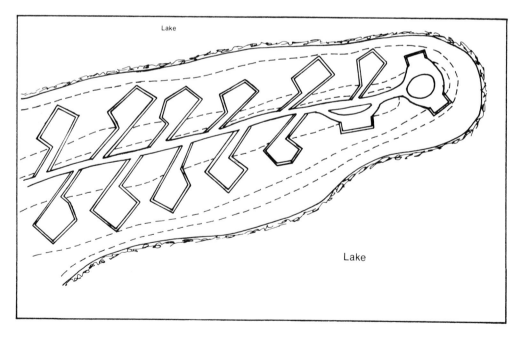

Figure 7.11

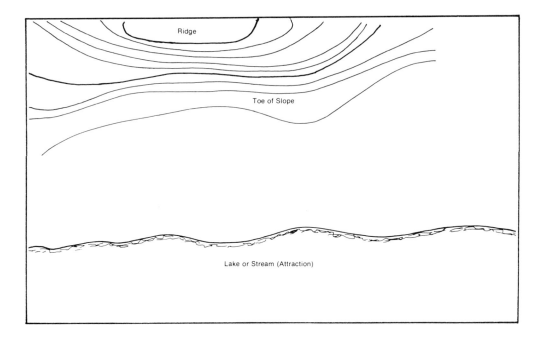

Figure 7.12

existing facilities dictate design to you, as we discussed in Chapter Two. Deciding on the road location first allows a support facility (the road) to dictate where camp units or other types of facilities can go.

Consider an alternative approach. Let's say we put on our field boots and tromp around the site for a couple of hours. After getting to know the area well enough to consider alternatives, we decide that the points indicated by X's on Figure 7.10 are the best locations for camp units. *Now* we have the information needed for an informed judgment about where to locate the loop road to reach these points. This process results in the design shown in Figure 7.11 because *the location of our camp units is the determining factor in the decision about where to align the center line of our road.*

Functionally, this design works; aesthetically, you could improve on the long

tangent shown. While the illustration shows how to develop a specific kind of facility on a specific resource base, the *point* has broader application: make sure your *primary facilities* dictate the location of *support facilities* rather than the other way around! Form indeed follows function here.

The Broad, Generous Site

On some occasions, you may be blessed with an ample land base for campsite development. The area might be the top of a wide ridge or a broad space between the edge of a ridge and a water attraction, as shown in Figure 7.12. Figure 7.13 illustrates one way of developing camp loops on this type of site, an approach the US Forest Service and a number of state-park systems have used frequently. One problem with this design is

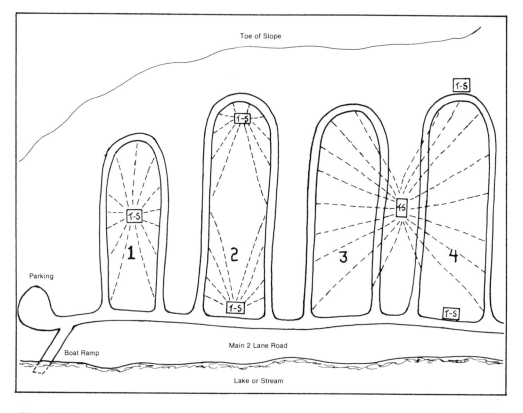

Toe of Slope

T-S

T-S

Parking

T-S

T-S

1

2

3

4

Boat Ramp

Main 2 Lane Road

Lake or Stream

Figure 7.13

the placement of the main road *between* the campers and the water attraction they use for recreation. Here again, we have a safety problem. Consider also situating the boat ramp beyond the camping area. If management wanted to keep the ramp open after closing the campground for the season, they would have to barricade *eight* entry/exit points to the camping area (two on each loop).

Further, the long, narrow, "finger-shaped" loops complicate placement of the toilet/shower buildings. In order to provide sanitary facilities for every loop, you could place them in the middle of each, as in loop #1, causing heavy pedestrian impact as discussed earlier. You could also place the

toilet/showers at the end of each loop, as in #2, necessitating twice the cost for two facilities and creating impact on the inside of the loop, or you could place the facilities between two loops (3 and 4), which again causes impact and inconveniences campers on the sides of the loops away from the toilet/shower.

Figure 7.14 shows another potential solution to the generous site — one used widely by the National Park Service and the private sector. But again the toilet/shower locations will contribute to environmental problems. Further, the site of these facilities is an inconvenience to campers. (Remember that this drawing represents an area perhaps a half mile or more in length in some larger

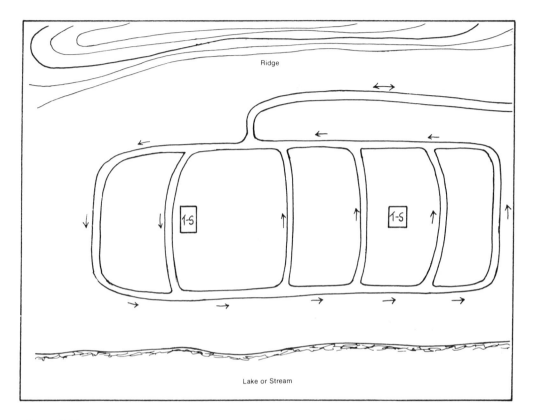

Figure 7.14

campgrounds.) Another design problem is the "fat" loops, wide spaces between parallel sections of road. We'll discuss appropriate loop dimensions shortly. For now, try and reason *why* fat loops would be a problem. (Hint: they waste space; but do you understand how?)

The traffic flow of this design can also create problems for visitors in terms of confusion. Remember, what you see in the drawing is not what confronts users on the ground. Entering this area in their vehicles, they find a series of *choices*. At several intersections, they have an option of moving left or right. A design is more "comfortable" for users if you as the planner make as many of these decisions for them as possible by

creating "pre-selected" traffic-flow options. That is, try to design intersections within camping areas so visitors can only go one way.

Figure 7.15 shows an even worse design for the generous site, yet, interestingly enough, both the public and private sectors use this sort of "plan" nationwide! The layout contains eight of the mistakes we've been discussing up to this point, and rather than going through them again, we'll let you find them. See the list below to check your answers.

Problems with Figure 7.15
— location of main road
— location of boat ramp

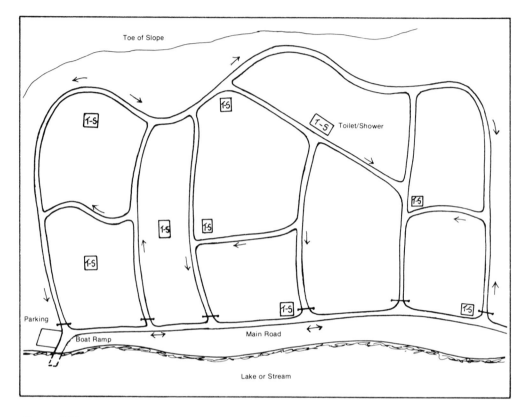

Figure 7.15

— number of toilet/showers
— number of gates and signs
— amount of road
— poor space utilization
— lost and confused campers!

Let's consider a better way of attacking the problem of camp loops on a broad generous site. Figure 7.16 shows one solution to the problem. What's better about this design? Several things. To begin with, the main road is located at the base, or "toe" of the slope, reducing the potential hazard of routing traffic between the campsites and the water attraction. Also, "keeping the road high," as this approach is called, moves the circulation pattern out of the area suitable for develop-

ment. Some designs we've seen start by locating the main road smack dab through the *middle* of the developable land — a real design error.

Consider also the potential for *managerial control* created by this design. The boat ramp is part of the development complex but away from the camping zone, so the manager has the options of closing the entire area (close Gate 1), opening only the boat ramp (close Gate 2), opening the campground while limiting camping to a smaller portion of the area during slow periods (close Gate 3), opening more of the area to camping as use increases (close Gate 4 or 5, depending on need), or opening the entire area. There are two advantages to this aspect

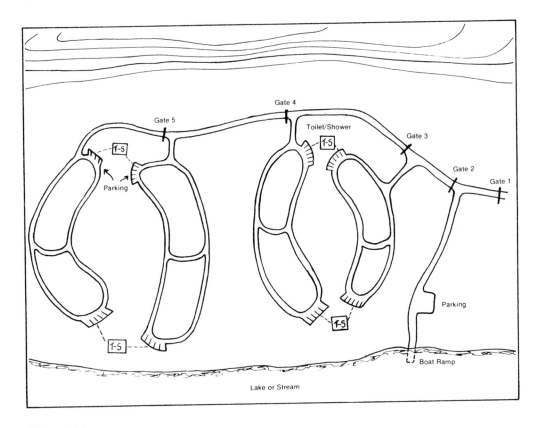

Figure 7.16

of the design. First, *management controls use.* The decision to open or close various portions of the area can be made on site as current conditions dictate. The "decision" to open or close portions of the area was *not* made by some far-off turkey designer during the planning stage. Second, *use controls management.* When use levels are higher than anticipated, this design can respond to the situation. If, at 11:00 am on Saturday, the loop nearest the boat ramp reaches capacity and campers are still arriving, it takes all of two minutes to meet demand by opening Gate 3 and closing Gate 4. If this second loop fills up at 4:00 pm . . . well, you get the picture.

Another problem this design addresses is environmental impact, or the "overuse" potential. Note how individual loops are "pointed" toward the toilet/showers at each end. With this orientation the most convenient way to approach these buildings is also the one which reduces impact most effectively. Rather than cutting across inter-site zones, the unprotected natural areas between units, the logical path from individual sites to the nearest sanitary facility is on the reinforced road surface. Even better, the placement of the toilet/showers keep them close enough to users to be convenient without spending all your capital dollars on more sanitary facilities than you really need. *Making your designs work for you* is a key design axiom!

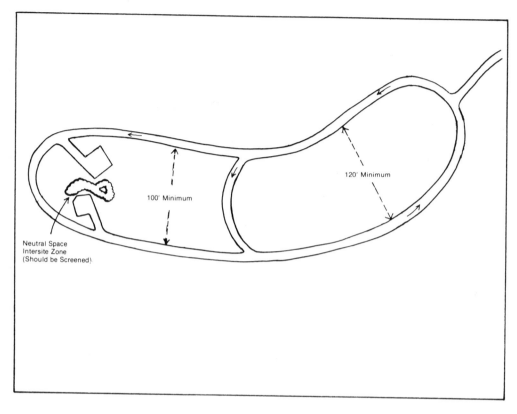

100' Minimum

120' Minimum

Neutral Space
Intersite Zone
(Should be Screened)

Figure 7.17

Basic Loop Design

Before we get any deeper into fitting together the various puzzle pieces in campground design, let's take a brief look at a few general techniques for developing loops. Specifically, how would you respond if we were to ask you, "How wide (or narrow) should loops be?" "How far apart should two loops be to meet user needs without wasting valuable land?" "How many (or few) camp units should you place on a single loop?" Answering these questions depends on a basic planning axiom: *know your users!* To make informed planning decisions, you need to understand what types of equipment recreationists use. While this holds true for

all types of areas, let's demonstrate the principle with camp-loop design.

Camp loops should be between a minimum of one hundred feet wide and a maximum of 120 feet wide. (See Figure 7.17.) To justify this, consider the size of most recreation vehicles. By law, camping trailers can be up to thirty-five feet in length; otherwise, they must be licensed as permanent house trailers. Add to this thirty-five feet the length of a tow vehicle, and you'll find you need between fifty and fifty-five feet to park a camper on a camp unit. Since you don't want folks bumping into users parked on the opposite side of a loop, you'll need a minimum of one hundred feet from a point on the *inside* to

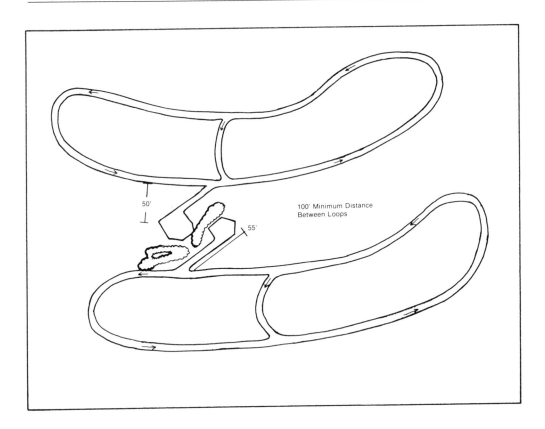

50'

100' Minimum Distance
Between Loops

55'

Figure 7.18

the point on the opposite *inside* of each loop. The answer is simple as long as you have the information about users' equipment you have to have. Conversely, you don't want to *waste* space by making loops too fat. If two thirty-five foot trailers with tow vehicles are parked opposite each other, the maximum space you'd need would be about one hundred feet. Add to this a neutral intersite zone or buffer between the backs of the two sites of about twenty feet, and the most width necessary for a loop would be about 120 feet. So why build it any wider?

This information about camping equipment can also provide you with the necessary "knowns" to decide how far apart two loops

should be. To accommodate the longest possible trailer and tow vehicle on a single site, you know you'll need about fifty-five feet. If you look at the schematic of the camp unit in Figure 7.18, you'll notice the site is not perpendicular to the loop road. Rather, the unit is angled at less than ninety degrees to allow users an easier approach when backing a long rig onto their site. This angle also keeps the back of the camp unit less than fifty-five feet from the edge of the loop on a straight line, although the unit itself is fifty-five feet long. You can also "stagger" camp units on adjacent loops as shown, and not *all* of your units need to be large enough to accommodate the maximum

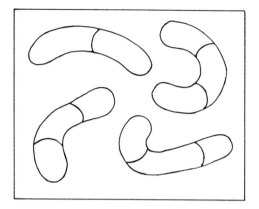

Figure 7.19

length trailer. (See the unit design discussion below.) Loops don't have to be quite as far apart as you might think. A good rule of thumb to prevent crowding while avoiding wasted space is to allow a minimum of one hundred feet between loops. Maximum distances will vary with terrain and vegetation for shading and screening, but in general loops should be as close together as possible, given the one hundred foot minimum.

If you look back at the several functional designs we've discussed up to this point, you'll find that all loops have one thing in common: a basic "peanut" or "hot dog" shape. There are several advantages to this configuration, most of which result from the flexibility it gives you. Peanut-shaped loops lend themselves to simple traffic patterns, easy control, efficient use of land, lessened amounts of roadway, and greater reduction in potential impact since the shapes can be manipulated to "point" at toilet/shower locations and other pedestrian destinations. Figure 7.19 shows a variety of ways in which you can sketch peanut loops.

The question of how many units to plan per loop is, in part, a function of capacities. If you build too few, you'll probably end up installing more toilet/showers than you need. But too many units per loop may lead to

congestion resulting from too much circulating traffic. There is no *exact* cut-off point for number of units per loop, but we've found that fifty is generally a good number. Since individual camp units *must* be designed in the field rather than on paper, it's hard to come up with exact numbers in advance. However, you need to provide engineers and architects with a fairly accurate "ballpark" figure so they can plan accordingly for utility lines, septic drainfield capacities, and the like. With practice, a planner should be able to estimate in advance, give or take three to five units, the number of campsites per loop.

Before moving on, we have one other "basic" comment about loops: *name them*. We've seen so many campgrounds with signs pointing to "Loop A" or "Camping Area 3" that they all blend together. Look for a *theme* for names, such as tree species occurring in your area, and identify loops accordingly. Campers will enjoy and remember "Dogwood Loop" or "Hickory Hollow" while letters or numbers — Loop A or Area 2 — leave us all cold!

Some Examples

Campground design requires attention to detail, a measure of creativity, a knowledge of users, an understanding of management, maintenance, and program requirements, and a smattering of information from a host of related fields from soils to sociology. Campground design is also not particularly difficult; *most* of the decisions you need to make regarding design can be arrived at by a combination of asking the right questions of the right people and plain old common sense. What is difficult about campground design is training yourself to see *potential* in the resource base rather than *limitations*. Let's look at a few examples of poorly designed campgrounds and practice the design concepts we've been talking about by developing a better alternative for each.

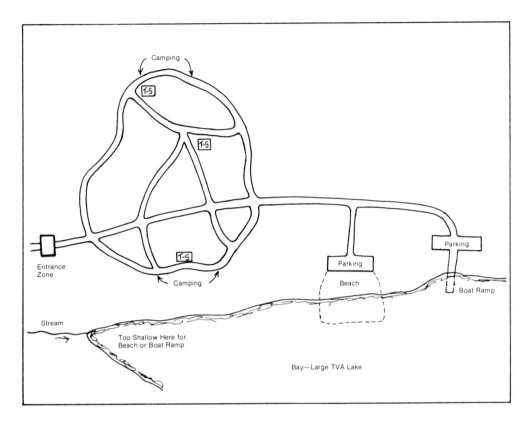

Figure 7.20

Figure 7.20 shows a typical combination day-use area and campground designed by the Tennessee Valley Authority.*

Let's list some of the problems with this area:

— The design moves day users (boaters and swimmers) through the camping zone, making the entire area difficult to manage.

*TVA has built dozens of areas like the one we've illustrated, when management obviously wasn't a serious design criterion. Some years after construction, TVA was forced to charge for camping use while most day-use facilities remained free. It doesn't take an exceptional I.Q. to understand the problems associated with allowing day users free access through charge-for-use campgrounds.

— The main road cuts through the center of the developable land, creating safety hazards and limiting the potential to design a functional area.
— The traffic pattern within the camping area is confusing for users.
— The layout of the camping zone and the location of sanitary facilities contribute to environmental impact.
— Pollutants from the parking lot above the beach will move downhill, directly into the beach zone.

These problems don't take a lot of expertise to see. The missing element in this design is anticipation of potential design challenges that include zoning the area for efficient

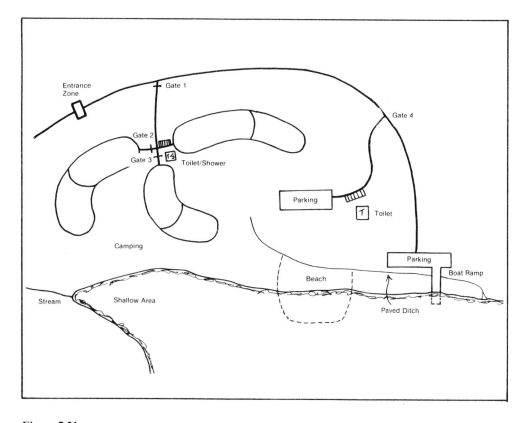

Figure 7.21

management, taking maximum advantage of the resource base, minimizing impact, and offering user convenience. Figure 7.21 shows an alternative design aimed at addressing these concerns and preventing the problems caused by the design in Figure 7.20. (In most instances, it's better to avoid mixing day use with overnight camping. This solution assumes that management policy wants them mixed.) Consider the following points.

— The main road has been kept high to avoid using up prime development land.
— The high main road makes it possible to separate day use traffic from the camping zone, increasing safety, camp control, and

fees paid via Gate 1. Gates 2 and 3 allow control of *where* users camp (not possible in Figure 7.20).
— Closing or opening Gate 4 allows management to decide when to use the beach zone.
— The paved ditch between the parking lots and the beach moves pollutants away from the beach zone.
— The camping loops are directed toward the toilet/shower building to reduce impact.

Other functional designs might be possible in this area, but this one begins to work *for* rather than *against* users, managers, and environment.

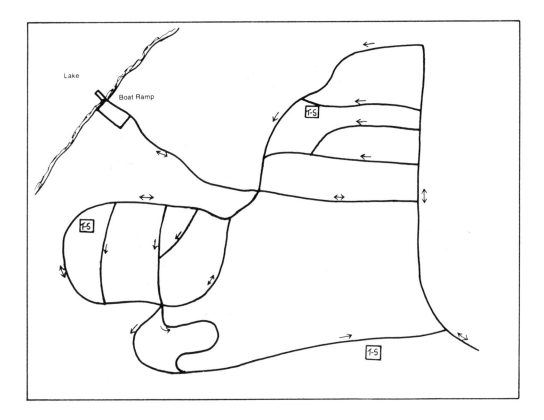

Figure 7.22

Figure 7.22 shows an existing private campground in the Midwest. The problems are basically the same: confusion and hazards for users; lack of control, increased maintenance costs, and wasted space for the manager; and degradation and loss of aesthetic appeal through overuse for the environment. In our experience we've found private campgrounds nationwide to be at least as poorly designed as those in the public sector. Figure 7.23 shows a better solution. Here again, the road to the boat ramp is a part of but apart from the camping zone, the potential for control is increased, confusion is reduced, and the two toilet/shower locations function better for the users

as well as decrease potential impact. Note that three sanitary facilities appeared in the initial "design;" note also how the peanut-shaped loops can be manipulated to aim all pedestrian use toward toilet/showers or other support facilities.

Figure 7.24 shows a state park campground in Mississippi designed by the Corps of Engineers. What mistakes do you see here? (You might begin with nine toilet/shower buildings.) We've suggested a solution to this problem at the end of the chapter. (See Figure 7.62.) Before you look at it, make a quick sketch of your own solution. Remember to maximize land use, minimize impact and user confusion, consider visitor

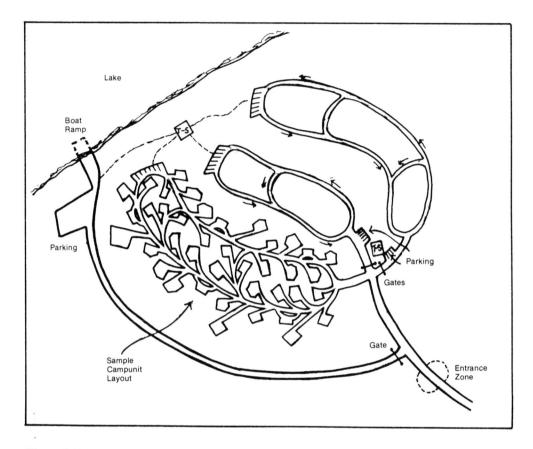

Figure 7.23

safety, and give management the power to make decisions *through your design.* The area is nearly flat, so topography didn't and shouldn't dictate design.

CAMP UNIT DESIGN

In the discussion of wrangler's camps in Chapter Five, we alluded briefly to a few planning considerations concerned with camp-unit design. Different types of campgrounds, because they attract specific kinds of users, require somewhat different approaches to laying out camp units. However, with the exception of backcountry or wilderness camps, some techniques *should be* common to camp-unit design regardless of the type of campground involved. Campsites in a family campground, due to management concerns and the amount of space and convenience users need and expect, probably require the most careful attention during field design. Thus in this section we'll focus on the types of considerations you need to think about when designing or rehabilitating camp units in a family environment.

The techniques discussed below should provide you with a general set of guidelines

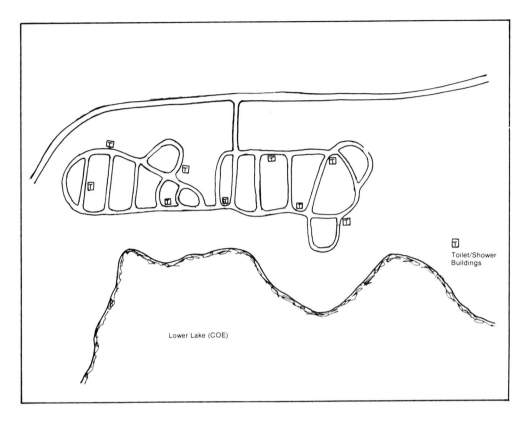

Toilet/Shower
Buildings

Lower Lake (COE)

Figure 7.24

for designing and building camp units in other types of areas as well. The differences in campsites for other types of facilities depend mainly on *size* and *level of development*. For example, units in sporting camps can generally be somewhat smaller than those discussed below because of the types of vehicles and camping equipment hunting-and-fishing parties normally use. Campsites in group areas may need to be somewhat larger since groups consisting of more members than a single family may want to use a particular site. Wrangler's camps, ORV, and other special-use facilities normally won't need the intensive, on-site management, diversified program opportunities, or number of camp units found in a large family campground. Thus campsites in these special-use areas may not need the unit numbering system, electrical outlets, or sewer and water hook-ups often found in family campgrounds. Basic layout and construction methods are generally the same for all developed (non-wilderness) campsites, and these techniques are what we'd like to discuss next.

There are probably as many solutions to the challenge of how to design functional camp units as there are plots of developable land. Before you begin to think about specific layouts for campsites, however, you need to keep two general considerations in mind. First, campsites, like other recreation facilities, should *never* be "paper designed." It's simply not possible to develop a good camp unit without the integral step of *field design*. Factors including shade, site aesthetics like scenic vistas, cuts and fills, location of units adjacent to the one you're designing, site type, size, and density, and understory vegetation must all be considered in final design and layout. These and other elements can be analyzed only after careful and frequent on-site inspections. Second, camp units, like the ball field at the private campground we discussed in Chapter Six, are best designed "in reverse." Instead of beginning the design or rehabilitation process by saying "let's put the entrance zone here, maintenance yard there, campsites here," and so on, begin by determining *what areas are most suitable for campsites*. Let shade, type of vegetation, terrain, and potential for access serve as your primary guides here. We'll discuss these topics in more detail shortly.

For now, allow your resource base to lead you to decisions about unit placement; let unit placement lead you to traffic flow patterns; traffic flow to camp-loop road alignment; loop road alignment to access to the camping zone. This may seem to be a backward approach to zoning. However, campsites (at least to users) are the focal points of campgrounds. From this perspective, we think it makes sense to locate units first and look at roads and other facilities as being supportive of the camping experience. We do suggest one exception to this approach. Can you guess what it is? To check your answer, turn to the *design* section of Chapter Eight.

Unit Site Selection

Once areas within the campground complex have been earmarked for camp units, on-site design can begin a cleared right-of-way for the loop or access road on which units are to be built. (Remember that traffic flow should have already been determined.) After clearing the right-of-way, the planner, or preferably design *team*, should go to the field and lay out individual units. Mark the perimeter of each unit with stakes and/or flagging tape, then clear the entire site, leaving all other understory vegetation between sites *intact* except for trees and brush within the marked perimeter. (See *Screening* below.) Once you've cleared these enclaves, stake the outline of each unit for construction, being particularly careful to indicate where corners of the campsite will fall.

Unit Size

The size of a camping unit depends largely on the physical characteristics of the selected site. When construction funds and heavy equipment are available, units can be built on marginal land since a bulldozer can level most any topography. However, heavy construction like extensive cuts and fills will cost more and, if not carefully undertaken, can create maintenance and environmental problems later on.

Assuming an adequate land base, a good unit size, excluding the parking spur, is an average of twenty-five by twenty-five feet or 625 square feet. Camp units don't have to be — in fact *shouldn't* be — all the same size and shape. Different angles, lengths, and widths will add variety to your design and better accommodate the different types of equipment and vehicles campers have. A site twenty-five by twenty-five feet is a good "benchmark" figure, because a unit this size should be large enough to contain the equipment used by an "average" camping family (the one with 1.8 children). Make some campsites larger than this for dual family use or for those groups with more children. Units smaller than 625 square feet are acceptable, and you may prefer them over the alternative of extensive cosmetic work on the land base.

In short, provide a *diversity* of unit sizes, shapes, and types. This approach allows you to accommodate different types and numbers of users, provide aesthetic appeal through variety, maximize the use of the resource base, and minimize the necessary amount of grading and other construction challenges.

Camp-unit Density

The USDA/Forest Service recreational manual strongly suggests that woodland areas contain no more than three camp units per acre. They are quite certain that this is what their campers want. At the same time, National Park campgrounds are likely to feature twelve to fifteen units per acre since their experts feel that this is what American campers want as a camping density. Unfortunately undefined campsites in these campgrounds look like environmental disaster areas. But this is another story!

Three units per acre in a Forest Service "family" campground means that campers are at least one hundred feet apart, that a resource is wasted, and that cost-per-unit for roads and sanitary facilities will be quite prohibitive. Further, most users prefer higher densities, although the National Park density may be a bit much for many (not most) users. Yet neither agency has designed loops of different densities to find out what users actually prefer!

Private-campground owners would likely tell us that the National Park Service density of twelve to fifteen units/acre is extremely low if you are at all concerned with land costs and profit margins. We've designed family campgrounds with densities from the ridiculous low of three units per acre to forty units per acre, which is much too high considering the types and sizes of American camping equipment. Experience tells us that campers have all sorts of preferences, and our advice is to design loops of different

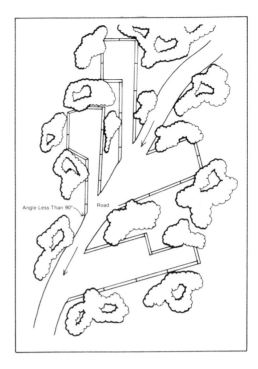

Figure 7.25

densities in your family campgrounds. The public-park camping unit density might range from a low of seven units per acre to a high of sixteen.

Types of Camp Units

You should design three functional types of camp units. These are the *back-in*, the *pull-through*, and the *pull-off*. Figure 7.25 shows several back-in units, the most space-efficient you can build because you can maximize the unit-per-acre density if this is a design goal. Further, roughly half the campers we've asked tell us they prefer back-in sites. Back-in units function well on *either side* of a camp-loop road as long as the angle of the

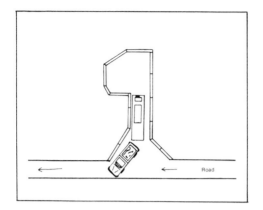

Figure 7.26

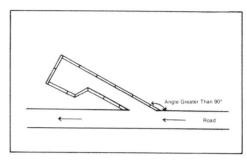

Figure 7.27

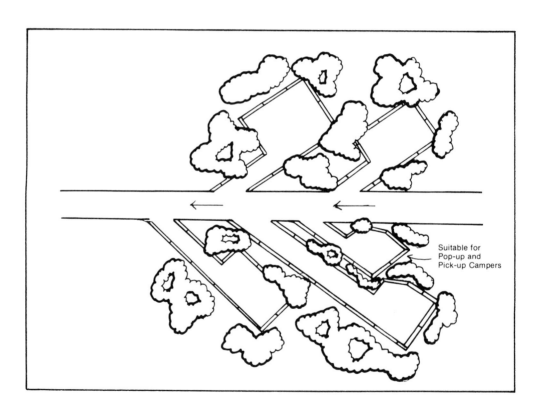

Figure 7.28

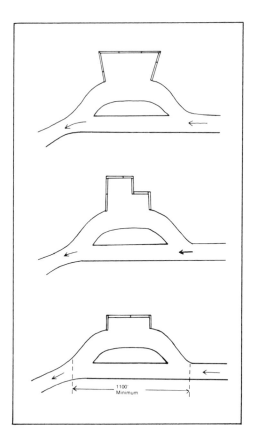

Figure 7.29

spur-to-road juncture is not greater than ninety degrees. (See Figure 7.25.) Occasionally, the lay of the land may dictate a ninety-degree spur-to-road juncture. You can make a perpendicular back-in unit usable if you flare the spur wide where it meets the road. (See Figure 7.26.)

Any unit where the spur-to-road juncture is greater than ninety degrees is a *pull-in* campsite. (See Figure 7.27.) *Do not build pull-in campsites!* If a camping group has a non-motorized RV like a trailer or fifth-wheeler, they must pull into these sites with their tow vehicle in front of their camping rig. Then they can't leave the site without

taking their camper with them. Manufacturers try to make camping trailers as convenient as possible, but they do require some effort to set up for camp use, like using a leveling jack to make sure the trailer rests level. Pull-in sites require users to break camp and take their trailer with them every time they leave the unit. Then they must re-level their rig upon returning. If a camping family intends to use your area as a "base camp" for a two-week sightseeing vacation, how favorably do you think they will feel toward you if they have to tow their camper with them everywhere because you built a pull-in campsite? Chances are, they'll simply drive the wrong way on your one-way roads so they can back into the unit, creating less-than-safe conditions and management headaches.

On a back-in unit, the spur should be a minimum of ten or twelve feet wide, though lengths can vary considerably. Not all sites you select for camp units will have enough depth for you to provide fifty-five-foot spurs without extensive grading, cutting, or filling. There are two solutions to this problem. One is to not worry about it. Not all users have thirty-five-foot trailers, and as a result you can build some camp units with shorter spurs. Those who come in compact cars and camp in tents may need only eighteen to twenty feet of spur for a functional site. Beyond this minimum, there is no set criterion for spur length. Some site topography may call for one hundred to 120 feet of spur to reach a good unit location, although more than this may cost more than it's worth. Spurs of different lengths also allow you to "stagger" adjacent camp units, letting you take maximum advantage of the land you have available. Compare the two designs in Figure 7.28. On the top portion of the drawing, we have two adjacent units with similar spur lengths. On the bottom portion, three units take the same amount of road space because the spur lengths are varied. Staggered spur lengths also help prevent

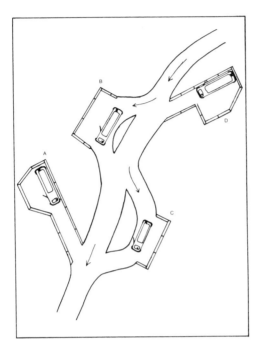

Figure 7.30

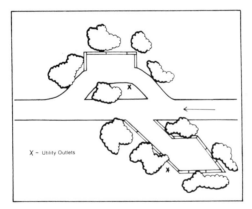

X – Utility Outlets

Figure 7.31

visual monotony among camp units. We call this an "up and back" principle of unit layout.

A second solution to narrow plots is to build some sites other than back-ins. One is the *pull-through.* (See Figure 7.29.) The pull-through unit requires more *linear,* or roadside, space than the back-in, but not as much *depth.* Also, since the pull-through doesn't require the user to enter the site in reverse gear, this may be the best type for inexperienced campers to negotiate. Pull-through sites function well on either side of a two-way road, but *only on the right-hand side of a one-way road.* To understand the logic behind this design requirement, you need to know a bit about camping rigs.

With the exception of pick-up camper shells, which have rear exits, camping vehicles like trailers and motor homes have doors on the *right-hand* or *passenger side* of the vehicle. Therefore one goal of camp-unit design is to place the living space to the *right* of the parking spur as you face the direction of traffic flow. This applies to *all* camp units, regardless of type. Consider the four camp-sites in Figure 7.30. Sites A and B are functional for users because the doors to camping rigs parked on these sites open directly onto the living space. Units C and D, however, because of their design, *force* users to walk around their camping vehicles to reach their living space. This design mistake — one we see in National Parks and *everywhere* else — won't prevent campers from using the site, but why inconvenience folks when it's so easy to design the site with the user in mind? Why, indeed, if you are a real professional?

As long as we're talking about user convenience, let's consider the correct location for utility hook-ups. On camping vehicles, the connections for electrical, water, and sewer hook-ups are on the rear of the *left-hand* or *driver's side* of the vehicle. This means that utility outlets, if you provide them, must be to the *left* of the parking spur as you face the direction of traffic flow. Figure 7.31 illustrates appropriate locations for utility outlets.

The third type of functional camp unit you can design is the *pull-off*. (See Figure 7.32.) Essentially "abbreviated" versions of the pull-through site, pull-offs are suited for locations where you don't have enough depth for a back-in and too little linear space for a pull-through. Again like the pull-through, the pull-off unit will function on either side of a two-way road but *only* on the right hand side of a one way road. If the pull-off unit is on a loop where utility hook-ups are provided, placing them to the left of the spur may increase the potential for collisions with utility outlet posts.* Thus you should place utility hook-ups as Figure 7.32 shows.

One important factor in designing camp units is *variety*. A long series of identical units may give the user a feeling of being in a "rubber stamp" campground. "Cookie-cutter" designs create monotony and prevent users from selecting the type they prefer. This does not imply that a particular type of unit should be forced onto a piece of land where it won't fit without extensive cosmetic work. Rather, unit types should be as varied as the land base permits. Altering the shapes and sizes of units of the same type, e.g., the back-in, can help reduce monotony as well, a practice which also helps you accommodate

*In order to minimize costs and allow managers to charge fees based on the types of amenities provided (electrical, water, sewer, or a combination of these), all units on a given loop should offer the same kinds of services; that is, one loop may have no utilities, while another has electricity only, another electricity and water, and so on. Separating loops by type of utilities provided is a good design technique. Conversely, segregating different types of *users*, tent versus trailer campers, for example, is *not* a good idea. Tent and trailer campers in developed family campgrounds don't seem to mind camping together, and trying to separate them into different zones can create a host of management problems.

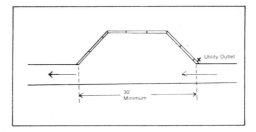

Figure 7.32

different types and sizes of camping rigs. (See Figure 7.33.) Another means of providing variety and accommodating a broader spectrum of needs is to build some camp-sites as double units. (See Figure 7.34.) These sites meet the requirements of two families who wish to camp together, although they can also function as independent units for separate groups. We've found that over thirty percent of campers in some family camp-grounds come as two families or as large groups of friends who want to camp together. Rules that require only one family per site, sites that are too small for two families, sites that are one hundred feet apart, or campgrounds that offer no double sites mean your facility isn't designed for all users!

Since you should now know a bit about camp-unit design, let's test your skills. Figure 7.35 shows a series of campsites on a one-way road, as indicated. Which ones are good? Which aren't? Why? To check your answers, see Table 7.1. No cheating, now. It may interest you to know that most of the rascals historically responsible for camp-ground design can't pass this test!

Unit Construction

Factors such as standards set by your agency or organization and availability of materials

Table 7.1		
Site #	Type	Remarks
1.	Back-in	Excellent, preferred by a majority of campers.
2.	Pull-through	Excellent, also high camper preference; however, takes up considerable space *if* it's designed right!
3.	Back-in	With rare exceptions the back-in, its living space located on the *right* side of the spur, is the *only* usable unit to place on the left side of a one-way road!
4.	Pull-off	Not a preferred unit, but it does function well.
5.	Back-in	Curved to the left to allow proper location of living space. A good camp unit. Owners of large trailers can easily back in on a *left* turning curve.
6.	Pull-through	One of the exceptions noted in #3. Living space is properly located for trailer doors which open on the *right*.
7.	Not Sure?!	"Designers" meant this to be a back-in, but they didn't widen the throat of the spur. (See dashed line.) This has to be done if you design units which are ninety degrees off the road.
8.	Pull-in	No! If your "designers" or planners locate a pull-in spur on their plan or field-locate it on site, shoot them!
9.	Back-in	This is used by many so-called designers, but the living space is located on the wrong side of the spur.
10.	Pull-through	Used by NPS, US Corps of Engineers, and others even though it functions poorly for the user. Trailer doors open on the right *away* from the living space.

If you said units 1 through 6 were O.K., and units 7 through 10 were not, you know far more about campsite location than *most* park designers!

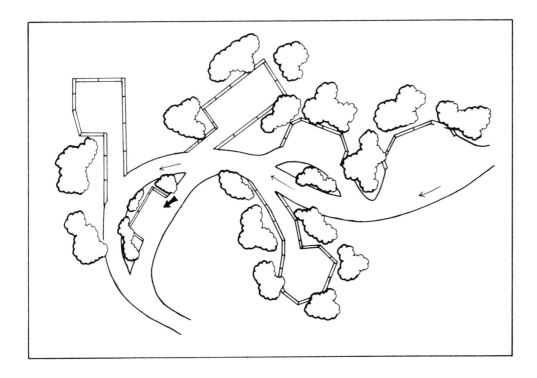

Figure 7.33

will dictate, to some extent, what you can and can't do with camp-unit construction. There are, however, some general guidelines to follow. If the site selected for a specific camp unit has minimal topographic problems, like a minor drainage difficulty or a depression, begin by grading the site fairly level. If these or similar problems don't exist, construction can start with the second step: place a layer of creek or river gravel (or clay) over the site to serve as a base for the unit. The length and width of this base should include space for the living and parking area of the unit plus an additional two to three feet of outsloped perimeter for use in final dressing. (See Figure 7.36.) The depth of this gravel base depends on the lay of the land. If you need fill to level a sloping section, portions of the base may be several feet deep. On level

ground, six inches generally is adequate. In some areas, the cost of river gravel may be prohibitive, but if this occurs you can substitute earth fill, particularly clay, for much of the gravel. However, the top three to four inches of fill should still be gravel to retard the settling caused by vehicle weight.

Next you'll place the unit surface on top of the base, but this final job requires two grades of limestone rock *and* a bit of a digression. Let's start with the digression. We've shown developed-site camp units to literally thousands of students and professionals. When we do so, comments such as, "I wouldn't camp on *rock* if you paid me" are thrown about frequently, mostly from young, environmentally oriented audiences and their professors. These, however, aren't the types of folks for whom developed site

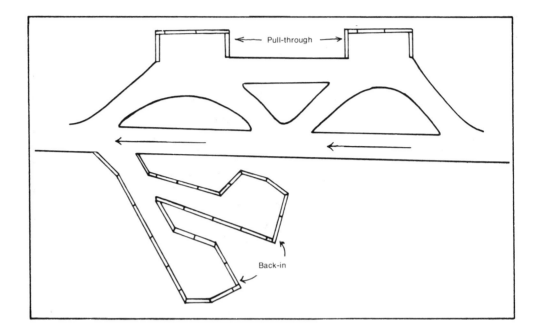

Figure 7.34

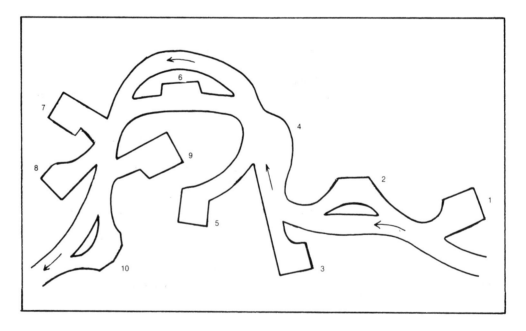

Figure 7.35

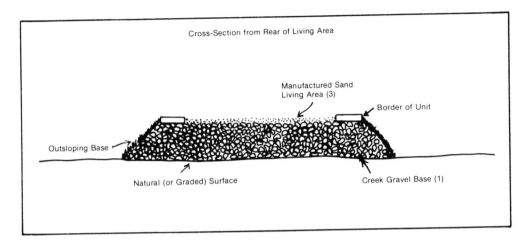

Figure 7.36

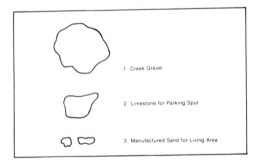

Figure 7.37 Sizes of Rock for Camp Units

campgrounds are built. Family campgrounds *are* attractive to people who look for convenience, safety, usability, and comfort. It's not our place (or yours) to dictate to people what type of camping experience is "good for them." We won't belabor this point, because we've discussed the need to provide areas and facilities for *all* types of users in several places throughout this book. We would like to clarify one thing, though: there are tent campers and there are tent campers. Some want backcountry experiences and won't settle for anything else. Others

enjoy the experience of a developed family campground. Often these individuals are "vehicle campers" at heart, though they may be too young to afford a recreational vehicle yet. Regardless of their motives, campers — tent or otherwise — in developed campgrounds almost always prefer sites surfaced with reinforced material. If you don't believe us, ask 'em.

To continue the discussion of camp unit surfacing, there are two grades of limestone rock you can use. The larger has an aggregate size of roughly one-quarter to one-half inch, and serves as surfacing for the parking spur section of the campsite. Cover the "living area" of the unit with the second grade of rock, a "fine" or manufactured sand. This is a flaked limestone with an aggregate size of roughly one-eighth inch. Figure 7.37 shows the sizes of the three types of rock used to build a campsite.

Two words on design philosophy are in order here. First, we suggest you *avoid* paving parking spurs. In many areas of the country, it's a good idea if funds are available to pave camp-loop roads for *reducing dust problems*. However, unless you have to build campsites on a loose *sand* base, paving

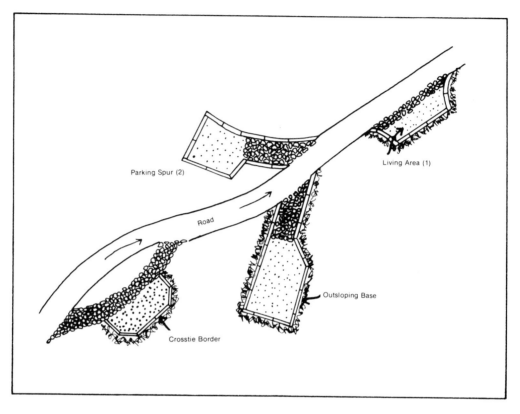

Parking Spur (2)

Living Area (1)

Road

Outsloping Base

Crosstie Border

Figure 7.38

the parking spur accomplishes very little except to increase the cost of development. Second, place the "living area" of the campsite immediately adjacent to *and not barricaded from* the parking spur. You should avoid second-guessing how campers will want to organize their living space. What a planner may envision as the ideal portion of the site for erecting a tent or parking an RV may not suit user preferences. By designing adjoining parking-living areas, you allow users to choose how they wish to arrange their own space, in effect letting them "design" their own site.

Once the gravel base and the limestone surfaces are in place *and graded as level as possible* for user convenience, you should outline or "define" the entire site with a border. Although they are becoming more expensive, we still recommend railroad crossties as the best choice here. They last several years, especially when treated with penta-chlorophenol, for which a *light* oil is used as a solvent, and they provide a well-defined, easily recognizable camp unit. By defining individual camp units, crossties serve as "property lines" for campers, psychologically containing each visitor in a predetermined area. Campers in other units tend to respect these property lines, so the borders actually reduce conflicts. From a management standpoint, they also help keep people within reinforced areas, protecting the adjacent environment and minimizing maintenance.

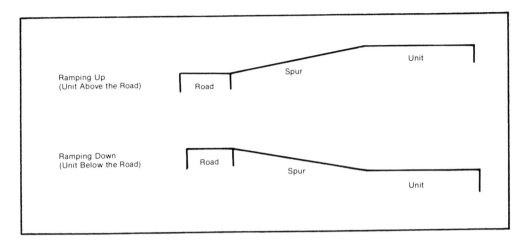

Figure 7.39

Crossties should be anchored in place by means of one-half-inch reinforcement bars thirty inches long driven through holes in the ties into the base material of the unit. Figure 7.38 shows some typical bordered campsites. It also indicates where you should place the two types of unit and spur-surface rock.

Ramps and Risers

Often a plot of developable land for a camp unit is situated higher or lower than the elevation where you hope to build the loop road. The most common methods of dealing with this problem are *cutting* (using construction equipment to lower the unit location to the elevation of the road) and *filling* (adding an earthen "fill" to bring the unit location up to the level of the road). In general, these methods: are costly, can alter the environment of the site by, for example, changing drainage patterns, tend to create maintenance problems, and are *normally unnecessary*. Figure 7.39 shows a profile drawing of how to avoid cuts and fills by constructing the parking spur in the form of a *ramp*. As long as the last twenty-five to thirty feet of the spur and the living area of the unit are level, ramping will function well for you. Some cut or fill may still be required; six percent should be the maximum allowable grade on a ramped spur.

For pull-off units and some pull-through locations, you may not have the linear distance needed to ramp the parking spur. If the road and spur are on one contour level and the area where you want the living space is higher or lower, risers, or railroad-tie steps, will work for you. (See Figure 7.40.) Risers should be permanently anchored and extend the length of the living space to prevent accidents and the erosion that would otherwise occur from foot traffic over the natural slope between the spur and the living area.

Unit Furniture

Careful placement of camp-unit furniture can enhance the opportunity for users to "design" their own living space within the borders of

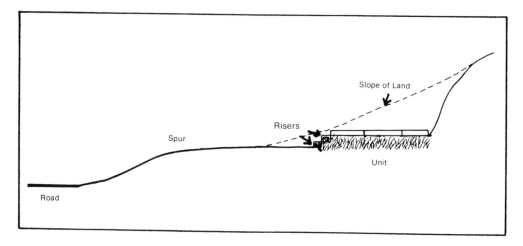

Figure 7.40

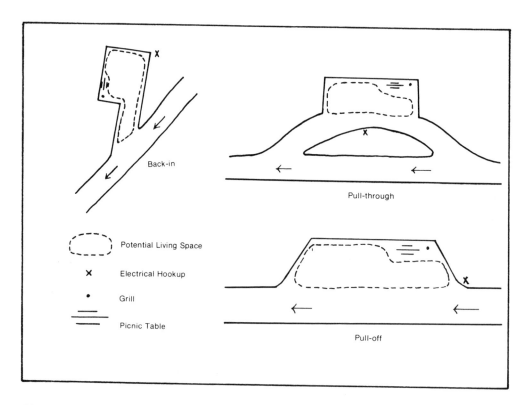

Figure 7.41

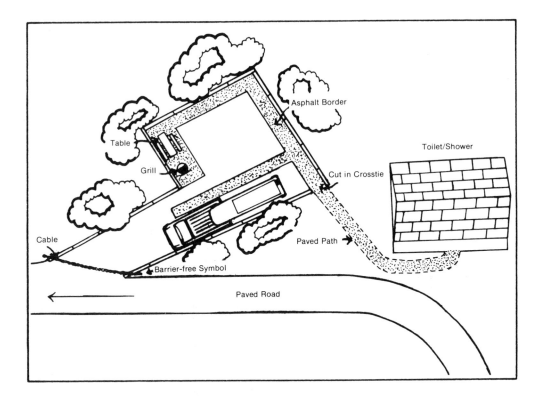

Figure 7.42

their site. Figure 7.41 illustrates several ways the table and grill can be "tucked" into a corner of the campsite. When deciding where to place furniture, remember our discussion about the different gradients of rock used in surfacing. It's better to put the table and grill within the portion of the unit topped with manufactured sand rather than in the area covered with the larger grade of limestone where you would expect (although not force) users to park their vehicles. Some planners tend to leave trees inside many of their defined sites — a poor practice since they get in the way of user equipment such as trailer awnings and dining flies and since the impact from camping will kill the trees. Before we elaborate on a discussion about unit furniture, a word about handicapped campers is in order.

Barrier-free Campsites. Camp units reinforced with limestone and manufactured sand are functional in part because they help prevent environmental impact. Another advantage of reinforced campsites is their accessibility for persons with ambulatory problems. Since these units are built level and since the surface tends to pack smoothly with use, they are easy to negotiate by people with canes, crutches, and wheelchairs. They have been praised by Easter Seal professionals as excellent for all but the most severely handicapped persons; thus, for these severely handicapped potential users we believe you should develop a small percentage, perhaps two of every one hundred of your units as barrier-free sites. Figure 7.42 shows this kind of unit, with only a few differences from the

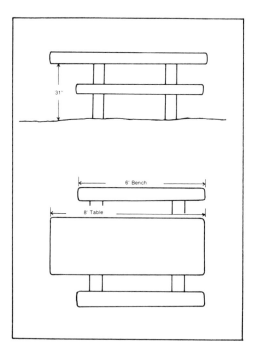

Figure 7.43

others you'd build normally. First, border the perimeter of the unit with asphalt, including a strip along the *inside* of the parking spur. Second, make an opening in the railroad-tie border as indicated to permit access from the back of the unit. This can, as shown, be coupled with a paved path leading to the sanitary facility, which must be barrier-free as well. We recommend modifying the unit nearest the toilet/shower facility when possible. Finally, *administer* the site as barrier-free with a locked cable and sign symbol at the road-spur juncture. With this arrangement, the on-site manager can "reserve" the unit or units for individuals who may need the smoother asphalt surface. If the campground approaches one hundred percent occupancy and the site hasn't been needed, it can also be opened for use by other campers. Our experience tells us that

provision of a few barrier-free camp units not only benefits the almost-forgotten severely handicapped camper but also provides excellent public relations for your agency or company.

Camp-unit Picnic Tables. In our opinion, the best type of table to use on *any* campsite is one with a concrete top and wooden benches. Wood is warmer to sit on during cool weather and the concrete top eliminates anchoring tables to prevent users from moving them to other sites — a real maintenance headache. When considering different types and sizes of tables, plan on at least two feet of seating space per user, or a six foot table that seats six people three on a side.

Some agencies provide barrier-free tables by removing one of the benches. This motive is commendable, but we don't like the results because they preclude use by parties with more than three persons if none of them is in a wheelchair. One advantage of the barrier-free site we described above is the capability to open it to all campers as use demands. So it should include tables for larger groups.

The best approach, in our opinion, is to build or buy tables for all your units that have one *cantilevered* end, as shown in Figure 7.43. These provide a two-foot space at one end of the table for a wheelchair and still leave seating for six along the benches. Another advantage of the cantilevered end is the *preparation space* it provides. Some campsites we've seen have both a six-foot table and a small additional table for preparing food or using a camp stove. The eight-foot cantivered table lets you combine preparation and eating in one area, takes up less unit space, and provides seating for wheelchair and ambulatory users.

When deciding where to place the table, you should consider both the afternoon shade and the location of our next piece of unit furniture, the grill. Also make sure the furniture will not be in the way of a trailer awning.

Camp-unit Grills. Probably one of the most common mistakes made in providing camp-unit furniture occurs with grills. Almost all campsites have grills, yet very few campers use them for cooking. We once surveyed campers in a four-hundred-unit Kentucky campground from early June to late August and found that about ninety-nine percent of the people we asked used their own portable camp stove or the cooking unit installed in their RV or trailer. We recommend providing grills since some folks will still want them, but you need to think about the *type* you install. Too many campgrounds have the stand-up, or picnic grill, a metal box-like structure mounted on a steel post. These units aren't a problem in themselves, until you consider the camper's companion, the campfire. In the survey mentioned above, we found that seventy percent of the campers built fires at night, a figure that would probably increase in cooler months or locations. The campfire is also part of the social experience that most campers want — and a phenomenon that too many planners don't want to deal with.

Campfires, simply put, create maintenance work. Fire spots have to be cleaned periodically. If a campsite gets too "messy," campers tend to build their fires all over, creating additional clean-up challenges. Aside from being messy, fires also contribute to the demise of nearby vegetation since they cook surface roots.

What's this have to do with grills? If you provide the almost worthless stand-up grill, nothing.* If, however, you provide a *ground level, tilt-back grill* (Figure 7.44) you may kill two birds with one stone. Some users will cook on these because they work about as well as stand-up grills, but the tilt-back grill

also provides a single, convenient spot for a campfire. Several models are available commercially, and they should be set in a cement form four feet across that is built into the base material of the unit. Then, when the unit is surfaced, the top of the cement form will be flush with the top of the campsite. We recommend a circular form since it suits the shape of a campfire better than a rectangular one. You should also instruct construction crews to set the grills so the grate, when in an upright position, is not between the user's campfire and the picnic table. The center of the grill pad should be between five and six feet from the end of the picnic table nearer the grill. This spacing leaves adequate room between the table and the fire without wasting space.

Lantern Hangers. Campers can be the cause of environmental impact without realizing it. An excellent example of this is lantern-burn damage. When a camping lantern is lit, it produces a considerable amount of heat that is transferred from the lantern element through the protective glass sleeve. If a lantern is hung on a tree limb or nail so that the sleeve is touching tree bark, something interesting happens. The heat passes through the outer bark to the *cambium,* the thin layer of cells between the outer bark and the wood. Only after several months does an open wound appear on the tree, so campers don't realize the harm they've done because the results aren't immediately noticeable. The next time you visit a campground anywhere in the world, however, look for wounds about six to ten inches long in the shape of a cat's eye five to eight feet above ground level: lantern burn. We'll bet you see *at least* one damaged tree in every camp unit; often you'll find half a dozen. The wound won't kill the tree itself, but it opens the door for insect infestation and disease that can damage the tree further. Also, lantern burns are not especially aesthetic. Several years ago when we helped begin research regarding this

---

*The stand-up picnic grill is excellent in a picnic area, but *not in campsites!* In campgrounds, visitors generally use these grills as stands for their commercial stoves. Yet we continue to perpetuate this mistake because it's how we've *always* done it!

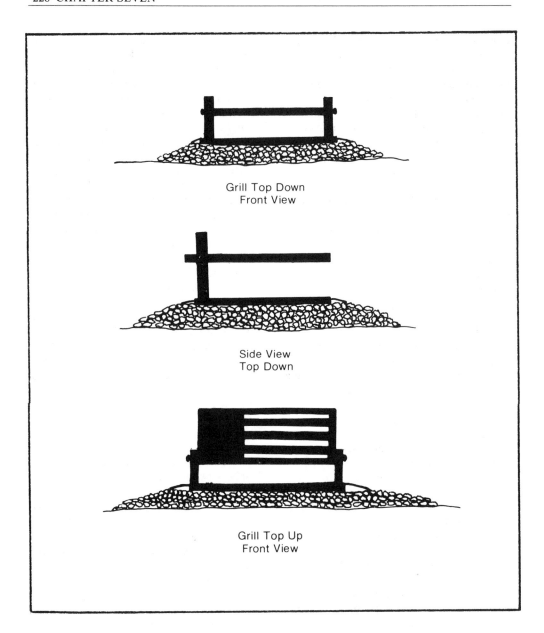

Grill Top Down
Front View

Side View
Top Down

Grill Top Up
Front View

Figure 7.44

problem we were surprised to find that campers weren't the only folks who didn't know what caused the "rare" tree scars. We found that students, professors, fellow professionals, and lantern manufacturers all lacked any knowledge of this phenomenon.

The solution to lantern burn damage is two-fold. First, you can educate campers by telling them about the problem. Second, you can provide a lantern-hanging device like a lag screw anchored in a tree. (See Figure 7.45.) As long as the lantern is kept four to six inches away from the bark, heat build-up won't be a problem. You may need to place two lantern hangers per unit to provide an option for campers, and when deciding where to put the hangers, try to "think like a user." Commercial hangers are available to park managers and campers. If putting a lag screw in a tree offends your environmental sensitivity (although it hardly hurts the tree), you might use lantern posts, though these are more expensive.

Off-site Facilities. You'll need an average of one garbage can per camp unit. However, if you put a can at each site, the trash collection crew for a three-hundred-unit campground will have to make three hundred stops. Therefore, if you use single cans it's a good idea to *cluster* them in groups of three to six depending on the density (units per acre) of your campground. Campgrounds with a higher density can have more cans clustered together without forcing users to walk too far to deposit their garbage, and can clusters offer an additional plus; some families have only small amounts of garbage while others may fill more than one can before you empty them.

Centrally located dumpsters are an alternative to single cans. These will reduce collection time further though campers may find them less convenient. Since this decision should be a managerial rather than a design issue, providing free garbage bags for

Figure 7.45

campers to fill and take to the dumpster is a management practice you should consider.

If you provide potable water in your campground, it's cheaper to place common-use fountain and faucet combinations along the loop road rather than putting an outlet at each unit. Depending on the campsite density, one outlet for every six to ten units should suffice. Be sure to recognize water points as potential impact sites and reinforce them. Water outlets should be boxed in and provided with a rock sump, as in Figure 7.46.

Figure 7.46

Water Movement. One advantage of reinforced units is quick drainage. Water
percolates well through manufactured sand
and doesn't "pool" or create mud on the
campsite. (This is why tent campers soon
learn to prefer them.) Care must be taken,
however, to prevent water from creating
erosion problems around camp units. Reinforced sites, since they are built above
ground level, can be used as berms to catch
run-off from a watershed and channel it
around the unit. In some instances a ditch
may be required adjacent to the base of the
campsite.

Cuts and fills, when necessary, may alter
existing drainage patterns and create the
need to redirect water. This can be accomplished if you provide a drainage channel
along the side of the loop road. Such a
technique can, however, create problems
where the road meets the spurs of camp
units, and the best solution is usually to
grade a slightly depressed paved channel on
the spur for water movement. If the erosion
potential is quite high, you could place a
culvert under the spur. However, a better
option is to build the road at a zero elevation (ground level) and eliminate the ditch
entirely. Engineers will likely question this
since they ofttimes insist that all roads, even
through flat areas, be bordered with ditches.

**Two Words about Vegetation: Shade and
Screening.** Optimum shade level depends, to
a degree, on factors such as climate, orientation of campsites to the sun, and geographic
location of the campground. Another deter-
minant of shade level is unit surfacing. Some
campgrounds still contain units with natural
ground surfaces. While these are environmentally poor ideas, many are still in use and
must be maintained. Even stranger, environmentalists tend to be the strongest detractors
of reinforced sites. Natural ground, particularly when heavily shaded, will not
withstand the compaction of recreational use.
On units with no reinforcement, you should
retain only minimum shading — about
twenty-five percent.

On the other hand, reinforced units withstand impact well. For these sites, the
amount of shade is primarily a matter of user
preference. (Again we suggest not leaving
trees within the defined site.) Although
campers may tell you they want heavy levels
of shade, they tend to select campsites with
moderate shade levels. Thus, when developing campsites, you should thin the overstory
vegetation somewhat. In general, it's good to
provide campsites with morning sun for
warmth and drying equipment and afternoon
shade for heat relief. When choosing which
trees to cut and which to leave, be sure to
consider the species able to withstand impact
in a recreation environment. (See Table 7.2.)
Young, vigorous hardwoods are good choices
to leave standing. Old-growth trees and
shallow-rooted species should be cut since
they won't withstand the pressure associated
with heavy use. Most planners use none of
these techniques. More often than not, they
will pick a grove of big trees, "plunk" in their
campground with little or no site reinforcement, and leave managers to find themselves
with a grove of dying trees. The camper is
then blamed for the site degradation and
"overuse."

Two other points to consider regarding
vegetation in camping areas are: *use existing*

Table 7.2*

SPECIES RANKING IN ORDER OF DECREASING ABILITY TO WITHSTAND RECREATION IMPACT

Hardwoods		Conifers
1. Hickories	12. Red Maple	1. Shortleaf Pine
2. Persimmon	13. American Holly	2. Hemlocks
3. Sycamore	14. Sourwood	3. White Pine
4. White Ash	15. Black Birch	4. Pitch Pine
5. Beech	16. White Oaks	5. Virginia Pine
6. Sassafras	17. Black Walnut	
7. Buckeye	18. Red Oaks	
8. Yellow Poplar	19. Black Locust	
9. Dogwood	20. Magnolia	
10. Blackgum	21. Black Cherry	
11. Yellow Birch	22. Blue Beech	

*From U.S. Forest Service Southern Experiment Station Research Note 171(1962): *Tree and Shrub Response To Recreation Use.* T.H. Ripley, Project Leader.

trees to your advantage and *plan for additional shade* where you'll need it. To demonstrate this point, consider the portion of a camping loop road in a Midwestern state park in Figure 7.47. The campsites here are reinforced, so the impact associated with too much shade isn't a problem. What *is* a problem is the total lack of shade in the camp units. The best solution would have been to move the loop road closer to the existing tree line, but since our planner created this design in the office, let's look at our best alternative after the mistake has been made. Figure 7.48 shows the road aligned in the same place. In this drawing, however, we've *extended* the length of some of the parking spurs to reach the shade of the trees. In between these longer spurs, we can now add additional units and plant fast-growing species such as sycamore in the East or red alder in the West to shade the units with shorter spurs. This design lets us take advantage of existing shade and increase our use of the resource base. It also assumes that a higher density of camp units is a design goal, and, as usual, should be a management decision. In practice you would, of course, place units on both sides of this road.

A second factor to consider relative to overstory shade is understory screening. Many plants which make excellent screens, such as Japanese honeysuckle *(Lonicera japonica)*, prefer sunlight to heavy shade. Establishing a fairly dense stand of understory vegetation between camp units has a number of advantages: the units in high-density camping areas can be separated psychologically from each other, the vegetation helps reduce the distance noise will carry, the screening can be aesthetic and help produce a feeling of being in the out-of-doors, the vegetation can be used to soften the effects of unsightly natural or human-made features like a badly eroded bank or sewage-treatment facility, and the screening can be used to "channel" people where *you*

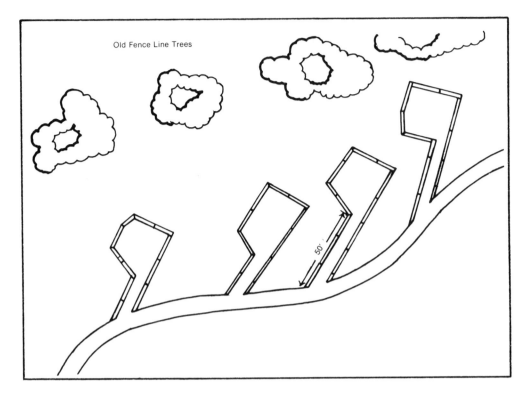

Old Fence Line Trees

50'

Figure 7.47

want them to go — onto reinforced trails and roadways. A majority of family campers prefer screening between campsites. This means you should design camp loops with varied screening densities.

One difficulty in establishing or keeping screening is the *mow, mow, mowing* fixation of most maintenance crews. Managers should instruct maintenance staff to avoid mowing between existing units where you are trying to establish screens. In new areas, construction crews should leave existing understory vegetation (the intersite zone), except within the perimeter of planned camp units. It appears that even with critical shortages of maintenance funds, the grass mowers are likely to survive us — and any campground vegetation.

Signing. In any recreation area it's a good principle of design to *minimize* signing as much as possible, remembering the need to avoid potential hazards and confusion. Generally, there are only two situations that require signs on camp units: when barrier-free sites should be so designated, and when all units should be numbered for easy identification. Since barrier-free units must be kept closed when not occupied by means of a cable across the spur, a good location for the barrier-free sign (preferably the international symbol for handicapped access) is on one of the cable posts. Signs should always be informative, unobtrusive, and inexpensive. Avoid the practice of installing a post at each campsite for the unit number. This is another way to waste maintenance dollars since these

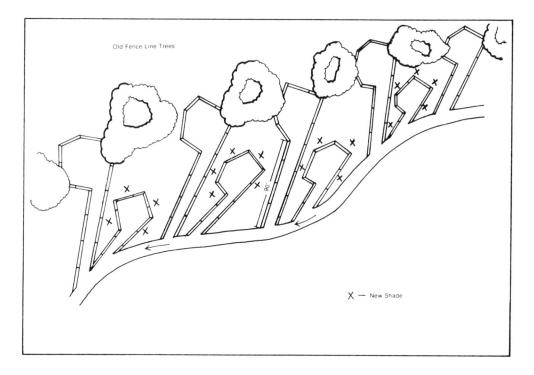

Old Fence Line Trees

90°

X — New Shade

Figure 7.48

posts are expensive, tend to get knocked down, and can become a safety hazard. The best numbering system we've seen involved a four-inch-curb-tape circle placed on the side of the picnic table facing the road — easy to see and hard to vandalize. Another good technique is to stencil the unit number on the paved loop road at the entry point of the properly built gravel spur.

"one swallow does not a summer make," understanding these basic amenities doesn't give you all the tools you need to develop a functional area. Let's briefly consider a few additional aspects important to managers and users: sewage dumping stations, placement of sewage-treatment facilities, administrative zones, and maintenance complexes.

ADMINISTRATIVE SUPPORT FACILITIES

Thus far, we've focused the discussion of planning developed sites or family camp-grounds on "meat and potato" issues — camp-loop layout and unit design. Just as

Sewage Dumping Stations

As we've tried to stress before, it's critical to know the needs of your users and how their equipment functions when designing parks and recreation areas. Waste-disposal facilities provide an excellent example of this principle

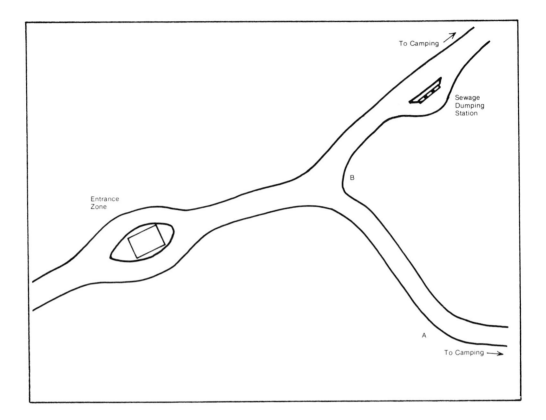

Figure 7.49

for discussion. Many RV's, built as they are for user convenience, have *sewage holding tanks.* These tanks are designed to hold several days' worth of raw sewage, drain on a gravity-flow basis, and be flushed out with water when emptied. Let's take a test here. In the preceding sentence, we've given you the basic facts you need to *zone, design,* and *build* a sewage dumping station. Did you get them? You probably need a little more to go on . . . .

Since sewage holding tanks in RV's will contain several days' worth of raw sewage, campers usually prefer to empty their tanks at one of two times: on their way *into* or *out of* a campground. Consider the location of

the sewage dumping station in Figure 7.49. Here, campers using the camp loops within the area designated (A) will have to drive out of their way to reach the dumping station. You also may need to place an additional sign at point B that indicates where the station is. Placing the dumping station as shown in Figure 7.49 causes an inconvenience for campers, costs you a few bucks for an extra sign, and violates the principle of zoning use areas. Figure 7.50 shows a simple alternative to avoid these problems. With this location, the dumping station is easy to find and convenient to campers, although from an aesthetic standpoint you may want to screen it. Another plus for this location is that it's a

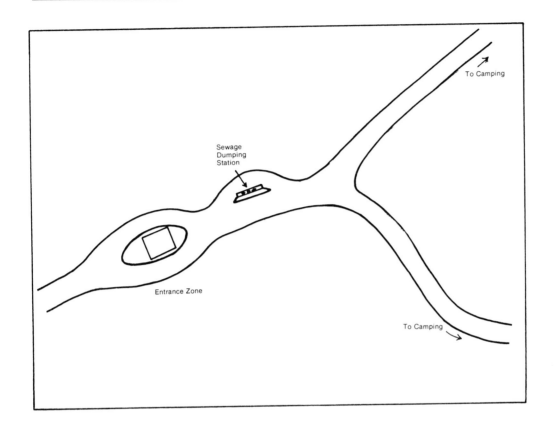

To Camping

Sewage
Dumping
Station

Entrance Zone

To Camping

Figure 7.50

possible turnaround zone for people who, after reaching the entry station, decide they want to leave the area.

From a design perspective, you need to remember that the connection for draining an RV holding or septic tank is on the left-hand or driver's side of the vehicle. Since the dumping station you provide is designed around a large, underground holding tank, campers need to be able to pull alongside it. The whole operation is rather like the design of a pump island at a gas station, and Figure 7.51 shows one way of designing it. With this layout, campers can reach the drain points from either side of the island, which means they have the convenience of

emptying their holding tanks as they enter or exit your campground. Between the two drain points a hose, or flushing outlet, lets them flush out their holding tanks. Since the tip of this hose may come in contact with raw sewage, you should sign the outlet for cleaning purposes only (not to be used to replenish drinking supplies).

Because RV holding tanks drain on gravity flow, the portion of road adjacent to the drain points need to be *insloped* two to three percent, as shown in Figure 7.52, for complete draining. The asphalt or concrete slab housing the drains themselves should be slightly *concave,* with the drains placed at the lowest point on the surface so any spillage

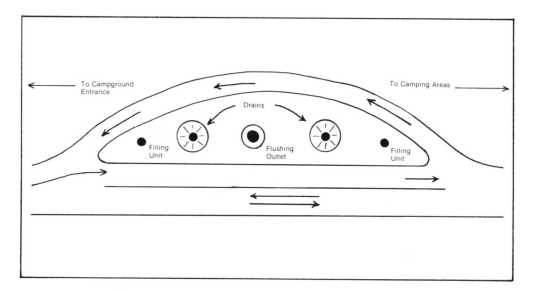

Figure 7.51

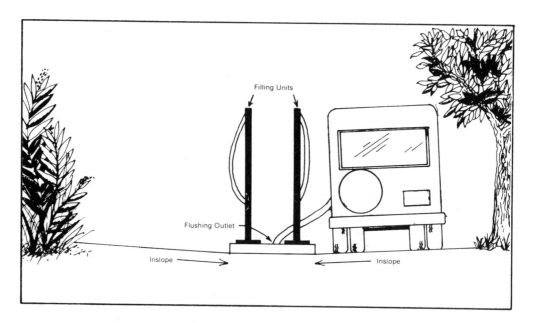

Figure 7.52

will run downhill into the drains. You should get help from your engineering staff when designing sewage dumping stations, but be sure they understand the needs of your users when they provide you with their input.

Placement of Sewage-treatment Facilities

The least expensive and visually obtrusive type of sewage-treatment facility for campgrounds is the sewage drain field. However, at times the soils' absorptive capacity in a large campground is inadequate for safe-functioning. In these instances you will have to build other more costly and potentially more obvious disposal facilities. Where possible, a second-best alternative is a sewage lagoon. The least desirable facility is a dollar-gobbling sewage treatment plant, a technical challenge to be coordinated with engineering personnel. Our purpose in mentioning the issue is to strongly suggest that you screen sewage-treatment facilities from public view. Some engineers seem to want their peers and the public to "enjoy" their dandy sewage structures. This approach to planning is an excellent example of the tail wagging the dog; sewage-treatment facilities are *support features*. Hopefully, you'll let common sense be your guide and not give an important, but supportive, facility top billing in your campground's visual array of goodies.

Administrative Zones

Administrative zones are to campgrounds what visitor centers are to parks. They are *initial contact points* and as such will play an important role in determining the impression your area has on campers. Thus convenience is a critical factor. The design of your check-in station depends, in large part, on how

management plans to administer the campground. Presuming your campground has *controlled access*, use limited to campers and their guests, you'll need to build a check-in station so that vehicles entering the area must drive adjacent to this point. Since vehicles leaving the campground may need to have contact here also, the best design for an entrance zone is probably one using a center island, as shown in Figure 7.53. As we suggested in Chapter Two, you should avoid making campers who have already checked in wait in line. To do so, provide a double-lane entry so that vehicles re-entering the area can skirt the check-in station. The double-lane portion of the entry road should be a *minimum* of two hundred feet long. Since all parties leaving the campground may not need to stop at the entrance zone, you should provide a double-lane exit as well.

It may also be a good idea to provide a parking area adjacent to the exit and/or entrance for service vehicles and campers who need to stop temporarily. Public telephones are a nice touch here, as is a bulletin board with emergency assistance numbers, area maps, regulations, other information, and a welcoming message (remember your hosting function). If you do provide parking here, remember to plan for large trailers and other RV's. You may also want to provide a turnaround inside the entrance zone for use when the campground is full, or for individuals who decide not to enter the area once they reach the check-in zone. (The dump station can double for this function.)

Maintenance Complexes

In Chapter Two we suggested that maintenance complexes in parks and recreation areas, including campgrounds, should be a part of, but apart from user-oriented facilities. Because of their function, maintenance complexes can be noisy, unsightly, and

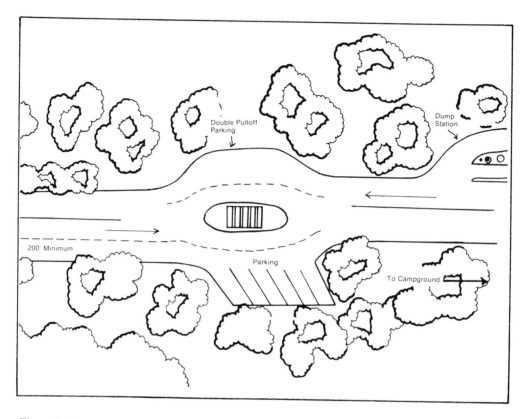

Figure 7.53

dangerous, especially for children. Therefore, these areas should be zoned away from camping and other support facilities. Vegetative screening and topography can help remove maintenance complexes from sight, and physical distance can help as well, but remember the need to keep maintenance areas conveniently near the facilities they serve. For example, if your crews have to drive or haul riding lawnmowers long distances to areas that need mowing, you use extra gasoline and increase the time it takes to mow. When possible, then, locate maintenance complexes *centrally* but keep them out of sight. Many campers enjoy sleeping a bit later than the 7:30 am time most maintenance folks like to crank up those mowers.

There are several other factors to consider when you build a maintenance complex. From the standpoint of protecting users and preventing vandalism, it will be necessary to fence in a maintenance yard, especially if the area has a gasoline pump for refueling vehicles. The maintenance building should serve several functions. Allocate some space for storage of inventory. If an electrical outlet at a camp unit blows a fuse on Saturday, campers shouldn't have to wait until the central storage area re-opens on Monday to have electricity. The maintenance building should also contain a well-lighted and ventilated "shop space" for making equipment repairs and adjustments and an area for the administrative functions associated with maintenance. This may not require much more than a desk, filing cabinet, and telephone or two-way radio, but it's better to have the space than to try and work without it. Finally, remember that your maintenance personnel have more than equipment needs. A "personal area" with a picnic table, drinking water, and toilet can help keep morale up and make maintenance personnel feel — as they should — that they are an integral part of your operation.

SOME PHILOSOPHICAL CONSIDERATIONS

Planning and designing campgrounds aren't tasks that exist in a vacuum. The strategies and approaches you use are closely tied to a number of other functions, among the most important of which are management goals and objectives for the area. While management of outdoor recreation areas is a subject for another book, you should consider a few miscellaneous subjects.

Fees

The question of camping fees — how much you should charge campers — depends on a number of factors. Generally, private campgrounds have a higher fee structure than those in the public sector since supply and demand has an impact here. We've discussed the need to build public campgrounds large enough to offset the cost of operations and maintenance with rates charged to campers, but agency or organizational policy also plays a role.

Even if all these factors and others are constants, it's not our place to tell you how much you should charge folks to stay in your campground. We do, however, have an analogy for you to consider. If you've ever

taken a course in biology, you probably heard a lecture about the food chain. For fisheries, it goes like this: the sun provides energy to microscopic plant life, which is eaten by small organisms, which are eaten by small fish, which are eaten by larger fish, which we try (often unsuccessfully) to catch. If you remove the first link in the chain, ultimately the entire system breaks down. It takes several years for the big ones to starve, but it does happen.

We can see a parallel in the "evolution" of campers. In developed-site family campgrounds you'll find people ranging in age from their late teens to post-retirement. We're generalizing here, but for the most part people tend to acquire more discretionary income as they get older, at least until they retire. The young (seed source) campers are those with the least money available for any sort of recreation — including camping. During the 1960's and 70's, the $2.50 to $4.50 per-night fees charged by most public campgrounds beckoned thousands of new young folks into the camping realm. This provided the people and the motivation for the purchase of millions of dollars worth of camping equipment *and* the potential source for a sizable increase in campers who would later prefer the extras offered in private-sector campgrounds. Sales of camping gear — tents, pop-up campers, stoves, and the like — were at peak levels. But then came special-interest groups, public laws restricting what agencies could and couldn't do, environmental emotionalism that painted RV users as bad folks who shouldn't be allowed to camp on our (their) nation's wild lands, and a continuing shrill cry from the private-campground owners' association. All these factors combined to force public park administrators to raise their camping prices drastically. As they did so, the private sector raised theirs, and the disastrous spiral began.

The young and the less-than-wealthy tent campers were the first casualities. Sales in stoves and lanterns, camping tents, and other vehicle camping gear dropped measurably. Sadly, some public agencies were relieved to be pushed out of the family camping realm because they were uncomfortable when confronted with campers like the elderly or the handicapped who often require on-site electrical hook-ups because of medical conditions. We hope you understand — unlike most public and certainly private sector folks — why elimination through pricing of the young and elderly or disabled tent campers parallels the loss of tiny organisms in the fisheries chain. Unless this fact is understood and remedied, developed-site family camping in all sectors will slowly disappear.

Research

What's the "best" way to keep campground users from causing lantern-burn damage to trees? The simple answer to this, telling them about the potential for harming the environment, isn't quite as straightforward as it might seem. A few years ago, a friend of ours, Dr. Ken Chilman of Southern Illinois University, studied ways of reducing lantern-burn damage to campground trees. One method he used was to have management staff pass out eye-catching flyers describing the problem to users as they checked into the campground. As it turned out, this method *alone* was actually associated with a slight *increase* in the incidence of campers hanging lanterns on trees! Instead, a combination of handing out flyers, talking to users, and providing lantern hangers was the most effective means of reducing damage. To understand this rather odd occurrence, you need to "think like a camper." When users check into a campground, they often get bombarded with literature — what some

folks call "gate garbage." This includes everything from area regulations to an ad for Aunt Bessie's sorghum mill and flea market. If the results of Dr. Chilman's study are any indication, users don't always read the wonderful handouts you provide at campground entrance stations.

The moral of this story emphasizes the need for research. Common sense is necessary to plan and manage campgrounds, but it ofttimes needs to be backed up with the results of *applied* research. (Note the emphasis on applied.) We mention this in a text on planning because campgrounds and other recreation areas can be planned and designed *with research potential built into them*. In order to find out how many camp units per acre users prefer, we need to build loops with different site densities into the same campground and see how users react. Simply asking campers how many units per acre they want may produce answers, but we'll bet they won't mean much. Do you know how many square feet there are in an acre? What this much space looks like on the ground?

Obviously, part of the decision on camp-unit density depends on management policy. But, management policy *should* be tied closely to user needs and preferences, and to determine these you need research. Try different kinds of garbage collection points (cans versus dumpsters versus trash bags); experiment with different levels of security lighting; install different types of ground-level grills; provide loops with various combinations of water, sewer, and electrical hook-ups; thin vegetation to different screening densities. These and other research opportunities should be management-sanctioned and carefully planned. We've found that the best approach is a cooperative effort involving park management, the academic sector, and the leisure-products community. The lantern-burn study we spoke of earlier prompted the Coleman Company to develop a lantern-hanging device which they now market — a solution brought about by research benefiting users, managers, business, *and* the environment. Note here how Coleman, a private leisure-products company, financed the study, located on a public park area, through a university.

Master Planning

Most of our discussion about campgrounds to this point has dealt with in-the-field design challenges: how to build loop roads, lay out camp units, and zone support facilities. These are all legitimate concerns, but actual development must be preceded by two other types of planning. The first is *strategic planning,* determining the goals and objectives you hope to accomplish by providing a use area. Too many managers and planners ignore this step. The second type is *master planning,* bridging the gap between intended strategies and actual field design. Master planning should let you know how the campground will be developed, zoned, and built before construction actually begins.

Master planning is in large part a matter of *synthesis,* or collecting information about 1) management opportunities and constraints, 2) site potential and limitations, and 3) user needs and characteristics and then *blending* these components into a functional solution. There are at least four reasons to use this process. First, developing a large campground or other recreation area is quite *complex.* If you don't look for potential problems, they'll almost certainly look for you. Second, you should be *accountable* for your designs. If a programmer says, "I'd rather have my playcourt here," you should be able to respond with, "Sorry, but that's the only spot we can put the drain field without having to install several sewage lift stations." Third, your technical-support staff will need to know *capacities.* Individual campsites *must* be designed on the ground,

but your plans should symbolically show thirty-five units on this loop, forty-five on that one, and so on. This gives engineers and architects the data they need to plan for utility lines, hook-ups, and other capacities. Finally, large areas are often built using *phased construction.* In other words, because of budget, construction-crew sizes, equipment availability, and other constraints, it may take two to ten years to complete an area once construction begins. Given the realities of staff turnover and, at times, the vagaries of shifting political winds, you need documentation showing the total concept toward which you're working. Figure 7.54 shows a master plan for the camping and road components of a campground we designed a few years ago. Note how various loops are developed with different unit densities and levels of utility hook-ups. Aside from meeting different user needs, this approach would lend itself to a variety of research opportunities focusing on user preferences.

REHABILITATION

We spend a lot of time thinking about the day an agency or corporation will call us to say they have three million dollars and a prime piece of undeveloped land and could we please help them design a new campground. We also keep expecting our golden retriever to develop differential equations and discover the Unified Field Theory. Unfortunately, the real world consists more of poorly planned existing campgrounds in need of fixing than it does of new opportunities. While planning a campground "from scratch" can be challenging, trying to rehabilitate an old one can be a nightmare. This doesn't have to happen, however, if you train yourself to look for site *potential* rather than limitations. The first lesson in rehabilitation is one you've heard before: don't let existing

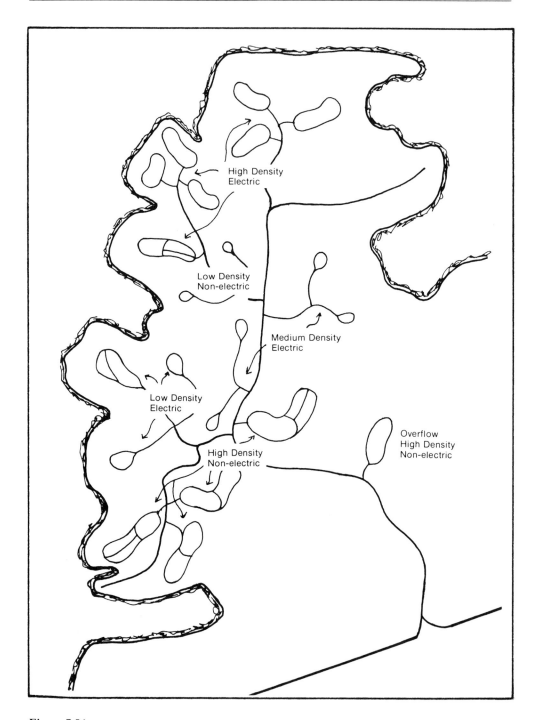

High Density
Electric

Low Density
Non-electric

Medium Density
Electric

Low Density
Electric

High Density
Non-electric

Overflow
High Density
Non-electric

Figure 7.54

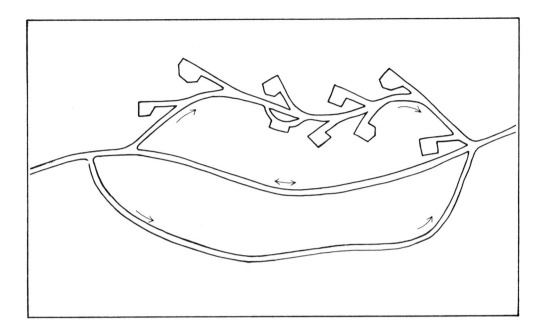

Figure 7.55

features like an in-place road dictate design to you. If you can't make an existing facility work for you, get rid of it. The short-term cost will probably be offset in the long run by saved maintenance dollars and increased user satisfaction, which tends to lead to repeat visits and additional income.

As always, however, planning should be a *balance*. It may be possible to use existing features if you learn to think creatively. For example, consider the road and camp-unit layout in Figure 7.55. Let's assume that one design goal of your rehabilitation project is to increase the number of available camp units. Given the available topography, you simply can't add more units with the circulation patterns as shown. However, circulation patterns aren't sacred; *maybe* if you were to reverse traffic flow, an entirely different solution with many more camp units would appear. (See Figure 7.56.) Obviously, this is only an illustration and reversing traffic flow

might make matters worse. But you should still learn to look beyond what you *have* to what you *might have*.

Figure 7.57 shows a more likely example of how rehabilitation can work. This type of road system is one you'll encounter frequently in campgrounds, one that's quite easy to fix by closing a few old sections and adding a limited amount of new road. Figure 7.58 illustrates a solution to this problem. The new design is easier to manage and control, offers a less confusing and more convenient layout to users, and discourages environmental impact.

Creating new designs for old sites can work at a broader level as well. In Chapter One, we looked at the existing campground in McCormick's Creek State Park in Indiana. (See Figure 1.9.) Figure 1.10 showed one solution aimed at reducing the user confusion that resulted from the original road design. Now let's look at an alternative

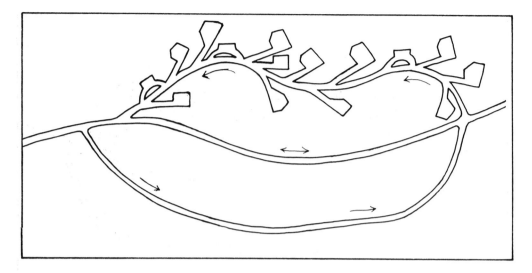

Figure 7.56

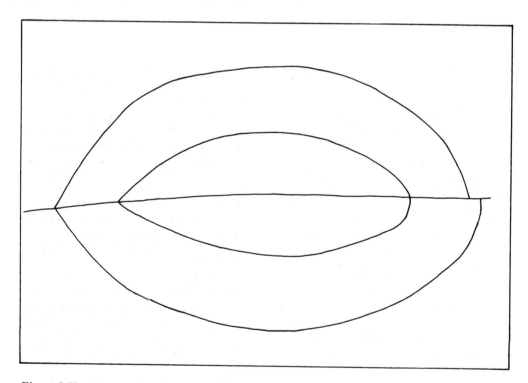

Figure 7.57

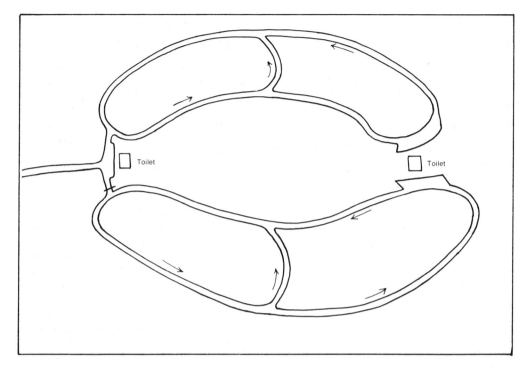

Figure 7.58

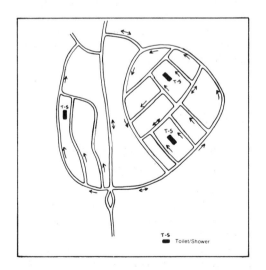

Figure 7.59

solution capable of achieving the same goals while using substantial portions of the old road system, reproduced here in Figure 7.59.

Figure 7.60 shows a new design for McCormick's Creek. In addition to using portions of the existing road system, this rehabilitation approach lets you keep the toilet/shower buildings in place, which would likely be a management constraint. Again the solution works for managers, users, and the environment.

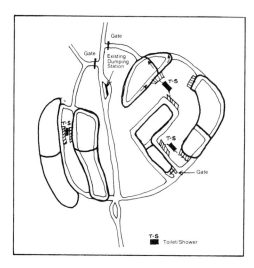

Figure 7.60

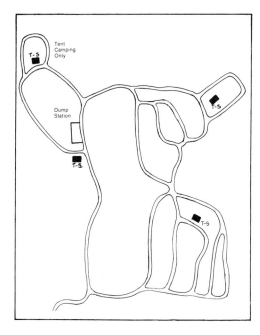

Figure 7.61

AN EXERCISE IN REHABILITATION

Since you're more likely to be faced with rehabilitation challenges than new designs, we thought you might like to practice your art. Figure 7.61 reproduces the existing Kentucky campground we showed you in Figure 1.17. Try your hand at improving this design by using as much of the existing road system as possible and all four toilet/showers. You may also have to move some facilities. (Hint: look at the location of the sewage dumping station.) To make the assignment more interesting, we'll impose two additional constraints on you. First, the area in the upper left corner of Figure 7.61 needs to be managed for tent camping only. How would you control this? Second, we may want to enlarge the campground next year. Can you provide us with some expansion opportunities? Appendix C shows one solution to this exercise. When you look at it, keep two things in mind: 1) there are better ways of designing this campground if we were starting from scratch; and 2) both Figure 7.61 and the solution in Appendix C would fail to get passing grades in our class in campground planning. To see an alternative solution to 1) and find the reason for 2), you're going to have to turn the page and read Chapter Eight . . . .

APPENDIX C

Solution to Chapter Seven Campground Design

As we suggested at the end of Chapter Seven, rehabilitating an existing recreation area can be quite a challenge. The constraints we imposed on you for this assignment probably made your task even more difficult, but they also lent a "real-life" flavor to your task. The solution we've

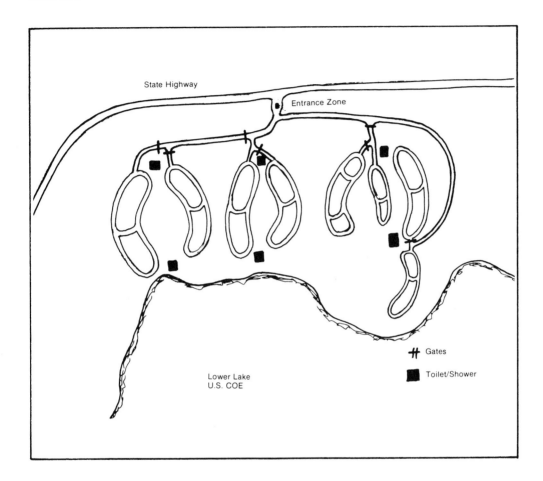

State Highway

Entrance Zone

Gates

Toilet/Shower

Lower Lake
U.S. COE

Figure 7.62

included shows one way of improving on the existing design while providing potential administrative control and opportunities for expanding the area. This solution, however, does *not* speak to the real problem with most campgrounds, a problem that has less to do with recreation design than with recreation, period. If you haven't read Chapter Eight yet, now would be an excellent time to do so. If you've already read the discussion on programming, how might you improve on the design we've shown here?

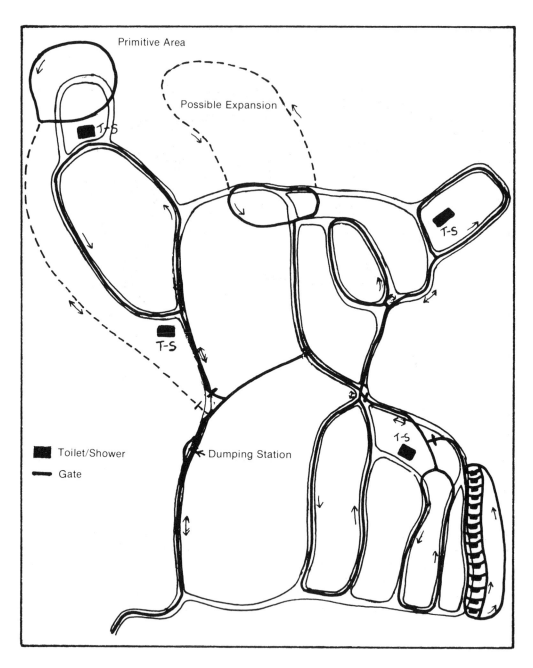

Primitive Area

Possible Expansion

T-S

T-S

T-S

T-S

■ Toilet/Shower

▬ Gate

Dumping Station

Appendix C

8

OUTDOOR RECREATION PROGRAMMING OR YES, VIRGINIA, CAMPING CAN BE FUN

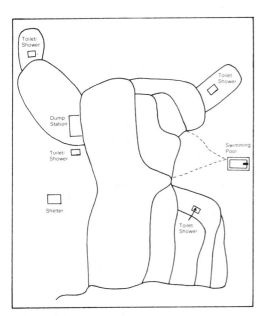

Figure 8.1

INTRODUCTION: SOME PHILOSOPHICAL CONCERNS

In Chapter Seven you were left with two challenges. One was to rehabilitate the poorly designed campground shown in Figure 7.59. The other, less straightforward issue was to determine the *real* problem with the area. If you haven't figured out what this was, don't feel too badly. Most outdoor recreation professionals — managers, support staff, and academics — have "missed the boat" on this question as well. As you've heard before, errors can be in both commission and omis-

sion. The poor design was *committed;* to fix it would require an investment of funds and some knowledge of rehabilitation techniques. The *omission* would be harder to correct, for the missing element in this campground, as is too often the case, was *programming.* There were neither the facilities — play courts, playfields, campfire theater, and the like — to *support* a diversified array of programs nor the *supportive attitude* of staff to make a move to correct such a lack.

To understand this second point, you need to see an expanded view of the facilities in Figure 7.59, and Figure 8.1 provides this view. The campground was adjacent to a large swimming pool, open from noon to 7:00 pm, and both facilities were managed by the same agency. When we first visited the area, however, we learned that no attempts had been made to use the pool as a program element for the campground. Campers could use the pool, but only in the same way as all other visitors to the park: on a pay-as-you-go basis. We see several things here: a *missed opportunity* for the agency to increase use of the pool, perhaps through early- and late-hour swimming sessions for campground users at a reduced entry fee; and less exercise and fun because of the lack of *incentives* to use the pool (decreased fees, organized programs directed toward them, or both). Mostly, we see an unfortunate attitude, one that suggests a management philosophy of indifference to programs. We don't try to hide being opinionated, but we think *the lack of outdoor recreation programming is the most serious shortcoming in the profession today.*

The most difficult aspect of the problem is the attitude responsible for it. Probably much of the reason for this stems from the resource-oriented, as opposed to people-oriented, background of many professionals working in outdoor recreation. How serious and widespread is the problem? Think back to your last few visits to resource-based parks and recreation areas, particularly those managed by state or federal agencies. How much recreation programming do you remember? (We aren't talking here of environmental or historical interpretation programs. *That* discussion comes later.) Chances are good that you won't remember much because, with a few notable exceptions, these programs simply aren't offered. Why? Read carefully the following scenarios, all of which we've encountered in visits to parks and recreation areas in the last few years.

— Once upon a time we talked with a young National Park Service ranger who had been *reprimanded* by his superiors for suggesting that campers be allowed to play softball at a Grand Canyon National Park campground; it seems that some campers had asked his permission to play, but you can read this reprimand as, "Visitors to National Parks shouldn't even *want* to play softball."
— Once upon a time a US Forest Service assistant ranger in a Southern National Forest committed heresy by mowing a half-acre space near his largest campground so that campers could play badminton and throw frisbees. Read this as a heresy because it suggests that visitors are not happy hugging trees and smelling flowers when they visit National Forests.
— Once upon a time we spoke to a US Army Recreation Service Officer who was upset because young children in one of her travel camps in Italy were playing in

and bringing dirt into the campground shower building. Read this as a problem resulting from a lack of anything else for the youngsters — or other campers — to do.
— Once upon a time a private-campground owner told a professor friend of ours that she didn't require research into user needs because she knew what her campers wanted — and it wasn't fun and games. Read this as a head-in-the-sand attitude some private-sector folks had better abandon before they start waking up to empty campgrounds.
— Once upon a time a GS-4 seasonal interpretive specialist with the Corps of Engineers got a reluctant "okay" to play softball with youngsters in her campground providing *and only providing* that she first interpret the wooden bat as a product of the natural resources the children were using. Read this as a management assumption that the *only* reason people — including children — visit the out-of-doors is to soak up as much environmental education as they can.
— Once upon a time a lady in a campground restroom in a Midwestern state park that lacked programming overheard teenage boys daring each other to run into the ladies room. Read this as a cause-and-effect relationship between boredom and unsociable behavior.

These "grim fairy tales" tell us that failing to *program* outdoor recreation areas is, in essence, failing to meet the needs of users *and* the cause of ever-increasing depreciative behavior problems. Several years ago, a number of federal recreation agencies had their collective hands smacked by the General Accounting Office (GAO) for "double counting" users (reporting inflated use figures). The reprimand by GAO resulted in new methods for tracking visitation rates — a positive step as far as it went. However, this situation reminds us of one you've seen before: fighting *effects* rather than *causes*. Since budget allocations are in part tied to quantitative measures (numbers of users), agencies needed to show high levels of use; thus many many figures got inflated. Could the *cause* of low-use levels — then and now — be tied to programs? When we travel, we keep a log of what we see in campgrounds. Consider the following "confessions of a campground snooper," some entries in this log during a recent summer.

— July 7th: A new National Park Service campground on Missouri's Current River, three hundred units, two hundred ninety built in areas without shade; no play equipment for children; programming limited to nature walks on weekends; no utility hook-ups; *four units occupied.*
— July 22nd (a Friday afternoon): A two-year-old Arkansas state park forty miles from Memphis; one hundred units, all in the sun; parking spurs barricaded from unit furniture; water and electric hook-ups provided; play amenities for young children *only*; all activities nature-oriented; *three units occupied.*
— September 2nd (the Friday before Labor Day): Seven hundred camping units in three family campgrounds in a Corps of Engineers area in southern Illinois; Seventy percent of the units built in the sun; nature programs only; *one hundred units occupied.* (Remember that Labor Day is one of the "big three" holidays for peak-use.)
— August 12th (another Friday): Backbone Rock Campground on the Cherokee National Forest; twenty units; a free area; no security or protection; no utilities; no programming; *no campers.*

We could go on, but the song remains the same. Obviously these areas and other, similar ones worldwide suffer from a variety of problems, many of which are design-

related. But we're talking about programming here. Consider the situation at a campground in Virginia's Hungry Mother State Park. Here the area was poorly designed and suffers from compacted soil, erosion, and dying trees. It has a trampled-on, no-grass, "overused" appearance *and* excellent use figures. The campground also offers a broad spectrum of recreation programs — programs which are fun for folks of all ages. There should be a message here.

Perhaps we should qualify our purpose at this point. We aren't trained or terribly experienced in terms of recreation programming. Further, this isn't a programming text, so we'll leave the goals, strategies, typologies of leisure, and the like to others more qualified than we to speak to these issues. We'll also limit this chapter to a discussion of programs in *campgrounds*, partly because this is where they seem to be the least in evidence and partly because we think programs are needed in campgrounds as much, if not more, than any other type of recreation area.

Over the past few decades, we've been involved in a host of different aspects of outdoor recreation — planning, design, administration, teaching, interpretation, and, unlike many planners, *extensive participation*. As a result, we've come to appreciate the benefits of all sorts of facilities and programs in campgrounds. Both personally and professionally, we're "up" on *all* elements of the outdoor realm and have discovered the following truisms:

1. Most resource-based recreation areas are "out in the boonies," removed from urban environments.
2. Most of the use in these areas originates from municipal settings; most of our park visitors are city folks.
3. Most of the recreation programs you'll find in cities and towns are flavored with *fun*; league sports, arts-and-crafts activi-

ties, dances, puppet shows, and similar activities for people from three to ninety-three.

4. When you go to the woods — to campgrounds in resource-based settings — you typically find one of two things: either no programming *at all* or only interpretive programs, usually limited to weekends and daylight hours (a nature walk on Wednesday and a dandy program on boater safety on Saturday night).

To make the point of this list clear, here are two more stories for you. The first involves a visit we once made to a California State Park in the Big Sur area. The campground was in the redwoods, but it was old, suffering from impact and poor design, and mostly devoid of campers. We did, however, see a campfire theater and asked a staff person we encountered if programs were held there. "Occasionally," he replied. "Next weekend, a Forest Service Ranger is coming in to tell the story of a forest fire."

Enjoyment is the key to campground programming, and the focus of our next story. Sitting in an Indiana restaurant, we overheard a conversation between two men who appeared to be in their forties. One was telling the other about how his two teenaged children had recently ruined the family vacation. It seems that two days after arriving in a state-park campground, the teens wanted to go home. Why? They had nothing to do. The next day the family left, spoiling Dad's vacation *and* reducing the number of visitor days the park could report at year's end.

These stories raise two questions you need to consider. First, *why?* Why hasn't recreation programming been a big deal in campgrounds? We feel there are three reasons for this. First, although it's not really their fault, in one sense the culprit is the National Park Service. TVA, the Corps of Engineers, the Forest Service, and most state-park systems have followed the

programming lead of the National Parks. In general, NPS interpretive and living-history programs are *excellent,* attracting millions of visitors each year. But where? And why? Visitors go to Appomattox, Gettysburg, Shiloh, and other Park Service areas *because of* their historical significance and to see the NPS programs. They go to nature centers and interpretive trails to learn about the environment. They want to be informed, to be educated, or they wouldn't stop in at these areas. But here's the kicker: visitors go to our *campgrounds* to relax, refresh, and recreate. To rest their minds, not to tax them. Personally, we think well-conceived historical and environmental programs are great. Professionally, we simply can't afford an attitude like "if I like it, it must be right for everybody."

Here's an example. A few years back, we attended a "camper's fair" weekend, a three-day special event in a campground where recreation programs were in effect. The potential audience for programs consisted of over one thousand campers ranging in age from tots to senior citizens. One program, a puppet show put on by teenagers from a local church, attracted over six hundred campers. Two nature walks, both of which were conducted by professionals, attracted a *total* of three campers (two of whom were one of your authors and his wife). We aren't suggesting that campers never attend nature programs; obviously they occasionally do. We do wonder whether, if *given a choice,* many might prefer something else. However, the real message in this story addresses two other points. One, *provide the choice.* Schedule interpretive programs, certainly, but make them a *small* piece of your programming pie. Second, and this is the focus of Chapter Eight, *camping should be fun!* Campers visit most of our parks to enjoy themselves. Park professionals don't have to *teach* everyone who visits their campgrounds something in order to justify their existence. Far too often in our programs, we've tragically *transposed* ideas appropriate for historical sites and nature centers into campgrounds where most users simply aren't interested. Camping should be fun, and given the success of recreation-oriented programs in municipal settings, what "logic" tells us not to transpose these into campgrounds for the same users who attend them at home?

A second reason that recreation programming hasn't been successful in campgrounds refers back to a topic we discussed in Chapter Seven: what the typical "campground" really is. With few exceptions, what most public agencies and some private concerns call "campgrounds" are really *sporting camps,* small areas of perhaps twenty to thirty units where services are limited to access and attraction (roads and the natural environment). On one hand, these areas are too small to justify either on-site programming personnel or the diversity of facilities you should have in order to offer a broad spectrum of recreation programs.

From a second perspective, think about the users of these areas. In large, developed-site family campgrounds where a variety of programs and support facilities are available, it has been our experience to find only about sixty percent of the visitors are interested in attending programs of any type. Therefore, if an average camping party consists of four people, you might, in a three-hundred-unit campground, have over seven hundred people as a potential market for programs. In a twenty-five-unit campground, the corresponding number would be sixty if the clientele were the same. At the opposite end of the spectrum, in small sporting camps a sizable proportion of the users is usually comprised of hunting and/or fishing parties, folks who mostly want you and your staff to let them alone to do their own thing. They are *not* the kind of clientele where recreation or interpretive programs are likely to succeed.

This situation is another argument for, as we suggested in Chapter One, thinking,

planning, and building big; developing areas large enough to protect, manage, maintain, and *program* for families. The Forest Service, Corps of Engineers, and TVA have all tried interpretive programming in small sporting camps, all three "enjoyed" the same negative results, all couldn't understand why, and all canceled programs in sporting camps *and* family campgrounds.

A final reason we feel recreation programming is not more evident in campgrounds brings us back to the point we raised earlier about attitudes toward programs. This point is best illustrated by another experience we encountered while camping in a Corps of Engineers area in North Dakota. Although the campground was relatively full, only a few campers appeared at an evening interpretive program we attended. After the program was over, we approached the naturalist who had conducted it and asked her if interpretive programs were the only type of activity offered and if the attendance had been typical. Her response was "Yes, this is all we offer, and I'm just doing my job — I don't care whether people come or not." Too bad, and all too typical of many "professionals" in many agencies.

Hopefully this was an extreme example. We haven't often encountered opinions like this one. However, we do frequently discover attitudes that reflect a lack of *introspection* relative to campers' program preferences. Managers and support staff, it seems, either don't know or, as in our example, don't care to know what campers want. In part, this lack of introspection may hark back to the training outdoor recreation professionals get while in school. In general, folks trained in forestry or other resource disciplines (if they take a programming course at all) learn interpretation — period. Conversely, program courses in many "people-oriented," HPER or education, curricula teach fun programming, but don't consider resource-based recreation areas as a medium for this message of enjoyment. Earlier we suggested you should think about two questions. The first was *why* recreation programming hasn't been an integral part of the campground services we provide, but the second was even more important: *so what?* What difference does it make if recreation programs aren't a big deal in campgrounds?

It seems to us that there are three responses to this question, each of which deals with an aspect of "planning parks for people" you've heard before — *users, management,* and *the environment.* The advantage of programming in campgrounds from the user's perspective is quite simple: programs provide opportunities for enjoyment, and maximizing the potential benefits of any recreation experience is a worthy goal for our profession. Offering a broad spectrum of recreation programs is one means of working toward this goal. From a management perspective, programming is an excellent way to enhance use figures in campgrounds. If people enjoy a particular recreation experience, they're inclined to do two things: repeat it and tell their friends about it. Over time, return visits and word-of-mouth can build a clientele for you.

From the standpoint of protecting the environment, programs also offer an alternative to negative pastimes in campgrounds. The philosophy of service provision limited to access and attraction has reaped a harvest of depreciative behavior in campgrounds worldwide. We've seen seven-year-olds sitting near their campsites aimlessly hacking on a tree with a hatchet. If we don't provide opportunities for enjoyment, users will try to entertain themselves, and, whether from ignorance or malice, much of this behavior ends up harming the environment and/or our facilities. Typically, we respond with more rules and more emphasis on law enforcement, and end up fighting effects rather than causes.

Let's dig a little deeper into the implications of failing to provide a diversity of campground programs. Consider a couple of seemingly unrelated topics — demographics and squirrels. First, demographics leads to consideration of camping-group composition. Who are our campers? If you drive through a typical campground *without* recreation programming, you'll see retirees, adults, and young children. Generally you *won't* see teenagers. Small children camp with their families because they have to. Teens, if given a choice, tend to avoid most campgrounds. It may be a painful revelation for resource-oriented professionals, but our experience tells us that teenagers, for the most part, are bored in a forest environment. Let's offer them nature programs, you say? We say these folks go to school nine months of the year; the *last* thing they want is an eager naturalist pushing educational programs at them.

We've talked to families of campers all over the country and what we find is this: only about twenty percent of the teenagers in these families camp with their parents. In other words, for every five camping households with teens, we get one teenager in our campgrounds. In facilities where recreation programs are offered on a regular basis, we've seen the percentage of teens camping with their families rise to between eighty and ninety percent. It's true that teens *don't* camp with their families. It's not true teens *won't* camp with them!

We suggested earlier that slightly less than two-thirds of the adults are interested in campground programs. After asking teens in a large, program-oriented campground the same question one summer, we found that eighty-seven percent said they attended at least one recreation activity each day they camped. The important point here, we feel, is a matter of *family unity.* If fun-oriented programs motivate teenagers to camp — and we're convinced they do — you can encourage entire families to recreate *together*. Maybe we're old-fashioned, but this strikes us as being a pretty nifty objective for recreation professionals.

Squirrels? Maybe this is stretching literary license a bit thin, but we're trying to get your attention on an important point here. Squirrels gather nuts and store them in anticipation of bleak times ahead. Similarly, recreation professionals need to think about "putting up a harvest" for the future. If teenagers don't go to campgrounds now, or go and don't enjoy themselves, who will be our campers in the next generation? We aren't suggesting that campgrounds are on the road to extinction without recreation programs; however, we are convinced that programs can lead to increased numbers of campers both now and in the years to come. Programming is a means of *beckoning* people to our campgrounds throughout their lives; this coupled with more enjoyment and positive behavior justifies a commitment to programming. "Secondary" benefits would also be increased camping-gear sales and increased revenue from user fees in both the public and private sectors.

Ask yourself a series of questions. Do you want people to enjoy themselves in campgrounds? Would you like to encourage entire families to camp together? Do you want campers to feel welcome in your areas? If you like the idea of building positive public relations, increasing your use rates, discouraging depreciative behavior, minimizing the money you spend on law enforcement, and enhancing the fun people have in your campgrounds — program. We've given numerous lectures across the US, heralding the exciting benefits of fun programming. Those in our audiences who have changed their less-than-successful nature dockets to fun activities have been delighted with the results.

TYPES OF CAMPGROUND PROGRAMS

The critical element involved in campground programming is *diversity*. In subsequent sections of this chapter, we'll discuss kinds of facilities helpful, though not indispensible, for successful programs; planning and design considerations for programming; and program promotion and conduct. Most important, however, is a broad spectrum of activity opportunities for all users: retirees, mature adults, young adults, teens, and preteens. Some programs, such as grocery bingo or shuffleboard tournaments, may appeal to more than one age group. Others, such as a bicycle race, may generate interest from a smaller proportion of your campers.

This raises two points you should consider. First, don't try to develop all your programs for "universal appeal." Getting entire families to enjoy a program together is great, but some simply won't attract all age groups. Therefore you should focus some of your efforts on specific target audiences. Second, successful programs aren't entirely dependent on maximum attendance. As we've suggested before, some campers will want to "do their own thing" and are perfectly happy whether you program or not. Shortly we'll talk about ways to increase the proportion of campers who attend programs, but attempting to "hard sell" or force activities on an entire camping clientele is both futile and aggravating.

The potential range of individual programs is limited only by the imagination and enthusiasm of the programmer. We can, though, classify most programs into one of six categories, including active, passive, interpretive, skills, nature arts and crafts, and a broad classification of activities we can refer to as special events.

Active Programs

Court games like basketball and volleyball, field sports like softball and touch football, and waterfront activities like races, relays, and water volleyball are examples of active programs, programs that will appeal to younger adults, teens, and preteens. Conducting active programs requires you to integrate all aspects of campground management into a comprehensive plan for providing user services. We've seen teenagers, when given the opportunity, play volleyball on a lighted playcourt until 2:00 am. We've also seen campground regulations enforcing a 9:00 pm curfew on activities. While quiet hours are an excellent management policy since many early risers retire early, simply enforcing a "no noise after 9:00 pm" rule suggests that managers and planners don't consider *all* campers. Campers are there to enjoy themselves. Going to bed and getting up when they want should be *their* decision as long as *you* plan areas where they can do their own thing without disturbing others. If teenagers want to stay up until after midnight and their parents don't object, managers, by enforcing early quiet hours, say, "Your needs aren't as important as those of other campers." Potentially noisy active programs *can* co-exist with quiet evenings if the facilities designed for these activities are zoned away from campground "bedroom areas" where quiet, at least after 10:30 or 11:00 pm, is a management goal.

Passive Programs

Storytelling, board games, campfire programs, grocery bingo, and other "quiet" activities are examples of passive programs. Depending on what you offer, these may appeal to a specific age group (fairy tales for children, a "senior-citizen checkers tournament") or a broader clientele (a "film festival" at your campfire theater with movies borrowed from the local public library). Passive programs can help salvage a camping trip dampened by poor weather, when "cabin fever" sets in quickly after one or two rainy days. An activity at a shelter building can be a welcome change from sitting inside a camping trailer wondering if the sun will ever come out again. Passive programs also provide an alternative to more strenuous activities. It may not be quite so difficult to explain to a six-year-old why he or she can't swim immediately after lunch if there's a toe-painting contest at the campfire theater at 1:00 pm.

Interpretive Programs

We have several comments to make about interpretation in campgrounds, most of which are philosophical. First, many of our earlier statements may have led you to conclude that we view interpretive programs negatively. We hope this isn't the case, because we strongly support a reasonable ratio of well-thought-out environmental and historical presentations. Our concern is your *approach* to these activities. Nature hikes, lectures on forest products, and talks on the nearby Civil War battlefield are typical of the activities many professionals think of when the subject of interpretation arises. This is unfortunate. Some "traditional" interpretive programs in campgrounds are well-received; some campers, us included, will get up at 6:00 am to go on an early-morning songbird walk. The problem with *limiting* interpretive programs to this approach is that *most campers won't*. For the majority of campground users, we feel that traditional methods of attempting to educate through programs simply haven't much appeal. To test our point, don't look at the *number* of campers you attract to a typical interpretive program; take a look at the proportion of users who *don't* attend.

In one respect, interpretive specialists are similar to some college professors we know; they may understand their material inside out and be terribly enthusiastic about it, but *conveying* this information and excitement is another matter. Just because *you* thrill over a woodpecker at work at dawn doesn't mean your campers will. Interpretive programs can make campers more conscious of the environment and their cultural heritage. Thus we advocate including these programs in the activities you offer. But *camping should be fun,* and this philosophy extends to educational programs as well.

We feel that traditional approaches to interpretation should be continued, with moderation, for the small percentage of campers who are inclined to learn for the sake of knowledge itself. Remember, however, the following guidelines. First, these programs should be *only* one dimension of a much broader spectrum of activity opportunities you provide; *please* don't assume that everyone has a burning desire to learn. No matter how important you think it is for people to appreciate nature and culture, you simply can't force-feed these topics to everyone. Offering only traditional interpretive programs attempts a strategy you've heard before: you can lead a horse to water . . .

A second consideration concerns potential *alternatives* to traditional approaches to interpretation, and we know of two you may find useful. First, conduct recreation programs with an *undertone* of interpretation. An excellent example of this is to plan a bike hike on which you have three or four scheduled rest stops. Make your first rest stop in the shade of a tree where squirrels nest (squirrels again?). Here you might talk about "homes in the forest" while participants stretch their legs and get a drink. Have your next stop planned under a bird's nest and ask riders if they see any other forest dwellings. In other words, keep the educational aspect of the ride low-key and secondary to the outing itself. Then users will enjoy themselves and learn a little in the process.

Another alternative to traditional interpretive programs is to conduct a "real" interpretive program around a fun theme. One of the most popular activities we've ever seen in a campground is one you've probably never heard of: the *critter crawl.* The critter crawl is a two-stage program. In the first stage, you meet with participants and tell them to find a critter in the woods — a frog, a turtle, or an insect — most any small critter will do as long as it can't fly. At this point, you should remind campers not to hurt the animal and use this as a springboard for an informative talk (*not* a lecture) on the need to protect natural resources. Next, give everyone half an hour to search. After they return with their discoveries, the critter crawl begins. To conduct this part of the program, mark a small circle perhaps three feet in diameter inside a larger circle about ten feet in diameter. Contestants place their critters on the ground within the inner circle and, at a signal, release their animals. The first critter that crosses the outer circle wins. You may need a few "ground rules," like any critter that eats another is disqualified. We've seen this happen, but a good interpreter can seize this opportunity to talk about the food chain. After the crawl, there's time to talk about returning the critters to the woods, again with the potential for "soft" interpretation.

With this program and the bike hike, you can plan around the common denominator of *fun.* If your programmer is a capable interpreter, participants will learn a few things, but the learning environments won't be "painful."

Skills Programs

In Chapter Six, we discussed planning facilities for bicycling- and archery-skills development and asked you to design an area for teaching fishing techniques. In addition to these activities, a camp-skills program can include tips on outdoor cooking and canoeing. Outdoor-cooking programs are a good way of "easing into" skills-development activities because they don't require much in the way of support facilities or equipment. A small open space for a campfire, a programmer who has had a bit of experience in camping, and a few cooking utensils are all you need. By asking campers to provide their own foodstuffs in advance, you can also minimize expenses. As with many, but not all other campground programs, outdoor-cooking activities offer some opportunities to incorporate low-key interpretive lessons: "This is how the pioneers did it." "Don't cut live saplings for firewood."

Canoeing-skills programs may require more of an investment, but costs can be kept low with a little foresight. You don't need new, expensive canoes since secondhand aluminum ones will work quite well. As an alternative, it may be possible to work out a cooperative agreement with a local outfitter. During slow, mid-week periods, canoe-rental businesses may be willing to rent you several at reduced rates, or even loan them to you in exchange for some free advertisement.

There are two points to consider here. First, programming creativity doesn't stop with thinking of good programs; the *how* as well as the *what* takes some thought and effort. Second, programs can create *opportunities* for positive recreation experience beyond the "now" of a camping trip. If you teach an eight-year-old how to canoe, he or she may develop a lifelong avocation.

Skills programs, regardless of the activity, can also function as an effective means of getting families to recreate together. If one of the main reasons a family visits your campground is for Dad to fish, you may be able to use his interest as a bridge to promote a family activity in a fishing-skills program. For example, when we worked for the TVA, we saw an interesting phenomenon occur. Traditionally, deer hunters who camped in Land Between the Lakes used the small sporting camps the agency provided. When programmers in the neighboring developed campgrounds started offering archery-skills programs, some of these hunters began, for the first time, to camp in these areas and *brought their families with them*. Since a variety of other programs was offered, all family members could enjoy the hunting trip, not just the hunters. The skills program attracted users, who brought other users, who attended other programs, which . . . there seems to be a "ripple effect" here.

Nature Arts and Crafts

Activities such as rock painting and making dolls from corn cobs and other natural materials are examples of nature-arts-and-crafts programs. These activities can be directed to a specific age group like preteens or focus on a broader campground population. As with skills-development programs, nature arts and crafts offer the opportunity for low-key interpretive messages. Depending on funds and staffing availability and limitations, nature arts and crafts can be organized with an extensive array of supplies or operated, if necessary, "on a shoestring." Most of the materials you'll need occur naturally; acorns, pine cones, sweet-gum balls, leaves, stones, and similar supplies can be picked up by participants before or during the program. This points out an important aspect of program provision. While it's *nice* to have a well-funded budget for recreation programming, it really isn't a requirement. The only things you really need to operate a successful activities program are a little creativity and a lot of enthusiasm.

Special Programs

The activities we've discussed to this point are by no means exhaustive, but with the preceding discussion as a guidelines, you should be able to develop a much broader set of program offerings. The types of activities described above also have one thing in common; they are examples of programs that you can conduct on an on-going, every-day basis in campgrounds. However, a good programmer shouldn't stop with the "ordinary." To make visiting your campground a *special occasion* — one user will remember — it's a good idea to plan and conduct some programs which are, well, special.

The range of opportunities for special programs is limited only by your imagination, though to ensure *successful* programs it helps to know who your users are. People who camp in developed-site, family campgrounds tend to be "just folks." You'll find chemical engineers and college professors camped next to retired janitors and twenty-year-old maintenance workers. Demographic and socio-economic variables are interesting to social scientists, but for you as a programmer or a planner who supports programming, there's a more basic variable at work here. Some people, regardless of their education, income, and career, simply enjoy camping in developed-site campgrounds. These individuals are basically down-to-earth, not a very scientific description but a fitting one. We once spent several minutes explaining understory vegetation to an unshaven, middle-aged camper who, we learned later, had a Ph.D. in forestry. He never said a word to discourage our less-than-learned lecture.

Special programs can be centered around a specific *theme* like a square-dance weekend, a special *event* like a star-gazing outing to view shooting stars, a particular *group* like a National Campers and Hikers retreat, a "*contrived occasion*," like Christmas in July, or simply a collection of programs like the Camper's Fair we mentioned earlier. Flea markets, auctions, food fairs, and clean-up weekends are other examples of special occasions — ones the user will remember. We once attended a successful weekend centered around pulling nails out of trees and installing lantern-hanging devices. The weekend worked because it was well advertised and organized, and offered a broad spectrum of fun activities throughout. By working with current and potential user groups, you can develop special programs to complement just about any interest, enhance the experience campers have, and boost your use figures considerably. While programming isn't difficult, it does take a commitment from management, hard work, and a little foresight. Let's turn our attention now to some campground features and facilities you can use to your advantage in activity programs.

PROGRAM SUPPORT FACILITIES

At the end of Chapter Seven we suggested that there was a problem with the campground in Figure 7.59 that our "rehabilitation efforts" in Appendix C didn't solve. The problem was *programming;* neither the "as built" design in Figure 7.59 nor the solution in Appendix C addressed it. Figure 8.2 shows the same campground with one possible set of program amenities added. However, this approach only creates the opportunity to program; it doesn't solve all the management and environmental problems resulting from poor *design*. Figure 8.3 takes one final look at the *potential* this campground could have

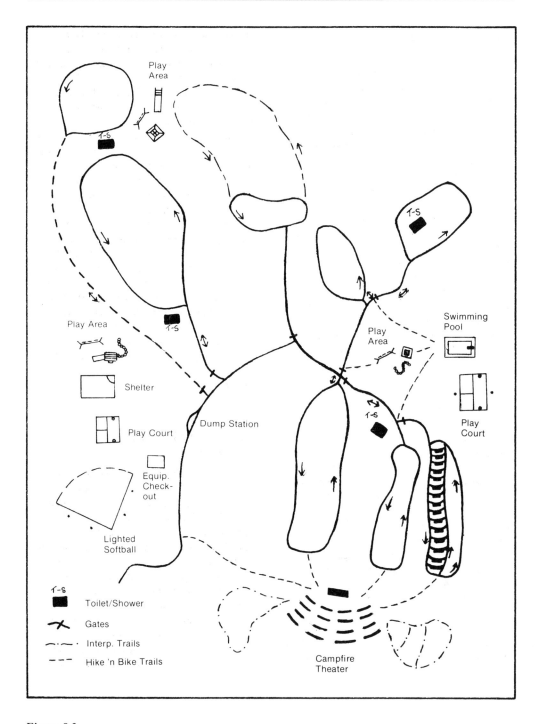

Figure 8.2

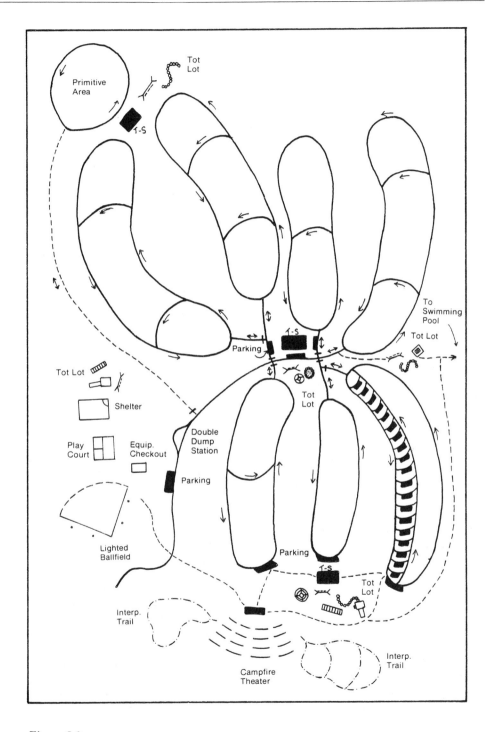

Figure 8.3

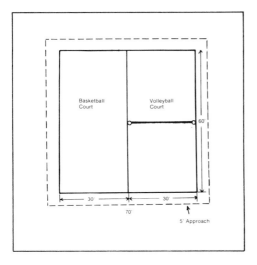

Figure 8.4

had if the planners responsible had designed for programming as well as for users, staff, and environment.

We'll leave it to you to identify the positive aspects of this solution. (Hint: think about control, circulation, design psychology, reducing impact, and programming.) We'd like to focus now on the features it's *desirable* to have in a campground from a programming perspective. Note that we said "desirable." *All you really need* to conduct programs is an audience and a desire to help users enjoy themselves. However, a few support facilities like the following will make life easier for program staff.

Play Courts

If we were asked to choose one single program-support facility, it would be the multipurpose play court. If well designed and zoned, this facility can support basketball, volleyball, children's games, teen dances, square dances, skills programs, and a host of other activities. Figure 8.4 shows a layout for a multipurpose play court. Ideally, it should be designed and built as a program facility with a paved surface. If development dollars are limited, however, there are alternatives. Ball courts may be "superimposed" on an existing paved parking lot by painting lines for court boundaries on the lot surface and erecting standards for nets and goals. Whichever approach you use, remember to orient the direction of play along a north/south axis. A flat, grassy area can be used as a volleyball court, though if the selected site is shaded you should scrape the turf and provide a fifty/fifty mixture of sand and soil packed smooth and graded. The value or utility of a multipurpose play court can also be extended by adding lighting and electrical outlets. When deciding where to site a play court, don't forget our discussions of screening, separation of conflicting uses, and the difference between regulation league play and the less structured form of play in campgrounds.

Campfire Theaters

Campfire theaters or amphitheaters are to passive programs what multipurpose courts are to active programs; they serve a variety of uses. Evening programs, daytime story hours, and staging areas for interpretive hikes are a few examples of their various applications. Campfire theaters also offer us an excellent opportunity to talk about how design decisions should be made, regardless of the type of facility involved. Consider this scenario: you've just been hired as the Assistant Manager of Cornfed State Park in Nebraska. Your first assignment is to supervise the development of a new campfire theater for the campground. The campground has 250 units and, because recreation programs are emphasized, use is quite high. Our question to you is how many linear feet of seating space should you provide? From a planning standpoint what we're really asking is how you should justify this decision. Put more simply, we're asking *why*. As we've said before, you should always be able to justify the planning decisions you make. Here, as usual, your decision should be based on minimizing costs balanced with meeting the needs of your users. We're sure you know the answer to this question as a good planner, but for the dummy seated next to you, let's walk through the logic you used to arrive at the solution: 1) you knew the campground had a maximum capacity of one thousand people (remember PAOT?), based on 250 units times four users per site; 2) you knew from looking at program records that only about fifty percent of your campers attended evening programs; 3) you knew from books on standards that the average adult needs about two feet of seating space, but since many of your campers are children, you amended this figure to 1.5 feet; 4) you then developed a simple formula which states that units times users per site times potential audience times individual seating space equals necessary seating space. Thus, using the numbers from Cornfed Campground, you arrived at 250 times four times fifty percent times 1.5 feet equals 750 linear feet of seating space. As a conscientious planner, this is the kind of approach you should always take.

You should also consider a few other design aspects of campfire theaters. First, it's a good idea to provide both barrier-free seating and ramped access to the stage area of the theater. You should also allow for user involvement in campfire programs, and an inaccessible stage may exclude some from participating. Access trails from the rest of the campground to the theater should be barrier-free as well, and if at all possible, choose natural slopes as locations for theaters to enhance the view of the program area or stage. If you don't have this option, you should elevate the stage so people seated in the rear of the theater will have unob-

structed views. *Within* a campground, distance from camp units to the theater doesn't seem to be much of a factor in determining who attends programs there. However, you shouldn't, as many state parks do, locate a theater *outside* the campground and expect high levels of camper attendance.

Many state parks have recreation buildings and evening programming near their park lodges. These are often two, three, or more miles from the family campground. Since programs open to all park visitors are scheduled at night in the recreation building, it appears that managers and programmers feel campers have an opportunity to participate — and if they don't, they must not be interested. We see this as another failure to plan parks for people. Campers, even those interested in programming, are quite difficult to "lure" from their sites at night. Thus we recommend that you program with enthusiasm at well-zoned program facilities *inside* your campgrounds. This doesn't imply that you should stop programming at facilities outside the campground; you just shouldn't expect to attract a large proportion of your campers to these activities.

From an administrative standpoint, it may not be a good idea to bring non-campers into a campground for programming, or you'll have an admission-control problem. If you're building a new area or adding program features to an existing park, one solution is to zone new program amenities on the edge of the campground nearest other park facilities so they can be reached on foot from both within and outside the campground.

Campfire theaters should be zoned away from active areas where noise may conflict with your quieter programs. Vegetative screening and a "buffer zone" of, for example, a system of interpretive trails can help reduce conflicts between programs going on simultaneously in the theater and an adjacent active area. If you provide parking for the theater, be sure either 1) that the lot is oriented *away* from the stage area of the theater, or 2) that you build an earthen berm to prevent vehicle headlights from shining onto the stage. You should provide "stage lights," however, to allow program staff the flexibility for a variety of activities. Since planning is a *support* function, work closely with program staff to develop the facilities that a projection stand in the seating area that they will need, a projection stand in the seating area with electrical outlet, for example.

Playfields

Playfields serve as a good example of how recreation programs in campgrounds can be implemented without major outlays of dollars. A relatively flat open field, cleared with a bush hog, can serve as a program zone for a variety of activities. Soccer, touch football, softball, frisbee, golf, a variety of children's games, and a number of other activities don't require expensive equipment or regulation play space. It isn't an environmentally sound practice to use a groundhog for home plate, but you don't have to provide major-league-quality bases either. As we suggested in Chapter Six, a perfectly level field isn't even a necessity. Gradually sloping terrain may drain more effectively and can shorten the distance balls will roll if you're short on space.

To reinforce a point we made earlier, regulation play and competition are not as important to campers as the opportunity to participate and have a little fun. If you have the funds available to build a backstop, do so. We feel it's more important, however, to provide an enthusiastic program person who has a little creativity. A good programmer can create activities with little in the way of support, whereas a well-designed play zone may go mostly unused unless someone is there to organize programs.

Shelter Buildings

Shelter buildings, if you have access to an architect, are easy to *design*. They aren't quite as simple to *plan*. The distinction we're making here is one of recreation *use*. If you commit the funds to build a shelter, you should make sure that what you get is what your programmer and users need. To determine what these needs are, it's therefore critical to talk to the people who use your campground. A well-designed shelter may mean one with a good roof, a floor, and support beams. A well-planned shelter might include shuffleboard-court surfacing, a large grill for group cook-outs, and other program amenities aimed at the types of users who come to your campground.

In addition to serving as an activity zone, the shelter can be a focal point of your programming efforts. If it is centrally located, a good idea, if possible, it can double as an equipment check-out building. Providing inexpensive and *durable* equipment — aluminum bats, frisbees, balls, and the like — either free or for small rental fees, can create activity opportunities. The shelter can additionally serve as a gathering point for hikes, nature walks, and other "diffused" programs. One advantage of using shelters for this purpose is getting your users to a protected spot should the weather turn nasty. Once you have a congregation, you can always substitute an indoor activity for the rained-out hike.

Fishing Piers

As we suggested earlier, some campers won't be interested in the campground programs you develop, and fishing piers are a good example of *unorganized* offerings. Designing and building a fishing pier creates the chance for campers to use an amenity without a formal program. While everyone may not be interested in an evening campfire program, for example, your campground may have a *water attraction* like a lake or stream that a large percentage of your users take advantage of. By providing a fishing pier you can, in effect, have a program even if you don't program. There's nothing to stop you from developing a planned activity around the pier or other facility, but these program features don't always require on-site staff to function successfully.

If you build a pier, be sure to locate it fairly close to your other campground facilities for use in organized programs. It should only be zoned just far enough away from beaches and boat ramps so these activities won't interfere with the quiet needed for fishing. You can sink fish attractors made from brush or old tires held together with bailing wire in the surrounding water.

It's a good idea to coordinate the location of your fishing pier with fisheries and/or wildlife staff, but the *final* decision on where to place it should be based on recreation program needs. (This will come as quite a shock to most wildlife and fisheries rascals.)

here since users from other loops must travel through this one to reach the beach. Because managers can't control traffic to the beach without barricading the camp-loop road, an administrative problem results as well. Our message here is "keep loop roads 'clean.' " *Don't rely on camping roads to provide access to program (or other) support facilities.*

Often, you'll find campgrounds and other recreation facilities on lakes used for transportation. For instance, the TVA system of reservoirs and many COE lakes have a steady flow of barge traffic, whose wave action can destroy a beach and be hazardous to weak swimmers. Barge traffic also provides an example of how complex recreation planning can be. We once found a perfect location for a campfire theater — a natural bowl, well-zoned, overlooking a lake. It was perfect until we spent a night camped on the site and heard barge traffic all night long, which would have destroyed a passive campfire program. Remember, then, that off-site conditions can really have an impact on your designs.

Beaches

We've already discussed the need to consider user safety and environmental protection when you locate beaches. Aside from these and the other basic concerns you found in the chapter on day-use areas, one important aspect of locating beaches in campgrounds is our old friend *zoning*. Beaches need to be zoned so they are convenient to, but not intrusive upon, camp units. This is true of all program amenities, but planners seem to violate this principle more frequently with beaches.

Figures 8.5 and 8.6 show two ways of designing a beach zone and camping-loop road. While the design in Figure 8.5 uses less road, it has a negative impact on campers

Trails

Although they may not be perceived as program zones, many campgrounds have a variety of natural amenities capable of supporting recreation activities, and a trails system is one example. Existing trails can be used for hikes, nature walks, scavenger hunts, and other programs. But since many organized groups, such as the National Campers and Hikers Association, award patches and other incentives for service projects, a little creative programming can turn a periodic trails-maintenance job into a theme weekend. This will result in a reduced workload for your maintenance crew, an activity for campers, an increase in your attendance figures, additional program

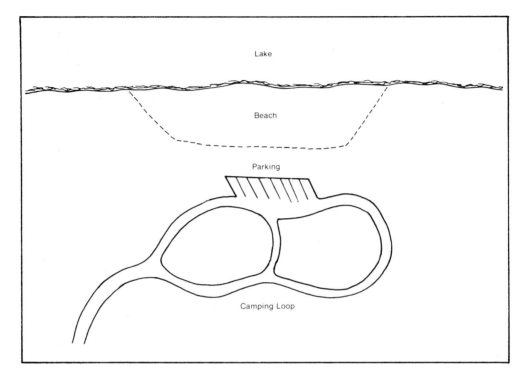

Lake

Beach

Parking

Camping Loop

Figure 8.5

opportunities, *and* a positive piece of public relations. With a little cooperation from local media, the weekend can even become something of a local "event" that provides you with free advertising. One trick we've learned over the years in organizing "joint venture" programs such as this is to take a back seat to other groups; let the camping club have the limelight for the work they do with a mention of your agency or organization as co-sponsor. You'll accrue the benefits you need, but it's good to make user groups feel important as well.

If you're considering the addition of a trails system to a campground, remember to avoid mixing trails with conflicting uses, as we discussed in Chapter Three. If your campground already has a number of trails for hiking, biking, and circulation, you'll always

be better off building an additional trail for interpretation than trying to superimpose this use on existing ones. The initial cost may be higher, but you'll save maintenance dollars over time because of reduced vandalism. A separate interpretive system will also enhance the experience for all trail users.

Whenever you consider developing trails — particularly in campgrounds — keep in mind the *potential* for program development. For specific tips on trail design and layout, refer back to Chapter Three.

Skills-and-Crafts Sites

In addition to the facilities for archery, fishing, canoeing, and bicycling we discussed

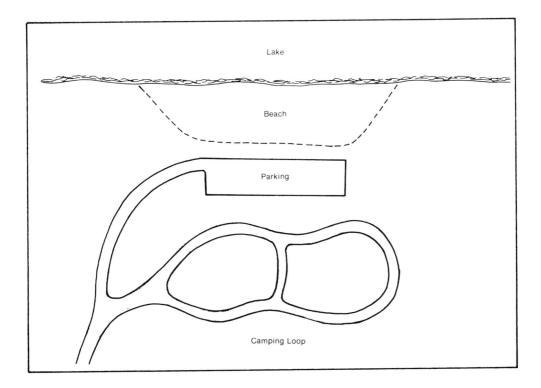

Figure 8.6

previously, a central location for skills and nature crafts can add another dimension to programming. You can use a shelter building as a focal point for activities such as cooking skills and nature crafts, but if a shelter is zoned to serve as the center of your active program feature, these activities may conflict with more passive skills, arts, and crafts programs. By adding a separate zone for the latter, you can create the opportunity to offer *concurrent* programs. Thus campers not interested in a mid-morning volleyball game can choose to attend a program on outdoor cooking or an activity focusing on nature art.

Many public recreation areas contain property formerly held by the private sector, like old farm buildings in various stages of disrepair. Using materials from these buildings, it's frequently possible to build a crafts cabin, and log or rustic wooden structures fit a campground environment, appeal to children and adults, and can provide you with a relatively inexpensive focal point for programs ranging from storytelling to crafts.

PUTTING THE PIECES TOGETHER

To this point, we've focused the discussion on justifying programming in campgrounds and highlighting a variety of programs and support features. Now, you need to consider the *how*. Once you've decided (and we hope

Figure 8.7

you have) that programming is an integral part of campground management, how do you go about doing it? We can break this process down into three general stages: design, program planning and preparation, and cost.

Design

There are two interrelated aspects of designing program facilities for campgrounds. One of these is *zoning*. Program areas need to be zoned so they won't conflict with each other or with the camping experience itself. Some program facilities like tot lots can, and often should, be built close to camping loops

so young children can reach them without parental concern for safety. You should locate play courts and fields and other active-program zones centrally, if possible, but certainly far enough away from camping loops and passive-program areas so noise won't interfere with other activities. Then campers can enjoy the fifty-person softball game until 1:30 am without causing problems for others. Where you place beaches, boat-launch sites, fishing piers, and other water-dependent facilities depends on location of good water, access without encroachment on camping-loop roads, and proposed sites for other program zones. As Figure 8.7 suggests graphically, the potential complexity of a good fit for all campground amenities, including program facilities, points out the

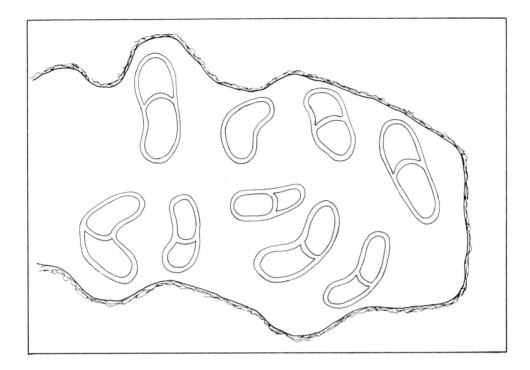

Figure 8.8

need for a second design consideration: *sequencing*.

In Chapter Seven we suggested that a good design technique is to "work backwards;" instead of locating your main road first, determine where camping loops can best be placed and then add the road for access and circulation. Figures 8.8 and 8.9 illustrate this principle. Let's assume for a moment that the land base shown in these figures is flat enough so topography isn't a limiting factor, but that the beach and boating site must be located as they appear in Figure 8.9. *Ignoring programming for a moment*, the campground in Figure 8.9 will work well from several perspectives. There is a single entry-exit point and good potential for controlling loop use, the design prevents confusion and keeps boating and beach traffic away from loops for users, the loops

are designed with environmental protection in mind, and the sewage-dumping station and maintenance complex are well-zoned. But we don't want to ignore programming.

To allow us to include potential programs in our campground, we need to carry the concept of sequencing one step further and *first* determine where the major active and passive program zones should go. Let's say the best locations are shown in Figure 8.10.

With these fixed, preferably with two or three alternatives, it's now possible to begin to "plug in" camping loops so all the zones begin to complement each other. Figure 8.11 shows this next step in the progression. Finally, we can work out the optimum circulation system to move users into and through the various zones, add support features like toilet/showers, and fine-tune

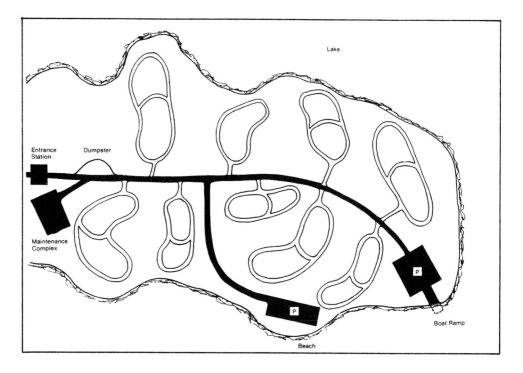

Figure 8.9

program zones. Figure 8.12 shows the completed campground.

Using a sequencing approach, the design challenge becomes a *logical process* as opposed to a guessing game in which Murphy's Law is almost certain to play a part. The main road is one of the last features you should plan. It is truly a subordinate piece of "hardware" rather than, as is usually the case, a poorly engineered dominant feature. From a programming perspective, contrast the final location of the main and subordinate roads in Figure 8.12 with the ones less well done in Figure 8.9.

Program Planning and Preparation

Planning and developing a broad spectrum of campground programs isn't especially difficult or too different from organizing recreation activities in a municipal setting. Recreation programs, regardless of environment, depend in part on 1) types of facilities available, 2) suitability of resource base, 3) capabilities and talents of program staff, and 4) kinds of programs emphasized, keeping in mind the needs of *all* users. There is a "psychology of programming" with

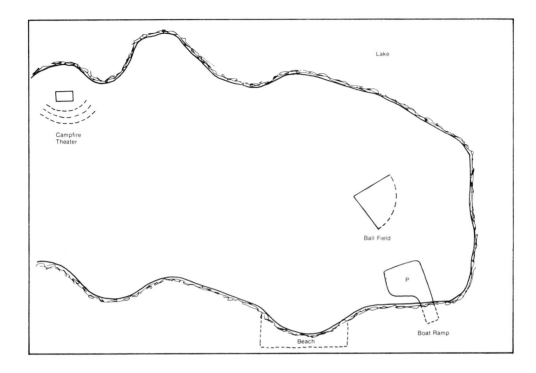

Lake

Campfire
Theater

Ball Field

P

Boat Ramp

Beach

Figure 8.10

respect to activities in campgrounds, however, and some aspects you'll want to consider include the following:

Preferences. Part of the challenge (and the fun) of working in a people-oriented profession is differences among people. What might be an excellent program for teens might flop with young adults. A superb program in a campground near Washington, D.C., could fail miserably in the State of Washington. Therefore the programs that you offer need to be based in part on who your campers are. You should find out what interests your users and give them what they want, not what you think they need. Various means of determining user preferences include talking informally to campers, developing and conducting a formal survey (graduate students in recreation-related curricula are always looking for research topics), and simply trying various programs over the course of a few use seasons to see which types of activities best suit your users' needs.

Timing. The simplest way to maximize attendance at different activities is to

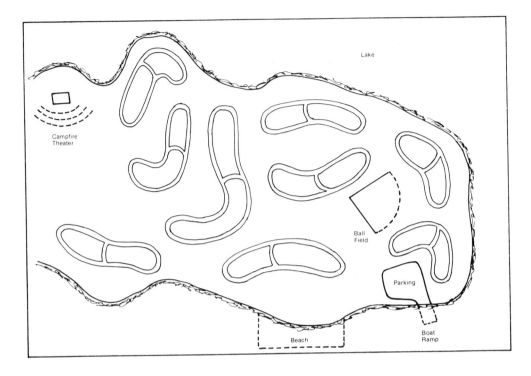

Campfire
Theater

Lake

Ball
Field

Parking

Beach

Boat
Ramp

Figure 8.11

program *where* people go *when* they are there. For example, you can plan a beach-oriented activity like a water-volleyball game in the hot, early afternoon hours when people will congregate in this zone without any outside motivation. Conversely, some activities such as active games for young children should be planned for early morning and early evening hours to avoid excessive exposure to sun and high temperatures. Knowing your campers' habits is important to timing. We used to assume campers ate at 8:00 am, noon, and 6:00 pm, until we asked them. Our *guesses* were an hour early for each meal.

Marketing. Like any other "product," campground programs can enjoy maximum success only if you make potential users aware of what you have to offer. Place eye-

catching, up-to-date signs where people are most likely to see them: on shower doors, in restrooms, at the campground check-in station, in program zones, and on bulletin boards. Do make sure that bulletin boards avoid looking overly cluttered. Please don't — as most folks do — use the entire space to tell *your* guests sixty-three things they can't do. These boards should be "designed" with a central focus for all information. Two excellent techniques involve using brightly colored construction paper and signs reading "Don't Look Under Here" with program announcements beneath.

Program schedules covering a seven-day period give campers an idea of what activities are pending. These can be posted and given to users when they check into the campground. If they have programming at all, most of the state and federal campgrounds

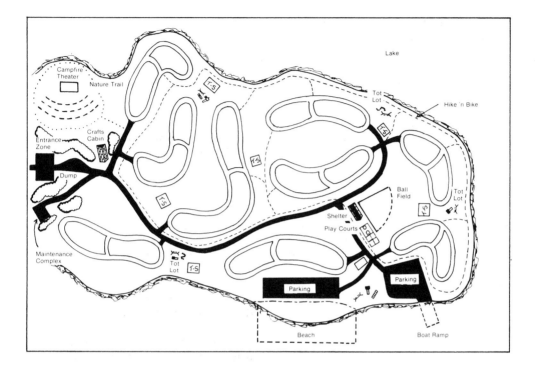

Figure 8.12

we've visited design a brochure for the entire summer season. This allows people to do the same things at the same hours of the same days *all summer!* Such an "enthusiastic" approach to creative programming is discouraging. Whenever you conduct a program, announce the times and locations of the next few activities to build a repeat clientele. Near mealtimes, programmers can drive, pedal, or walk through camping areas to *invite,* not force, users to attend upcoming activities.

Naming. Use creative names for your programs, particularly those aimed at young children. You're more likely to attract youngsters to a "Water World Series" than to a program imaginatively entitled "beach activity." We know a programmer who periodically held "green submarine hunts" at

her beach, and people often came to find out what it was — a greased watermelon tossed into a shallow swimming area for contestants to try and "capture." Wouldn't it be *awful* to hear teens and other youngsters shouting and having fun chasing a greased watermelon at a beach in a National Forest or National Park campground when they could be learning the differences between parasitic and symbiotic relationships in the natural environment?

Certificates and Awards. Although some might disagree, we recommend *against* using awards as program participation incentives. Ours is a highly competitive society, and recreational settings should offer a change of pace from this norm. It isn't necessary to have a "winner" in a critter-crawl contest; if you do, you have to have perhaps twenty or thirty losers as well — many of whom may be quite young. The alternative we prefer is to provide *certificates of enthusiastic participation,* given to all who join in the activity. These can be printed in bulk with blank spaces for the programmer to fill in name of participant and activity. By printing colorful certificates with your logo, you can provide a memento of the occasion not tied to competition and a fantastic source of advertisement for your campground. (By the way, did you know the vast majority of campers come to both public and private campgrounds through word-of-mouth recommendations?) If you do offer competitive programs like horseshoe tournaments, trophy and athletic supply houses normally stock inexpensive ribbons for awards in quantity.

Cost

The issue of expense — the cost involved in providing campground activities — often seems to be a stumbling block in programming. "We'd like to provide programs, but the budget's too tight" is a frequent comment. Yet successful programming doesn't have to be tied to major outlays of funds. Consider two examples — bicycles and bingo. As we suggested earlier, many campers tend to bring bicycles with them. In addition to the bicycle-skills program we mentioned in Chapter Six, you can center more than a dozen others around bikes, none of which requires much in the way of special facilities or equipment:

— a bike repair workshop
— a bicycle safety program
— a bike "show"
— a family bike hike
— a bicycle exhibition in cooperation with local retailers
— a bike-decorating contest

— first aid for bike-related injuries
— a cross-country biking workshop (packing, touring, maps . . .)
— a road rally
— bicycle games (follow the leader, frisbee tag)
— a bike olympics
— an overnight bike trip
— a bicycle "weekend" centered around bike-related activities

The cost of an inexpensive bingo game can provide all the support you need for an evening program popular enough to conduct two or three times a week. (Remember that campground populations "turn over" frequently.) One of the best and cheapest bingo games we've seen is grocery bingo. Prior to this event, post advertisements asking campers to attend and bring with them as an "entry fee" some item of food: a bottle of soda, can of beans, piece of fruit, or box of crackers. To begin the game, issue a bingo card in exchange for each food item, placing the collected goods on a table. The winner of each round then gets to select two or more food "prizes." We've seen a program like this run successfully for two hours with fifty participants. Conducted twice a week for fifteen weeks, this would work out to three thousand person hours of entertainment for a capital outlay of perhaps six or seven dollars. Expensive programming?

Building a complete inventory of program-support equipment (games, sports equipment, arts-and-crafts supplies and the like) will require some funding, but there are ways of keeping costs low. Some expenses can be reduced by buying in quantity. Often you may also be able to find sporting-goods stores and other suppliers with factory seconds available; a blemished basketball will save you money and function perfectly well in a campground environment. Your agency or company may already have audiovisual equipment available for campfire movies and slide shows. Some programs such as a "trash scavenger hunt" don't need support equipment and can even save you money for ongoing maintenance tasks. Several years ago, before can manufacturers started producing ringless tabs, we attended a campground carnival where the "admission" for each of several programs was two pop-tops. The program collected seven large grocery bags of "fees." You should also consider developing cooperative agreements with local merchants. If Wilbur, Jr., wins a coupon for a double-dip cone at the Tastee Possum, the rest of the family may spend several dollars there. Local business benefits, your campers are happy, and you earn some positive PR.

Sources of Programs. A creative friend of ours once programmed a campground alone for a summer. On many occasions, he had three or four activities running *concurrently:* he'd start contestants hunting for critters for a critter crawl, organize a softball game and a volleyball game with two poles and a rope for a net, begin a grocery bingo game and leave a willing camper in charge, and return in time to conduct the critter crawl. Enthusiasm? You bet. Buying a hatful of goodwill and eliminating depreciative behavior? You bet some more! It helps to have several people involved in programming, but there are ways of getting free support from several sources. "Cruising" for talent in your campground can produce a wealth of activities. Since programmers will spend considerable time with your camping population, they should continually look for campers with program talents and a willingness to perform or share their skills; an entire evening campfire program might be planned around a camper with a guitar. Often older campers also have skills such as whittling with appeal to younger campers. When you do develop programs using the talents of your visitors, get their names and addresses to write them a letter of thanks on your letterhead stationery.

Other recreation agencies in your area may also have programs you can use. We once worked out an agreement with the director of a nearby National Park Service park to conduct living-history programs in our campgrounds. The programs were well-received and they beckoned many of our campers to the NPS area where they originated. Churches and local civic organizations are other sources of activities at little or no cost. Local manufacturers of, for example, fishing or camping equipment are often more than willing to co-sponsor demonstration programs. And special-interest groups such as Bass Masters or a parachute club, are often willing to conduct demonstrations.

You can create successful programs with little more than a fertile imagination. For instance, you'd be surprised at the interest campers will have in a dog show. Dog-food companies have, at times, provided free kits with instructions, rules, and ribbons. In fact, if you dig a bit, there are all types of "freebies" available to conduct all sorts of programs.

Staffing. Probably the least expensive means of providing programming personnel is working through college and university practicum programs. While there are several ways of coordinating a practicum program, we recommend the following procedures:

1. Each year, several months in advance of the camping season, you and your staff should determine the number of students needed and the various types of talents you want. The intent here is to provide each program area with a balanced mix of expertise. For example, if a campground has three practicum positions, you might look for students with respective backgrounds in urban community centers and playgrounds, natural resources and interpretation, and skills certification. A spin-off benefit of this approach is the opportunity to let the students share their

talents with co-workers, thus broadening the background of each. By pairing students from different schools together, you can also expand the teaching experience the students receive. Hundreds of two- and four-year curricula across America include recreation. Many of these require their students to complete practicum experiences in park settings.

2. After determining the required number of students and the talent you want, initiate the hiring process with university practicum supervisors or contact professors. We recommend avoiding attempts to hire students directly. By developing close working relationships with faculty, you make arrangements with individuals who will be more familiar than you with the potential and limitations of particular students. Faculty should also be familiar with university practicum requirements, and once a professor knows you and your needs, he or she can match your requirements to specific students. Because of placement, early enrollment, competition for top students, and other considerations, it's important to start the hiring process well in advance of the use season.

If you hire students with backgrounds in recreation, it *isn't difficult* to teach them the actual programming techniques they need. Thus the most important qualities to seek in potential students are *enthusiasm* and *initiative*. These intangibles are often difficult to identify in a resume or a brief interview, which reinforces the need to establish a relationship with faculty representatives. We also recommend having a formal orientation to familiarize incoming practicum students with your policies, goals, objectives, management practices, and particular programming approaches. Once they are oriented, students should be able to develop and conduct programs with minimal day-to-day supervision.

3. Once specific students are selected, you should initiate a service contract with the university — not the student — that allows him or her to be employed by the school rather than your agency or company. From your standpoint, this simplifies procedural matters such as insurance and wage-and-tax reporting. It also formalizes the relationship between you and the school involved. With this arrangement, direct payment for services enables schools to handle student requirements according to their policies. Some schools do not allow students to be paid for a practicum; others compute taxes and handle the payments as a salary; still others treat the payment as a cost of living stipend and make few, if any, deductions.

CONCLUSIONS

A well-planned and conducted array of recreation programs in a campground is similar to a three-ring circus; campers choose from a variety of diversions to make their stay in your area more enjoyable. The key to successful programming is twofold, and the first critical element is the programmer. Whether you use practicum students, seasonal employees, or full-time staff, programmers *must* be enthusiastic, creative, and imaginative. Support facilities and well-funded program budgets are nice to have, but the people responsible for programs and your supportive attitude, including careful and unannounced critiques, will ultimately determine the success of your activities. The second aspect necessary for good programs is an understanding that activities must *build a bridge between the known and the unknown*. To many urban-oriented recreationists, camping is a somewhat unfamiliar, foreign, and perhaps frightening experience. If you want to beckon minorities and other "non-users" that agencies would like to host but rarely entice, you *can* do so. By providing activities from municipal recreation settings that these users recognize and are comfortable with, you can bridge the gap between the familiar and the unfamiliar. To us, failing to recognize the potential of fun-oriented recreation programs in outdoor recreation settings represents one of the biggest missed opportunities in the profession today. If you're serious about wanting all types of users — young and old; black, brown, red, yellow, and white; handicapped and not; wealthy and poor; *and* the "unforgotten" majority of average campers — give fun programming a try. If you aren't interested in these folks, don't program; you'll still have the environmentalists, fishing parties, and good ole boys. You'll also have empty units and depreciative behavior, but what else is new?

Hopefully, you won't miss this opportunity to program. To give you a chance to try your creative hand at programming, here's an exercise for you. Haunted Hollow Campground is located in a large Western state park. The campground has a shelter building, beach, skills court, playcourt, playground, interpretive trail, archery range, fishing pier, ball field, boat ramp, activity building, campfire theater, log cabin, horseshoe pits, and hike n' bike trail system. Your assignment is to plan a week-long activity calendar for the campground. You have three practicum students as programmers, each of whom needs two consecutive off days during the week (not on weekends when use is heaviest). You should plan a broad spectrum of programs — some for all users and some for specific age groups — including concurrent programs for campers with varying interests. We've included a sample calendar as Appendix D, but you should also use the information in this chapter to develop a strategy for advertising that involves users

and finds other program sources. You can assume you have a good inventory of support equipment. You can also assume that you can do better than we did since we're just planners.

APPENDIX D

Haunted Hollow Campground

Program Schedule
Week of June 21-27

Facility or area code: * S — shelter, B — beach, SC — skills court, PC — play court, P — playground, IT — interpretive trail, A — archery range, F — fishing pier, BF — softball field, G — entrance gate, R — boat ramp, AB — activity building, CT — campfire theater, LC — log cabin, HP — horseshoe pits

Monday, June 21
6:30 am   Bicycle Hike for Wildlife (S)
7:00 am   Early-bird Jog (G)
9:00 am   Fishing Skills (F)
          (For children 13 and under)
10:00 am   Nature Crafts (S)
11:00 am   Critter Gathering (G)
1:00 pm   Critter Races (S)
2:00 pm   Water Volleyball (B)
3:30 pm   Green Submarine Hunt (B)
7:00 pm   Soccer Skills (BF)
8:30 pm   Cartoons for Little Folks (CT)
9:00 pm   Teen Disco (S)
9:00 pm   Grocery Bingo (CT)
10:00 pm   Family Softball (BF)

*Code indicates where program begins.

Tuesday, June 22

8:30 am   Archery Skills (A) (For teens)
9:00 am   Scavenger Hunt (G)
          (For those 12 and under)
9:30 am   Checker Tournament (S) (All ages)
10:00 am Paint a Practicum Student (CT)
11:00 am Cooking Skills for Moms (LC)
1:00 pm   Raft Races (B)
1:00 pm   Water Volleyball (B)
2:00 pm   Storytelling (S)
3:30 pm   Nature Crafts (S)
5:00 pm   Bike Hike (G)
7:30 pm   Puppet Show (CT)
8:30 pm   Square-dance Skills (SC)
9:00 pm   Teen Volleyball (PC)
10:30 pm Teen Coffeehouse (S)
          Bring your guitar!

Wednesday, June 23

8:00 am   Rowing Skills (R)
9:00 am   Solar Food-drying (S)
9:00 am   Archery Skills (A)
          (Dads and children under 13)
10:00 am Rowboat Races (R)
11:00 am Horseshoe Tournament (HP)
1:00 pm   Water Volleyball (B)
2:00 pm   Outdoor Cooking (LC) (For teens)
3:00 pm   Dog Show (CT)
3:30 pm   Bicycle Skills (SC)
4:30 pm   Sand-castle Creations (B)
6:30 pm   Pillo Polo (BF)
8:00 pm   Paris Fashions (CT)
8:30 pm   Grocery Bingo (AB)
9:00 pm   Singalong (CT)
10:30 pm Family Softball (BF)

Thursday, June 24

7:00 am   Early-bird Jog (G)
8:30 am   5-mile Family Bike Hike (C)
9:00 am   Canoe Skills (B)
9:00 am   Sack Races (BF)
10:00 am Badminton (PC)
11:00 am Raft Races (R)
1:00 pm   Water Volleyball (B)
2:00 pm   Rowing Races (R)
4:00 pm   Storytelling (AB)
7:00 pm   Bait-casting Contest (F)

7:00 pm   Tug of War (BF)
8:30 pm   Square Dance (PC)
9:00 pm   Teen Disco (S) Bring Your Records!
9:00 pm   Nature Campfire Program (CT)
10:30 pm Family Volleyball (PC)

Friday, June 25

6:30 am   Early Morning Hike & Nature
          Walk (G)
9:00 am   Scavenger Hunt (AB)
9:30 am   Egg Fight (BF) Bring your own
          boiled eggs.
10:30 am Nature Crafts (AB)
10:30 am Critter Gathering (G)
11:00 am Water Frisbee (B)
1:00 pm   Critter Races (S)
2:00 pm   Green Submarine Hunt (B)
3:00 pm   Water Volleyball (B)
4:00 pm   Learn to Swim (B)
5:00 pm   Bicycle Skills (SC)
7:00 pm   Horseshoe Tournament (SC)
8:00 pm   Living-history Program (CT)
8:30 pm   Square Dance (PC)
9:30 pm   The Late Show (CT)
10:30 pm Family Softball (BF)

Saturday, June 26

9:00 am   Badminton (PC)
9:00 am   Rock and Seed Crafts (AB)
10:00 am Storytelling (CT)
11:00 am Water-balloon Toss (B)
1:00 pm   Water Whiffleball (B)
2:00 pm   Canoe Races (B)
2:00-7:00 pm Camper Flea Market (S)
4:00 pm   Adult Learn-to-Swim (B)
7:30 pm   New Town Band (CT)
8:30 pm   Teen Disco (S)
10:00 pm Saturday Night Movies (CT)
10:30 pm Teen Volleyball (PC)
10:30 pm Family Softball (BF)

Sunday, June 27

8:30 am   Worship Service (CT)
10:00 am Family Swim Time (B)
11:00 am Water Volleyball (B) (Moms and
          Dads against children)
11:00 am Shuffleboard Contest (S)

2:00 pm Fishing Skills (F)
3:00 pm Nature Walk (IT)
8:30 pm Grocery Bingo (CT)
9:00 pm Family Softball (BF)

You are invited to learn and have fun throughout the day and evening with all sorts of
activities. College students who are majoring
in parks and recreation from several universities are your program hosts. They receive
credit and are carefully graded during their
twelve- to fifteen-week practicum experience.

A variety of outdoor play equipment is
available (free) for your use at the equipment checkout building. Hours are 9:00 am-
12n; 3:00 pm-5:00 pm; and 6:00 pm-10:00 pm
each day.

Enjoy your stay at Haunted Hollow and
please come again!

9

MISCELLANEOUS
GOODIES

INTRODUCTION

When we first discussed this text with our editors, they wanted an estimate of how long a book we expected to write. Crossing our fingers, we suggested 350 typed pages, wondering how on earth we could possibly fill up so much space. Having exceeded our original estimate with two chapters left to write, we now find ourselves facing the problem of where to stop. In Chapter Five, we barely "scratched the surface" of what *could* be said about group camps, and Chapter Seven easily could have become a book on camping and campground management. The difficulty is one of *connections*. With so many topics either directly or indirectly related to recreation planning, we could add another dozen chapters and still fail to provide you with a comprehensive background covering all aspects of the discipline. Therefore the purpose of this chapter is to touch quite briefly on a *few* of the many topics related to designing functional and pleasing parks and recreation areas.

One concept professionals use frequently when discussing outdoor resources is *multiple-use management:* devoting resources, in varying degrees, to *forage, timber, wildlife,* and *watershed management* as well as to *recreation*. Since multiple-use management makes good sense from the perspective of resource stewardship, we'll show how it can affect recreation. First, however, to increase your sensitivity of how complex recreation planning and design can

be and how carefully you need to consider *all* aspects of design, let's start with another topic: signing.

SIGNING DO'S AND DON'TS

In Chapter Two you read about possible problems resulting from the build-up of gases, oils, and waxes on parking lots. This was potential *physical* pollution about which recreation planners should be concerned. Signing in parks can cause another type of pollution, too, one that is *psychological* and often harder to correct because it is less apparent. We've seen sign pollution in the city (Figure 9.1); sign pollution on the way to the park (Figure 9.2); and sign pollution in the park itself (Figure 9.3). One of the biggest problems with poor signing in recreation areas is that once someone installs a sign, it seems to take an act of Congress (or an act of vandalism) to take it down. Since signs cost money, there seems to be a tendency on the part of park managers to leave them in place. Thus, as is the case with other planning decisions, you should ask yourself whether or not a sign is necessary in the first place.

You need signs in parks to *inform, instruct,* and *warn* visitors. A well-designed sign can enhance user convenience as long as you remember three concerns. First, signs should *support* a visual experience rather than *dominate* it. Second, an over-

Figure 9.1

Figure 9.4

Figure 9.2

Figure 9.5

Figure 9.3

Figure 9.6

Figure 9.7

Figure 9.8

Figure 9.9

dependence on signs may point to a more basic problem of poor design. If an area is confusing in terms of circulation, for example, chances are good that signs will multiply like rabbits. Finally, if you don't need a sign, don't install it. This last point may seem to be overstating the obvious, but many signing mistakes result from precisely this problem. How many of you knew, for instance, what the purpose of the support facility in Figure 9.4 was *before* you read the accompanying sign?

Admittedly there may be instances when some seemingly evident situations require signing, as in some primitive parks where you need to warn visitors about water unsafe for drinking. Again, however, we must ask how many of you knew the purpose of the container in Figure 9.5 without having to read the sign. Humorous, yes; expensive, yes; necessary, no. While it's unfortunate, signing is occasionally necessary to remind visitors of the obvious. Such is the case with no-litter signs in parks like the one in the picnic area in Figure 9.6. Do you think, however, that the planner needed to go to the lengths shown in an expanded view of this area in Figure 9.7? Signing mistakes fill a continuum from obvious errors to subconscious problems. To illustrate this point, let's consider a few of these.

Spelling

People who work in recreation have different types and levels of intelligence. We've known maintenance workers barely able to read who could rebuild an engine without having to think about it. Thus, while it seems unlikely, it's not impossible to find signing errors resulting from someone's inability to spell, as in Figure 9.8. The important point illustrated here is the need to pay *close attention to detail.* If you assume something will be done correctly just because *you* know how to do it, the results can be embarrassing. In recreation planning, never take *anything* for granted.

At times, human nature being what it is, people have a tendency to *see what they expect to see.* If you've ever proofread a term paper half a dozen times and then had someone point out a typing error, you'll know what we mean. After taking the picture of the sign in Figure 9.9, we asked the park employee accompanying us how long it had been in place. It turned out that the sign had been installed three years earlier and that no one had noticed the misspelled word. People — users and management alike — saw the word "scenic" because it was what they *expected* to see.

In addition to paying attention to detail, you need to train yourself to look for problems and head them of at the the pass. (We assume you saw the incorrect spelling of the word "off," but did you catch the "double the" as well?)

Readability

In addition to conveying correctly spelled information, signs in recreation areas must be *legible.* Therefore the size of the lettering you use is a consideration, particularly as it relates to *distance* and *scale of motion.* Signs placed a few feet away from a trail to reduce incidental damage must have lettering large enough to read. Printing on signs you expect people to see from a car travelling at forty-five miles per hour should be larger than lettering read from a stationary position. The type of sign you use can have a positive or negative effect on legibility as well. For example, the slat sign in Figure 9.10 is quite difficult to read because you have a tendency to try and focus on both the foreground — the sign itself — and the background visible between the slats.

When installing a sign, you need to consider not only how legible it is *now* but how easy it will be to read *later.* For instance, you could argue that the problem in Figure 9.11 was caused by poor maintenance, and our response would be that better maintenance would have cured the *effects* of the problem. The *cause,* however, can be attributed to poor signing techniques since sign installations must be high enough to *prevent* problems like this from occurring in the first place. As we've tried to point out to you on other occasions, design decisions are always a matter of *balance:* too much balanced with not enough; too expensive with too cheap; and, in this case, too low with too high. You *should* place signs high enough to keep weeds from obscuring them in the future. You *shouldn't* expect your users to come equipped with stilts. The person responsible for the interpretive sign in Figure 9.12 apparently made this mistake. Interestingly enough, the "tree top" sign saying "Mulberry" wasn't on a mulberry at all!

While readability can be influenced by physical factors like sign height, psychological considerations play a part as well. When we discussed displays in visitor centers, we suggested that a good rule of thumb for message length was a maximum reading time of twenty seconds. This holds true for most signing situations. One of the most popular attractions at TVA's Land Between the Lakes is a buffalo range. When we worked there, we *rarely* saw anyone take the time to read the sign in Figure 9.13. Now contrast the message in Figure 9.13 with the one in Figure 9.14. From a psychological perspective, which would you be more likely to read? Neither topic was likely to attract visitors, yet the Forest Service sign was well

Figure 9.10

Figure 9.13

Figure 9.11

Figure 9.14

Figure 9.12

Figure 9.15

Figure 9.16

Figure 9.17

Figure 9.18

done; the TVA sign wasn't. Remember that in order for people to *learn* from your signs, they have to read them. We think it makes more sense to tell folks two or three things and have them remember one or two than to try and tell them twenty things and "turn them off" to reading at all.

Sign Psychology

Signs are not simply signs. They are part of an environment visitors perceive when they use parks and recreation areas. As a result, you need to go beyond limiting your attention to signs themselves and think about sign *placement*. For example, the directional sign in Figure 9.15 is perfectly *functional*. Directly and simplistically it conveys the information users need. What, however, does the environment in which the sign is placed *say* to users, from a psychological perspective, about the recreational experience awaiting them? Contrast the sign environment in Figure 9.15 with the setting in Figure 9.16. Which would you prefer?

The *shape* of signs can have a positive or a negative effect as well. While it's physically possible to frame a square sign, the psychological effect on viewers is quite negative. Your eyes have a tendency to look for *dominance* in what you see, and a rectangular sign like the one in Figure 9.17 lets you perceive either a vertical or a horizontal dominance, depending on which way the sign is oriented. A square sign appears to be out of balance because there is no dominant direction for your eyes to follow.

The informational aspect of signing is another factor you need to watch carefully. Since you're trained in recreation, you could probably determine that the camping fees for the area in Figure 9.18 are based on level of services such as electrical versus non-electrical sites; do you think, though, that some users might find this message a bit confusing? Even when information on signs doesn't conflict with other messages the results can be puzzling to the public. Consider the message on the sign in Figure 9.19. How can you launch your boat if you have to stay clear of the ramp? Avoid signs with incongruous meanings. Even when the message on a sign isn't confusing, the impact can be negative. For example, what kind of a mental picture do you get of the gardens in Figure 9.20?

Not all signing errors result from too much verbiage or too many sign installations. Sometimes "not enough" can be a culprit as well. Consider the blank back of the sign in Figure 9.21. Essentially, this is wasted space. Sign posts are expensive and too many of them tend to clutter the environment, so you can reduce costs and minimize the number of sign installations you need by taking advantage of both sides of sign posts. The sign back in Figure 9.22 contributes to both a good use of the installation *and* your efforts to have visitors experience a positive feeling about your area.

One of the most frequent signing mistakes we see results from designers assuming that every sign needs a sign post. The camp unit number sign in Figure 9.23 may be necessary from a management perspective; the sign *post* isn't. Figure 9.24 shows an alternative solution if your campsites are electrified: place the unit-number sign on the electrical-outlet post. If this isn't a possibility, try the solution in Figure 9.25. Put the unit number on the side of the picnic table facing the loop road. Sign installations can be minimized further by *stencilling* information directly on paved roads, as Figure 9.26 demonstrates. If

Figure 9.19

Figure 9.20

Figure 9.21

sign posts are necessary, and the information isn't conflicting or confusing, it's possible to reduce the number of installations by *stacking* several signs on the same post as in Figure 9.27. This installation also demonstrates the best way we know to reduce verbiage: using *symbols.* Consider the sign in Figure 9.28. There isn't any wording at all, yet the message is clear to anyone.

In an earlier chapter we discussed the importance of *lines, forms, textures,* and

Figure 9.24

Figure 9.22

Figure 9.25

Figure 9.23

Figure 9.26

colors in recreation design, which you can use quite effectively in signing parks.

Figure 9.29 shows an excellent application of *line* in signing. The linear shape of the sign reinforces the line of the message contained on it. Similarly, the *form* of the sign in Figure 9.30 is aesthetically pleasing and conjures up an image of the physical resource to which it refers. The sign in Figure 9.31 carries this technique a step further. Here the sign installation reinforces the form of the sign. In Figure 9 ʾ2 the sign

Figure 9.27

Figure 9.29

Figure 9.28

Figure 9.30

Figure 9.31

Figure 9.32

makes good use of *texture,* giving the message a sense of depth. You can clarify information on signs by using *color* as well. Colors contrast effectively and make the message as well as the sign attractive.

In summary, signs in recreation areas need and deserve careful attention since they provide a way for your management personnel to interact with visitors without face-to-face contact. This interaction can be negative and expensive if you approach signing with a casual attitude; it can be positive if you learn to think of signing as yet another aspect of planning parks for people.

MULTIPLE-USE MANAGEMENT AND RECREATION PLANNING

The term "multiple-use management" carries with it two levels of meaning. On one level, it refers to managing resources by allocating varying degrees of emphasis to recreation, forage (or range), wildlife, watershed, and timber. For example, a management plan might have recreation as a primary focus in a given resource-base "unit" with a secondary emphasis on wildlife and watershed while allocating an adjacent unit primarily for timber with a subsidiary purpose of forage.

Various textbooks focus on the "hows" of this aspect of resource management. Thus we want to consider a second implication of the concept: *resource coordination.* By this we mean opportunities and shortcomings in planning and administration techniques to ensure that all components receive equitable emphasis in management plans. Note we didn't say *equal* emphasis. Some resources, because of unsuitability or the need to stress other aspects of multiple-use management, shouldn't focus on recreation. Since this is a text about recreation, let's start by using this aspect of multiple-use management to demonstrate the need for a *comprehensive* approach to allocating resources.

Recreation

One of the underlying concepts we've tried to stress throughout this book is the need to plan and manage recreation resources to meet the needs of *all* users — from the backpacker to the RV camper. An extension of this approach should be the philosophical basis for multiple-use management: using resources to meet the needs of the entire *community* of plants, animals and people. Aldo Leopold probably stated the case most eloquently in *A Sand County Almanac* when he spoke of the land ethic. Our concern, limited here to the topic of recreation, is for what we feel is a failure on the part of resource managers to consider the entire spectrum of recreationists. Perhaps a more basic problem is what we feel is the cause of this failure: far too many outdoor recreation professionals aren't "people persons."

To demonstrate this point, consider the following story. We once represented a major federal agency at a meeting to discuss the recreational use of a white-water river that was also being used to produce hydroelectric power. Participants at the meeting included staff from two federal agencies, several state offices, commercial rafting outfitters, and river users. After driving for two hours to reach the town where the meeting was to be held, we had dinner with the federal agency representative who was to chair the meeting. We finished our meal ten minutes before the 7:00 pm meeting time, yet the person in charge of the meeting sat and drank coffee until 7:15. When we suggested leaving the restaurant, his response was, "Hell, they can't start without me — I'm running the show."

We aren't suggesting that this is a typical occurrence, but it does point out the distinction between a public servant and a bureaucrat, it does speak to the issue of professionalism, and it does demonstrate the lack of sensitivity, in an extreme case, that some recreation "professionals" have for the need to work *for* and *with* people. Although this insensitivity rarely occurs in such a direct fashion, we feel that outdoor recreation today often suffers from an undercurrent of the same attitude responsible for the behavior of the person in our story. Such behavior can negatively affect users several ways. For example, in Chapter One we suggested that outdoor recreation professionals need to be concerned with people and the environment. In looking at the situation in outdoor recreation today, we feel that

concern for the *environment* has been confused with an emphasis on the *environmental*.

This is a difficult point to make, because it seems to imply we are anti-environmental, and we aren't. Simply put, we feel the management direction most resource-based recreation agencies take stresses environmentally oriented use *at the expense of neglecting the needs of users interested in other forms of recreation.* The problem with this approach occurs because, quite frankly, the majority of people who recreate in the out-of-doors simply aren't the users at whom this environmental emphasis is directed. Our "community" of outdoor recreationists is made up in large part of people who don't want to "rough it," yet our allocation of resources, both fiscal and physical, emphasizes wilderness use. This strikes us as being an inequitable distribution of resources which, aside from failing to address the needs of all users, causes considerable harm to the public relations of the agencies involved.

Particularly in times when social programs receive less governmental emphasis, those public agencies involved in service delivery must address the interests of all segments of the population. To fulfill their purpose effectively, we think that public recreation agencies, particularly those with a resource emphasis, must develop goals and objectives with a stronger social orientation. They need to understand the demographics of outdoor recreation and the social forces and motivations leading to recreation behavior. The mission of public recreation should be to meet the demands of all users — minorities, the aged, the handicapped, and the "forgotten majority" of mainstream recreationists as well as those with a preference for backcountry camping. This is what we mean by an equitable distribution of resources focusing on a broad spectrum of people.

Accomplishing this mission requires a coordination of resources to ensure we take into account all members of the outdoor recreation community. If reading this book does nothing else than motivate you to ask all sorts of questions as you visit parks, then we will feel greatly rewarded. Ask national forest, state park, national park, and other folks to describe their recreation mission to you. If they've ignored fun programming and turned off teens, failed to host senior citizens who need refrigerated medicine by not providing electrical hook-ups, ignored "mainstream" campers and the handicapped by overemphasizing wilderness use, or conveniently "forgotten" certain legitimate recreation pursuits like off-road riding, ask *why*. Your questions may make resource-oriented professionals think — some, perhaps, for the first time ever. Expanding on this theme of resource coordination, let's briefly consider the other components of multiple-use management.

Forage

Just as efforts *within* recreation need to be coordinated to provide a judicious approach to service delivery, planners and managers need to balance strategies *between* recreation and other components of multiple-use management. To illustrate this point, consider the situation Figure 9.33 depicts. In this example, the TVA developed a beach at point B on our schematic. From a *recreation standpoint* only, point B might have been an acceptable location for a beach. Thinking back to the chapter on day-use areas, you could assess this location from such perspectives as slope, erosion potential, safety, water quality, and adjacent recreation-use zones. If all these factors "check out," however, you still would need to consider other aspects of multiple-use management. In this case, the critical factors were watershed and forage. As it turned out, point B was unacceptable, although the beach was

actually located there, because: 1) point B was at the base of a watershed, where surface water drained into the lake; and 2) point A at the upper end of the watershed in Figure 9.33 happened to be a hog lot and grazing area. Forage and recreation should be considered equitably in multiple-use management, but they are often not *compatible* with a given resource base.

Forage or range management, while at times in conflict with recreation use, does offer a good analogy for discussing a concept pertinent to recreation planning: *carrying capacity*. There are different types of carrying capacity, one of which is *biological*, involving the physical ability of an area to withstand use from humans or animals both domestic or wild. Some ecosystems are more fragile than others and as a result are less able to physically accommodate use. This topic leads us back to our soapbox forum. Too often, research designed to assess biological carrying capacity gets used as a smokescreen to hamper intensive recreation development. Some managers, citing the potential damage developed sites can do to the environment, will argue for low-density, dispersed use. The fact is that it doesn't take intensive use at all to harm an *unprotected* environment. Stepping on natural ground a very few times will destroy much of its resiliency and capability for percolation or absorption. Further, designers of low-density recreation developments often neglect to recognize and reinforce areas of known impact even though using *several* low-density areas spreads impact over a larger proportion of the resource base. Thus techniques advocated in the name of protecting the physical carrying capacity often do the environment more harm than good *and* work against our principle of an equitable distribution of resources for recreation.

A second type of carrying capacity is *social*, the impact people have on people within a given area. On a broad level, the problem with carrying capacity seems to be a

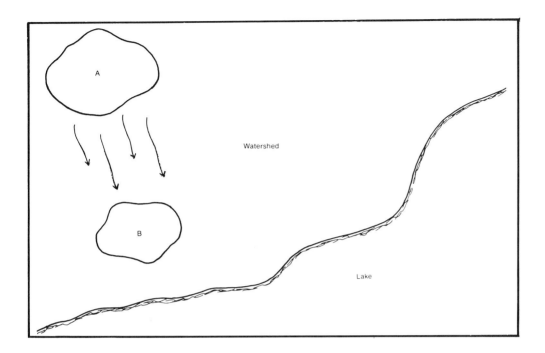

Within the figure: A, B, Watershed, Lake

tendency on the part of some recreation planners to confuse the two types, sort of a cow-hour per person-acre approach to management. *Physical* carrying capacity is just what the term implies: it takes "x" number of acres to support "y" number of feathered, furry, or simply unshaven critters. Physical carrying capacity is more or less an absolute that can be maximized through careful application of resource management practices but beyond a certain point exceeded. Continuing to introduce four- or two-legged users beyond the limit of physical carrying capacity generally results in damage to the ecosystem *and* the users.

There are limits to social use as well, but planners can use the differences in this type of carrying capacity to their advantage by providing high levels of quality recreation. *Social* carrying capacity is less concrete than physical because it is primarily influenced by

psychological factors, factors which are easier to manipulate through design. Environmental planners, for example, have recognized for some time how light-colored rooms create a *perception* of less crowding than darker-colored rooms of the same physical dimensions. In effect, a ten by twelve room painted beige has a greater social carrying capacity than a ten by twelve room painted dark brown.

While we don't advocate painting tree trunks a lighter color, we do suggest that the principle of perceptual manipulation has its uses in recreation design. Screening between camp or picnic units can provide a sense of privacy that users will associate with feeling less crowded. Curvilinear design will reduce encounters on trails, contributing to the *sense,* if not the actuality, of being alone in a natural environment. And simple zoning of conflicting use areas minimizes the potential for conflict with users who have different needs.

These aren't novel concepts; we've discussed all of them previously. The point is to learn how to use design techniques to accomplish management goals. Whatever the recreation *context,* one should be to maximize the resource base. This doesn't imply that you should always choose to build a three-hundred-unit campground in lieu of providing a wilderness experience. Such a decision should be based on user needs and the compatibility of the resource base with the use alternatives you're considering. In fact, it may be necessary in some wilderness areas to limit the amount of use to protect both physical and social carrying capacity. However, and this is the focus of our argument, it *is* possible to increase social carrying capacity through design. Completing the analogy between recreation and forage, planners should use the tools available to them to ensure that limits of use are defined by *physical* factors rather than social constraints.

Wildlife

If individuals, agencies, and corporations involved in multiple-use management practice resource coordination, the results can benefit more than one activity. For example, fishing is a wildlife-management technique valuable from a recreational perspective as well. Building fish attractors can lure the population in a lake and may increase potential angling. Yet in our experience, we've found that wildlife-management efforts that benefit recreation are too often *incidental* and quite often accidental. Fish attractors may enhance fishing, but rarely have we seen efforts to place them coordinated with recreation planners, managers, or programmers.

This problem stems from the tendency of most resource-oriented professionals to be arrogant toward recreation, though notable

exceptions exist. We've seen this attitude create problems and limit opportunities for recreation staff time and time again. Consider our example of fish attractors. If fisheries or wildlife staff fail to coordinate placement of these with recreation personnel, a missed opportunity may result. Hypothetically, a fisheries biologist might have two locations — A and B — acceptable for an attractor. If he or she places it at point A when point B is adjacent to a stretch of shoreline that has excellent potential for a fishing pier in a group camp, what happens? The fisheries program reaps the same benefit in either case, but an enhanced recreation program falls by the wayside.

Recreation professionals must understand yet another idea when dealing with most resource-trained folks, the belief that users, if they are of any value, visit our nation's wildland parks either to hunt or to fish. Further, resource people believe any camping associated with hunting or fishing is acceptable *but* that it's inconceivable that people would want to camp for fun or a social vacation. "These kinds of less-than-desirable city dwellers should stay away from *my* forests, lakes, and streams," they imply. One of your authors has a forestry degree and subscribed to this shortsighted thought process as recently as fifteen years ago.

We aren't suggesting that the resource professional *purposely* takes steps to limit potential recreation, but failing to coordinate efforts with others whose work may be affected by their decisions is still a breech of professionalism. The resource arrogance we're discussing may be a matter of perspective. Unfortunately, some of these professionals tend to view their work as "hard science" when compared to the "soft science" of people-oriented disciplines such as recreation. In one sense, the point is well taken. Generally the physical sciences, which include resource disciplines, are more exact than the social sciences. If we introduce a given quantity of rotenone into a lake embayment, we can predict with some accuracy the resulting fish-kill percentage. Conversely, if we superimpose water skiing on a lake previously limited to fishing, it's much more difficult to predict the social implications. Although recreation, because of this element of uncertainty, may be more challenging, it is in an absolute sense a "softer" science.

When resource professionals adopt the attitude that "We're scientists and recreation workers are baby sitters," we still have a problem. We once drew up plans for a campground which was to be built several years in the future. The plan anticipated a five-year growth on several young trees and shrubs which, by the time the campground was built, would have provided shade and screening for camp units. Without checking with recreation, wildlife staff then had the area bush hogged as part of a wildlife enhancement program. Prompted by arrogance based on lack of understanding, rather than malice, they didn't even understand why we were angry over their actions.

Resource coordination is a necessity in successful multiple-use management. Wildlife watering holes and woods openings that create the "edge effect" beneficial to wildlife can, if well placed, enhance the aesthetics of roads and trails travelled by recreationists. Cover plantings of shrubs and coniferous trees for deer and upland game birds can provide screening helpful in separating conflicting recreation zones. Natural salt licks can aid wildlife as well as serve as observation points for people interested in viewing animals. These examples and other wildlife-management techniques can be useful from a recreation perspective if they are coordinated with the appropriate staff. In fairness, recreation developments created in a vacuum can be harmful to wildlife management. You owe it to co-workers to keep them informed of your plans; you should expect the same in return.

Watershed

Watershed management can affect recreation in a variety of ways. We've already discussed the potential for erosion and siltation around beaches and other waterfront zones if planners ignore preventive maintenance measures. However, let's dig a little deeper and explore other water-related concerns that planners must consider relative to recreation. In general, water can be harmful to recreation when there is too much of it or not enough. Typically, we tend to recognize the former problem more frequently since the results of erosion and siltation are usually quite evident.

Often, however, the problem of too much water isn't solved as readily as it should be. In many cases this seems to result from planners' *reluctance* to cope with the situation. In most instances the solution to too much water is channelization: altering the land base to provide drainage patterns compatible with recreation development. Here's an axiom of design for you: *directing runoff water where you need it to go is not a sin against nature.* If you make a decision to develop a given resource base for recreation, you've already committed to changing the site environment. (The same would be true of implementing a program of cover plantings for wildlife.) The challenge is to make the changes in ways not harmful to resources.

Channelization (ditching) has suffered in some cases because self-styled environmentalists have criticized the practice. Ditching does alter the landscape, but if a potential for damage exists without it, the technique is a positive measure. The point to remember is that more often than not, people sincerely concerned with environmental protection will make judgments based on personal opinions and superficial appearances rather than professional knowledge. Part of professionalism is living with criticism when you know your decisions are based on accepted management techniques, one of which is channeling runoff water to prevent damage. We remember a situation in Kentucky where a local judge criticized a mowing program because it was harming wildlife. The purpose of the mowing was to create the edge environment necessary *for* wildlife, yet the criticism originated entirely from a position of ignorance, resulted in negative public relations for the agency involved, and slowed the mowing program, negatively affecting wildlife.

A second and often less-evident problem with recreational water is a lack of it. To demonstrate this point, consider the following two examples. During the planning stage of a living-history complex in Tennessee, program staff decided to designate a well near the homestead as the focal point of the interpretive zone. The plan called for the well to be drilled at the base of a heavily wooded ridge directly behind the house, but soon after the complex opened, the well went dry. This problem was the result of a phenomenon known as *evapotransporation*. The heavy tree cover on the ridge literally pumped the available water out of the watershed serving the well. As a result, water had to be piped into the well house from another location. The mistake was a failure to recognize the effect watershed considerations can have on recreation developments.

Our second example takes us to a campground and beach area on a human-made lake in the Jefferson National Forest in West Virginia. Here, as elsewhere, ponds and lakes need a sizable watershed behind them feeding a year-around flowing stream in order to provide an adequate water supply for the lake during the hotter months of the year. In this instance the lake water, including the swimming area at a beach, became stagnant since evaporation and evapotransporation combined to reduce the inflow of water from the watershed to the beach zone.

Let's consider next a situation in which attention to resource coordination and watershed considerations can enhance recreation and other components of multiple-use management — in this case, fisheries. Figure 9.34 shows two ponds created by damming two points along a feeder stream. If our objective is to enhance both recreation use and fisheries, we could devote pond A to recreation and implement fisheries management techniques, including fertilization, on pond B. This approach would work *if* the water in the feeder stream remained clean and clear at all times. If water quality and siltation, however, were problems, a solution would be to add a third pond as shown in Figure 9.35. Here, pond A serves as a *filter* in which sediments will settle. Pond B, for recreation, will now have a higher water quality, and pond C can be intensively managed for fisheries, which require a heavy fertilization and dark green water. The critical element in this approach is understanding the interrelationships among the components of multiple-use management and *coordinating* them in a comprehensive way.

Timber

Outdoor recreation without trees would be like, as the song goes, a day without sunshine. Trees provide parks with shade, screening, interpretive opportunities, erosion control, and aesthetic value. They also exemplify the complexity involved in coordinating resources in multiple-use management. Consider the scarlet oak. It provides a good mast crop (acorns or food) for wildlife; it's a fast-growing tree and, while not particularly useful for lumber, produces a good cubic volume for pulpwood so that foresters like it; it has good fall color and is a well-formed tree. But when it comes to intensive recreation development, it is a poor

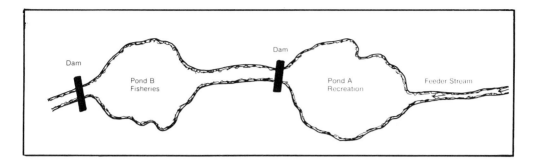

Figure 9.34

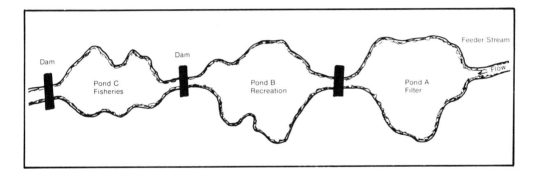

Figure 9.35

tree indeed! The scarlet oak is very shallow rooted, which means it won't stand up under the impact associated with intensive recreation use. On the other hand, it makes an aesthetically pleasing "background" tree when removed from zones where people and vehicles will circulate. Thus planners need to balance several factors with respect to only the scarlet oak: where intensive use zones will be; which trees can be left to avoid unnecessary cutting; which trees can be cut prior to construction to avoid maintenance problems and potential hazards later on.

This last issue — pre-construction thinning — can be a problem in itself. Planners worldwide are often reluctant to cut trees for recreation development. While you shouldn't cut trees indiscriminately, you should learn when it is appropriate to cut and do so. To complicate matters, there is no standard or simple answer we can give you. As an example, think about the Douglas fir for a moment. If you happen to be working in the Rocky Mountain section of the country, the Douglas fir is somewhat shorter and stockier than its relatives to the west, but in general it isn't a bad tree for recreation. In the West, however, the taller, more slender version of the tree causes planners problems. Western Douglas firs, which are also shallow rooted, depend on the branches of adjacent trees for support. When you thin a stand for recreation development, taking away their support, the fir becomes susceptible to wind damage. Thus part of understanding the relationship between the timber and recreation components of multiple-use management is knowing when not to cut, when to cut quite heavily, and when to keep intensive use areas *out* of certain stands of trees.

Understanding when to cut is quite critical. In the West planners often build campgrounds and other recreation areas in groves of aspen. Since aspen is a rather short-lived species with a low tolerance for people and impact, these areas often end up without trees. In general, old-growth or mature trees don't withstand impact as well as young, vigorous ones, and this raises two points. First, you need to know which trees and species to leave and which to cut. Second — and this is critical — resource management practices, including timber thinning and new plantings, need your attention *several years* in advance of actual development. This aspect of design points directly to the need for long-range master planning. Strangely enough, we've found that foresters who make a living harvesting timber are almost as reluctant as environmentalists with regard to cutting trees in *park* areas.

Recreation planning and management aren't just "now" activities. They both require *advance work* in the form of master planning and foresight in the form of discovering the *future implications* of the designs you implement. If you don't plant in advance, you may have to live without shade and screening when you open an area. If you don't consider the implications of your design relative to impact, you may have to live without shade and screening a few years after you open an area. Since this isn't a text on master planning or resource management, we'll leave these topics at this point. The important element for you to remember is that recreation doesn't and can't exist in a vacuum. You may have a personal and professional bias toward the importance of recreation, but downplaying the importance of the other components of multiple-use management can result in problems we'd rather not have to face.

Forage, wildlife, watershed, timber, and recreation, as we've considered them in this chapter, are rarely easy to interrelate. It would be helpful to us all if *coordination* were a required course in resource *and* recreation curricula. The elements of multiple-use management often conflict with each other, but they can also coexist as long as managers make informed judgments about how to allocate resources equitably. Perhaps the "saving grace" of multiple-use management is that the potential and the solutions to most problems are for the most part *tangible*. If you know, for example, that white pine is a shallow-rooted species, you can avoid a headache by coping with it through design and pre-construction cuts. The really difficult problems in recreation, as in life, are the intangible ones. For a brief look at some of these recreation "toughies," turn to Chapter Ten.

10

ACCESS TO A HERITAGE:
ROADBLOCKS OR ASSURANCES?

"The outdoors lies deep in American tradition. It has had immeasurable impact on the Nation's character and on those who made its history . . . . When an American looks for the meaning of his past, he seeks it not in ancient ruins, but more likely in mountains and forests, by a river, or at the edge of the sea . . . . Today's challenge is to assure all Americans permanent access to their outdoor heritage."

INTRODUCTION

For those of us who deal with planning and management of outdoor recreation facilities and programs, the last sentence in the above statement is *or should be* a guiding principle. You will find this quotation on the back covers of all volumes of the Outdoor Recreation Resources Review Commission (ORRRC) report. The ORRRC report was presented by Chairman Laurance S. Rockefeller to President Kennedy and the Congress in January of 1962, so park planners, designers, and administrators have had over twenty-five years to " . . . assure all Americans access to their outdoor heritage." Our purpose in this chapter is to explore the success with which we have met this challenge. Have we strived to "assure access" or have we created roadblocks that impede maximum enjoyment of the out-of-doors by *all* Americans?

Before addressing this question, we need to lay a foundation with four cornerstones. First, we are supporters — *ardent supporters* — of recreation. Both personally and professionally, we think the continually growing popularity and acceptance of leisure, recreation, and parks is one of the most important and positive societal phenomena today. We are not, however, so myopic or shortsighted in our support to believe, or to try and portray, recreation services without their problems. Throughout this book, we've tried to share with you a variety of planning- and design-related mistakes. In this chapter, you'll find very little discussion related directly to these topics. Indirectly, however, we feel the discussion to follow suggests some of the reasons why, in our opinion, parks have not been planned for people historically.

Our second cornerstone contains multiple realities. One of the most, indeed, probably *the* most, important aspects of your education is learning about and accepting the existence of multiple realities. In Chapter Seven we alluded to how the US Forest Service "knew" that three camp units per acre was appropriate, while the National Park Service "knew" that twelve units was. We feel neither is right, but in an absolute sense, neither the agency nor our opinion is wrong. It's a matter of *perspective.* If you ask a park planner, administrator, programmer, and maintenance worker to identify the most important facet of service provision, chances are you'll hear, respectively, "planning," "management," "programming," and "maintenance." One's answer depends on one's viewpoint.

As you grow professionally, you need to move from a *dualistic* perspective in which someone is either right or wrong to a *relativistic* perspective in which a continuum of ideas exists that is based on outlook with none more "correct" than another. Our perspective is simple. We want the best for the most for the least; the best recreation areas and services for the most possible people at the least possible cost in dollars and damage to the environment.

Our third cornerstone is closely related to the second. We don't feel we are alone in wanting cost-effective, ecologically sound recreation areas for all people. We do, however, suspect we are in a minority by suggesting that these efforts are much less successful than they could or should be for a variety of reasons we'll discuss shortly. Our third cornerstone, then, is that many professionals, educators, and students aren't going to like what we have to say in the next few pages, but we're going to raise these points anyway for two reasons. First, we are rather tired of what seems to us to be the prevalent attitude in recreation, parks, and leisure services today, an attitude reflected in textbooks, professional society meetings, and much of our day-to-day business. "God's in heaven and all's right with the world," is

what most professionals in our field believe. We don't perceive that all *is* right with the world of recreation, and we feel a commitment to tell you why. Second, controversy is the fuel to feed the fires of change. If ninety percent of you who read this chapter simply get mad at us, so be it; we hope the remaining ten percent will be moved to help effect some changes.

Our fourth and final cornerstone is a definition of the word "essay" in its original sense. An essay historically meant an *attempt*, and here we want to attempt to point out issues for your consideration. We aren't going to pretend to have all the answers for the concerns we have. In most cases, there aren't tangible ones because the problems we want to discuss are primarily abstractions.

It's quite simple to suggest corrective measures for erosion problems caused by water movement. It's easy to prescribe techniques of design psychology aimed at improving the aesthetic value of a parkscape. It is more difficult to solve or even describe concerns focusing on conceptual issues like those which follow. Keep in mind as you read, then, that we are offering you a perspective on several issues. We do so out of care and concern for the profession, we expect our comments to anger many of you, and we don't have all the answers. We do, however, have a variety of questions to share. Most of the individuals who read this book will be either students, educators, or recreation professionals. Thus we'll organize our comments into sections dealing with these three groups. Since most of you are students, let's begin here.

TODAY'S STUDENT — TOMORROW'S PROFESSIONAL

In the last ten years alone, we've had the opportunity to interact on a rather close basis with perhaps five thousand recreation students. If we were in the place of an outdoor recreation manager looking to hire a staff assistant, we would consider hiring maybe — maybe — five percent of this group. In fairness to students, part of the blame for this situation falls on your curricula. As we've discussed before, there are basically two types of university departments turning out recreation majors: the department housed in a school or college of health, physical education, and recreation (HPER), and the department housed in a school of forestry or natural resources. In general, HPER schools do a reasonably good job of teaching "people-oriented" skills such as programming and administration. However, most of these departments *don't* have the faculty expertise (or the inclination) to teach courses relevant to resource management, courses like dendrology, hydrology, soils science, and the like.

How many of you who are HPER students, for example, would recognize a scarlet oak? Without a course in dendrology, you might not even think about the need to consider the properties of this tree relative to recreation. Try, however, putting a campground or picnic area in a stand of mature scarlet oaks and watch how quickly your shade disappears because these shallow-rooted trees simply can't withstand the compaction. On the other hand, graduates of resource-oriented schools may know these things, but they all too often fail to learn how to provide a *people-oriented* experience in our outdoor recreation areas.

While part of the "student problem" lies with curricula, students aren't blameless either. We've seen far too many undergraduate *and* graduate students interested only in a "quick fix" education with attitudes like "I'll take easy courses for less work and a higher GPA." We've seen graduating seniors who are literally incapable of writing a grammatically correct, much less comprehensible, report; who don't even know the

names of our research journals, let alone read them; and who seem to feel the profession "owes" them a job just because they have a degree. We aren't so old to not remember how tough it can be to get through school, but it can also be hard getting a job. If you want to market yourself, you need to be ready to make some sacrifices.

Try to find summer work in recreation settings. You may make less money, but you can pick up some great experience and make some good contacts. Join professional societies and *get involved* in them. Volunteer to serve on committees, help organize conferences, and attend meetings. Professional societies don't exist *for* you, they exist *because* of you. Talk to teachers and professionals and find out the kinds of skills you need to have to function effectively — then go get them. Take courses in technical writing, business administration, and computer programming. Your grade-point average may suffer a little, but you'll be a better professional for it. Finally, demonstrate that you're capable of being a professional by acting like one. For example, don't wait to read the articles and editorials in *Parks and Recreation* until they're assigned. Read them because it's your responsibility to know what's happening in the field.

Maybe you feel that what we've been saying doesn't apply to you. If you're right, you're the type of student we'd want to hire. If you can look at yourself and say, "I've honestly done all I can to get the most out of my education," then good for you. If you have challenged yourself (and your professors), congratulations. If you've taken people- and resource-oriented courses and management classes to prepare for a career in outdoor recreation, you should feel positive about yourself. If you are eager and willing to learn, you are already thinking like a professional should. If you fit this description, we'd feel pretty good about you, too, but we would also guess — unfortunately — that you represent a minority of students.

"PROFESSORING" AND OUTDOOR RECREATION

Let's turn our attention now to the individuals primarily responsible for training recreation students: university professors. Although there are exceptions, most of the academics we know are intelligent, well-meaning, and personable. When it comes to outdoor recreation, many professors have only two problems: teaching it and researching it. The fact is that being intelligent, well-meaning, and personable, while commendable, doesn't qualify someone to teach or research a particular area. You also need a sensitivity to and an understanding of the subject at hand. Too many academics we have met over the years lack these qualities in relation to outdoor recreation. Part of the problem, as we perceive it, stems from professors receiving their training in either an HPER or a resource-oriented curriculum — the same one that detracts from the capabilities of their students.

Back in the early- and mid-1960's, many forestry schools made the decision to "get in on" or climb aboard the recreation bandwagon. Unfortunately for the profession and the students they were to instruct, many of the forestry-school professors selected to teach outdoor recreation were not trained to do so, and some were quite upset at being given this challenge. Others were excited about their new assignments, and these folks did all they could to fill in the gaps in their knowledge. Still others decided not to invest the time or energy to learn their trade, and this lack of background (and interest) has been quite harmful to the "production" of enthusiastic, well-trained outdoor-recreation-resource professionals. Curiously, too, many of the graduates they produced were extremely wilderness-oriented and anti-mainstream — a result contributing measurably to the many parks which haven't been planned for people.

Another factor contributing to the deficiencies of outdoor-recreation-oriented educators is the discrepancy between academic environments and the "real world" of recreation management. The faculty members we feel are "good" in the sense of being concerned with the needs of professionals are those who work closely with field-level personnel and keep abreast of the issues facing these folks. The academic types we have problems with are the ones who teach about and profess an expertise in outdoor recreation without ever having worked in a professional setting or who haven't kept up with what happens in the field.

To make our point, let us share a couple of stories with you. When we worked for the TVA, our office once received a "windfall appropriation." In other words, we had about 90,000 dollars dumped in our laps that we weren't expecting to get. The only catch was that we got it on June 15th and had to either spend it by the end of our fiscal year or lose it. Our fiscal year ended June 30th.

Now every planning course we've ever taken or taught has said that first you conduct a needs assessment, then prepare a master plan, then devise site plans, work up alternative designs, select the best options from among the alternatives, and lay out the design in the field. The day we found out about the money we had a staff meeting to decide how to spend it. At 7:00 am the next morning, we were flagging a bicycle trail. At 7:30, a truck unloaded a bulldozer, and two weeks later, the trail was finished. This wasn't an ideal situation, but it *was* the real world, and sometimes the classroom is a long way from it.

Our second story also stems from our TVA days. In the mid-1970's, we were involved in planning an outdoor recreation consortium for five university recreation departments. While the TVA was to host the event, it was up to the university faculty to develop the objectives and curriculum for the consortium the way they felt it should be done. We met for two days. By suppertime on the second day, with our available time drawing to a close, we had managed to agree on a statement of purpose and a handful of objectives for the consortium — and hadn't even discussed the curriculum. We put that together rather quickly the last evening before we left. What happened? The purpose and objectives were important, but sometimes academicians tend to think in lofty terms and forget the nuts and bolts in the process. As Howard Tinsley suggested by quoting Bacon, people who dwell in ivory towers sometimes have heads made of the same material.[1]

In defense of recreation educators, we need to share with you what we feel is one of the major problems these folks face: the university rewards system. Basically, the problem is that too many universities reward faculty activities having little value to most professionals. To understand this point, you need to consider the nature of the term "value." In essence, there are two kinds, intrinsic and extrinsic, and most things can be judged according to either type. A wedding ring, for example, can be evaluated extrinsically by how much it costs and intrinsically by the significance of the marriage it symbolizes. Similarly, the activities of a faculty member can be judged extrinsically by how well he or she prepares students for professional careers and researches topics relevant to professionals and intrinsically by publications in basic research journals.

In our opinion, the rewards of tenure and promotion associated with academic productivity are too often tied to activities judged on the basis of intrinsic value. We

know faculty members who have been granted tenure because of success in publishing articles, yet they are less-than-good teachers and they don't really understand the needs of professionals. We know others who have been denied tenure, i.e., fired, because they devote time and energy to excellence in teaching and fail to publish regularly. This is a touchy issue, and we should qualify our position with two comments. First, good teaching and valuable research are not mutually exclusive activities. As a friend of ours named Tony Mobley has said, "Research is to teaching like sin is to confession: if you don't do the first, you don't have much to talk about at the second." Universities have the right to expect their faculty to be both scholars and teachers. Unfortunately most schools seem to reward scholarship more readily than teaching.

Our second qualification deals with the research for which faculty are rewarded. From the perspective of outdoor recreation professionals, we feel the most serious problem with research today is a lack of applicability. In other words, the results of much of the research being conducted are, for various reasons, of little utility to managers, planners, and programmers trying to improve the facilities and services they provide for the public. The way university reward systems are set up, research doesn't count for much unless and until it gets published, and for the most part recreation journals tend to publish basic research instead of applied findings. In order to publish — and win tenure points — academics are encouraged to do basic research. Thus field-level professionals don't find much to interest them in journals, tend not to read them, and miss out on most of the applied information that is available.

Another problem with application is the way in which research results are written. Any scientific discipline, ours included, has

[1] Tinsley, H.E.A. (1984). "Limitations, Explorations, Aspirations: A Confession of Fallibility and a Promise to Strive for Perfection." *Journal of Leisure Research,* 16, pp. 93-98.

its own jargon and style. Most recreation journals thrive on terms such as "statistical significance," "regression coefficients," and "orthogonal factors." Research reports also tend to be formatted with an introduction, a methods section, a review of results, and a discussion. From a research standpoint, this is both desirable and necessary for the advancement of knowledge. If another researcher can scan a journal article and learn how a particular variable explains only six percent of the variance of the dependent measure, he or she will learn something from it. But it probably doesn't help the average manager very much. For research to be useful to the practitioner, it must lay out, in plain English, a set of *recommendations* based on research results for consideration. If, for example, a study finds that "perceived isolation" is one of the most important factors in choosing a campsite, the researcher could recommend leaving vegetation growing between camp units. However, this bridge between results and recommendations is neglected far too often.

A final barrier to research application that we can blame on researchers is the lack of understanding they often have for the problems facing the practitioner. When we were with the TVA, we were called by a well-known researcher from a northeastern university. He asked us to serve as state coordinators and distribute a research-needs questionnaire to resort owners, federal and state administrators, user groups, and recreation equipment suppliers. We agreed. The questionnaires arrived on June 16th with a note saying they were to be returned by the respondents by June 20th! Remember that the pre-Fourth-of-July period is the professionals' busiest season. The researcher simply didn't understand this.

Too often also, researchers decide what they want to study without adequate input from professionals. If you asked managerial folks why they don't pay more attention to research, most would probably tell you it's because the studies don't help them do their jobs. If you asked them why not, they'd probably tell you they aren't asked what they need to have researched. This is partly the fault of the professional for not seeking help from academic types by letting researchers know their needs. Partly also, though, researchers are to blame for not seeking input from practitioners when they develop topics to investigate. Several of the larger federal agencies established outdoor research staffs. Included were the National Park Service, USDA-Forest Service, TVA, and US Corps of Engineers. Some good things came from these staffs and the millions of dollars spent, but the basic problem we discussed earlier occurred here, too. Essentially, researchers decided what sorts of problems or questions needed their attention without adequate input from managerial types. Thus the usefulness or relevance of their reports for managers and others who wanted answers was missing. In summary, there must be more communication among field professionals, researchers, and academic types. Unfortunately we don't anticipate this happening given the current university rewards system and the tendency of many academics and agency researchers to remain aloof to the needs of the practitioner.

PROFESSIONAL ISSUES: TELLING IT LIKE (WE THINK) IT IS

Those of you who have had an introductory course in recreation should be aware of the inception and evolution of parks in the US, from Central Park to Yellowstone and the latter-day Great Smoky Mountains National Park. What we would like to address in this section is the modern era of outdoor recreation. In our view, this era was ushered in as a result of the twenty-seven-volume Outdoor

Recreation Resources Review Commission Report we mentioned earlier. Out of this report grew a new coordination agency, the Bureau of Outdoor Recreation (BOR); the seeds of all sorts of legislation from the Land and Water Conservation Fund Act to National Recreation Areas to National Scenic Trails; *and,* for the first time, a serious effort by a number of agencies to provide the staff, time, and money for outdoor recreation that many had barely tolerated before.

Ultimately, there were over ninety agencies, boards, commissions, and committees in the federal government alone concerned in one way or another with outdoor recreation. Understandably there was also a tremendous amount of inexperience and mistakes aplenty, but America was moving with excitement toward providing access to outdoor recreation for *all* its diverse peoples. Shortly after the BOR became a working agency, states appointed liaison officers to work with federal officials in making sure Land and Water Conservation Fund grants and other monies were properly channeled and spent on carefully prioritized projects. The USDA Extension Service, USDA Soil Conservation Service, and others hired trained staff to help towns (large and small), counties, the private sector (including farmers and ranchers), and countless others with planning, design, and guides for management. Other federal agencies had roles, too, but they and the BOR carried most of the known technological transfer to others without adequate or trained staff.

In sum, the 1960's and early 70's saw great strides in providing outdoor recreation areas, programs, and facilities for the young and not-so-young, the mainstream users and minorities, the well-to-do and the rest of us. Professional societies blossomed and even tried to nurture those of us who were trying to become knowledgeable about the vast realm of outdoor recreation opportunities. Then something happened.

Almost imperceptibly at first, the enthusiastic outdoor recreation movement geared toward providing "all Americans permanent access to their outdoor heritage" slowed, stalled, and finally stopped. Outdoor recreation for *all* Americans ceased to be a watchword or a guiding principle.

What happened and why is a multi-faceted story and one with many causes. To our knowledge, few of what we feel are the real issues in outdoor recreation today have found their way into textbooks. In the following sections, we'd like to cite some of these omissions, factors we feel have been and are currently barriers to outdoor recreation opportunities for the public at large.

The Special Interest Syndrome

The 1960's and 70's were a time of tremendous social upheaval. These days were also the era of "movements" — from civil rights to anti-war to environmental protection. Causes became the "in" thing, and much of what happened was good. American society began to correct, or at least become aware of, prejudices based on race, beliefs, or gender; the immorality of a military-industrial approach to foreign policy; the disdain for environment of self-serving corporate interests; and other problems inherent in a society pushed too quickly into the future. Relative to our discussion here, one problem stemmed from the realization by a variety of special-interest groups of the power of the news media. In effect, nearly any issue could become a celebrated cause if its proponents argued loudly enough to attract media attention. The question of whether "movements make news" or "news makes movements" is one for journalism classes. The point for us to consider is the effects special-interest groups have had on outdoor recreation. Essentially the progress toward outdoor recreation for *all* Americans halted when special-interest groups began demanding *more than their fair share* of the pie, and some of these include the following.

The Environmentalists. The extremely vocal environmental movement gave added voice and political clout to proponents of wilderness use. This halted all sorts of *development-oriented* recreation activities in most of the federal sector. Anything not connected with wilderness was bad, bad, bad. The National Park Service, USDA-Forest Service, and other agencies backed away from development and closed or tried to close some of their park and recreation areas to all sorts of legitimate users while increasing manyfold their money and emphasis on wilderness and the environment. The Forest Service now heralds wilderness and winter sports as their main recreation components, yet history and research have both shown these activities to be the pursuits of the wealthy, the well-educated, and the physically fit. This hardly includes all Americans — in fact, it excludes most of them. We are not anti-wilderness; we are simply opposed to emphasizing wilderness use *at the expense of* the "silent majority" of Americans who are either unable or not inclined to carry their recreation gear on their backs. A tangible example of this deemphasis on opportunities for all Americans is the almost exclusive policy of the National Park Service, the Bureau of Land Management, and the Forest Service of providing no electrical hook-ups in their campgrounds. To those individuals, including many older Americans, who need refrigerated medicine or air conditioning because of health problems, this policy says "We don't want you."

The Private Sector. Pointing a finger at public parks nationwide, owners of private campgrounds said, "We could really make money if you (the states and the federal government) weren't in the business." This caused all sorts of anti-public-development

problems, from a moratorium on campsite development in the National Park Service to elimination of the entire Washington office outdoor recreation staff in the USDI Fish and Wildlife Service to Congressional legislation almost destroying construction of outdoor recreation facilities in Corps of Engineers areas, even to the point of severely limiting how poorly designed facilities can be renovated. Public Law 8972 means that existing and potential campers and other users across the nation have been further shortchanged in access to their own park areas. The private sector has been quite successful in its efforts to have public agencies increase their fees for recreation use in the name of unfair competition. As public areas charged more, the private sector was able to raise their prices as well. But rather than encouraging more users to move to the private sector, the result of this price spiral has been to discourage use. From the perspective of the private sector, this is ironic. From the perspective of the user, this is unfortunate.

The Municipal Factor. Land and Water Conservation funds were initially intended to be used for true *outdoor* recreation developments and lands to host these developments. This did not sit well with many municipal recreation professionals who also wanted "a piece of the action." Since most National Recreation and Park Association members are municipally oriented, NRPA has lobbied

*The topic of LWCF expenditures raises an interesting side issue. Particularly in the East, the Forest Service has, in our opinion, taken advantage of a "loophole" in the LWCF acquisition guidelines. This loophole permits use of land-and-water conservation funds for acquisition of lands if they are suitable for small or big game hunting. Since any sort of land would meet this criterion, the Forest Service has used it to fill in their checkerboard ownership. In most instances, the land acquired has not been used to enhance outdoor recreation enjoyment.

for a change in basic priorities for LWCF Act money. They have been quite successful in diverting funding to cities.* Special-interest groups, including ethnic minorities, have also lobbied successfully for a stronger emphasis on inner-city development, so the National Park Service has moved into urban areas and away from priorities associated with areas of national significance. Again, we are not anti-municipal or anti-minority; we *are* against using funds intended for *outdoor* recreation for purposes other than those for which the LWCF Act was created.

The Career Problem: Who Am I and What Am I Doing Here?

Attempting to deal with the demands of special-interest groups is a major impediment for outdoor recreation professionals. For the most part, however, these groups represent "outside interests" and are at least easy to identify. A more difficult problem arises when factors impeding "access for all Americans" become internal to the profession. This is the topic we'd like to discuss now, situations existing under the general heading of personnel-related issues.

Top Dogs. The bottom line is the top; ultimately the decisions affecting recreation policy rest with the individuals responsible for managing agencies involved in the profession. Consider some parallel situations. If you check into a hospital, presumably you would feel more secure if the person in charge has a medical background. Similarly, academic institutions need educators in decision-making positions. Somehow this logic has escaped many public agencies involved in providing outdoor recreation areas and facilities. For the most part, the "top slots" in agencies which manage recreation resources are not filled with people who have backgrounds in recreation. In a typical

Corps of Engineers district, personnel are ultimately responsible to a career military officer, usually a colonel. Directly under this individual and responsible for day-to-day operations, you'll find a district engineer. This person typically has engineers and landscape architects as assistants. Perhaps at the next level down (the fourth from the top), you'll find a recreation-trained person; more often, however, even these slots are filled with LA's, foresters, or wildlife biologists.

We aren't picking on the Corps. Similar situations exist in the Forest Service, TVA, other federal and many state agencies. We aren't even being generally critical of the individuals involved; many of these folks are competent and well-meaning. *But* they generally aren't recreation-oriented. Regardless of how professional or how nice an individual is, he or she is going to have personal and discipline-oriented biases that will influence decision making. Simply stated, we feel that outdoor recreation interests — access for all Americans — would be better served if some of the people responsible for recreation management were trained in recreation.

First-level Positions: No Jobs or Snow Job?
If you follow the job markets at regional and national conventions and watch job-announcement bulletins, you'll find probably fewer openings advertised for outdoor recreation positions than any other branch of the profession. One of the obvious reasons for this is the government job situation in general. Whether you agree or disagree with administration policy, there are fewer jobs available today in the public sector. We feel, however, that there is another reason behind the lack of entry-level positions available to graduates of recreation curricula; we perceive a disdain for these graduates — probably you included — on the part of resource-oriented agencies. Historically, recreation jobs in these agencies, for example the Forest Service, were filled with resource-trained

individuals. In the "early days" of recreation — the 1950's and early 1960's — this was more understandable since there were fewer people being trained in recreation, although even then there were problems. In some instances, recreation jobs were used as "dumping grounds" for individuals perceived as incompetent by their superiors.

Today, however, available recreation graduates rarely find their way into the few job openings that exist. People get promoted, retire, or leave public service, so jobs open up and we don't object to seeing foresters, landscape architects, and wildlife biologists get them. We do object to seeing these individuals get *recreation* jobs because the hiring decisions are made by foresters, landscape architects, and wildlife biologists.

Watch Where You Step: The Career Ladder. To put it bluntly, recreation-related jobs in resource-oriented agencies tend not to be career-structured. Ideally, professions such as recreation should consist of *career ladders*. Under these circumstances, an individual fresh out of college with a degree in recreation is hired in an entry-level position. After some on-the-job training and experience, our now-seasoned professional moves up the career ladder to a mid-level recreation position. After several more years, the more talented individuals with equal parts of dedication and creativity become the next generation of decision-makers.

Such a system perpetuates excellence for two reasons. First, people learn as they grow professionally, becoming more competent. Second, promotions create new entry-level positions which can be filled by younger folks who can then be helped along by those who preceded them. Problem is, things don't seem to work this way in practice. Recreation jobs in many public agencies have tended to evolve into stepping stones for administrative careers. Instead of moving *vertically* up a career ladder in recreation, people are often "stair-stepped," moved up

and over to recreation temporarily from another discipline within the same agency. They then stair-step back up and over to an administrative position.

In addition to defeating the purpose of the career ladder, the real problem stemming from this practice is that recreation expertise never materializes. If you take a forester or other resource-oriented individual and place him or her in a mid-level recreation position for a year or two and then promote this person to an administrative position, there isn't much time and even less inclination to learn recreation. Thus when the people answering to this "temporary" recreation person make mistakes, particularly in their guidance or critiques of lower level personnel, we shouldn't be too surprised to see the results of these mistakes become reality in our parks and recreation areas. Using recreation positions as stepping stones rather than creating a career ladder very likely accounts for most of the planning, design, and management mistakes we've described throughout this book.

Strange Bedfellows. Another personnel-related issue in recreation today is the question of unionism. Should recreation professionals belong to and support them? Our perspective on the matter is an emphatic *no*. For many workers, unions, particularly through the first half of the twentieth century, were a source of salvation. Poor and often hazardous working conditions, low pay, and insufficient benefits all received attention and were largely eliminated for many workers due in significant part to the efforts of unions. There is, however, a basic difference between workers and recreation professionals. The difference is professionalism. Until the early 1970's, the unionization of recreation professionals was a rare occurrence. Then, starting with maintenance personnel, unions slowly began working their way through recreation programs in both municipal and resource-based agencies.

We can't argue that recreation professionals haven't benefited personally from the growth of unions; they tend to bargain from positions of strength. Our concern is for what we feel is a resulting decline in both the quality and quantity of professional work. Unions tend to breed self-interest, and individuals who become concerned with increased wages, more benefits, and the fruits of seniority have less time to devote to quality work. Requiring that professionals be promoted because of seniority rather than expertise and diligence works against the progression of a profession. In a very real sense, unionism and professionalism work at cross-purposes. Unions are by definition formed to advance self-interests; professionals are dedicated to advancing society through selflessness.

This may be an unpopular opinion, but we continually hear recreation workers lamenting that they are not recognized as professionals. Assembly-line workers unionize and aren't viewed by the public as professionals; doctors don't unionize and are. In essence, you are what you are perceived to be.

A Final Roadblock. We have a friend who recently lost his hob, a chief of recreation for one of the nation's most progressive state-park systems. He lost his job not because he was incapable or because of cutbacks in funding, but simply because he belonged to the losing party in a state election. His replacement, who belonged to the winning party, was a park maintenance worker.

The spoils system — rewarding campaign assistance with jobs — has been around for some time; however, this doesn't make it any more palatable from a professional perspective. Early in his career, one of your authors aspired to a resource position with a federal agency. As it turned out, there was no opportunity for the aspiration to become reality, for the individual who approved the selection filled those slots with candidates

who happened to have the same religious affiliation as his.

Hiring practices based on political or religious inclinations are both a shoddy and poor way to ensure quality in professional work. Yet these injustices are no different from government-sanctioned quota systems in which people are hired and promoted because of, rather than in spite of, race or gender. Here again we need to qualify our position. We aren't against civil rights or the women's movement. In fact, the cause of the problem is likely the typical white male manager who for years hired only other white males. This practice and the seeming unwillingness of these folks to break out of their molds necessitated a reaction — resulting in quota systems — to afford equal employment opportunities. Our quarrel is with *reactive* policies. Professionalism does not have room for hiring based on *anything other than professional capabilities and potential*. Race, gender, political affiliation, and religious preferences are *personal* attributes and shouldn't even be a factor in deciding who to hire. Throughout this book, we've attempted to stress the importance of separating your personal preferences from your professional decisions regarding the provision of facilities and programs. To us, it seems the same logic should apply to hiring practices.

Other Barriers To Progress. Earlier in this chapter we discussed the outdoor recreation delivery systems of the USDA Extension Service, the USDA Soil Conservation Service, and the USDI Bureau of Outdoor Recreation. These agencies brought help to all sectors of the outdoor recreationr realm and were particularly helpful to the private sector. As we bring this book to a close, the *one* remaining outdoor-recreation specialist position in the USDA-SCS is about to be eliminated. The extension service no longer has a guiding staff in their Washington office. Their state specialists are best adrift on their own. The BOR is no more!

This agency, which once had so much promise, fell prey to special-interest groups. In its final HCRS form (Heritage, Conservation, and — oh yes — Recreation Service), elimination was the prudent action to take. However, from a federal (and national) perspective, who now provides the leadership and guidance so needed by everyone? Remember, we said this chapter heralds questions rather than answers.

We began with a marvelous quotation from the ORRRC report challenging future generations of professionals to "assure all Americans permanent access to their outdoor heritage." As you can see, there have been and are far too many roadblocks and far too few assurances. During about one-third of the time we've taken to write this book, a second ORRRC called the President's Commission on Americans Outdoors has been established and has just now finished gathering new data to guide us into the next century. We had — and still have — high hopes that this group speaks for the quiet majority of unorganized Americans interested in all sorts of outdoor enjoyment. However, the make-up of the Commission's assistant directors and some of its staff tells us that the special interests and those who are radically against public park development for *all sorts of users* are firmly in control.

In a letter containing many of the points we've raised here, we have given the Commission an account of what we feel are the roadblocks preventing outdoor recreation access for all Americans. Frankly, we doubt if our voices will be heard above the din of the special-interests. We hope our assessment is in error, and that the new Commission will give us a people-oriented park mission for future generations. Only time will tell.

We suggest you read the Commission's report and judge for yourself. Read it, however, from the perspective of a wheel-chair-bound child, a teenager, a senior citizen, and a factory worker seeking a re-creative experience on a safe, generous, level usable, modern campsite. Does the report guarantee *you* access, or must you embrace wilderness and other special camping to avoid roadblocks to your outdoor heritage?

CONCLUSIONS

This has been a difficult chapter — and book — to write primarily because we think recreation is such a positive phenomenon and we felt a need to take a negative approach at times to make the points we wanted to make. Not so very long ago, friends either laughed or didn't understand when we told them we studied and worked in recreation. But as recreation becomes more a part of our culture, this attitude is changing. Acceptance by the public may make your life a bit easier, but it will also make your work more challenging as people demand more and better services and programs from recreation professionals. Our purpose in writing this book has been to share mistakes we and others have made in the hope of keeping you from repeating these and similar errors.

Ours is an ever-changing, dynamic profession. New opportunities for service provision appear almost daily, and with these comes the chance to improve access to our heritage of recreation *and* the potential for making further errors.

Mistakes will continue to occur. The only *real* mistake, however, the only one you shouldn't accept, is perpetuating the errors of those who have gone before you. Whether you agree with our arguments or not; whether you've found our discussions meaningful or "just another assignment to read;" whether you learn from us or someone else, we hope you will at least accept a challenge: *plan parks for people.*

OTHER BOOKS FROM VENTURE PUBLISHING

Acquiring Parks and Recreation Facilities through Mandatory Dedication: A Comprehensive Guide, by Ronald A. Kaiser and James D. Mertes

Adventure Education, edited by John C. Miles and Simon Priest

Amenity Resource Valuation: Integrating Economics with Other Disciplines, edited by George L. Peterson, B.L. Driver and Robin Gregory

Behavior Modification in Therapeutic Recreation: An Introductory Learning Manual, by John Dattilo and William D. Murphy

Beyond the Bake Sale - A Fund Raising Handbook for Public Agencies, by Bill Moskin

The Community Tourism Industry Imperative - The Necessity, The Opportunities, Its Potential, by Uel Blank

Doing More With Less in the Delivery of Recreation and Park Services: A Book of Case Studies, by John Crompton

Evaluation of Therapeutic Recreation Through Quality Assurance, edited by Bob Riley

The Evolution of Leisure: Historical and Philosophical Perspectives, by Thomas Goodale and Geoffrey Godbey

The Future of Leisure Services: Thriving on Change, by Geoffrey Godbey

Gifts to Share - A Gifts Catalogue How-To Manual for Public Agencies, by Lori Harder and Bill Moskin

International Directory of Academic Institutions in Leisure, Recreation and Related Fields, edited by Max D'Amours

Leadership and Administration of Outdoor Pursuits, by Phyllis Ford and James Blanchard

The Leisure Diagnostic Battery: Users Manual and Sample Forms, by Peter Witt and Gary Ellis

Leisure Diagnostic Battery Computer Software, by Gary Ellis and Peter Witt

Leisure Education: A Manual of Activities and Resources, by Norma J. Stumbo and Steven R. Thompson

Leisure Education: Program Materials for Persons with Developmental Disabilities, by Kenneth F. Joswiak

Leisure in Your Life: An Exploration, 3rd Edition, by Geoffrey Godbey

A Leisure of One's Own: A Feminist Perspective on Women's Leisure, by Karla Henderson, M. Deborah Bialeschki, Susan M. Shaw and Valeria J. Freysinger

Outdoor Recreation Management: Theory and Application, Revised and Enlarged, by Alan Jubenville, Ben Twight and Robert H. Becker

Playing, Living, Learning: A Worldwide Perspective on Children's Opportunities to Play, by Cor Westland and Jane Knight

Private and Commercial Recreation, edited by Arlin Epperson

The Process of Recreation Programming Theory and Technique, 3rd Edition, by Patricia Farrell and Herberta M. Lundegren

Recreation and Leisure: An Introductory Handbook, edited by Alan Graefe and Stan Parker

Recreation and Leisure: Issues in an Era of Change, 3rd Edition, edited by Thomas Goodale and Peter A. Witt

Recreation Economic Decisions: Comparing Benefits and Costs, by Richard G. Walsh

Risk Management in Therapeutic Recreation: A Component of Quality Assurance, by Judy Voelkl

Schole: A Journal of Leisure Studies and Recreation Education

A Social History of Leisure Since 1600, by Gary Cross

Sports and Recreation for the Disabled - A Resource Manual, by Michael J. Paciorek and Jeffery A. Jones

A Study Guide for National Certification in Therapeutic Recreation, by Gerald O'Morrow and Ron Reynolds

Therapeutic Recreation Protocols for Treatment of Substance Addictions, by Rozanne W. Faulkner

Understanding Leisure and Recreation: Mapping the Past, Charting the Future, edited by Edgar L. Jackson and Thomas L. Burton

Wilderness in America: Personal Perspectives, edited by Daniel L. Dustin

Venture Publishing, Inc
1999 Cato Avenue
State College, PA 16801
814-234-4561